A
PARLIAMENTARY
HISTORY OF THE
GLORIOUS REVOLUTION

'A parliament with one consent
Is all the cry o'th'nation'

*A New Song: On the calling of a
free Parliament January 15, 1689**

* In *Poems on affairs of state*. Vol.4:1685-1688,ed. by Galbraith M. Crump.
New Haven: Yale University Press, 1968:323.

A
PARLIAMENTARY
HISTORY OF THE
Glorious Revolution

DAVID LEWIS JONES

LONDON

HER MAJESTY'S STATIONERY OFFICE

Printed in the United Kingdom for Her Majesty's Stationery Office
Dd289430 6/88 C10 G443 10170

Contents

Preface

THE SUBJECT OF THIS BOOK IS THE ROLE PLAYED during the Glorious Revolution by the Parliaments of England and Wales and of Scotland. The introduction describes how the various factions in both kingdoms viewed their Parliament and includes a narrative of the debates and proceedings at Westminster and at Edinburgh. At the appropriate place, I have included the text of the Declaration of Rights presented by the Parliament of England and Wales to William and Mary, and the texts of the Claim of Right and the other documents presented by the Parliament of Scotland.

The main part of the book is a collection of the surviving reports of the debates held at Westminster – there is little surviving evidence for the debates held in the Scottish Parliament.

I am grateful to Professor Lois G. Schwoerer of the George Washington University for the kind permission to reprint her edition of 'A Jornall of the Convention at Westminster begun the 22 of January 1688/9'. Professor Henry Horwitz of the University of Iowa showed equal generosity with regard to his edition of Danby's notes. Professor Michael Thompson of the Institute of Historical Research gave the necessary permission to reprint these two texts which were first published in the *Bulletin of the Institute of Historical Research*. 'Notes of a Noble Lord' are published by permission of the Master and Fellows, Magdalene College, Cambridge.

The Bodleian Library; the British Library; Dr. Williams's Library; and, the House of Lords Record Office allowed me access to manuscripts in their charge and I wish to acknowledge the help given by the staff at these institutions.

Dr. Isolde Victory and Mr. David Johnson were kind enough to comment on the introduction; any faults which remain are mine.

This publication is part of the parliamentary celebrations of the tercentenary of the Revolutions of 1688-89 and of the Bill of Rights and Claim of Right authorised by the Lord Chancellor and the Speaker of the House of Commons with the advice of a committee under the chairmanship of Lord Pym.

D. L. J.
(Deputy Librarian, House of Lords)
25 January 1988

Introduction

The downfall of James II

M R JUSTICE POWELL ENDED HIS CHARGE TO THE jury in the trial of the seven bishops with a stern warning: 'I can see no difference, nor know of none in law between the King's power to dispense with laws ecclesiastical, and his power to dispense with any other laws whatsoever. If this be once allowed of, there will need no Parliament; all the Legislature will be in the King, which is a thing worth considering, and I leave the issue to God and your consciences.'[1] The jury acquitted the bishops. Powell was dismissed from the bench for his open defiance of the King.

This verdict at the end of June 1688 marked yet another rebuff for James who had sought since his accession on 6 February 1685 to remove the legal disabilities on his fellow Catholics. He had prorogued the Parliament held in 1685 because both Houses, but especially the House of Lords, had refused to countenance any attempt to repeal the Test Acts which prohibited Catholics from holding offices and from sitting in Parliament. James had pursued his policy by other means. Fortified by the decision in the test case *Godden v Hales*, he dispensed with the laws and appointed individual Catholics to offices. He increased the size of the army and placed Catholics among the officers. He established the Ecclesiastical Commission to discipline the clergy and the universities. He used this Commission to punish clergy who preached against Catholicism and to appoint a master and Catholic fellows to Magdalen College Oxford against the wishes of the college. He sought to pack Parliament by turning out those Lord-Lieutenants and sheriffs who refused to accept the need to repeal the Test Acts. He remodelled borough charters to produce obedient electors in the borough constituencies which selected 78 per cent of the members in the Commons. He conducted a survey to find suitable candidates. He pursued, at the same time, extra-parliamentary methods and used the suspending power which the House of Commons had declared illegal in 1672. The first Declaration of Indulgence published in April 1687 was a failure because the Dissenters refused to accept the Declaration and foiled James's aim of dividing the Protestants. Many of his subjects reflected that if the King could suspend certain laws by a Declaration then he could well suspend other laws in the future. James reissued the Declaration in April 1688 but it attracted little attention until he ordered on 4 May 1688 that it should be read in all the churches. The authority of the Church of England would be placed behind the Declaration. Seven bishops, led by the Archbishop of Canterbury, petitioned against the Declaration and found themselves accused of seditious libel in the Court of King's Bench.

When the bishops were taken to the Tower, the banks of the Thames were crowded with men angry at the King's actions. The same men rejoiced when the bishops were acquitted. Yet the fact that the bishops, the most obedient of subjects, were the men who had stood forth against the King shows the lack of significant opposition to James. Political opposition had remained mute because the heir to the throne was Mary, the wife of William of Orange and a dedicated Protestant. On 10 June, two days after the bishops went to the Tower, Queen Mary secured the Catholic succession when she gave birth to a son, James Francis Edward.

William of Orange maintained a close watch on events in England. He was concerned not only for his wife's rights but also for his own country because James's policies were forcing the English court to rely more and more on Louis XIV who threatened the Netherlands. Englishmen in flight from James found a refuge in the Netherlands and they urged William to invade England. He hesitated until April 1688 when he requested an invitation from persons of consequence who would be prepared to support him. William's decision was prompted by the sturdy rumour that the Queen's pregnancy was an imposture and a spurious child would be named the heir.

While the trial of the bishops was in progress, leading Englishmen were canvassed. A number refused to sign the invitation but kept silent. The invitation was finally signed by seven men: The Earls of Danby, Devonshire and Shrewsbury; Lord Lumley; the Bishop of London; Edward Russell and Henry Sidney. Not one of them was of great importance politically at that time; all of them had been slighted or injured by James. Arthur Herbert, once a Rear-Admiral, disguised himself as an ordinary sailor and carried the invitation to the Netherlands in the week after the acquittal of the bishops.

James decided to call a Parliament and gave his approval for the issuing of writs at a Council held on 24 August. The proclamation, published on 21 September, announced 'that as it is our royal purpose to endeavour a legal establishment of an universal liberty of conscience for all our subjects; it is also our resolution inviolably to preserve the Church of England ... And for the further securing not only the Church of England but the Protestant religion in general; We are willing the Roman Catholicks shall remain incapable to be Members of the House of Commons.' One week later, the writs were recalled and another proclamation informed the King's subjects that 'We have received undoubted advice, that a great and sudden invasion from Holland, with an armed force of foreigners and strangers, will speedily be made in a hostile manner upon this Our Kingdom.'[2]

Concessions were rapidly offered by the King in early October: the charters of the City of London and other municipalities were restored; the Ecclesiastical Commission was dissolved; the justices and deputy-lieutenants dismissed for their opposition were restored to office in several counties; the Fellows of Magdalen College were reinstated. The news that the Dutch fleet had been driven back by a storm led James to suspend any further concessions. But the fleet was seen sailing past Dover and on 5 November Lord Preston, a Secretary of State, received a note from Cowes Castle that at break of day an officer of the Customs had seen 200 sail off the east coast of the Isle of Wight[3].

William of Orange landed at Torbay on the same day – Monday, 5 November. He entered Exeter on the following Friday and published his Declaration at the Market Cross. In this document, already published in the Netherlands and seen by James on 1 November, William recited James's misdeeds, attacked his counsellors, cast doubt on the paternity of James Francis and proclaimed his intention of ensuring a free Parliament: 'we now think fit to declare, that this our expedition is intended for no other design, but to have a free and lawful Parliament assembled as soon as is possible.'[4]

Before James left to join his army on Salisbury Plain, he summoned a council on 17 November and told his counsellors that he had intended to call a Parliament at this time but because foreign troops were in his kingdom it could not be a free Parliament. When he emerged from the Council, the Archbishops of Canterbury and York presented an address: 'the only visible way to preserve your Majesty and this kingdom, would be the calling of a Parliament, regular and free in all its circumstances.' Six bishops and twelve peers signed this address; other peers refused to sign because they could not see how two armies could be maintained in the land until a Parliament was called. The King rejected the address[5].

Almost every day, James received the bitter news of defections to William's cause. Lord Delamere rose in Cheshire; the Earl of Danby in Yorkshire; the Earl of Devonshire in Nottinghamshire. A spate of rumoured defections from the command of his army greeted the King when he arrived on Salisbury Plain. His nerves collapsed and he suffered from severe bleeding in the nose. These rumours were confirmed when Lord Churchill, whom the King had raised from obscurity, and the Duke of Grafton, his illegitimate nephew, deserted to William. They were soon followed by Prince George of Denmark, the King's son-in-law, and the

Anne, the King's younger daughter, fled from London to Nottingham. James left his army – four times the size of William's forces – and returned to London.

All the peers and bishops in town – around twenty peers and ten bishops – were summoned to a council at Whitehall on Tuesday 27 November. The King referred to the petition presented ten days ago and remarked that there appeared to be a general feeling abroad that a Parliament should be summoned. He asked the peers for their present advice. There was a warm debate: Lord Clarendon, James's brother-in-law, spoke vehemently and angrily against those who had invaded their laws and liberties. He told James that he had warned him often of the consequences of his actions and if James had listened more then his affairs would not now be in disarray. Lord Nottingham spoke softly but severely while Lord Halifax attempted to smooth the meeting and to reach a conclusion. One peer demanded that all Catholics should be dismissed from public offices especially that of sheriff which had an important role in elections. James indicated that he intended to call a Parliament and would consider the other matters raised in the council[6].

Lord Jeffreys, the Lord Chancellor, remarked in the Law Courts at Westminster the next morning that the writs would be sealed on the following day and that Parliament would meet on 15 January. On the same day, the Grand Jury in Westminster Hall handed a paper to the judges of the King's Bench in which they petitioned the King for a Parliament. The judges hastily decided that it was none of their business. At a council on 30 November, James announced that he was issuing the writs for a Parliament on 15 January and anyone could stand for election even those in arms for the Prince. He also issued a general pardon and sent the Marquess of Halifax, the Earl of Nottingham and Lord Godolphin – one from each rank of the peerage – as Commissioners to treat with the Prince[7].

The message carried by the Commissioners was brief: 'The King commanded us to acquaint you, that he observeth all the differences and causes of complaint alledged by your Highness, seem to be referred to a free Parliament. His Majesty, as he hath already declared, was resolved before this to call one, but thought that in the present state of affairs; it was adviseable to deferr it, till things were more composed: Yet seeing that his people still continue to desire it, he hath put forth his proclamation in order to it, and hath issued his writs for the call of it. And to prevent any cause of interruption in it, he will consent to every thing that can be reasonably required for the security of all those that come to it...' William told the Commissioners that if the King remained in London during the Parliament, then he should also be there with an equal number of guards; if the

King stayed outside London then William would also stay away and at the same distance[8].

The news that James intended to call a Parliament was greeted with general relief. Richard Warre, Under-Secretary to Lord Preston, wrote to a friend in Stockholm: 'Almost all the people in the nation of all ranks & condition are set upon a Parliament as the only means that can restore and settle a lasting peace in the Kingdom... God send us a good issue at last and preserve the King.' The Navy sent Lord Berkeley with a congratulatory address: 'To give His Majesty their most thankfull acknowledgements for calling a Parliament, the only proper means for securing our lawes and the Protestant religion in defence whereof they would sacrifice their lives.' On hearing the news, the Duke of Norfolk sent the gentlemen who had risen in Norfolk back home after they had publicly declared their approval of the King's decision. Henry Barker ejected in April from his post as Clerk of the Crown – an office with a vital role in the despatch and receipt of writs – in favour of the Catholic Sir Robert Clarke was suddenly restored to his post. Although the writs had not been sent out, a Common Hall was summoned to meet at the Guildhall on 18 December to choose members for the City of London[9].

James's main concern during the first week of December was for the safety and postion of James Francis whose legitimacy might be denounced by William's supporters in Parliament. Disguised as a laundress, Queen Mary left Whitehall during the early hours of 10 December and fled with the child to France. Later that day, James ordered Jeffreys to surrender the Great Seal and the writs which remained to be issued. He received both that evening. The writs were destroyed and, around two in the morning of 11 December, the King attended only by Sir Edward Hales left Whitehall Palace. As they crossed from the Horseferry at Westminster to Lambeth, James dropped the Great Seal into the river. This foolish action was intended to foil the planned Parliament[10].

The Interregnum

Close observers of the King had realised that he was contemplating flight; the loyal Earl of Ailesbury 'fell on my knees with tears, humbly beseeching him not to think of going'[11]. The Earl of Rochester, James's brother-in-law, and the Bishop of Ely had drawn up a declaration and written notes summoning the lords to the Guildhall once the King had left. Both men were loyal to James and intended that the meeting would safeguard the King's throne.

Six bishops and twenty-two peers gathered at the Guildhall around mid-day. The meeting began well for the loyalists: Sancroft, the Archbishop of Canterbury, took the chair and Francis Gwyn, Rochester's secretary, was appointed secretary. The most immediate problem was public order: the mob had attacked several Catholic dwellings and the Earl of Feversham had followed James's orders to disband the army but he had not disarmed the soldiers. Popular violence against Catholics had occurred on several occasions since October and James had turned down, on 22 November, a proposal by Sir Edward Hales that mortar pieces should be mounted in the Tower. The King pointed out that this would destroy the city and the wealth of the nation and the King and would 'so far exasperate the people all over England as to cause a general defection.' With his order to disband the army, James had increased the likelihood of considerable violence from the mob[12]. The Lords took prompt action: Skelton, Lieutenant of the Tower and a Catholic, was summoned; the Earl of Craven was ordered to raise the militia of Westminster and Middlesex to preserve the peace; the Earl of Feversham was ordered to remove the troops under his command to quarters distant from the city; the Earl of Dartmouth was ordered to prevent hostilities between his fleet and that of the Prince of Orange and also to remove Catholic officers. When Skelton arrived, he was told that the Lords could not trust him to hold the Tower and Lord Lucas was named in his place.

Four lords: Rochester, Weymouth and the Bishops of Ely and of Rochester were asked to prepare a declaration to be issued at the end of the meeting. A text had already been drafted by the Bishop of Ely and the Earl of Rochester. When the meeting considered their draft, Wharton together with Montague, Newport and Culpepper argued that the paragraph relating to the King should be omitted. Wharton, a friend of Oliver Cromwell and practised in opposition, had visited William when he spent several months travelling in Europe during the early part of James's reign. The other three were lesser men: Montague was an opportunist who failed to obtain employment under James; Newport, described by Ailesbury as the most violent and waspish of all, had lost his posts when he refused to support the repeal of the Test Acts; Culpepper had been without official employment for a long time. The bishops argued strongly that the declaration should favour the King's interest which led a choleric peer to exclaim: 'These Bishops are returning to their vomit of Popery.'[13] The radical faction gained their point because they collected support from peers who lacked employment and from peers who had been members of the Council or the Household and were disappointed by the King's flight.

The declaration emphasised the need for a Parliament and requested

William to aid them in obtaining one. All the lords present signed; the Archbishop of Canterbury pointed out to Lord Ailesbury that if they refused they would be marked men. The four lords who drafted the declaration were sent to present it to the Prince. They obtained a cool reception because the Lords had not conferred any power on William and, unlike the City of London, they had not invited him to London[14].

On the following day, Lord Halifax arrived back from his journey as one of the King's Commissioners. Halifax had carefully avoided a commitment to either the King or the Prince; he had changed his mind because the King had duped the Commissioners by preparing for his flight while they were negotiating with William. It was known that James had ignored a letter he received from his Commissioners a few hours before his flight[15]. While at the Prince's camp, Halifax spoke briefly to Gilbert Burnet, an English clergyman who came over with William, and he knew that William and his supporters were content that the King should depart. As the leading politican among the peers, Halifax took the chair for the remainder of the sitting of this assembly.

The number of peers in London was increasing daily. The Earl of Nottingham urged his father-in-law, Viscount Hatton, to come to London: 'when every day produces such extraordinary things: & tho you can't remove your family on a sudden yet you might immediately come yourselfe, & I should be glad you would come hither, that we might consider ye present circumstances & how to behave ourselves; & London is not yet a safe place ye rabble committing every night great disorders & that is ye Prince of Orange may be here tomorrow but there is no doubt but he will be here on Saturday.'[16]

The maintenance of public order was still the most pressing concern of the Lords because rumours were causing great alarm and fears. Colonel Selwyn of the Footguards and Colonel Baggott of the Hereditary Prince of Denmark's Regiment of Foot were ordered to quell and disperse the mob '& in case of necessity to use force and fire upon them with bullett.' The Lords were also worried about the fate of the writs issued by James. Lord Jeffreys, the former Lord Chancellor, tried to escape from London when he learned of the King's flight. At their meeting on 12 December, the Lords were informed that he had been caught at Wapping and they ordered Lord Lucas to take him to the Tower. Lucas questioned Jeffreys and, on his report, three peers were sent to seal the King's closet. Jeffreys claimed that he sent out all the writs to places where there were Protestant sheriffs and had returned to the King all the writs out of counties with Catholic sheriffs. Sir John Ernley reported that 16 writs had been sent out and 36 held back while the Earl of Thanet remarked that he was a Protestant sheriff and had asked three or four times for the writs but had been refused.

The Lords were thrown into confusion when a messenger arrived from Kent with a hearsay report of the King's whereabouts. After an excited discussion, Halifax successfully argued that there were many reasons to doubt this information and he suggested that they should meet at four that afternoon. When they met later that day, the Sword-Bearer of the City appeared with a seaman called Robert Clinton who described how the men of Feversham detained the King. The Bishop of Winchester argued that they had sufficient evidence about the King and they should send a number of Lords together with his servants to the King. This suggestion led to some argument and Halifax showed himself very reluctant to do anything. Finally, it was agreed that one peer should go immediately to warn the King that a number of Lords with a troop of guards were on their way to him. Lord Ailesbury volunteered and he set out in search of his beloved master who greeted him with an air of displeasure and the remark: 'You were all Kings when I left London.' The Lords sent a message to William, now at Windsor, explaining what they had done[17].

The Lords continued to sit until 15 December and they turned their attention again to the fate of the Great Seal and the writs. William Chiffinch, the Page of the Backstairs and the Keeper of the King's Cabinet-Closet where all his papers resided, was questioned as was his servant Joseph Hough. Popular feeling against Lord Jeffreys was still high and it was considered unsafe to bring him from the Tower. North & Grey, Chandois and Ossulstone were sent to examine him. The Lords wished to know: (1) what he had done with the Great Seal; (2) whether he had sealed the writs and what had he done with them; (3) whether he had sealed the several patents for sheriffs for the ensuing year; and, (4) whether he had a licence to go out of the kingdom[18]. The answers arrived that evening: Jeffreys claimed that he had surrendered the Great Seal to the King during a private audience the previous Saturday afternoon; the writs he had sent by his servant Gosling to the King and they were delivered the same Saturday afternoon; he had sealed the patents for new sheriffs but could not remember the details; he had received several passes to go abroad. Jeffreys thanked the Lords for securing him from the rabble[19]. James provided considerable ammunition to his enemies when he threw away the Great Seal: 'It is the Great Seal that is the dead spring of our government, as the King's presence, or the presence of any that are deputed by him, gives life to it: when this disappears, and the King withdraws himself, without naming any persons to represent him, the government is certainly laid down and forsaken by him.'[20]

Around six in the evening, shortly before listening to the evidence from

Jeffreys, Halifax received a letter from the Earl of Middleton, dated 7.30 a.m. that morning at Feversham, which reported that the King was well and would be at Whitehall the next morning[21]. James rode through the city, around three in the following afternoon, and some of the people ran bareheaded before him. When he arrived at Whitehall, 'a great number of persons, before that, suspected to have left England, did appear in a very brisk manner at court.'[22]

Halifax and other peers who did not wish to meet the King left London to join William at Windsor where the 'foolish men of Feversham' were abused for stopping the King. William asked the peers for their advice. Twelve peers held a secret meeting with Halifax in the chair. They were all in agreement that James should not go to one of his own houses. Lord Delamere, seconded by Mordaunt, moved that he should go to the Tower but this was opposed by Grafton, Churchill and Shrewsbury. Not one of the peers wished to do anything to help James. The heated meeting ended with a decision that James should be advised to withdraw to Ham where the Duchess of Lauderdale, away in Scotland, had a mansion. When Clarendon, arriving too late for the meeting, asked why the King should not go to Windsor or Hampton Court, Lord Delamere 'very angrily (a little thing put him into a passion) said, he did not look upon him as his King, and would never pay him obedience.' William made the peers carry their decision to the King who asked if he could go to Rochester rather than to Ham. On the morning of 18 December, James was rowed down the river to Rochester while, about two in the afternoon, William attended by large numbers of nobility and gentry entered London and went to the house of the Duke of Grafton. A meeting of peers declared themselves for William, and Princess Anne, wearing orange ribbons, went to the theatre[23]. In Ashford, Sir Edward Dering presented venison to the town and Sir John Knatchbull attended the celebrations at the Saracens Head where he drank the Prince of Orange's health and told the company: 'it was my oppinion still (as it always was) that his Majesty would be gone againe for all that he was now att London.'[24]

William addressed sixty-five Lords at a meeting on 21 December: 'I have desir'd you to meet here to advise the best manner how to produce the end of my Declaration in calling a free Parliament for the preservation of the Protestant religion, & returning the rights & liberties of the Kingdom & settling the same that they may not be in danger of being again subverted.' He left them to their deliberations. The Declaration published by William at the beginning of his invasion was read and Culpepper moved that thanks be given to the Prince for his Declaration and for calling the peers together. Halifax agreed with the thanks for the Declaration but suggested a tenderness about the thanks for calling the peers together because they had a birth-right which might be prejudiced. There was some debate upon this point until Halifax urged them to keep to the thanks for the Declaration. It was resolved that they should meet tomorrow at ten and Halifax suggested they meet in the House of Lords because it was more convenient for hearing than any other place. At the end of their sitting, the Prince replied to the thanks of the Lords: 'I will do all I can for the good of ye Nation, which I think myself oblig'd to do both in honour and conscience.'[25]

The only business done by the Lords on 22 December was a debate on the removal of all Catholics from London. There was no dispute over their removal but there were pleas for exception: Clarendon asked that the servants of the Queen Dowager, Charles II's widow, should be exempt. The main business, 'to consider of a way to have a Parliament', was deferred until Monday.[26]

King James 'hufft and talkt at Rochester how he would not stirr' but stole away in disguise early on Sunday morning. He left a letter to Lord Middleton in which he explained that he had withdrawn until his subjects returned to their obedience. Francis Gwyn complained to another loyalist, Lord Dartmouth, that the King 'chose as ill a time now, as he did before, for tomorrow the Lords are to meet concerning a Parliament, and I wish he had stayed to hear what their method had been.'[27]

The loyalists led a heated discussion on the fate of the King and the contents of his letter when seventy-three Lords met on Monday. Godolphin claimed that he had seen the letter and that it would provide no satisfaction for the Lords. A motion that the Lords should send to Lord Middleton - not present being a Scottish peer – was defeated and Paget turned their attention to the business of calling a free Parliament. The Lords fell into a discussion as to whether the King's departure was a demise in law. Pembroke suggested 'that it is to be consider'd whether this is an abdication that the Prince of Wales's right is to be considered into & that all this cannot be better done than by a Convention, but there should be a power in the mean time there being no officer.' He failed to bring his fellows to the point and the loyalists continued to argue for an enquiry into the King's departure until Culpepper pointed out that their meeting was a certain sign that there was no government and thus no need of any proof or enquiry.

Paget again turned their attention to the matter of a Parliament and the question of the writs arose. The sixteen writs issued by James II would result in the election of around 180 members. Devonshire suggested that a way be found for electing members of the Commons while Halifax argued that an address be made to the Prince to issue circular letters for electing members and that he should take the administration on himself. Clarendon wanted the Parliament to consist of the 180 members elected on the writs already issued. Nottingham, the careful constitutionalist, pointed out that if they held a convention there would be no need for oaths as in a Parliament. He proposed that, in the meantime, there should be a regency on the precedent of John's regency when Richard I was imprisoned. The Convention would send propositions to James. Nottingham suggested what these should be: the legitimacy of James Francis would be left to Parliament; the King would follow the advice of Parliament in matters relating to the religion, liberties and security of his subjects; the members of Parliament would be bound by oath from which they would be absolved if the King broke his promise; on his return the King would call a free Parliament which would sit for thirty days every year.

In the end, the Lords agreed to ask the Prince to send circular letters to the coroners for the election of members and he should take upon himself the administration of the kingdom. Coroners were choosen because they were elected by all the freeholders in the county court unlike the sheriffs who had been appointed by James. On the afternoon of Christmas Day, the Lords met and signed fair copies on vellum of the address requesting the Prince to issue the circular letters and of the address asking William to take charge of the administration of the government. Francis Gwyn wrote again to Lord Dartmouth: 'But it is now all over; neither he [the King], nor his (if the child be so), are like ever to set foot here again.'[28]

When the Lords went in a body to present the addresses to William, the Prince refused to give them an answer until he had spoken with the gentlemen formerly of the House of Commons. He was shrewd enough to want more support than the Lords alone. On 23 December, he issued a proclamation which summoned all the members of the Commons in the Parliaments of Charles II and who were near London to meet him at St James's on Boxing Day. Men who had sat only in James's Parliament were pointedly excluded[29]. William also summoned the Lord Mayor and Court of Aldermen of London as well as fifty members of the Common Council. When they arrived at St James's, the Prince asked them to advise the best manner for 'calling a free Parliament, for the preservation of the Protestant religion, and restoring of the rights and liberties of the kingdom, and settling the same, that they may not be in danger of being again subverted...'

When the meeting moved to the House of Commons, it was estimated that there were 400 men present and 220 of them had been members of the Commons. They followed the practice of the House: Henry Powle was elected Speaker while Paul Jodrell and Samuel Gillham, the Clerk and

Clerk Assistant, were present to assist Powle. A few thought that the Lord Mayor and the citizens of London should depart and hold their discussions separately as William had suggested if the chamber proved too small. Serjeant Maynard, a member of almost every Parliament since 1640, replied that the citizens were now the chief magistrates and this was a time for amity between Protestants[30].

An influential group was prepared to argue that William should assume the Crown immediately. They did not press this argument because several of those present were still loyal to James and, more important, the Lords had given contrary advice the previous day. There was some uncertainty as to what the Lords had said and Francis Gwyn appeared with copies of their addresses which were read, debated and agreed. When they discussed the resolution that the Prince should take charge of the government, Sir Robert Sawyer asked for an explanation of the term 'administration civil.' This provoked a tart response from Maynard who pointed out that, as a fellow lawyer, he had seen Sawyer in Westminster Hall where that term was daily explained – 'but if we sit here till that Gentlemen understand, no man can tell when we shall rise.' Maynard's great age drew respect; when William congratulated him on being the oldest lawyer in the country, Maynard replied 'I was afraid, had not your Highness come just when he did, that I should have outlived the Law itself.' Sawyer was being devious rather than foolish in his question because he wished the meeting to consider the question of civil administration and thus provide him with an opportunity to introduce the idea of a regency. He was silenced effectively by Maynard[31].

After William had accepted the addresses presented by both assemblies, he sealed the circular letters for summoning a Convention and ordered them sent to the proper officers. Offers from private gentlemen to deliver them as they went to canvass in the country were firmly refused. On 5 January, the Prince issued an order restricting his soldiers to their barracks while the election was in progress. The public reason for this order was that the Prince wanted to prevent disorder but he also wished to thwart the suggestion that Englishmen were voting under the direction of Dutch soldiers[32].

An early historian of the Revolution boasted that the elections 'went on with the greatest liberty that could possibly be conceived; every man giving his vote for whom he pleased without the least sollicitation from the Prince or any of his.'[33] William was tied by his Declaration which promised a free Parliament. Moreover, with only three weeks between the despatch of the circular letters and the election, there was not enough time for the Prince to manage the elections. Free meant that the elections were free from influence excercised by the royal government. Local powers were left to exercise their influence on the result. William had realised this soon after the King's first flight when he wrote to Danby and the gentlemen who had risen at York: 'Therefore I desire you, to give them my hearty thanks for their zeal to the cause and for my service, and to let them know, that it is best for them and that can doe me no better service for the present than to go back for their respective dwellings, and stand for to be chosen Parliamentmen in their counties, and keeping their inclination for me..' Danby advised the Major of Pontefract: 'I hope you will make such distinction in the elections of Parliament men to serve for your borough that you will not choose any who have only looked on whilst others have ventured their all to preserve you, or if you do I am sure you will not have deserved your preservation.'[34]

Contests have been recorded for thirteen seats in nine counties and for fifty-six seats in forty-one boroughs. The vast majority of seats were not contested. The question of who should rule the country did not play a large part in the elections because electors and candidates recognised that this was a matter best left to the Convention. Resentment against those who had acted for James did influence a number of the contests: Samuel Pepys failed to be elected at Harwich and there were false rumours in the constituency that he had attended mass; Robert Price, attorney of South Wales, was voted down in Weobley because he had consented to the repeal of the penal laws – he lost by 47 votes to 53; soldiers intervened at Wallingford in favour of Dormer, a former officer, and the frightened mayor made a double return which had to be resolved by the House of Commons; Sir Robert Sawyer was alarmed by the machinations of his Williamite opponents at Cambridge University but he did obtain a seat[35].

The meetings of the Lords in December had established that there were four parties with a solution to the national crisis: 1. for recalling the King; 2. for a regency; 3. for crowning Princess Mary as the next heir; 4. for crowning William[36].

Few men had the steadfast loyalty of Lord Ailesbury who wished to recall his master. James had lost goodwill and respect after the disgraceful way in which he abandoned the government during his first flight. James made no effort to support or aid those struggling on his behalf. Popular rumour still held that the King would be asked to return but persons with more knowledge realised that this was very unlikely[37].

Failing a recall, the loyalists were prepared to unite with a larger party which argued for a regency on the grounds that England was a hereditary monarchy. Nottingham supported a regency because he feared that upsetting the succession would create an elective monarchy. Rochester and

Clarendon, James's brothers-in-law, were also counted among this party. Rochester had served James and he was disliked intensely by William. Clarendon lacked money and wished to regain the post of Lord Lieutenant in Ireland. William avoided discussing Irish affairs with Clarendon because he wanted an accomodation with the present Lord Lieutenant, Tyrconnell, who hated Clarendon[38]. The disappointed Clarendon followed his natural tendency and, in his muddled and bustling fashion, he argued for a regency. When he called on his niece, Princess Anne, she remarked that it would not be safe for her father to return again. In the strange conversation that followed, Clarendon tried to establish the Princess's opinion while she was polite and evasive[39].

The natural ally of the regency party was the Church of England. Nottingham, Rochester and Clarendon pleaded unsuccessfully with Archbishop Sancroft that he would emerge from the retirement he had maintained at Lambeth since 11 December. However, Lambeth was the scene of several meetings where the clergy discussed their dilemma. Dissenters suspected that the bishops were conspiring to maintain the predominance of the Church in the state. The bishops were concerned because William as a Calvinist was favourable to the Dissenters but the main reason for their reluctance to change their allegiance was the oath they had sworn to James. A regency would enable the calling of a Parliament in the King's name and thus follow the laws of the land. The Bishop of St Asaph joined in their discussions although he favoured William. The Bishop of London was not present and he showed his support for the Princess Mary when he directed his clergy to omit James Francis from their prayers. Sancroft made a feeble protest[40].

The natural head of the regency party should have been Danby but his disenchantment with James had led him to sign the invitation to William and to place himself at the head of the gentry who rose for William in Yorkshire. When Danby arrived in London on Boxing Day, he was piqued to find that Halifax, his great rival, had won the Prince's confidence while he himself received little attention from William. The Prince's supporters were also cool towards Danby; his name was absent from a list drawn up by Burnet in the middle of December, 'of men in whom the Nation trusts' and suitable for employment by the Prince[41]. Danby had been absent from the meeting on 24 December when Lord Paget proposed that Mary should succeed to the throne. Paget had been supported by the Bishop of London, Danby's ally, and by Lord North. These men believed that because James had withdrawn himself and James Francis was not his son then Mary as the heir had succeeded to the throne[42]. In the first week of January, Danby wrote to Mary and assured her that he would be 'strictly devoted to your personall interests.' Clarendon also wrote to his niece but on the eve of the Convention when he warned her: 'it is too much to be feared a Crown thus obtayn'd, will never sitt fast.'[43]

Englishmen who had returned from their Dutch exile argued that James had ceded the throne. The most busy of these men was Gilbert Burnet who wrote a memorandum, before the King's first flight, which gave the reasons for and against both a regency and a deposition[44]. Burnet favoured deposition by mid-January and argued, in an anonymous pamphlet, that: 'his deserting is still to be dated from his first going from White-Hall; and he having given that first advantage against himself, which came after all that series of injustice and violence that had gone before it, no man can think it was not very fitting to carry it as far as it would go, and not to treat with him any more upon the foot of acknowledging him King.' James loathed Burnet and had sent the royal yacht on an unsuccessful mission to kidnap him from the Netherlands. Robert Ferguson, surnamed the plotter, had also returned from exile and he expressed himself more boldly: 'we are willing to acknowledge the kindness we have received from him at last, in his leaving the Nation and retiring beyond the seas. And that which is now incumbent upon us ... is to bolt the door after him and so foreclose his return.'[45]

Neither Burnet nor Ferguson were in the inner circles of the Prince's advisers but they reflected the opinions of many who did have the Prince's confidence. Halifax remained aloof from the discussions; a newsletter sarcastically observed of his behaviour on 24 December that 'Lord Halifax trims it like himself.'[46] Clarendon complained after Halifax visited him on 4 January that 'he seemed very dark, and to be much upon the reserve in his discourse.' Halifax had one great advantage over his friends and enemies: he knew the Prince's mind. In a private conversation on 30 December, William told Halifax that 'hee would not stay in England, if K. James came again. He said with the strongest asservations, that hee would go, if they went about to make him a Regent.'[47]

William's supporters encountered a major difficulty in the sentiment many Englishmen felt for Mary. William Herbert, on hearing that there was a plan to crown William alone, 'protested against ever drawing a sword on the Prince's side, if he could have imagin'd him capable of such usage to his wife.' Bentinck, the Prince's Dutch favourite, who had argued for William on this occasion, as he had done often, left immediately to consult the Prince and returned within half an hour with the assurance that William would be content with 'conjunctive sovereignty.' This was accepted even by the Prince's most extreme supporters. 'That which remains to be done, is to declare the Prince of Orange King and settle upon him the sovereignty and regal power; allowing in the mean time to the Princess, the privilege of being named with him in all leases, patents and grants.'[48]

William had confessed to Halifax his concern about the Commonwealth Party which appeared to him the strongest in England. He feared they would make him a 'Duke of Venice' – a powerless monarch. The presence of so many radicals among the exiles in the Netherlands had coloured William's views although Princess Anne was also perturbed about their influence. A commonwealth party was not a republican party: 'to dream of reducing England to a Democratical Republick is incident only to persons of shallow capacities.' The aim of the Commonwealth Party was to reduce the monarch to a figure-head and transfer power over the executive to Parliament. Royal fears were exaggerated; this was an insignificant group of men like Wildman who had been a radical plotter since the time of Oliver Cromwell[49].

The Convention

Once the elections were over, the members set out for London. The total number of members in the Commons was 551: 183 had been elected for the first time; 196 sat in the Parliament called by James in 1685; 176 sat in the Parliaments of Charles II. The vast majority, around 70 percent, were country gentlemen without any mercantile or professional interests. The crisis caused by the attempt a decade earlier to exclude James from the succession had given rise to two parties: the Whigs being exclusionists and the Tories being against exclusion. These party labels had not been used during the election and they appear infrequently in the sources for the Convention although they returned to common use soon afterwards. A study of the individual members has shown that the majority had Whiggish sympathies. However, the attitude of members towards James did not always follow their Tory or Whig beliefs and we will describe the parties as loyalist or Williamite.

The House of Lords consisted of 181 peers: 11 dukes; 2 marquesses; 66 earls; 9 viscounts; 67 barons; 2 archbishops; 24 bishops. It was in the House of Lords that James II had encountered outspoken criticism of his wish to repeal the Test Act. There was a majority of loyalists in the House but they were also devoted members of the Church of England.

Attendance in both houses was unusually high during the Convention as compared to the normal attendance in previous and succeeding Parlia-

ments. The average attendance in the Lords was 95 while the same figure
for the Commons was 346. Approximately two-thirds of the lords did not
speak while four-fifths of the members of the House of Commons remained
silent and their numbers included Isaac Newton and Christopher Wren.

The Convention had been summoned to settle the national crisis but
both houses appointed the committees usual in Parliament. John Locke
was vexed: 'People are astonished here to see them medle with any small
matters and when the setlement of the nation upon sure grounds of peace
and security is put into their hands, which can noe way soe well be don as
by restoreing our ancient government, the best possibly that ever was if
taken and put togeater all of a piece in its originall constitution.' The Lords
also appointed a committee to investigate the death of the Earl of Essex.
After his arrest in June 1683 for complicity in the Rye House plot, Arthur
Capell, Earl of Essex, was sent to the Tower where he was found, a few
days later, with his throat cut. The evidence pointed towards suicide but
the opposition believed he had been murdered. The Lords could now
investigate the matter but despite several meetings during the Convention
and later the committee failed to reach any conclusion[50].

Tuesday, 22 January

There was no ceremony when the Convention met. The first task of the
House of Lords was to select a Speaker *pro tempore* who would guide, in the
absence of royal ministers, the business of the House. Danby's supporters
put his name forward but Halifax was the natural choice because he had
filled this role in the meetings held in December. In place of a speech from
the throne, Halifax read out a letter from the Prince who urged 'that no
interruption may be given to a happy and lasting settlement.' William
reminded the Lords of the dangerous situation of the Protestants in Ireland
and the peril facing the Netherlands engaged since November in a war with
France. The House went on to name the assistants who were normally the
judges and whose role was to advise committees of the House on bills and
other matters. Because the judges had been too obedient to the wishes of
both Charles II and James II, the House named lawyers who had shown
independence of the government. The men named were Sir Robert Atkins,
William Montague, Sir William Dolben, Sir Creswell Levinz, Mr. Bradbury, Mr. Petyt, Sir John Holt, William Whitlock and Sir Edward Nevill.
Objections were raised against Bradbury as a second-rate lawyer but the
Earl of Dorset employed him in family affairs and insisted on his nomination[51].

In the House of Commons, the Earl of Wiltshire nominated as Speaker

Henry Powle who had acted in this post during the meeting of the members of Charles II's Parliaments. Sir Edward Seymour had a number of supporters but his nomination was not pressed to a vote. Seymour was a magnate in the West Country and he had joined the Prince following the publication of the Declaration in Exeter but by January he realised, to his dismay, that William intended to be King[52].

After the House had been called and defaulters noted, the Speaker read the Prince's letter. Sir Henry Capel moved that the state of the nation be considered on the following day in view of the urgency and the fact that the House was full. Sir Thomas Clarges argued that the debate on national affairs should be postponed until Monday because not all the members had arrived. This was agreed. Halifax later spoke with warmth to Clarges about this delay which had been deliberately planned by Clarges, Heneage Finch and the latter's brother, the Earl of Nottingham. The loyalists hoped that if the House of Lords held their debate on the state of the nation first then it might forestall radical action by the House of Commons[53].

Throughout the day, both Houses had been negotiating over the text of an address of thanks to the Prince. When the address was ready, both Houses adjourned and led by their Speakers went to present it to the Prince[54].

Wednesday 23 January.

William's reply to the address was read in both houses. The Lords selected the usual committees and ordered that no Catholics should appear in the Palace of Westminster. The Commons ordered that a letter be sent to the Prince requesting him to authorise elections in vacant seats which had arisen where a member had been elected for two constituencies and then chose to serve in one of them. Both houses adjourned: the Lords until the next day and the Commons until 26 January.

During the intervening days, members consulted among themselves and paid their respects to the Prince. Sir John Knatchbull, on the evening of this day, met with fellow-members and other gentlemen from Kent. Knatchbull and Sir Vere Fane were selected to present the Association to the Prince – the Association was a document drafted in November by Sir Edward Seymour for English gentry to sign as a mark of their support of William. Two days later, the gentlemen from Kent gathered at Locketts around eleven in the morning and went in a body to St James's. When Sir Vere approached William, he was told: 'Sir lett the Gentlemen come in (for they staid att the doore) first that I may see them for they will not know me else and when Sir Vere had read over the Assossiation the Prince said I thank the gentlemen for their kindness and will be ready to doe them any service I can.' William was behaving with unusual affability[55].

Thursday 24 January

The House of Lords considered the petition of the Duke of Norfolk against the representatives of the Dowager Duchess who wished to auction on this day statutes, pictures and drawings from the great collection of the Duke's great-grandfather, the Earl of Arundel. Faced with conflicting opinions from the legal assistants, the House came to a sensible decision and ordered the auction stopped until the courts in Westminster Hall were open and the Duke could present his case in the Court of Chancery[56]. Halifax had noted that the Speaker of the Commons was accompanied by the mace when both Houses presented the address to the Prince; the Clerk of the Parliaments was instructed to find out if a Speaker *pro tempore* in the Lords should have a mace[57].

Friday 25 January

This was the day appointed for the calling of the House of Lords. Thirteen peers were under age while Holderness and the Bishop of Hereford were excused on the grounds of great age. Jeffreys and Peterborough were in the Tower for their misdeeds under James II. Howard of Effingham was in Virginia. Langdale, Sunderland, Powis and Berwick had fled abroad and the last two were with James as was the Bishop of Chester. Twelve peers and three bishops were sick but seven of them appeared for a number of the sittings of the Convention. Twenty peers and two bishops were recorded as absent: eight peers attended later meetings of the Convention; nine peers were Catholics and could not attend; the Archbishop of Canterbury and the Bishop of Coventry & Lichfield stayed away throughout the Convention as did Conyers, Newcastle and Willoughby of Parham. The Speaker was ordered to summon the absent lords. The Duke of Newcastle who had played an ignominious role in the rising in the North pleaded ill-health: 'I am soe very weake, I have noe stomack, eate noething but a little broth.' Conyers excused himself because of the death of a son and ill-health. Willoughby of Parham was in his late eighties and was probably excused on the grounds of age[58].

The calling of the House was interrupted by the introduction of the Duke of Northumberland despite the fact that the King had fled and that this was not a Parliament. When all the names had been called, the Earl of Berkeley rose to protest that Lord Griffin had not been introduced. Griffin, a hunting companion of the King, had been created a peer on 17 November

and he replied that he had received a writ of summons and that his patent
was at the door. Lord Delamere strongly opposed the presence of Griffin
but Lovelace moved that he should be introduced. Lovelace realised that
this would allow the introduction of Lord Carteret, a Williamite, and
Griffin was introduced between Delamere and Lovelace – both men
violently opposed to James.

Nottingham and his friends pursued their strategy and moved that the
House should consider the state of the nation either now or tomorrow.
Devonshire argued that they should wait until Tuesday when they would
know what the Commons had resolved on Monday. Winchester and Halifax supported Devonshire as did several other peers and Tuesday was
appointed as the day for considering the present state of the nation. William's supporters had passed the initative to the Commons[59].

Saturday 26 January

The Commons listened to petitions relating to the elections and they appointed Dr. Sharp, the Dean of Norwich, to preach before the House at St
Margaret's Westminster on 30 January, the anniversary of the death of
Charles I. Sir Thomas Lee argued that no day at such a distance should be
kept for anything but the business of the House but he was ignored[60].

Monday 28 January

Sir Edward Seymour moved that the House of Commons resolve itself into
a Committee of the Whole House to discuss the state of the nation. Col.
Birch and Serjeant Maynard, both Williamites, argued that the debate
should be in the House itself. The latter course would be quicker because
members could only speak once in the House while there was greater
freedom in the Committee. The majority were for a Committee and Richard Hampden, the son of John Hampden of ship money fame, was called
to the chair.

A long pause was broken by a young member, Gilbert Dolben, who
made a learned speech which ended with the motion that 'it is the opinion
of the committee, that King James is demised; by voluntary departure, in
consequence of which the government is without a king.' Dolben's remarks implied that the crown should pass to the next successor. Another
pause ended when John Arnold, a radical, seconded the motion. More
determined and sensible opponents of James were soon on their feet. Sir
Robert Howard recited the arbitrary acts of the King and described his
departure as above a demise being an abdication. He recalled that James
had departed without making any provision for the government and ended

with the motion that 'King James the 2nd by advice of Jesuits or some ill Advisers has violated all laws in Church & State, has subverted & thereby & by withdrawing himself has abdicated the government & is no longer our King.' He was seconded by an angry Sir John Morton.

The loyalists were less united than the Williamites: Dolben had argued for a demise; Sir Christopher Musgrave doubted that the House had the power to depose the King and wanted the opinion of the lawyers; Sir Robert Sawyer made a confused speech in which he wondered if they were representative of the people but believed that the King had abdicated; Heneage Finch argued weakly for a regency; Sir Thomas Clarges made a good point when be suggested that the House keep to the Prince's original declaration. Not one of these speakers expressed a wish to see the King return. Williamite speakers dominated the debate. Pollexfen, the distinguished lawyer, put their position succintly when he remarked 'I conceive the crown is vacant & that wee need not trouble our heades over a demise or differ about words, but wee must agree in this, that to avoid confusion to make a settlement is absolutely necessary.'

The House was full and impatient members grew angry as the arguments were rehearsed again and again. A number of speakers could not be heard and there were cries of 'Speak out Speak out' which led Sir William Pulteney to remark 'It is a time & indeed to speak out' as he began a masterly indictment of James II. Sir Henry Capell criticised Finch for blaming the King's advisers which led Howe to make even more vebement criticisms. From the chair, Hampden rebuked Howe and he was rebuked in turn by Harbord for usurping the authority of the House which alone could censure a member. Hampden pleaded that he wished the debate to be conducted moderately.

As the younger loyalists saw the Williamites and especially the lawyers among them – Treby, Williams, Maynard, Boscawen, Pollexfen and Somers – dominating the debate, they began to filibuster in order to delay the question. Lord Fanshaw argued strongly in favour of the King while Lord Cornbury, Clarendon's heir, asked for the question to be explained. These tactics failed and the majority shouted Ay when Hampden asked whether the question should be put: That King James the second having endeavoured to subvert the constitution of the Kingdom by breaking the originall contract between King and people, and by the advice of Jesuits and other wicked persons having violated the fundamentall laws And having withdrawn himself out of the Kingdom has abdicated the Government and that the Throne is thereby vacant. The majority shouted Ay ay in answer to the question; one member went out immediately before it was put. Three members voted against: Lord Cornbury; Lord Fanshaw; Sir

Edward Seymour. The vote of the Committee was reported to the House and the question being put whether the House agreed with the Committee only Lord Fanshawe voted against. Fanshawe, an Irish viscount, held a sinecure office which was widely seen as the reason for his vote. The clumsy motion represented the views of the majority who were unwilling to accept the view of their more radical colleagues that James had forfeited the throne because of his misgovernment[61].

Hampden carried the vote to the House of Lords which had adjourned so the Commons did likewise. The Lords had begun the day, as usual, with prayers but Halifax whispered to the Bishop of St David's that he should omit the King's name. The Bishop refused and, on Halifax's motion, the House ordered prayers suspended until further notice. On the previous Wednesday and Thursday, the Bishop of Bristol had omitted the King's name but on Friday the Bishop of Oxford had prayed for the King. In the Commons, the prayers for the King had been skipped over from the beginning. Other business concluded by the Lords on this day was the introduction of the Duke of Southampton and a request to the bishops to draw up prayers for the Prince to be read on Thanksgiving Day[62].

Tuesday 29 January

The House of Lords adjourned into a committee, with Danby in the chair, to consider the present state of the Nation. The Bishop of Ely spoke first and said that there was still a lawful King over the kingdom but by reason of his lunacy he was incapable of administering the government. He moved that they should either send to the King to appoint a Regent or appoint one of their own. This was the argument used in the Commons by Heneage Finch and it is not surprising that his brother, the Earl of Nottingham, seconded the Bishop. The Prince's supporters countered that abdication and dereliction was the same thing in law which was answered by the argument that a regency was the only remedy that came nearest the law. A powerful point argued by the Williamites was that if the King invaded England with an army then the Regent must, in the King's name, pronounce those who supported the King to be traitors. It was a very warm debate; Macclesfield, Abingdon and others made sharp speeches against the bishops. Old enmities surfaced; Clarendon spoke with his usual zeal and led Lord Wharton to demand that he be called to the Bar for describing the Civil War a rebellion. Rochester, Clarendon's brother, was equally passionate while another peer denounced any attempt to keep James out of his kingdom as treason. The debate ended with a division on which the motion for a regency was defeated by three votes. Almost all the bishops voted for a regency except the Bishop of London who voted against while the Bishop of Bristol left before the division and the Bishop of St Asaph was absent. Abingdon, one of the first to join the Prince, voted for a regency as did the Hyde brothers, Ailesbury, Nottingham, Pembroke and most of the dukes. The Duke of Norfolk voted against as did the two Marquesses: Halifax and Winchester. Lord Churchill stayed away because of a sore leg which some noted was an excuse he had used before at times of crisis.

Danby had been a fair chairman and did not vote although his supporter Ferrers had been fierce in the debate and voted for a regency. It had been a long day; Lord Winchelsea stood in the twilight and remarked that he saw the supporters of the regency intended to prolong the debate by long speeches and he prayed that God would give them strength to maintain the debate. The House adjourned at eight o'clock after the vote in the Commons on the previous day had been read. The Lords agreed to sit the next day despite its solemnity as the anniversary of the death of Charles I[63].

The House of Commons formed a Committee of the Whole House to give further consideration to the state of the nation. Col. Birch was a blunt man who began by stating that the King deposing himself showed the hand of God. He moved that it was 'inconsistent and ruinous to a Protestant state to be governed by a Popish Prince.' Only Lord Falkland among the twelve speakers who followed disagreed and it was voted that it had been found, by experience to be inconsistent with the safety and welfare of this Protestant kingdom, to be governed by a Popish Prince. This vote was taken to the House of Lords which interrupted its debate to give unanimous approval to the vote. While many Lords were prepared to defend James because of the oaths they had sworn, they were not enthusiastic to repeat the experience of a Catholic monarch[64].

The Commons continued their debate. Wharton moved that William and Mary be declared King and Queen and that the lawyers be asked to find a way of achieving that end. Lord Falkland intervened to suggest that 'before the Question is put, who shall be set upon the Throne, I would consider what powers we ought give the Crown, to satisfy them that sent us hither.' This suggestion was greeted with enthusiasm: William Williams referred to the money given to Charles II and cited the Militia Act and the controversy as to whether the power over this Act should be with the Crown or the people: 'now we speak for England. This is the time to be free, now the throne is vacant.' It was agreed that before the Committee filled the Throne, they would proceed to secure 'our religion, laws and liberties.' Serjeant Maynard warned the House against trying to do too much: 'Many speak, in Coffee-Houses and other places, of fine things for you to do, that you may do nothing but spend your health, and be in confusion – Take care of over-loading your horse, not to undertake too many things.' Sacheverell pointed to their central duty: 'secure this House, that Parliaments be duly chosen, and not kicked out at pleasure; which never could have been done, without such an extravagant revenue that they might never stand in need of Parliaments. Secure the right of elections and the legislative power.' Pollexfen thought that Falkland's motion was excellent in itself but it might cause dissensions; he argued, as did Maynard, that they should have a King first. The great majority of speakers were enthusiastic and the loyalist Sir Christopher Musgrave said: 'You must have wheels, before you can put the cart upon them. In the first place, put the Question, that you will proceed in asserting the Rights and Liberties of the Nation; and that you will appoint a Committee to bring in general Heads of such things as are absolutely necessary for securing the Laws and Liberties of the Nation.' After an excited debate in which heads were proposed, it was moved, with some oppostion, that a committee should consider these heads at eight o'clock the following morning. Thirty-five members were named to the Committee[65].

Wednesday 30 January

The anniversary of the death of Charles I. Shops were closed. The House of Commons went to a service in St Margaret's Westminster where Dr Sharp, Dean of Norwich and a man who had offended James II, preached. There was no service in Westminster Abbey for the House of Lords.

At three in the afternoon, the House of Lords met to consider the vote passed by the Commons on 28 January. The legal assistants were consulted over the meaning of 'original contract' – a concept which had been mentioned frequently during the debates in the other house. Atkyns suggested that the contract originated in the mists of time with the '1st originall of Government' and he referred to a remark made by James I in 1609 that there was 'a Paction between ye Pr. and people;' to a number of statutes; to the opinion of the learned Grotius; and, to the covenant between King David and Israel. Petyt thought that the contract originated in Germany and came over with the Saxons and he traced its development up to the reign of James I. The other lawyers were even more vague. The Lords were not greatly enlightened.

The debate ended with a vote on each of the first three paragraphs of the vote passed by the Commons: 'That King James the Second having endeavoured to subvert the constitution of the Kingdom by breaking the originall contract between King and People' was accepted by 54 votes to 43; 'and by the advice of Jesuits and other wicked people having violated the fundamental laws' was accepted as was 'And having withdrawn himself out of this Kingdom.' Another debate arose over 'has abdicated the Government.' The message from William to the King on 17 December was read and it moved that *deserted* should be inserted instead of *abdicated*. This was agreed and the House adjourned until the next day when the lords would consider the final clause, 'and that the Throne is thereby vacant.'[66]

The Commons Committee met in the morning to consider what should be done for the security of religion, laws and properties and agreed on a number of heads:

1. Parliament should meet at least once every three years and should not be dissolved until they had finished their business. The same Parliament should not sit for too long as in Charles II's reign when one Parliament lasted for seventeen years.

2. Municipal charters should not be altered by the sovereign.

3. Trials for treason should be regulated so that there were two witnesses to the fact and counsel should be allowed to the prisoner; excessive fines and punishments like whipping to be abolished; judges should only be allowed to sit during good behaviour and were not to be suspended by the King while their salaries should come from the public revenue and not from their fees.

4. Penal laws were not to be dispensed with and only the legislative power could suspend laws.

5. Only Parliament could raise money.

6. Information in the King's Bench to be abolished and proceedings were to be by indictment only.

7. Fees of judicial officers to be regulated.

8. The Commission of Ecclesiastical Affairs was illegal and pernicious; its acts were to be voided.

9. A standing army was to be kept in peace time only with the consent of Parliament.

10. The Militia Acts were a grievance to the subject in matter of religion. There should be effectual provision for the liberty for Protestants in the exercise of their religion.

Other matters were prepared by the Committee but they rose to attend the service at St Margaret's[67].

Thursday 31 January

Thanksgiving Day. Mr Gee preached before the House of Lords because the Bishop of St Asaph was unwell. Gilbert Burnet preached before the Commons on the text 'Happy is that People that is in such a case: yea, happy is that People whose God is the Lord' (Psalm 144,15). He ended by referring to the 'great Salvation' that they had recently experienced and urged them 'to carry it on to those glorious ends of settling our religion, and delivering our nation, not only from all oppression and injustice at present, but from the danger of falling under it for the future.'[68]

At three in the afternoon, the House of Lords met to debate the final part of the Commons' vote 'and that the Throne is thereby vacant.' The legal assistants were unanimous that they could not provide an opinion because this was a matter of state and not of common law. It was, they insisted, a matter for Parliament.

In the angry debate that followed, William's supporters spoke harshly against the bishops. The Earl of Oxford, an old Cavalier who had joined William, denounced them for being the principal promoters of every act of Parliament prejudicial to the interest of the nation during the past fifty years. Macclesfield who had come over with the Prince quoted his ancestors as saying that the bishops were the principal authors of all the public mischiefs since the time of Archbishop Whitgift in Elizabeth's reign. White, Bishop of Peterborough, retorted that those who had drawn their swords against the King were rebels and traitors and their only way out was to return to their loyalty. Devonshire and Delamere both declared that they had drawn their swords for their religion, lives and estates and would keep them drawn until they were secure. Outside the chamber, Macclesfield had shouted to three or four bishops that he had ventured his life and estate and had been exiled several times for them but now he was determined to die or to bring them to a better understanding or to drive them out of the kingdom. Feelings ran so high among the Lords that there were fears the whole dispute would be ended by the sword.

There were two votes. The first, early in the debate, put the question that instead of 'the throne is thereby vacant' should be inserted 'the Prince and Princess of Orange should be declared King and Queen.' This was defeated by 52 votes to 47. All the bishops, except London, voted with the majority. Danby placed himself with the minority as did his followers: the Bishop of London, Fauconberg, and Lindsey. However, Ferrers who was regarded as Danby's creature voted with the majority. The vote showed that the loyalists commanded a majority in the House. At the end of the debate, the House voted on the last clause in the Commons' vote, 'and that the throne is thereby vacant.' This was rejected by 55 votes to 41. On the second vote, Danby and his followers voted with the majority. Mordaunt observed with satisfaction that there were not above four of the ancient nobility who voted that the throne was not vacant. Most of the Lords in the minority entered a protest against disagreeing with the Commons[69].

The Commons Committee considering the security of laws, religion and property sat again and agreed on more heads:

1. In cases of attainder for treason or felony, the Attorney General should not refuse his warrant for a writ of error because it was a petition of right.

2. Abuses about sheriffs should be complained about and they should be appointed by judges in the Exchequer Chamber.

3. Complaints were made about juries where the freeholders books omitted many names or gentlemen had crosses against their names so that only 'sure cards' sat on the juries. This should be regulated.

4. The right of the subject to petition the King should be asserted.

5. Sovereigns ought to take an oath before administering the government that they would preserve the Protestant religion, the law and liberties; the Coronation oath should be inspected because it had not been changed since before the Reformation.

Other matters raised were irregularities in administering the excise and also the chimney acts. Other members pointed out that these could only be amended by a bill and that 'the proper work of this Committee was chiefly to agree on such grievances as had endangered our Constitution and thereupon to declare what that law was which had bin born down, and what further was necessary to secure the same.'[70]

Friday 1 February

The House of Commons resolved that Dr. Sharp and Dr. Burnet should be thanked for their sermons. Sharp had preached on the text 'Deliver me from blood-guiltinesse' (Psalm 51, 14). In his sermon, he had denounced the killing, dethroning or deposing of kings as a popish doctrine and he had prayed before the sermon for the King and Queen. On the afternoon of 30 January, there had been a short sitting of the House when the Speaker had been keen to condemn Sharp for his actions but it was pointed out that he would not have known that the Commons had voted the throne to be vacant because their business was secret. It is possible that the House agreed to vote thanks to both preachers to avoid controversy but one account claims that Sharp had asked the Speaker's pardon. The short debate at the beginning of this day suggests otherwise and that the Williamites allowed the thanks in order to concentrate on greater matters[71].

Thanks were voted to the clergy who had opposed both James II and Catholicism. Heneage Finch objected to the word *late* being used to describe the reign of James II in the text of the vote but he confessed that his objection was of little consequence. Whereupon another member remarked that if Finch wanted it kept out then it must be of consequence and should be left in. It was left in the text. Wharton moved that thanks be given to those in the army 'for having testified their steady adherence to the Protestant religion, and been instrumental in delivering this Kingdom from Popery and slavery.' The fleet and all who appeared in arms for that purpose were added to the vote.

Sir George Treby, chairman of the Committee considering that which should be done to preserve religion, laws and liberties, had a heavy cold and did not arrive before the House rose. There was a feeling that the report of the Committee should be left for another day because of the disagreements likely between the two houses. Before noon, a motion that the House should adjourn until the next day was carried by 229 votes to 143[72].

The House of Lords sent down to the Commons their amendments to the Commons' vote of 28 January. After ordering that the Earl of Peterborough, in the Tower, should have access to his trunks holding his papers, the Lords adjourned until ten the next morning. Halifax reminded the Lords of Ireland and warned those who were making divisions to take heed that the blood of Protestants might not be laid at their door[73].

Saturday 2 February

Sir George Treby reported to the Commons on the work of the Committee for bringing in the general heads absolutely necessary for the better securing of religion, laws and liberties. The following heads were read once throughout and then one by one and agreed:

1.   The pretended power of dispensing or suspending of laws, or the execution of laws, by royal prerogative, without consent of Parliament is illegal.

2.   The Commission for erecting the late Court of Commissioners for Ecclesiastical Causes, and all other Commissions and Courts of the nature, are illegal and pernicious.

3.   Levying of Money for the use of the Crown, by pretence of prerogative, without grant of Parliament, for longer time, or in other manner, than the same shall be so granted, is illegal.

4.   It is the right of the subjects to petition the King: and all commitments and prosecutions for such petitioning, are illegal.

5. The acts concerning the militia are grievous to the subject.

6. The raising or keeping a standing army within this Kingdom in time of peace, unless it be with the consent of Parliament, is against the law.

7. It is necessary for the publick safety, that the subjects, which are Protestants, should provide and keep arms for their common defence: and that the arms which have been seized, and taken from them, be restored.

8. The right and freedom of electing members of the House of Commons; and the rights and privileges of Parliament, and Members of Parliament, as well in the intervals of Parliament, as during their sitting; to be preserved.

9. That Parliaments ought to sit frequently and that their frequent sitting be secured.

10. No interrupting of any session of Parliament, till the affairs, that are necessary to be dispatched at that time, are determined.

11. That the too long continuance of the same Parliament be prevented.

12. No Pardon to be pleadable to an impeachment in Parliament.

13. Cities, universities, and towns corporate, and boroughs, and plantations, to be secured against Quo Warrantos, and surrenders, and mandates, and restored to their ancient rights.

14. None of the Royal Family to marry a Papist.

15. Every King and Queen of this realm, at the time of their entering into the exercise of their regal authority, to take an oath for maintaining the Protestant religion, and the laws and liberties of this nation; and that the Coronation oath be reviewed.

16. Effectual provision to be made for the liberty of Protestants in the exercise of their religion, and for uniting all Protestants in the matter of publick worship, as far as may be.

17. Constructions upon the statutes of treason, and trials, and proceedings, and writs or error in cases of treason, to be regulated.

18. Judges commissions to be made *quamdiu se bene gesserint*; and their salaries to be ascertained and established, to be paid out of the publick revenue only; and not to be removed, nor suspended, from the execution of their office, but by due course of law.

19. The requiring excessive bail of persons committed in criminal cases, and imposing excessive fines, and illegal punishments, to be prevented.

20. Abuses in the appointing of sheriffs, and in the execution of their office, to be reformed.

21. Jurors to be duly impannelled and returned, and corrupt and false verdicts prevented.

22. Informations in the Court of King's Bench to be taken away.

23. The Chancery, and other courts of justice, and the fees of offices, to be regulated.

The lawyers in the House had some reservations; Serjeant Maynard disliked the wholesale abolition of information in the Court of King's Bench but it was pleaded that the intent of this clause was to point to the misuse of informations and any necessary qualifications could be made in a future bill. Col. Birch rightly remarked: 'If this take so much time here, what will it do in the House of Lords. Therefore pen it clearly.'

Five more heads were added as a result of the debate:

24. That the buying and selling of offices, may be effectually provided against.

25. That upon return of writs of *habeas corpus* and *mandamus*, the subject may have liberty to traverse such returns.

26. That all grants of fines and forfeitures are illegal and void; and that all such persons as procure them, be liable to punishment.

27. That the abuses and oppressions in levying and collecting the hearth-money, be effectually redressed.

28. That the abuses and oppressions in levying and collecting the excise, be effectually redressed.

Some of these clauses had been discussed by the committee and rejected but members of the committee successfully pleaded on the floor of the House for their inclusion.

Then the Commons came to consider the amendments made by the House of Lords to their vote of 28 January. Despite an attempt by the loyalists to support the amendments, the Williamites rejected the changes and a committee was appointed to prepare reasons for rejecting the amendments and to present the reasons to the Lords at a conference[74].

Halifax informed the House of Lords that he had received a letter addressed to the Speaker. He knew the hand to be that of Lord Preston, a Scottish peer and one of the Secretaries of State under James. When Halifax asked whether the House wished the letter read, some cried 'read it,' others 'no.' Warr, Preston's secretary, had delivered the letter and, when questioned, he claimed that he knew nothing about it. Preston was sent for and, within an hour, he told the House that he had received that letter and one for the Commons about three o'clock yesterday morning from Hayes, a Scottish gentleman, who told him that the letters were from the King. Preston undertook to find Hayes and ensure that he would attend the House on Monday morning. The House of Commons laid their letter aside[75].

Towards the end of their sitting, Lord Lovelace presented a petition to the House. When Clarendon, seconded by Ferrers, demanded that following standing orders the petition should be read, Lovelace rapidly withdrew the petition. Rowe presented the same petition to the House of Commons and said it was from 'great numbers of persons, for crowning the Prince and Princess of Orange King and Queen.' Serjeant Maynard objected: 'if you read it, the Parliament is without doors, and not here.' He was supported by Sir Edward Seymour who pointed out that on the previous day the Lords had been threatened by a mob which was not yet dispersed. Seymour emphasised that if the debates were to be free, they should be preserved from the mob. Earlier in the day, the House of Lords had ordered the High Steward of Westminster to keep the passages to Old Palace Yard clear. Crowds were standing around the doors of Parliament and either blessing or cursing the peers according to their opinion.

Lovelace withdrew the petition because it had not been signed. The petition asked that William and Mary be settled on the throne in order to defend the Protestant religion and to secure Ireland. After the violent debate in the Lords on Tuesday, people feared an armed struggle and sought to aid a speedy and peaceful settlement. The people of London were busy in signing the petition on Saturday night and Sunday but the Prince, not wanting open pressure placed on the Convention, ordered, on Monday, that the petition should be suppressed[76].

Monday 4 February

Richard Hampden reported from the Committee preparing the reasons why the Commons could not agree to the Lords amendments: (1) *deserted* only covered the withdrawing while *abdicated* covered all factors mentioned in the vote; (2) there was no need to omit 'and that the Throne is thereby vacant' because the Lords had agreed to most of the vote which pointed to that conclusion; the Lords had addressed the Prince to take upon himself the administration of affairs; they had appointed a day of thanksgiving; they had agreed that a Catholic sovereign was incapable of governing; there was no person on the throne from whom they could have royal protection and therefore they owed allegiance to no person, consequently the throne was vacant. Tredenham tried to plead that the throne was not entirely vacant but he was brought to order by the Speaker because the House had resolved that the throne was vacant.

After the conference, Clarendon reported to the House of Lords that the Commons refused to accept their amendments. The legal assistants gave their opinion that *abdicated* was not a word found in English law and, after a debate, the House voted again for *deserted* by 54 votes to 51. Another debate followed on 'That the throne is thereby vacant' which was rejected by 54 votes to 53. A committee was appointed to draw up the Lords' reasons for not agreeing with the Commons[77].

Hayes was called to the bar and he explained that he had been ordered by the King at St Germains last Monday to attend Lord Melfort who gave him the letter for Preston. The reference to the distrusted Melfort annoyed even the King's friends and nothing more was said about the letter[78].

Col. Birch urged haste during a short debate in the Commons on the heads for securing religion, laws and liberties: 'Put some title to them, and send them to the Lords immediately.' Wildman argued that the heads requiring new laws should be listed separately from those declaratory of ancient rights. The committee was instructed to do this and to consider the question of a title[79].

Tuesday 5 February

Nottingham read out the reasons why the House of Lords insisted upon their amendments to the vote of the House of Commons on 28 January: (1) *abdicate* is not a word known in the common law of England and, in the usual meaning accepted in civil law, it is a voluntary act; (2) while the exercise of government by the King has ceased, this does not mean that the King has abdicated or the throne is vacant because this is an hereditary not an elective monarchy and no act of the King can bar the right of his heir to whom allegiance is due. The House accepted these reasons and they were presented to the Commons at a conference[80].

The loyalists in the Commons spoke in favour of the reasons presented by the Lords. Clarges, Tredenham and Sawyer argued vehemently that the Crown was hereditary and that it had fallen on the next heir – the Princess of Orange. Col. Birch retorted that the throne was vacant and suggested that Parliament had taken the power to dispose of the Crown. Heneage Finch, in a learned speech, denounced this as making the monarchy elective when the succession lies with the right heirs. Sir Robert Howard pointed out that 'All things are not so clear as we would wish; but let us preserve ourselves, which must be our supreme law.' Pollexfen argued against making the Princess sole sovereign.

The members who had attended the conference reported that the Lords suggested that their original vote on 28 January had not been unanimous. The hint was taken and another divison was held. The Commons voted against accepting *deserted* without a division. Powle then called for a vote on 'That the throne was thereby vacant' and requested those who agreed with the Lords to withdraw from the House while those who held to their original vote should stay: 151 withdrew and 282 stayed. The House was full; counting the 4 tellers and 2 observers there was an attendance of 439 members[81].

The House of Lords sat on during the day. Ill-feeling over the vote on the previous day was reflected in the resolution that when the House divided the Lords should go on either side of the House to be exactly counted and not go below the bar. Halifax kept the House sitting while they awaited the decision of the Commons on their amendments. Impatient peers pressed for an adjournment until he was forced to agree to adjourn at three if nothing had been heard from the Commons. The House of Lords rose around half past three[82].

Wednesday 6 February

The anniversary of the accession of James II; both Lords and Commons had passed a resolution that it should not be observed.

Following their rejection of the Lords' amendments, the Commons requested a free conference with the Lords. Freedom of debate was permitted in a conference. When the managers for the Commons arrived in the Painted Chamber, a great crowd of spectators hindered their passage to the table. The Serjeant at Arms was sent to summon back to the House all the members except Maynard, Sir Robert Howard and Pollexfen who were lame. Few members were prepared to return and the Clerk was sent to record the names of those who refused. Inquisitive strangers were cleared and the free conference began[83].

The proceedings were dominated on behalf of the Commons by Williamite lawyers and on behalf of the Lords by the loyalists. Hampden, the Commons' chairman, began the debate by emphasising the two points under consideration: the word *abdicated* and 'That the throne is thereby vacant.' The young Somers enhanced his reputation with a very learned speech on *abdicated*. However, Nottingham and the other lords wanted to discuss the vacancy which should be settled first because the controversy over *abdicated* stemmed from it. The inconclusive debate ended when Rochester conceded: 'I believe my lords would be induced to agree, that the King hath abdicated, that is, renounced the government for himself.'

A little pause ended when Hampden agreed to discuss the vacancy. The Lords maintained that the throne was not vacant but, despite repeated requests from the members of the Commons, they declined to name the person who occupied the throne. This led to some exasperation. Treby remarked: 'You are the persons that usually are, or ought to be, present at the delivery of our Queens, and the proper witnesses to the birth of our Princes. If then your Lordships had known who was on the Throne, we should certainly have heard his name from you, and that had been the best reason against the vacancy as could have been given.' After the failure of their proposal for a regency, the loyalists wished to preserve the true succession: 'The consequence of this abdication in the opinion of the majority of the Lords & of 152 of ye Commons of which my brother & I [Sir Robert Sawyer] went, was that ye Princess now Queen as ye only visible & unsuspected heir should succeed.' Nottingham and other lords expressed their abhorrence of an elective monarchy which, to them, was implied in the vacancy of the throne. The members of the Commons were unanimous in denying that this was their intention. None of the lords wished to irritate William by standing forth and openly declaring Mary as Queen. The Conference ended at three in the afternoon. The Commons adjourned when their managers returned[84].

Nottingham reported on the conference to the House of Lords. On the word *abdicated*, he remarked that the Commons believed that acting contrary to a trust was a renuciation of that trust while both deserting and abdication were unknown to English law. As for the vacancy, the Commons had accused the Lords of implying as much in their acceptance of most of the vote of 28 January. If the Lords believed that the King had merely left the exercise of government, then he could return to that exercise again. While the Commons insisted on *abdicated*, they acknowledged that this was an hereditary kingdom and that it was necessary to fill the throne. Nottingham ended by remarking that they had not received an answer to the Lords' arguments on *abdicated*. Clarendon recalled that one member had said that the succession was not elective perpetually but that it should be declared how the throne should go. Nottingham added that when the Commons were asked how succeeding Parliaments would be prevented from electing there was no reply but the Commons disclaimed the pretence of an elective kingdom[85].

Halifax argued that necessity required that they should agree with the Commons. Churchill brought a letter from Anne who earnestly desired the Lords to concur with the Commons. Around ten loyalists including Chesterfield, Weymouth, Ferrers, Hatton (Nottingham's father-in-law), Godolphin and the Bishop of London stayed away following Nottingham's advice to let the Williamites prevail and thus avoid another civil war. Four peers who had not attended regularly before were brought to the House by the Williamites: Lincoln who announced that he would do whatever Mordaunt wished; Lexinton who had only recently returned to England; the Bishop of Durham who had been waiting for a ship to carry him into exile when he was persuaded to obtain a pardon by using his vote; and, the Earl of Carlisle who came in on his crutches. Five years later, Mordaunt requested a dukedom for persuading not only the Bishop of Durham but also Lord Huntington who had recently abjured his Catholicism and Lord Ashley to vote both against the regency and for the vacancy.

In a division between four and five o'clock, the House of Lords voted by 65 to 45 to agree with the Commons in accepting the word *abdicated* and in declaring the throne vacant. The ever loyal Ailesbury was the teller for the non-contents[86]. The House then turned its attention to filling the throne. The Marquess of Winchester – a man who feigned considerable eccentricity during the reign of James II – reminded the Lords that this day was the anniversary of James II's accession and they had done much to blot the memories of the mischiefs that followed in the past four years by making this a day to be remembered with gratitude. He moved that the Prince and Princess be declared King and Queen; Devonshire and the impetuous Delamere in a surprisingly good speech seconded him. Nottingham thought this could never be justified by reason or law but only by the sword – it was contrary to the oaths; it made an hereditary monarchy elective. Clarendon and Rochester supported him. The Williamites responded with the argument that this was the only way to obtain a settlement and union at home and an union with Protestant states abroad which would prevent any nation warring against them. Moreover, it was perfectly reasonable to place on the throne the one who had delivered them which was based on good precedents when the two Houses had placed the best candidate on the throne. It was malicious to say that the crown would become elective for when they had departed from the lineal descent the crown was never reckoned elective. The constitution was the best in the world and if the two houses would not peaceably fill the throne it was the worst and they were the most miserable people.

Nottingham raised the question of the royal title. The usual title was King and Queen of England, Scotland, France and Ireland; Scotland was an independent kingdom and could act independently. The business of crowning should be left until this question had been resolved. Many of the lords were impressed until Halifax quickly suggested that they should proclaim William and Mary King and Queen of England with all the appurtenances thereunto belonging and they could consult with Scotland later. Nottingham turned to another difficulty; they were obliged by the oaths of supremacy and allegiance and could not obey another king while they were under these obligations. Danby supported Nottingham. Halifax feared that this would ridicule the title of William and Mary and also the proceedings of the House of Lords. Danby demanded to know if the Lord in the chair wished to argue him into perjury and he pointed out forcefully that they had resolved to make William and Mary King and Queen because of the present crisis but nobody could assert that they were rightfully sovereigns by the constitution. Halifax would soon learn of disaffected persons. This did not defeat Halifax's agile management and he moved that they should vote but not send their vote to the Commons until they had debated the question of the oaths on the following morning. This was agreed and the question whether the Prince and Princess of Orange should be declared King and Queen was carried without a division. The House rose at ten in the evening[87].

Debates on the vacancy had not been confined to the floor of the House of Lords. Several peers had met at the Earl of Devonshire's house where a fierce argument had developed between Halifax for the Prince and Danby for the Princess. Halifax appealed to Fagel, one of the Prince's advisers, but he demurred at reporting the Prince's opinion. His own belief was that the Prince would not wish to be his wife's gentleman usher. Danby said that he hoped they all knew enough now; for himself, he knew too much; he left in a huff. Princess Mary wrote, around this time, to Danby and warned him against any attempt to divide her from the Prince. This meeting led to another when William summoned Halifax, Danby, Shrewsbury and other peers and told them that 'he could not think of holding any thing by apron-strings nor could he think it reasonable to have any share in the government, unless it was put in his person, and that for a term of life: if they did not think it fit to settle it otherwise, he would not oppose them in it: he would go back to Holland, and meddle no more in their affairs.' This second meeting, probably held on 3 February, concentrated the minds of those who heard the Prince and helped to bring agreement between the two houses[88].

Popular opinion had been alarmed at the disagreement between the two Houses and cautious men made provision: 'the publique sense of things is, that we may yet be in farr greater straites than hitherto brought too, People drawes in their money they lent for the publique service of the nation as fast as it becomes due, and every supposes that commodity in a verry litel tyme will become more valluable than ever, on wch account all persons haveing any foresight are accordingly provoiding'[89].

The *Orange Gazette* reported that 'We are filled this afternoon with such an excess of joy at the agreement of both Houses of the Honourable Convention.' Bonfires were built at the doors of many noblemen and all over town; bells rang in churches that evening and the following morning in London and the neighbouring villages[90].

Thursday 7 February

Two loyalists (Nottingham and Rochester); two radical Williamites (Delamere and Wharton); and, the loyalist Bishop of Peterborough were named as a committee to draft oaths to replace the oaths of allegiance and supremacy. Their suggestions were accepted and it was resolved that the oaths taken to James were abrogated. The bishops were instructed to bring before the House the form of an oath of obedience which they were to take on their appointment. Messengers had been sent to the Commons with the Lords' agreement to their vote of 28 January. Messengers were now sent with the texts of the oaths of fealty and the vote for declaring the Prince and Princess of Orange King and Queen. On their return, the Lords ordered the guns in the Tower to be charged and a message was sent to the Commons that they intended to sit at four in the afternoon[91].

When the Commons received the Lords' agreement to their vote of 28 January, the Earl of Wiltshire pressed that the House of Commons should immediately consider filling the throne. He emphasised that they should preserve the ancient government and other members raised the question of the heads for preserving religion, laws and liberties. Hampden argued against haste in order that the committee might 'consider well what must be for the benefit of all posterity, when you are dead and gone.' The committee was revived and instructed to withdraw into the Speaker's Chamber to draw up a text of the heads which distinguished between those declaratory of ancient rights and those requiring new laws, and to prepare a title for the heads. The Commons adjourned until the afternoon when they received the Lords' vote for proclaiming William and Mary King and Queen and also the texts of the oaths.

Treby presented the text of the heads at the beginning of the afternoon session. The committee had worked with commendable speed although they had not prepared a title. Dissensions within the committee over one of the heads, 'that no pardons should be pleadable to an impeachment in Parliament,' had led them to omit it. Danby had benefitted from a pardon after an impeachment in Parliament and the committee might have felt it would be tactless to include this head. Moreover, it was a considerable curtailment of the royal prerogative.

Instead of considering these heads, the Commons fell into a debate on the succession; Sir Robert Sawyer moved that Catholics should be incapable of inheriting the Crown or of succeeding to the Crown. This gained support and it was added to the list of heads. Sacheverell wanted the succession declared if either William or Mary died and after the death of the survivor. Col. Birch suggested this should be added to the heads drawn up by the committee. Sir Thomas Lee brought them back to the work of the committee and pointed out that it proposed a declaration of the rights of the subjects linked to a declaration for filling the throne. His suggestion that the question of the throne and of the succession should be left until tomorrow was agreed.

The House sat until two in the afternoon, adjourned until four and then sat late into the night. Some members did not dine while others did; some members were weary and some were angry. The debate was disorderly. One member complained that he had not heard the question which led another to retort that he would have heard if he had left the bottle sooner[92].

The Lords met at four in the afternoon and sat until seven but no message came up from the Commons[93].

Friday 8 February

Serjeant Holt, one of the legal assistants in the Lords and a determined Williamite, began the debate in the House of Commons on the Lords' vote that William and Mary be declared King and Queen. He argued for an additional clause which would clarify the administration of the government and he moved that William should have the sole administration which would avoid confusion and secure his position if Mary died. This drew some debate despite Hampden's plea that time should not be lost.

The task of amending the Lords' vote was passed to a committee which was instructed to sit immediately. Somers reported that the committee found itself in difficulty because the amendment of the vote had to be linked to the declaratory part of the paper containing the heads. The House instructed, after some debate, the committee to link to the vote and the amendments those heads which declared ancient rights and to omit those heads requiring new laws. The new oaths should also be added. When the text was complete, it was read and approved by the House before being presented to the Lords at a conference. The House adjourned until nine the following morning after a vote of 185 to 94[94].

Little business was done in the Lords. The paper sent up by the Commons was read and the House adjourned until nine the following morning[95].

Saturday 9 February

On Friday evening, William granted an audience to certain bishops and peers who warned him that the heads for preserving religion, laws and liberties implied distrust of the Prince and they were, moreover, an usurpation on the rights of the crown by enemies of the monarchy. Acceptance of these heads was unnecessary because the House of Lords could achieve a settlement without them. Sir Edward Seymour told the House of Commons on Saturday morning that he had learned from Bentinck that the Prince was dissatisfied with the restrictions and limitations they were placing on the crown and he would have done better for their security himself. This caused a commotion in the Commons while, in the House of Lords, Nottingham snapped that William might regard the crown of England with limitations far more than anything he could have received in the Netherlands. The House of Lords which had been considering the heads for the past two hours requested confirmation of the remarks made by Seymour. Colonel Sydney, one of the Prince's closest advisers, went to court and argued that any hesitation over the heads would have dangerous consequences for those who had spoken for them were the Prince's most faithful servants. The heads contained only the known laws and were not intended as a snare for the Prince. If they were rejected, the Prince's supporters would be uneasy. William claimed that he had not expressed any opinion on the heads and he desired to do what his Declaration had stated which was to preserve their religion, laws and liberties. He would do what the Lords and Commons thought fit. The Prince's view was promptly reported at Westminster.

William's displeasure over the heads had been the subject of rumours since 1 February. He was unwilling to accept the crown with these conditions attached to it. The crisis in the relations between the Prince and the Convention did not appear in the open until the heads had been sent to the Lords where a number of peers saw an opportunity of gaining the Prince's favour by offering to undo the work of the Commons. This failed. However, the sudden decision by the Commons to omit those heads requiring new laws may well have been caused by their knowledge of the Prince's attitude[96].

The House of Lords continued their consideration of the heads. The main problem for the Lords was the dispensing power. When they consulted the legal assistants, Atkyns thought that the sovereign had no power but others thought that there was such a power but with limitations. The relevant clause in the list of James's misdeeds was amended to read [with the changes in italics]: By assuming and exercising a power of [*dispensing and* omitted] suspending of laws, and the execution of laws, without consent of Parliament, *and by such dispensing with law, as by consequence, would subject all the laws to his will and pleasure*. The clause in the list of rights was also amended to omit *dispensing*: That the pretended power of [dispensing or] suspending of laws, or the execution of laws, by regal authority, with consent of Parliament, is illegal. The House spent some time on this and Roger Morrice believed that it was part of the plot to sabotage the heads. However, the Lords gave a most proper reason for their amendments in that many patents and grants depended on dispensation.

The clause in the list of James's misdeeds on raising a standing army was strengthened by the addition of 'quartering soldiers contrary to law.' This led to the only division of the day when the amendment was approved by 44 votes to 33. Schwoerer argues that this amendment embarrassed the Williamites because the Prince had obtained free quarter for his soldiers. They were also defeated in their attempt to remove *in time of peace* from the clause in the list of rights: that the raising or keeping a standing army within the kingdom in time of peace, unless it be with the consent of Parliament, is against the law. The stipulation that 'Parliaments ought to be held frequently, and suffered to sit' was amended to omit 'suffered to sit' because the statutes on the assembling and holding of Parliaments did not cover this. In the final paragraph which declared William and Mary King and Queen and granted William 'administration of the government,' the latter phrase was altered to 'sole and full exercise of the regal power' which emphasised the monarchical nature of the government. The Lords postponed consideration of the clause on James's use of information in the Court of King's Bench until the end of their sitting when they decided to delete it. The lawyers in the Commons had been uncertain about this and their opinion was probably mirrored in the Lords[97].

The Commons listened to a report from the Committee of Elections and Privileges on a dispute over the election at Poole and then rose after a short sitting[98].

Monday 11 February.

The Lords sent their amendments to the Commons and adjourned until four o'clock in the afternoon. However, they did not sit again on this day.

The deletion of the clause on information in the Court of King's Bench was opposed in the House of Commons. Treby explained that it had been included at the request of Sir William Williams who had been punished by this court for publishing as Speaker and at the order of the House material relating to the Popish Plot. The lawyers in the House spent some time on this clause until they produced an alternative wording: 'By prosecutions in the Court of King's Bench for matters and causes cognizable in Parliament and by divers other arbitrary and illegal courses.'

Nor were the members prepared to accept the amendments to the clauses on the dispensing power. They refused to consider the amendment to the clause on the dispensing power among the list of James's misdeeds. However, they left the clause among the list of rights as amended by the Lords but added another clause immediately after it: 'That the pretended power of dispensing with laws, or the execution of laws, by regal authority, as it has been exercised of late, is illegal.' This took account of the objections raised by the House of Lords and echoed in the House of Commons but acknowledged the way in which James had used his power to dispense with the Test Acts[99].

Tuesday 12 February

The Lords debated the amendments made by the Commons to their amendments. The words 'and assumed' were added after 'exercised' in the clause condemning the dispensing power. The House insisted on a number of their amendments but these were minor. It was resolved that the paper drawn up by the Commons should be enrolled in the Court of Chancery and in the Parliament Office and it should be given the title of a Declaration. The conclusions reached by the Lords were discussed with the Commons at a free conference and taken back to the House of Commons where they were accepted.

Meanwhile, the House of Lords ordered the drafting of a proclamation for declaring the Prince and Princess of Orange King and Queen. When the agreement of the Commons to the changes in the text of the Declaration had been received, the Lords sent the Duke of Norfolk to ask William and Mary to receive both houses. The text of the proclamation was delivered to the Commons for their agreement. Norfolk returned and told the Lords that the Prince and Princess would receive both houses at ten the following morning. After a message had been sent to inform the Commons, the Lords ordered the printing of the proclamation and adjourned until eight o'clock the next morning. The House of Commons ordered that the door-keepers of the House should attend in the morning to ensure that none but members be allowed in to their audience with the Prince and Princess[100].

Wednesday 13 February.

Ash Wednesday. The House of Lords ordered the heralds and pursuivants to proclaim King William and Queen Mary in the usual manner and at the usual places. The Declaration was read before the House. And the Lords and Commons went to the Banqueting House where the Lords led by Halifax stood on the right and the Commons led by the Speaker stood on the left. William and Mary entered and stood beneath the canopy; members of both Houses led by their Speakers were brought up by Black Rod to perform three obeisances to their Highnesses.

Lord Halifax informed their Highness that both Houses had agreed upon a Declaration and, on their permission, the deputy to the aged Clerk of the Parliaments read the Declaration:

THE DECLARATION OF THE LORDS SPIRITUAL AND TEMPORAL, AND COMMONS, ASSEMBLED AT WESTMINSTER.

Whereas the late King James the Second, by the assistance of divers evil counsellors, judges, and ministers, employed by him, did endeavour to subvert and extirpate the Protestant religion, and the laws and liberties of this Kingdom.

By assuming and exercising a power of dispensing with and suspending of laws, and the execution of laws, without consent of Parliament;

By committing and prosecuting divers worthy prelates, for humbly petitioning to be excused from concurring to the said assumed Power;

By issuing and causing to be executed a Commission, under the Great Seal, for erecting a court, called, The Court of Commissioners for Ecclesiastical Causes;

By levying money for and to the use of the Crown, by pretence of prerogative, for other time, and in other manner, than the same was granted by Parliament;

By raising and keeping a standing army within this Kingdom in time of peace, without consent of Parliament; and quartering soldiers contrary to law;

By causing several good subjects, being Protestants, to be disarmed, at the same time when Papists were both armed and employed contrary to law;

By violating the freedom of election of members to serve in Parliament;

By prosecutions in the Court of King's Bench, for matters and causes cognizable only in Parliament: And by divers other arbitrary and illegal courses: And whereas, of late years, partial, corrupt, and unqualified, persons have been returned, and served on juries in trials, and, particularly, divers jurors in trials for high treason, which were not freeholders;

And excessive bail hath been required of persons committed in criminal cases, to elude the benefit of the laws made for the liberty of the subjects;

And excessive fines have been imposed;

And illegal and cruel punishments inflicted;

And several grants and promises made of fines and forfeitures, before any conviction or judgement againt the persons upon whom the same were to be levied;

All which are utterly and directly contrary to the known laws, and statutes, and freedom, of this realm:

And whereas the said late King James the Second having abdicated the government; and the throne being thereby vacant;

His Highness the Prince of Orange whom it hath pleased Almighty God to make the glorious instrument of delivering this kingdom from Popery and arbitrary power, did, by the advice of the Lords Spiritual and Temporal, and divers principal persons of the Commons, cause letters to be written to the Lords Spiritual and Temporal, being Protestants; and other Letters, to the several counties, cities, universities, boroughs, and cinque ports, for the chusing of such persons to represent them as were of right to be sent to Parliament, to meet and sit at Westminster upon the 22th day of January, in this year 1688, in order to such an establishment, as that their religion, laws, and liberties, might not again be in danger of being subverted: Upon which letters, elections having been accordingly made;

And thereupon, the said Lords Spiritual and Temporal, and Commons, pursuant to their respective letters, and elections, being now assembled in a full and free Representative of this Nation, taking into their most serious consideration the best means for attaining the ends aforesaid, do, in the first place, (as their ancestors, in like case, have usually done) for the vindication and asserting their ancient rights and liberties, declare;

That the pretended power of suspending of laws by regal authority, without consent of Parliament is illegal;

That the pretended power of dispensing with laws, or the execution of laws, by regal authority, as it hath been assumed and exercised of late, is illegal:

That the Commission for erecting the late Court of Commissioners for Ecclesiastical Causes, and all other Commissions and Courts of like nature, are illegal and pernicious:

That levying of money for or to the use of the Crown, by pretence of prerogative, without grant of Parliament, for longer time, or in other manner, than the same is or shall be granted, is illegal:

That it is the right of the subjects to petition the King; and all commitments and prosecutions for such petitioning, are illegal.

That the raising or keeping a standing army within the Kingdom in time of peace, unless it be with consent of Parliament, is against law:

That the subjects, which are Protestants, may have arms for their defence, suitable to their conditions, as allowed by law:

That election of members of Parliament ought to be free:

That the freedom and debates or proceedings in Parliament ought not to be impeached or questioned in any court or place out of Parliament:

That excessive bail ought not to be required; nor excessive fines imposed; nor cruel and unusual punishments inflicted:

That jurors ought to be impanelled and returned; and jurors, which pass upon men in trials for high treason, ought to be freeholders:

That all grants and promises of fines and forfeitures of particular persons, before conviction, are illegal and void:

And that, for redress of all grievances, and for the amending, strengthening, and preserving of the laws, Parliaments ought to be held frequently.

And they do claim, demand, and insist upon, all and singular the premises, as their undoubted rights and liberties; and that no declarations, judgements, doings, or proceedings, to the prejudice of the people, in any of the said premises, ought, in any wise, to be drawn hereafter with consequence, or example.

To which demand of their rights they are particularly encouraged by the Declaration of his Highness the Prince of Orange; as being the only means for obtaining a full redress and remedy therein.

Having therefore an entire confidence, that his said Highness the Prince of Orange will perfect a deliverance so far advanced by him; and will still preserve them from the violation of their rights, which they have here asserted; and from all other attempts upon their religion, rights and liberties;

The said Lords Spiritual and Temporal, and Commons, assembled at Westminster, do resolve,

That William and Mary, Prince and Princess of Orange, be, and be declared, King and Queen of England, France, and Ireland, and the Dominions thereunto belonging; to hold the Crown and Royal Dignity of the said Kingdoms and Dominions to them the said Prince and Princess, during their lives, and the life of the survivor of them: And that the sole and full exercise of the regal power be only in, and executed by, the said Prince of Orange, in the names of the said Princes and Princess, during their joint lives; and, after their deceases, the said Crown and Royal Dignity of the said Kingdoms and Dominions to be to the Heirs of the Body of the said Princess: And, for default of such issue, to the Princess Ann of Denmark, and the heirs of her body: and, for default of such issue, to the heirs of the body of the said Prince of Orange.

And the said Lords Spiritual, and Temporal, and Commons, do pray the said Prince and Princess of Orange to accept the same accordingly.

And that the oaths, hereafter mentioned, be taken by all persons of whom the oaths of allegiance and supremacy might be required by law, instead of them; and that the said oaths of allegiance and supremacy be abrogated.

I, *A.B.* do sincerely promise and swear, that I will be faithful, and bear true allegiance, to their Majesties King William and Queen Mary. So help me God.

I, *A.B.* do swear, that I do from my heart abhor, detest, and abjure, as impious and heretical, this damnable doctrine and position, That Princes excommunicated or deprived by the Pope, or any authority of the See of Rome, may be deposed or murdered by their subjects, or any one whatsoever. And I do declare, that no foreign prince, person, prelate, state, or potentate, hath, or ought to have, any jurisdiction, power, superiority, preheminence, or authority, ecclesiastical or spiritual, within this Realm. So help me God.

William, with Mary's hand in his, rose and accepted the Declaration: 'This is certainly the greatest proof of the trust you have in Us that can be given; which is the thing that maketh Us value it the more, and we thankfully accept what you have offered Us. And, as I had no other intention in coming hither, than to preserve your Religion, Laws, and Liberties, so you may be sure, that I shall endeavour to support them; and shall be willing to concur in any thing that shall be for the good of the Kingdom; and to do all that is in My power to advance the welfare and glory of the nation.'

The Lords and Commons left the Banqueting Hall and proceeded to Whitehall Gate where, in their presence and in the presence of a great crowd, Garter proclaimed the Prince and Princess of Orange King and Queen. From where, in a long procession with members of both Houses in coaches, they went to the Temple Bar where they entered the City of London and proclaimed the King and Queen three times – between the two Temple gates; in the middle of Cheapside; and, at the Royal Exchange. The streets were lined by trained bands and the members of both Houses were escorted by the Aldermen, Sheriffs and Recorder of the City.

At very short notice, an effective ceremony had been organised to mark the presentation of the Declaration and the proclamation of the King and Queen. That night there were bonfires in the streets and the bells rang out[101].

Thursday 14 February

The Speaker reported to the House of Commons that he had requested a copy of the speech made by the King yesterday. He probably wished to confirm that the Prince had accepted the Declaration[102].

The House of Lords did not sit.

Friday 15 February

The Speakers of both houses read out the King's answer to the Declaration. Lord Shrewsbury in the Lords and Mr Hampden in the Commons informed each House that it was the King's wish that they adjourn until Monday. The royal barge had been prepared but the royal robes were not ready and King William postponed his visit to Parliament until Monday[103].

Monday 18 February

King William came down to Parliament in the royal barge. He entered the House of Lords wearing the royal robes as well as the crown which was unusual because he had not been crowned but was designed to increase confidence in the settlement of the nation. In the speech from the throne, he thanked the Convention for the confidence they had shown in him and referred to the dangers facing English allies both abroad and in Ireland. The King left it to the Convention to 'consider of the most effectual ways of preventing the inconveniences which may arise by delays, and to judge what forms may be most proper to bring those things to pass for the good of the Nation...'

Later that morning, the House of Lords read for the first time a bill for turning the Convention into a Parliament. This had been planned the previous Thursday when Pollexfen and Sir Robert Atkins attended the King to advise him of the best way of obtaining a Parliament. The crisis in Irish and European affairs was used as an excuse for avoiding the delay which would arise from an election. That afternoon, the bill was given a second reading and amended during the committee stage. There is no record of the debate on the bill.

The House of Commons adjourned shortly after the members had returned from the House of Lords. Consideration of the King's speech was postponed until the following morning.

Tuesday 19 February

Thomas Medlicott began the debate in the House of Commons by referring directly to the real reason for haste which was the need to raise money. An obscure lawyer whose election was declared void in May, Medlicott quoted a number of historical precedents, especially that of 1660, to justify turning the Convention into a Parliament. The loyalists opposed him; Clarges suggested that they might have a new Parliament in 25 rather than 40 days. The House of Lords had spent the morning on the third reading of the bill which arrived in the Commons at this point. Hampden urged haste although he advised the House to keep to their standing orders and not follow the Lords who read the bill twice in one day. His care for the forms of the House was a tactic to silence the loyalists who anwered that they were debating the King's speech not the bill. They were not strong enough to carry their argument and the House adjourned.

Wednesday 20 February

Sir Henry Capel delivered a message from the King who requested haste on the matters recommended in his speech. After a long silence, Falkland, Howe, Maynard, Lee and Howard spoke for the bill. Sir Edward Seymour disputed fiercely that there was need for haste to deal with Ireland or France: 'I should be glad to see us a legal Parliament, that we may have the people's hearts along with us; and then we shall be sure of their money.' His main point was difficult to answer: if they had not been a Parliament before how could they, in law, be a Parliament now. If they were a Parliament then they would be liable to the Test Act but they had not taken the oaths prescribed under that act. Maynard, despite his age, answered Seymour vigourously; he dismissed the argument about the oaths which were taken to the King who had abdicated and claimed that necessity demanded that they preserved this course as the best one available. Col. Birch recalled the debate in 1660 and warned that plots against them might arise if they waited another three weeks. He conceded that there was merit in the objections arising from the oaths. The debate continued until the early afternoon when it was resolved that the 'Lords Spiritual and Temporal, and the Commons, now sitting at Westminster, are a Parliament.' The loyalists were less concerned for James II than for their own party — soon to be called Tory again — and they wanted an election to bring them greater strength in the Commons. The bill was read a second time without a division; it was estimated that 100 members opposed the bill but there were only five noes when the question was called. A committee was appointed to consider the bill and almost all the members who had spoken on the floor of the House were included among its members. The major amendment made to the bill by this Committee was intended to meet the objections relating to the oaths: all members had to take by 1 March the oaths included in the Declaration of Rights and this was to be regarded as equivalent to taking the oaths at the beginning of a Parliament.

The House of Commons approved the amendments and gave the bill a third reading on 22 February. On the same day, the House of Lords approved the amended bill. King William gave his assent to the bill on 23 February[104].

The Aftermath

Within ten days, a committee had been appointed to prepare a bill for turning the Declaration into law. The title of the bill contains the first reference to 'rights': 'An Act for declaring the rights and liberties of the subject, and the settling of the succession of the crown'. Again, the House of Lords objected to the prohibition imposed on the use of the dispensing power. Two additional clauses were introduced in the upper house:

(1)   the sovereign was to take the Test Oath before his proclamation; and,
(2)   the succession after Anne and her issue was vested in the next Protestant heir, Sophia of Hanover and her issue.

William had urged the clause on the succession but it was rejected by the Commons and the debate on the bill dragged on until William adjourned Parliament in August.

Another committee was appointed by the Commons on 24 October and a bill was drafted, discussed and passed to the Lords by 6 November. This time, the succession was left out of the bill and the Lords accepted, with some amendment, the prohibition on the use of the dispensing power. The Lords added again a clause requiring the sovereign to take the Test Oath but this time it was to be either at his coronation or before Parliament which made it more public than in the clause added to the previous bill. Thus amended, the Bill of Rights received the royal assent on 16 December 1689. Religious toleration made a small advance in this year with the Toleration Act which allowed freedom of worship but only to Protestant Dissenters who accepted the divinity of Christ.

The reign of William saw further legislative measures to increase the power of Parliament and restrict the royal prerogative. The Triennial Act of 1694 required that general elections be held every three years and this enlivened political life considerably until it was replaced by the Septennial Act of 1716. William's desire to safeguard the Protestant succession resulted in the Act of Settlement of 1701 in which Sophia of Hanover and her issue were named to succeed Anne and her issue. The long title of this act is 'An Act for the further limitation of the crown and better securing the rights and liberties of the subject.' Under this act, office-holders were prohibited from serving as members of the Commons although this section was soon repealed; judges could not be dismissed without the permission of Parliament; a royal pardon could not prevent impeachment by the Commons. The clauses relating to judges and impeachment had been matters of concern for the Convention as was the misconduct of elections by sheriffs which was the subject of the Elections Act of 1696.

During the Convention, a number of members had pointed towards the supply of money as the crucial link between King and Parliament. James II had been granted a generous financial settlement for the duration of his reign and, but for his obsession with the repeal of the Test Acts, he could have ruled for many years without calling a Parliament. Charles II had also managed without Parliament at the end of his reign. This mistake was not repeated; William and Mary were granted the customs but not until 1690 and then for a term of four years which was renewed in 1694 for another five years. The war with France consumed the King's income and he was forced to return to Parliament for extra funds. While the Bill of Rights had given the status of a statute to the Declaration of Rights, it was the financial settlement of 1690 which gave force to these rights by requiring the frequent sittings of Parliament and thus enabling it to increase the liberties of the subject. Since 22 January 1689, Parliament has met every year[105].

Scotland

James's Scottish subjects, like the great majority of Englishmen, were mere witnesses during the making of the Revolution. Once the news of James's departure and the arrival of William in London reached Edinburgh, many of the nobility and gentlemen departed south. Government came to a halt and, by January, there was not even a quorum left in Edinburgh for the Privy Council[106].

William did not consider Scottish affairs until the arrangements for the Westminster Convention were complete. At a meeting on 7 January with the nobles and gentlemen from Scotland at St James's, he asked for their advice on the matter of 'securing the Protestant religion, and restoring your laws and liberties.' Adjourning to the Council Chamber in Whitehall, the Scots choose the Duke of Hamilton as their President. Hamilton had a clear advantage over the other Scottish magnates because he had been in London since early December when he had attended the meetings of the Lords at the Guildhall. Guided by Hamilton, the meeting resolved to prepare an address in reply to the Prince's speech.

Heated objections were raised on the following day to that part of the draft address which dealt with the summoning of the estates of Scotland. There was considerable argument over whether the assembly should be called a meeting or a convention of the estates, – in Scotland a convention was a recognised part of the constitution and acted as an abbreviated form of a full parliament. James had interfered with the Scottish electorate in his attempt to repeal the penal laws against the few Catholics in Scotland and there were fierce disputes over the following points: (1) whether the orders for the election should be addressed to the sheriffs of shires and magistrates in burghs or only to the clerks in both; (2) whether the election should be restricted to those who were qualified to stand and to vote according to law or whether there should be a larger franchise because of the need to obtain the advice of the nation how a legal and free Parliament might be called; (3) whether all the burgesses should elect members to represent the burghs and for their own magistracy or, as in England, the magistrates that were in office before 'their liberties were infringed should be reinstated and so proceed to the elections in the usual forme.' Hamilton intervened to suggest that the address should be in general terms while the details could be left to the Prince.

Permission was requested, at the end of their meeting, by Hamilton's son, the Earl of Arran, to read a paper because he was unaccustomed to speak in public. He surprised everyone present by suggesting, in his paper, that they should apply to the Prince to bring back King James in order to get a free Parliament for securing the Protestant religion and the laws and liberties of the country. One of the tactics used by the Scottish nobility before, during, and after the Revolution was for the father and son to support opposing sides and thus ensure the future of the family and estates whichever side prevailed. This explanation is unlikely on this occasion.

Arran's parents were often baffled by his behaviour and Hamilton now indicated his dissatisfaction.

Sir Patrick Hume asked, on the following day, if anyone was prepared to support Arran. Nobody stood forth and Hume asked the meeting to declare Arran's proposal inimical to the Prince's speech but he was quashed by Hamilton who insisted that their business was to prepare an address to the Prince. The revised address was put to the vote and accepted unanimously. William was asked to accept the administration, both civil and military, of Scotland until a general meeting of the estates to be held on 14 March. Elections would be held fifteen days before the meetings of the estates which was 'to deliberate and resolve what is to be done for securing the Protestant religion, and restoring the laws and liberties of the Kingdom, according to your Highness Declaration.' William accepted the address on 14 January[107].

Passage north was denied to the Scotsmen in London until William had been declared King of England. On 6 February, Commissioner Munro departed for Edinburgh with William's orders for the Convention and a proclamation commanding all men to lay down their arms and keep the peace[108]. Sir James Dalrymple's advice that all Protestants should be allowed to vote was accepted by William despite the fact that it 'was out of all rules ever before heard tell of.' Furthermore, men who had been forfeited under James VII were permitted to sit in the Convention. The Earl of Mar protested unsuccessfully on the first day against the 'Earl of Argylle being called as an Earle in respect of the sentence of forefaulters past against the late Earl of Argylle standing unreduced.'[109]

Alexander Ross, Bishop of Edinburgh, read the prayers when the Convention met on 14 March 1689; he prayed 'for God to have compassion on King James and to restore him.' The estates assembled in one house: 9 bishops, 2 dukes, 2 marquesses, 28 earls, 5 viscounts and 21 lords for the estate of the nobility; 57 commissioners for the shires; and, 65 commissioners for the burghs. There was not a clear division between the parties of James and of William; many men were waiting to follow the great magnates. The nine bishops present were loyal to James. A trial of strength between the two parties came with the election of a President. Hamilton was William's candidate. James's supporters selected with reluctance the vacillating Earl of Athol as their nominee. Athol had remained in Scotland during January with the intention of establishing himself in charge of the government. The result of this foolish blunder was that the presbyterians who loathed him ensured in London that Athol was pushed to the sidelines. Against his will, Athol became the candidate of the loyalists and the episcopalians which placed him in the unfortunate position of urging his own followers to vote for Hamilton who was elected with a majority of forty votes[110].

Military matters were the first concern of the Convention. Edinburgh Castle was held by the Duke of Gordon and his cannon menaced the city. The Earls of Lothian and Tweeddale were sent to negotiate Gordon's surrender but an initial agreement which permitted his withdrawal with honour fell through when the Convention received further demands from which they concluded that Gordon was only trifling with them. Hamilton and other lords from the presbyterian counties in the west had brought several companies of foot into Edinburgh as well as hiding many men in the city until the first day of the Convention when they emerged to strengthen the presbyterian party[111].

On 16 March, the macer reported that a Mr Craine was at the door with a letter from King James. Some of the members wished the letter read immediately. Hamilton insisted that they had met on this day to consider the address presented to William in January and a letter sent to the Convention by William. He reminded the Convention that they met by William's authority. William's letter, dated 7 March, was read: 'Now it lyes on you to enter upon such consultations as are most probable to setle you on sure and lasting foundations which Wee hope you will set about with all convenient speed, with regaird to the publick good, and to the generall interest and inclination of the people. That after soe much trouble and great suffering they may live happily and in peace, and that you may laye asyde all animosities and factions that may imped soe good a worke.' William also commended the benefits of an union between the two kingdoms.

Before the letter from James was read, the Convention resolved that notwithstanding anything contained in the letter 'they are a frie and lawfull meeting of the Estates and will continue undissolved until they setle and secure the Protestant Religione, the Government lawes and liberties of the Kingdom.' Loyalists hoped that the letter would strengthen their cause but the hectoring tone in which it was written dismayed them. James demanded obedience and loyalty: 'Eternise your names by a loyalty suteable to the many professions you hav made to us.' The letter was signed by Melfort who was disliked as much in Scotland as he was in England[112].

Negotiations continued with Gordon over the surrender of Edinburgh Castle. Loyalist lords met on Sunday 17 March and they resolved to convene a loyalist Convention at Stirling. Athol dithered as usual but John Graham of Claverhouse, Viscount Dundee, believed that his life was in danger if he remained and he left Edinburgh on Monday. On his way out of the city, on the Stirling road, Graham clambered on to the rocks below the castle and held a conference with Gordon. News of this meeting was immediately brought to the Convention which forbade all correspondence with Graham and sent a major with 80 horse after him. Graham's impetuous action had foiled loyalist plans[113].

The Convention was especially concerned that the militia were prepared in the western counties facing Ireland. An appeal for help had been received from Irish Protestants and the Convention responded by sending agents to obtain intelligence in Ireland while two frigates were ordered to cruise off the west coast. James's letter had been sent from aboard the *St Michael* on 1 March and Ireland was his probable destination. This was confirmed on 25 March when Gordon informed the Convention that James was in Ireland and he would therefore not surrender; James's standard was flown above the castle and the cannon fired. Gordon sent a courteous message that the Convention should not fear the cannon because they would be fired without bullets[114].

These affairs delayed the Convention's answer to William's letter until 23 March when they assured him that they would 'secure the Protestant religion and establish the Government lawes and liberties of this Kingdome upon solid foundations most agreeable to the generall good and inclinatione of the people.' The proposal for an union was described as 'the best means for secureing the happiness of these Nations and setleing a lasting peace.'[115]

Three days later, the President moved that a committee be named to prepare 'overtures for setleing of the government of the nation.' An attempt to keep this subject in the whole house was defeated on a vote but permission was granted for any interested member to attend the meetings of the committee. Hamilton proposed that eight members from each estate should be named to the committee. The six bishops present argued that they were a separate estate but they were quickly quashed. The loyalists then moved that each estate should select its own representatives but this was defeated on a division in favour of the proposal that each member should hand in, on the following day, a list of the twenty-four members he wished to nominate. When the lists were counted, the Williamites had a clear majority on the committee[116].

Major General McKay arrived at this time with Scots regiments despatched north by William. The Convention gave him command of any forces standing or to be raised in Scotland[117].

By 30 March, the committee had decided that the throne was vacant on the grounds of maladministration rather than desertion or abdication. There were various opinions as to the next step: some members argued that the crown descended by succession to the Queen of England and that to the King of England should be granted, by right of marriage, the administration during life; others thought that the crown should be granted to both with an union of the two nations; and, a third party considered it would be best to grant the crown first and then discuss the union. A sub-committee of four members was appointed to draft the reasons for the vacancy and proposals for settling the government. On 1 April the reasons for the vacancy were approved by the full committee. Each reason was read and debated at length by the Convention on 3 April but a final decision was postponed until the following day when the clerks would note the attendance in order to establish who were the members who had appeared at the Convention but were now absent. The macers were sent to inform the members in town that they should be present.

The reasons were read and debated one by one on the following day and the entire text put to the vote when it was approved by all the members except twelve of whom seven were all the bishops present. Following Scots law, the Convention declared that King James 'hath forefaulted the right to the crowne and the throne is become vacant.' The Committee was ordered to bring in an act for settling the crown on William and Mary; to consider the terms of the destination of the heirs of the crown; and, to prepare an Instrument of Government to be offered with the Crown for securing the people from the grievances which affected them. Radical counsels carried greater weight in Scotland where James was deposed in a straightforward manner and the offer of the crown was tied to an Instrument of Government which was a term redolent of the Commonwealth period. At the end of their sitting on 4 April, a bishop volunteered to say the usual prayers whereupon it was moved that as James was no longer King he would pray for him at his peril. The bishop contented himself with reciting the Lord's Prayer. Before the Convention adjourned, it was ordered that the vote of the house should be carried to absent members for their assent or dissent[118].

During the following week, the Committee considered the settlement of the government. Urgency was brought to its work on 9 April when a person who had recently arrived from Dublin informed the committee that he had seen the late King there. If James had ships at his disposal, he might soon be in Scotland. The Declaration of the Estates containing the claim of right and the offer of the crown was submitted to the Convention on 11 April. It was read several times and, after several amendments, put to the vote and approved. As in England, the text incorporated a revised oath of allegiance. The Convention ordered that the Declaration be recorded in the Register Books of Parliament and that William and Mary be proclaimed King and Queen of Scotland at the mercat cross of Edinburgh immediately after the adjournment. On this day in London William and Mary were crowned King and Queen of England. Before the Convention adjourned, an act was passed declaring that it would continue undissolved until the King and Queen of England should accept the crown. Hamilton read the proclamation at the mercat cross – 'an action thought below his dignity, and mean from one of his haughty temper.'[119]

The Committee now turned its attention to the grievances which were presented and agreed, after argument, on 13 April. On the same day, a proclamation was published against the owning of the late King James and appointing public prayers for William and Mary King and Queen of Scotland. Further grievances were added during the following week and a new text of the coronation oath was approved by the Convention. By 24 April, all the arrangements were complete and a letter was prepared informing William that he had been proclaimed with Mary as King and Queen of Scotland with the unanimous approval of the whole house. The Earl of Argyle, Sir James Montgomerie of Skelmorlie and Sir John Dalrymple were appointed as the three commissioners who would attend the King and Queen with the "chearfull offer" of the crown and would also present the Claim of Right and represent the things found grievous to the nation. William and Mary were urged to swear and sign the coronation oath. As for the Union, the Convention had nominated commissioners to treat of the terms of an entire and perpetual union between the two kingdoms with the reservation that church government should remain in Scotland as it would be established at the time of the union. The letter ended with a reference to the common danger facing both kingdoms from the situation in Ireland[120].

When the Committee presented the draft of the letter on 22 March, the Earl of Crawford suggested an additional clause requesting the King to turn the Convention into a Parliament. This was approved on the following day after a long debate and a vote. The offer of the crown was approved unanimously by the Convention but Queensberry, Athol, Cassels and Kintore voted against the clause relating to the Claim of Right and the grievances[121].

Before the three Commissioners departed for London, they were instructed to see that the letter from the Convention and the Declaration of the Estates were read in their presence as well as the grievances and the address for turning the Convention into a Parliament. They were also to offer the coronation oath and to see that it was sworn and signed. Afterwards, the three commissioners were to return immediately to Scotland with an account of the proceedings. The Convention was concerned that the ceremonies in London should be properly witnessed and the Scots nobility and gentlemen in London, especially members of the Convention, were ordered to wait on the King when the commissioners presented the offer of the crown. As well as the three commissioners named above, twenty-four other commissioners were on their way to London to treat of the union. In this matter, the only other action of the Convention before adjourning on 29 April until 21 May was a proclamation for a public thanksgiving[122].

William and Mary received Argyle, Montgomery and Dalrymple in the Banqueting House at Whitehall on 11 May. Before presenting the letter from the Convention, the Earl of Argyle spoke briefly: '... It is from the grateful and dutiful sense of so happy and unexpected a delivery, as well as from the respect due to the blood of their ancient monarchs, that the Estates of Scotland have commissionate us to make a humble tender to your Majesty, and your Royal Consort, of that crown and kingdom, with the firm persuasion and assurance of this rooted in their hearts, That the care and protection of religion, liberty and property, could be no where so well lodged as in the hands of Your Majesties, their great and glorious deliverers.' Then the documents from Scotland were read:

'MAY IT PLEASE YOUR MAJESTIE

The setleing of the monarchie and antient government of this kingdome admitting no delay, Wee did upon the eleavinth instant proclaime your Majestie and your Royall consort King & Queen of Scotland, with so much unanimity, that of the wholl house ther was not one contrary vote, We have nominate the Earle of Argyle Sir James Montgomerie of Skelmorlie and Sir John Dalrymple In our name to attend your Majesties with the chearfull offer of the croune And humbly to present the Petitione or Claime of Right of the subjects of this kingdome, As also to represent some things found greivous to this natione, which we humbly intreat your Majestie to remeid by whollsome lawes in your first Parliament And in testimony of your Majestie and the Queens acceptance, We beseech your Majesties in presence of these sent by us to swear and signe the oath herewith presented, which our law hath appoynted to be taken by our Kings and Queens at the entry to their government, till such tyme as your great affairs allow this kingdome the happiness of your presence in order to the coronation of your Majesties. We are most sensible of your Majesties kyndnes and fatherly care to both your Kingdomes in promoveing ther union, which we hope hath been reserved to be accomplished by you, that as both Kingdomes are united in one head and Soveraigne so they may become one body politick, one nation to be represented in one Parliament, And to testifie our readines to comply with your Majestie in that matter We have nominated comissioners to treat the termes of ane intire and perpetuall union betwixt the two kingdomes, with reservatione to us of our church government, as it shall be established at the tyme of the union, These commissioners doe wait your Majesties approbatione and call, that they may meet and treat with the commissioners to be appoynted for Ingland at what tyme and place your Majestie shall appoynt. And if any difficulty shall arrise in the treatie, we doe upon our pairt refer the determinatione therof to your Majestie And we do assure ourselves from your Majesties prudence & goodness of a happy conclusione to that important affair, so as the same be agreed to and ratified by your Majestie in your first Parliament, Wee doe lykewayes render your Majestie our most dutyfull thanks, for your gracious letter brought to us by the Lord Ross (a persone well affected to your service) And for your princely care in sending doune these troupes which may in the mean tyme helpe to preserve us and when the season offers may be imployed towardes the recovery of Ireland, from that deplorable condition and extream danger, to which the protestants ther are exposed, the guarding our coasts with a good fleet, preserves Ingland as well as us from ane invasion, and as it is the interest of Ingland to contribute to secure us from the first impressiones of the common danger So we shall not be wanting on our pairt to give our assistance for reduceing of Ireland that all your Majesties kingdomes may flourish in peace and truth, under the auspicious influence of your happy reignes Signed at the desyre of the Estates and in our name by our President.

The Declaration of the Estates of the Kingdom of Scotland containing the Claim of Right and the offer of the Croune to the King & Queen of England.

Whereas King James the Seventh being a profest papist did assume the regall power, and acted as King without ever takeing the oath required by law, wherby the King, at his access to the government is obliged to swear, To maintain the protestant religion, and to rule the people according to the laudable lawes; and did by the advyce of wicked and evill counsellors, invade the fundamental constitution of this kingdome and altered it from a legall limited monarchy, to ane arbitrary despotick power; and in a publick proclaimation, asserted ane absolute power, to cass annull and dissable all the lawes, particularly arraigning the lawes establishing the protestant religion and did exerce that power to the subversion of the protestant religion, and to the violation of the lawes and liberties of the kingdome.

By erecting publick schooles and societies of the Jesuites and not only allowing mass to be publickly said But also inverting protestant chappels and churches to publick mass houses contrair to the express lawes against saying and hearing of mass.

By allowing popish books to be printed, and dispersed by a gift to a popish printer, designeing him Printer to his Majesties household, Colledge and Chappell contrair to the lawes.

By takeing the children of Protestant Noblemen and gentlemen sending and keeping them abroad, to be bred papists, makeing great fonds and dotationes to popish schooles and colledges abroad, bestowing pensiones upon preists, and perverting protestants from ther religion, by offers of places, preferments and pensiones.

By disarmeing protestants while at the same tyme he imployed papists in the places of greatest trust, civil and military; such as Chancellor, Secretaries, Privie Counsellors, and Lords of Sessione, thrusting out protestants to make roome for papists, and intrusting the forts and magazines of the Kingdome in ther hands.

By imposeing oathes contrair to law

By giveing gifts and grants for exacting money, without consent of Parliament, or Conventione of Estates

By levying or keeping on foot a standing army in tyme of peace without consent of Parliament which army did exact localitie free and dry quarters.

By imploying the officers of the army as judges through ye Kingdome and imposeing them, wher ther were heretable officers and jurisdictiones by whom many of the leidges were put to death summarly, without legall tryall, jury or record.

By imposeing exorbitant fines, to the value of the pairties estates exacting extravagant baile, and disposeing fines and forefaultors befor any proces or conviction.

By imprisoning persones without expressing the reasone, and delaying to put them to tryall.

By causeing persue and forefault severall persones upon stretches of old and obsolete lawes, upon frivolous and weak pretences, upon lame and defective probationes as particularly the late Earle of Argyle, to the scandal and reproach of the justice of the natione.

By subverting the right of the Royal Burghs, the third Estate of Parliament, imposeing upon them not only magistrats, But also the wholl toune Councill and Clerks, contrary to their liberties and express chartours, without the pretence either of sentence, surrender or consent, so that the Commissioners to Parliaments, being chosen by the magistrats and Councill, The King might in effect alswell nominat that entire Estate of Parliament; and many of the saids magistrats put in by him were avowed papists, and the Burghes were forced to pay money for the letters imposeing these illegall magistrats and councils upon them

By sending letters to the chiefe courts of Justice, not only ordaining the judges to stop and desist *sine die* to determine causes But also ordering and commanding them how to proceed in cases depending before them contrair to the express lawes; and by chainging ye nature of the judges *gifts ad vitam aut culpam*, and giveing them commissions *ad beneplacitam*, to dispose them to complyance with arbitrary courses, and turneing them out of their offices when they did not comply.

By granting personall protectiones for civill debts contrair to law

All which are utterly and directly contrairy to the knoune lawes, statutes and freedomes of this realme.

Therefor the Estates of the kingdom of Scotland find and declaire that King James the Seventh being a profest papist, did assume the regall power and acted as king, without ever taking the oath required by law, and hath by the advyce of evill and wicked counsellors, invaded the fundamentall constitution of the kingdome, and altered it from a legall limited monarchy to ane arbitrary despotick power, and hath exercised ye same, to the subversione of the protestant religion, and the violation of the lawes and liberties of the kingdome, inverting all the ends of government, whereby he hath forefaulted the right to the Crowne, and the throne is become vacant.

And whereas His Royal Highness William then Prince of Orange now King of Ingland, whom it hath pleased Almighty God to make the glorious instrument of delyvering these Kingdomes from Popery and arbitrary power, did, By the advyce of severall Lords and Gentlemen of this Nation at London for the tyme call the Estates of this Kingdome to meet the fourteenth of March last, In order to such an establishment, as that your religion, lawes and liberties might not be again in danger of being subverted, And the said Estates being now assembled, in a full and free representative of this nation, takeing to their most serious consideratione, the best meanes for attaining the ends aforesaid do in the first place, as ther ancestors in the like cases have usually done for the vindicating and asserting their antient rights and liberties, declare

That by the law of this Kingdome no papist can be King or Queen of this realme, not bear any office whatsomever therin: nor can any protestant successor exercise the regall power, untill he or she swear ye Coronation Oath

That all proclamations asserting ane absolute power to cass annull and dissable lawes, the erecting schools and colledges for Jesuits, the inverting protestant chappells and churches to publick mass houses and the allowing mass to be said are contrair to law.

That the allowing Popish bookes to be printed and dispersed is contrairy to law.

That the takeing the children of noblemen, gentlemen, and others, sending and keeping them abroad to be bred papists, The makeing fonds and dotations to popish schooles and colledges The bestowing pensiones on priests and the perverting protestants from ther religion by offers of places preferments and pensiones are contrary to law.

That the disarming of protestants and imploying papists in the places of greatest trust, both civil and military, the thrusting out of protestants, to make roome for papists, and the intrusting papists with the forts and magazines of the Kingdome are contrary to law.

That the imposeing oaths without authority of Parliament is contrair to law

That the giveing gifts or grants for raiseing of money without the consent of Parliament or Convention of Estates is contrary to law

That the imploying the officers of the army as judges throughout the Kingdome, or imposeing them wher ther were heretable offices and jurisdictiones and the putting the leidges to death summarly, and without legall tryall jury or record are contrary to law.

That the imposeing of extraordinary fynes, the exacting of exorbitant baile, and the disposeing of fynes and forefaultors befor sentence are contrary to law.

That the imprisoning persones without expressing the reason therof and delaying to put them to tryall, is contrary to law.

That the causeing persue and forefault persones upon stretches of old and obsolete lawes upon frivolous and weak pretences, upon lame and defective probation, as particularly the late Earle of Argylle, are contrary to law.

That the nominating and imposeing the magistrats councils & clerks upon burghes contrary to ther liberties and express chartors is contrary to law.

That the sending letters to the courts of justice, ordaining the judges to stop or desist from determining causes, or ordaining them how to proceed in causes depending befor them, and the changeing the nature of the judges *gifts ad vitam aut culpam* into commissions *durante beneplacito* are contrary to law.

That the granting personall protectiones for civil debts is contrary to law.

That the forceing the leidges to depone against themselves in capitall crymes however the punishment be restricted is contrary to law.

That the useing torture without evidence, or in ordinary crymes is contrary to law.

That the sending of ane army in one hostile manner upon any pairt of the kingdome, in a peaceable tyme, and exacting of locality and any manner of free quarters, is contrary to law.

That the chargeing of the leidges with lawborrowes, at ye Kings instance, and the imposeing of bonds, without the authority of Parliament, and the suspending advocats from their imployment for not compearing when such bonds were offered were contrary to law.

That the putting of garisones in privat mens houses in tyme of peace without their consent, or the authority of Parliament is contrary to law.

That the opinions of the Lords of Sessione in the two cases following were contrary to law viz (1.) That the concealing the demand of a supply for a forefaulted persone altho not given is treason. (2.) That persones refuseing to discover what are their privat thoughts and judgements in relation to points of treason, or other mens actions, are guilty of treason.

That the fyneing husbands for ther wives withdrawing from the church was contrary to law.

That prelacy and the superiority of any office in the church, above presbyters is, and hath been a great and insupportable greivance and trouble to this nation, and contrary to the inclinationes of the generality of the people ever since the reformatione (they haveing reformed from popery by presbyters) and therfor ought to be abolished.

That it is the right and priviledge of the subjects to protest for remeed of law to the King and Parliament against sentences pronounced by the lords of sessione, provydeing the samen do not stop execution of these sentences.

That it is the right of the subjects to petition the King, and that all imprisonments and prosecutiones for such petitioning are contrary to law.

That for redress of all greivances, and for the amending strenthneing and preserveing of the lawes, Parliament ought to be frequently called, and allowed to sit, and the freedom of speech & debate secured to the members.

And they doe claim, demand, and insist upon all & sundry the premises as ther undoubted right and liberties, And that no declarationes, doeings or proceedings, to the prejudice of the people in any of the said premises ought in any wayes to be drawne hereafter in consequence or example, but that all forefaulters, fynes, loss of offices, imprisonments, banishments, pursuits, persecutiones tortures, and rigorous executiones be considered, and the pairties laesed be redressed.

To which demand of ther rights and redressing of their grievances they are particularly encouraged by his Majesty the King of England his declaration for the Kingdom of Scotland of ye   day of October last, as being the only means for obtaining a full redress and remedy therein

Haveing therfor ane entire confidence, that his said Majesty the King of England will perfect the delyverance so far advanced by him and will still preserve them from the violation of their rights which they have here asserted, and from all other attempts upon their Religion lawes and liberties

The said Estates of the Kingdome of Scotland Doe resolve that William & Mary King and Queen of England, France & Ireland be, and be declared King & Queen of Scotland to hold the crowne and royall dignity of the Kingdome of Scotland, To them the said King and Queen dureing ther lives, and the longest liver of them, and that the sole & full exercise of the regall power, be only in and exercised by him the said King in the names of the said King and Queen, dureing ther joynt lives, And after ther decease the said Croune and Royall Dignity of the said Kingdome, to be to the heirs of the body of the said Queen which failing to the Princess

Ann of Denmark and the airs of her body, which also failing, to the aires of the body of the said William King of England.

And they do pray the said King and Queen of England to accept the same accordingly.

And that the oath hereafter mentioned, be taken by all protestants of whom the oath of allegiance, and any other oathes and declarationes might be required by law, instead of them, And that the said oath of allegiance, and other oaths and declarationes may be abrogated.

I A:B: do sincerely promise and swear, That I will be faithfull and bear true allegiance to their Majesties King William & Queen Mary So help me God

THEN THE GRIEVANCES WHICH THE ESTATES WISHED THE KING TO REDRESS WERE READ:

The Estates of the Kingdome of Scotland doe represent that the Committee of Parliament called the Articles, is a great greivance to the Nation, and that there ought to be no committees of Parliament but such as are freely chosen by the Estates to prepare motions and overtures that are first made in the house

That the first act of Parliament sixteen sixtie nyne is inconsistent with the establishment of the church government now desyred and ought to be abrogated.

That forefaultors in prejudice of vassalls, creditors and aires of entaile are a great greivance.

That the oblidging the leidges to depone upon crymes against delinquents utherwayes then when they are adduced in speciall processes as witnesses is a great greivance.

That the assyses of error are a greivance, And that juries be considered by Parliament.

That the eighteinth act of Parliament sixteen eighty one declareing a cumulative jurisdiction is a greivance.

That the commissariot courts as they are now constitute are a greivance.

That the twenty seventh act of Parliament sixteen sixtie three giveing to the King power to impose custome at pleasure upon forraigne import and trade is a greivance and prejudiciall to the trade of the nation.

That the not takeing ane effectuall course to repress the depredations and robberies by the Highland clannes is a greivance.

That the banishment by the Councill of the greatest pairt of the advocates from Edinburgh without a process was a greivance.

That most of the lawes enacted in the Parliament anno sixteen eighty fyve are impious and intollerable greivances.

That the marriage of a King or Queen of this realme to a papist is dangerous to the protestant religion and ought to be provyded against.

That the levieing or keeping on foot a standing army in tyme of peace without consent of Parliament is a greiveance.

That all greivances relateing to the manner and measure of ye leidges ther representatione in Parliament be considered and redressed in the first Parliament.

That the greivances of the Burrowes be considered and redressed in the first Parliament.

There followed the address for turning the Convention into a Parliament. William made a brief reply accepting these documents. Argyle then read out the coronation oath distinctly word by word, and the King and Queen repeated it after him, holding up their right hands, according to the custom of taking oaths in Scotland:

'We   faithfully promise and swear by this our solemne oath in Presence of the eternall God, that dureing the wholl course of our life, we will serve the same eternall God to the uttermost of our power, according as he has required in his most holy word, revealed and contained in the new and old testaments, and according to the same word shall maintain the true religion of Christ Jesus the preaching of his holy word and the due and right ministratione of the sacraments now receaved and preached within the realme of Scotland, and shall abolish and gainstand all false religion, contrary to the same, and shall rule the people committed to our charge, according to the will and command of God revealed in his aforesaid word, And according to the loveable lawes and constitutiones receaved in this realme nowayes repugnant to the said word of the Eternall God, and shall procure to the utmost of our power, to the Kirk of God, and wholl christian people true and perfect peace in all tyme comeing that We shall preserve and keep inviolated the rights and rents, with all just priviledges of the croune of Scotland, neither shall we transferr nor alienate the same, That we shall forbid and repress in all estates and degrees, reise, oppression, and all kind of wrang And We shall command and procure that justice and equity in all judgements be keeped to all persons without exceptione As the Lord and father of all mercies shall be mercyfull to us, And we shall be carefull to roote out all hereticks and enemies to the true worship of God that shall be convicted by the true Kirk of God of the forsaids crymes out of our lands and Empire of Scotland And wee faithfully affirme the things above written by our solemne Oath.'

William objected to the clause in the oath about the rooting out of heretics. The Convention had authorised the Commissioners to answer that by the law of Scotland no man could be destroyed or persecuted for his private opinion and even obstinate heretics, convicted for perverting other men, could only be denounced or outlawed with the confiscation of their moveable goods. Before reciting the last clause, the King said before all present that he did not mean by these words to be under any necessity to become a persecutor and he ordered the Commissioners to bear witness that he had made this reservation. They replied that persecution was neither intended by the oath, nor required by the law of the land[123].

The Claim of Right and the grievances were accompanied with the strong implication that the offer of the crown was conditional on their acceptance. William, on the other hand, wished to maintain the prerogatives of the monarchy intact and Lord Melville assured him that the Claim of Right and the Grievances 'are loosely drawn and may be helped in Parliament what dissatisfies.' William was displeased that the Convention had demanded the abolition of prelacy and the Lords of the Articles. Presbyterian influence in the Convention had insisted, on a vote of 106/7 to 32, that the grievance about prelacy should be adopted and included, rather oddly, in the Claim of Right. The King, naturally, wished to keep royal influence over the church and also to maintain the control over Parliament exercised by the Lords of the Articles, a nominated committee which managed the business[124].

Hamilton, now named the King's High Commissioner in Scotland, opened Parliament on 5 June when the first business was the act for declaring the meeting of the estates to be a Parliament. This act, copied from England, was strictly illegal in Scotland but it was introduced, voted and touched with the sceptre on the same day William's attempts to preserve episcopacy and the articles were defeated by a radical faction in Parliament. Known as the Club and noted for its sophisticated organisation, this faction argued for a radical interpretation of the Claim of Right and the grievances with some success when they obtained the abolition of both episcopacy and the articles. Parliament became unmanageable.

William had proposed the union to avoid difficulties in Scotland but the

English proved lukewarm. Preoccupied with the war in Europe, the King allowed the proposal to lapse. However, the continued difficulties in Scotland during the reign of Anne combined with the Scottish Parliament's failure to follow England's adoption of the Hanoverian family as the next successors led the ministers in London to turn again to the union which was finally achieved in 1707[125].

Sources for the debates at Westminster

The five texts published below are the main sources for the debates in the Convention held at Westminster. They are all unofficial records because both Houses considered their debates and proceedings to be matters of concern only to their own members. Sir Henry Hobart was quickly rebuffed when he moved, on 22 January, that 'the votes of this House might be printed for the satisfaction of the nation at this juncture.'[126].

Notes of a Noble Lord

The original copy of these notes is Pepys MS 2179, pp.41-63, at Magdalen College, Cambridge. The text was available to early historians of the Revolution. Alan Simpson established the close connection between these notes and the published version of Lord Clarendon's diary. It is probable that the notes form an initial version of Clarendon's account of the Revolution and we have printed additional material from the published diary in the notes following the text below. In editing the text, we have extended the abbreviations, adopted modern usage with regard to capitals and added punctuation where necessary but the spelling is as in the original[127].

Danby's notes of the debate in the Lords on 29 January

This text from BL Egerton MS 3345, bundle 3, was edited by Professor Henry Horwitz as an appendix to his valuable study on Parliament and the Glorious Revolution. The Earl of Danby was the chairman of the committee to consider the present state of the nation and his notes are the only detailed record of a debate in the House of Lords[128].

Grey's debates

Anchitell Grey, member for the borough of Derby, kept a diary recording the debates in the Commons from 1667 to 1694. While his diary only records those debates in which Grey was interested, it is still valuable as the only source for many debates. The text we possess was first published in 1763 and reprinted in 1769; we have reproduced below the 1769 edition. It is possible that the editors made a muddle of their manuscript original because the two other sources for the important debate on 28 January, printed below, show that the sequence and number of speakers as recorded by Grey is incorrect. The order of speakers, using the pagination in the original, should read: Dolben-Temple, pp.7-10; Howe, p.24; Howard-Pulteney, pp.19-24; Clarges-Finch, pp.15-19; Lee-Treby, pp.10-15; Finch-Howard, pp.24-5[129].

Notes of what passed in the Convention... 28 January 1689

These notes were taken with a pencil by John Somers, a young Whig lawyer, whose reputation was considerably enhanced by his participation in the Convention. The text was first published in *Miscellaneous State Papers from 1501 to 1726* (London: W. Strahan and T. Cadell, 1778), 2:401-25. It is a more accurate report of the debate than that recorded by Grey.

A Jornall of the Convention

This text (HLRO, Hist. Coll. 155) contains a valuable account of the debate in the Commons on 28 January and has been edited by Professor Lois G. Schwoerer with a detailed introduction. We reprint the text below. Professor Schwoerer suggests that the compiler of this *Jornall* may have been Sir Henry Hobart, the member for Norfolk. More valuable as a source than Grey or Somers, the *Jornall* records not only a summary of the speeches but also notes the atmosphere in the House[130].

The debate at large... at the Free Conference, 6 February

Unlike the other texts, this is a verbatim account recorded by 'Mr Blaney in a private place to take down all that was said.' It was first published in 1695, with an improved second edition in 1710 and a third edition in 1714; we publish below a reprint of the second edition. The published text includes an useful summary of the proceedings in the Commons from 22 January to 5 February. The first edition must have been approved by the government presumably with the intention of emphasising the reasons for James's abdication[131].

Notes

Abbreviations

Ailesbury	*Memoirs of Thomas, 2nd Earl of Ailesbury*; ed. by W. E. Buckley. 2 vols. London, 1890.
APS	*Acts of the Parliament of Scotland, vol. 9*. Edinburgh, 1822.
Balcarres	*Memoirs touching the Revolution in Scotland* MDCLXXXVIII-MDCXC; by Colin Earl of Balcarres. Edinburgh, 1841.
Ballard 45	Bodleian Library. Ballard MS 45. Newsletters to Dr. Richard Charlett about English public affairs, 1688-1706.
BL	British Library.
Burnet	Gilbert Burnet. *History of his own time*. 6 vols. Oxford, 1823.
CJ	*Journal of the House of Commons*
Clarendon	*Correspondence of Henry Hyde, Earl of Clarendon, and of his brother Laurence Hyde, Earl of Rochester*; ed. by S. W. Singer. 2 vols. London, 1828.
CSPD	*Calendar of State Papers, Domestic Series*.
Foxcroft	H. C. Foxcroft. *The life and letters of Sir George Savile, Bart., 1st Marquess of Halifax*. 2 vols. London, 1898.
Grey	*Debates of the House of Commons, from the year 1667-1694*; by Anchitell Grey. 10 vols. London, 1769.
Henning	*The House of Commons 1660-1690*; ed. by B. D. Henning. 3 vols. London, 1983.
HMC	Historical Manuscripts Commission
HLROMM	House of Lords Record Office. Manuscript Minute.
LJ	*Journal of the House of Lords*.
Luttrell	Narcissus Luttrell. *A brief historical relation of state affairs from September 1678 to April 1714*. 6 vols. Oxford, 1857.
Morrice	Dr. Williams's Library. Morrice MS Q – a political diary kept by Roger Morrice.
Procs	*An account of the proceedings of the Estates in Scotland, 1689-1690;* ed. by E. W. M. Balfour-Melville. 2 vols. Scottish History Society, 3rd series, vols 46-47.
Rawl D1079	Bodleian Library. Rawlinson MS D1079

Stowe 370   British Library. Stowe MS 370. The proceedings of the
              Lords Spiritual and Temporal from their first meeting at
              Guild Hall, London.

1. *A complete collection of state trials*; comp. by. T. B. Howell. (London, 1816),
   1:427.

2. The texts of the proclamations will be found in *London Gazette*, no. 2384 (20/24
   Sept. 1688); no. 2386 (27 Sept./1 Oct. 1688).

3. BL Preston Papers. Volume entitled '1688 Letters from England,' fol 11.

4. Morrice: 316; Foxcroft, 2:8. The text of the declaration is in *CJ*, 10:1-5; for the
   drafting of the declaration, see Burnet, 3:286-88.

5. *To the King's Most Excellent Majestie the Humble Petition*. (London: Printed for H.
   Jones, 1688); Morrice: 319, 321; Clarendon 2:201-05; Foxcroft 2:10-13.

6. Morrice: 329; Clarendon, 2:208-11; Foxcroft 2:14-15; Ailesbury, 2:185, 192-3.

7. Morrice: 331-2, 336; Clarendon, 2:211; Ailesbury, 2:193; Luttrell, 1:480; *London
   Gazette* no. 2406 (29 Nov./3 Dec. 1688).

8. *The Commissioners proposal to His Royal Highness the Prince of Orange with His
   Highness's answer*. (London: R. Bentley, 1688).

9. BL Add MS 45731 fol 71, R. Warre – E. Poley 4 Dec. 1688; Morrice: 338-9, 341.

10. A R Wyon, *The Great Seals of England* (London, 1887): 109. The Great Seal was
    retrieved by a fisherman.

11. Ailesbury, 2:194; James described this as a coffee-house report until Ailesbury
    pointed out that he knew horses were ready at Lambeth.

12. R. A. Beddard, 'The loyalist opposition in the interregnum: a letter of Dr.
    Francis Turner, Bishop of Ely, on the Revolution of 1688,' *Bulletin of the
    Institute of Historical Research* 40(1967): 106; *CSPD James II*, 3:359; HMC
    Dartmouth 11th Report, App, Pt.5: 230, 232; HMC Dartmouth 3, 15th Re-
    port, App. I:135; W. L. Sachse, 'The mob and the revolution of 1688,' *Journal
    of British Studies* 4 no. 1 (Nov. 1964): 23-40.

13. R. A. Beddard, 'The Guildhall Declaration of 11 December 1688 and the
    counter-revolution of the loyalists,' *Historical Journal*, 11 (1968):414

14. Stowe 370, fols 2-6; another copy of the minutes of 11 Dec. meeting are printed
    in *CSPD James II*, 3:378-80. The excellent account of the proceedings found
    in Stowe 370 was probably prepared by Francis Gwyn; Philip Jenkins, 'Fran-
    cis Gwyn and the birth of the Tory Party,' *Welsh History Review* 11 (1982-83):
    283-301 gives an account of Gwyn's career. Morrice: 347-8; Clarendon, 2:224;
    Ailesbury, 2:197-99. The meeting of the lords is discussed by Beddard in the
    two articles cited above and in " 'The violent party:' the Guildhall revolu-
    tionaries and the growth of opposition to James," *Guildhall Miscellany* 3(1970):
    120-36.

15. F. A. J. Mazure, *Histoire de la Révolution en Angleterre*, (Paris, 1825), 3:233.

16. *Correspondence of the Family of Hatton*; ed. by E. M. Thompson, (Camden Society, n.s. 23):123.

17. Stowe 370, fols 20-23; Ailesbury, 2:209.

18. Stowe 370, fol 38.

19. Stowe 370, fol 42.

20. [G. Burnet], 'An enquiry into the present state of affairs. Published by authority. December 1688,' *State Tracts* (London, 1705), 1:129.

21. Stowe 370, fol 40.

22. *London Courant*, no. 3(15/18 Dec. 1688); Burnet, 3:334.

23. Halifax's note on the Windsor meeting in Dorothy H. Somerville, *The King of Hearts: George Talbot, Duke of Shrewsbury*, (London, 1962):50; Clarendon, 2:229-31; Ballard 45, fol 21.

24. P. C. Vellacott, 'The diary of a country gentleman in 1688,' *Cambridge Historical Journal* 2(1926-28):62.

25. Stowe 370, fols 46-60; Morrice: 384-85; Ballard 45, fol 22.

26. Stowe 370, fols 61-66.

27. BL Add MS 20007, fol 54a; Morrice: 390; HMC Dartmouth 3:139.

28. Stowe 370, fols 66-76; BL MS Althorp 8 (Halifax's notes of this debate); Clarendon, 2:234-5; Morrice: 392; Nottingham's notes for his speech are in Henry Horwitz, *Revolution politicks: the career of Daniel Finch, Second Earl of Nottingham*, (Cambridge, 1969):69; HMC Dartmouth 3:141.

29. *Whereas the necessity of affairs*, (London: 1688). An anonymous memorial suggesting the summoning of members of Charles II's Parliament was sent to Halifax, BL MS Althorp 8.

30. *London Courant*, no. 6 (25/29 Dec. 1688).

31. *CJ*, 10:5-7; *English Currant*, 26-28 Dec. 1688; *London Courant*, no.6 (25-29 Dec. 1688); Morrice: 396-8, 409; Henning, *sub* Sawyer; Maynard's reply to William is quoted by Michael Landon, *The triumph of the lawyers*, (University, 1970):220.

32. *CJ*, 10:7-8 (text of the circular letter); *Universal Intelligence*, no. 10 (5/8 Jan. 1688/9); Morrice:348.

33. 'History of the Desertion. Part the Second,' *State Tracts* (London, 1705), 1:103.

34. J. H. Plumb and Alan Simpson, 'A letter of William of Orange to Danby on the flight of James II,' *Cambridge Historical Journal*, 5(1937/38): 107-08; HMC 14th Report, App., Part 9:454.

35. The best account of the elections is the history of the constituencies in Henning, vol. 1; also valuable is Alan Simpson, *The Convention Parliament 1688-1689*, (Oxford, DPhil, 1939):14-36; J. H. Plumb, 'The elections to the Convention Parliament of 1689,' *Cambridge Historical Journal* 5(1937/38):235-54.

36. For contemporary accounts of these parties, see Ballard 45, fol 24; Morrice: 434-5; Luttrell, 1:497.

37. HMC Portland 3:421; 'my opinion is the King will be deposed and the Prince's favourites will push him on to a crown,' Earl of Lindsay – Countess of Danby (18 Dec. 1688), HMC 14th Report, App., Part 9:452; a similar view was expressed in Francis Gwyn – Lord Dartmouth, HMC Dartmouth 3:141.

38. Burnet, 3:355-56.

39. Clarendon, 2:249.

40. Morrice: 400, 424, 426, 433 where they are called Hierarchists; Clarendon 2:252; St Asaph's attitude is recorded in *CSPD James II*, 3:381.

41. BL Add MS 32681, fol 317.

42. Clarendon, 2:235; Morrice: 434.

43. Andrew Browning, *Thomas Osborne Earl of Danby and Duke of Leeds* (Glasgow, 1951), 2:156-7. Clarendon's letter is quoted in Simpson, *Convention Parliament*:61-3.

44. Henry Sidney, *Diary of the times of Charles the Second*; ed. by R. W. Blencowe, (London, 1843), 2:288-91.

45. [G. Burnet], *An enquiry*:133; Richard Ashcraft, *Revolutionary politicks & Locke's 'Two treatises of government'*, (Princeton, 1986):526; [R. Ferguson], 'A brief justification of the Prince of Orange's descent into England,' *State Tracts* (London:1705), 1:141.

46. Ballard 45, fol 22.

47. Clarendon, 2:241; Foxcroft, 2:203-04.

48. John Sheffield, Duke of Buckinghamshire, *Works* (London, 1726), 2:84-5; Ferguson, *Brief justification*:146

49. Foxcroft, 2:203; Clarendon, 2:248; Ferguson, *Brief justification*:141.

50. The membership of the Commons is analysed in Henning, 1; attendance is calculated by Andrew Browning, *English Historical Documents 1660-1714* (London, 1953):956-7. For the names Tory and Whig, see James Fox and Clayton Roberts, 'John Locke on the Glorious Revolution: a rediscovered document,' *Historical Journal* 28(1985):387. There is a reference in Rawl D1079, fol 11b/12a for 5 Feb. to 'Portman, Rich cum multis aliis Toriorum.' Locke's vexation is mentioned in his letter to Edward Clarke (29 Jan./8 Feb. 1689), *The correspondence of John Locke*, ed. by E. S. de Beer (Oxford, 1978), 3:545-6.

51. Morrice: 437; for the role of the assistants, see Elizabeth Read Foster, *The House of Lords 1603-1649* (Chapel Hill, 1983):71-86.

52. BL Add MS 40621, fol 5; Clarendon, 2:238.

53. BL Add MS 15949, fol 10; Clarendon, 2:252-3

54. *LJ*, 14:103; *CJ*, 10:12.

55. BL Add MS 33923, fol 462; 'the Prince is mighty reserved and hard of access,' Barbara Lady Dartmouth to Lord Dartmouth, HMC Dartmouth 11th Report, App., Part 5:241.

56. *LJ*, 14:106; HLROMM 24 Jan. 1688/9.

57. Clarendon, 2:253.

58. *LJ*, 14:107-08; HLROMM 25 Jan. 1688/9; HLRO Main Papers 6 Feb. 1689 for the excuses by Conyers and Newcastle, for the latter, see A. S. Turberville, *A history of Welbeck Abbey and its owners* (London, 1938), 1:215. A list of the peers present each day from 22 Jan. to 13 Feb. is printed in the appendix at the end of Laurence Echard, *The history of the Revolution*, (London, 1725).

59. Clarendon, 2:253-4.

60. Morrice:443.

61. Morrice:444; the main sources for the Commons' debate are Grey, 9:6-25; Somers's notes and the *Jornal* reprinted below.

62. HLROMM 28 Jan. 1688/9; Clarendon, 2:255; HMC Portland, 3:422-3.

63. Danby's notes reprinted below; Rawl D1079, fol 4; Ballard 45, fol 25; Morrice:446-7, 450. HLROMM gives the figures for the division as 51 votes to 48, see also Eveline Cruickshanks, David Hayton, Clyve Jones, 'Divisions in the House of Lords on the transfer of the Crown and other issues, 1689-94: ten new lists,' *Bulletin of the Institute of Historical Research* 53(1980):59-60. Churchill's absence is noted sourly by Morrice:450-51.

64. Henry Horwitz, '1689 (and all that),' *Parliamentary History* 6(1987): 23-32.

65. Grey, 9:25-37.

66. *LJ*, 14:111; HLROMM 30 Jan. 1688/9.

67. BL Add MS 15949, fol 12a, Stanley West – Mr. Rich. Tucker, Merchant, Weymouth, Dorset 31 Jan. 1688/9.

68. Gilbert Burnet, *A sermon preached before the House of Commons. On the 31st of January 1688*, (London: John Starkey and Richard Chiswell, 1689):35.

69. Morrice: 451-2; BL Add MS 40621, fol 12, E. Harley-R. Harley; Cruickshanks, Eveline, et al, 'Divisions in the House of Lords':60-61.

70. BL Add MS 15949, fol 12a.

71. Grey, 9:37-40, the report for 1 Feb. is obscure; HMC Portland 3:426; Morrice:452; Rawl D1079, fol 5.

72. *CJ*, 10:16; Grey 10:40-2; Morrice:455.

73. HLROMM 1 Feb. 1688/9; Rawl D 1079, fol 7b.

74. Grey, 9:42-5; *CJ*, 10:17.

75. HLROMM 3 Feb. 1688/9; Clarendon, 2:258; Grey, 9:45-6.

76. Clarendon, 2:258; 'Notes of a noble lord' 2 Feb. 1688/9 printed below; the text of the petition is described by Morrice:453-4, and printed in *London Intelligencer*

no 7 (2/5 Feb. 1688/9); Grey, 9:45-6. Some of the lords may have recalled the trial of Strafford when the House was 'so encompassed with multitudes that their lordships may be conceaved not to be free,' Paul Christianson, 'The 'obliterated' portion of the House of Lords Journals during the attainder of Strafford, 1641,' *English Historical Review* 95(1980):349.

77. *CJ*, 10:18-19; Grey, 9:49-52; HLROMM 4 Feb. 1688/9; Cruickshanks, Eveline, et al, 'Divisions in the House of Lords':61-62.

78. HLROMM 4 Feb. 1688/9; Clarendon, 2:259.

79. Grey, 9:50-2.

80. *LJ*, 14:117.

81. Grey, 9:53-65; Rawl D1079, fols 11b-12a; Eveline Cruickshanks, John Ferris, David Hayton, 'The House of Commons vote on the transfer of the Crown, 5 February 1689,' *Bulletin of the Institute of Historical Research*' 52 (1979):35-47.

82. HLROMM 5 Feb. 1688/9; Clarendon, 2:259.

83. *CJ*, 10:20; *LJ*, 14:118; HLROMM 6 Feb. 1688/9.

84. The debate during the conference is reprinted below with Rochester's speech on p.29 and Treby's on p.49; Bodleian Library Rawl D1232, fol 7, Sawyer to Dr. Cook 19 Feb. 1688/9. The use of *abdication* is considered by Thomas P. Slaughter, "Abdicate' and 'Contract' in the Glorious Revolution,' *Historical Journal* 24(1981):323-37; John Miller, 'The Glorious Revolution: 'contract' and 'abdication' reconsidered,' *Hist Jnl* 25(1982):541-55; Slaughter, "Abdicate' and 'contract' restored,' *Hist Jnl* 28(1985):399-403.

85. Fragments of the speeches are recorded in HLROMM 6 Feb. 1688/9; Rawl D1079, fol 12b.

86. Rawl D1079 fol 12b; Ballard 45, fol 27; Morrice:459-60; HLROMM 6 Feb. 1688/9; G. Burnet, *History of his own time*, 3:377; John Dalrymple, *Memoirs of Great Britain and Ireland*, 2nd ed. (London, 1773):340; Henry Horwitz, *Revolution politicks*:81-2; Rawl D1079, fol 13b (Lords agreed with *abdicated* by 3 votes), fol 12b (majority for vacant was 20 votes).

87. Ballard 45, fol 27; Morrice:460-61.

88. G. Burnet, *History of his own time*, 3:371-74; L.Echard, *History of the Revolution*:257-8; H. Horwitz, *Revolution politicks*:79.

89. N. Pinney-J. Pinney 6 Feb. 1689, *Letters of John Pinney 1679-1699*, ed. by Geoffrey F. Nuttall, (London, 1939):64-5.

90. *Orange Gazette* no. 10 (5/8 Feb. 1688/9); Morrice: 462; Rawl D1079, fol 12b.

91. *LJ*, 14:119-20; HLROMM 7 Feb. 1688/9.

92. Grey, 9:70-5; *CJ*, 10:20-22; Morrice:461.

93. Clarendon, 2:262.

94. Grey, 9:75-81; *CJ*, 10:22-24.

95. *LJ*, 14:121.

96. HLRO Willcocks Papers Sect. VI Letter 21, Yester-Tweeddale 11 Feb. 1689; Morrice: 463-5, printed in part by H. Horwitz, 'Parliament and the Glorious Revolution,' *Bulletin of the Institute of Historical Research* 47(1974):48-9; Robert J. Frankle, 'The formulation of the Declaration of Rights,' *Historical Journal* 17(1974):265-79.

97. *LJ*, 14:122; HLROMM 9 Feb. 1688/9; Lois G. Schwoerer, *The Declaration of Rights, 1689*, (Baltimore, 1981):243-47.

98. *CJ*, 10:24.

99. *LJ*, 14:123; HLROMM 11 Feb. 1688/9; *CJ*, 10:24-26; Grey,9:81-3.

100. *LJ*, 14:124-27; HLROMM 12 Feb. 1688/9; *CJ*, 10:26-28.

101. *CJ*, 10:29-30 for an account of the ceremony which has been studied by Lois G. Schwoerer, 'The Glorious Revolution as spectacle: a new perspective,' In *England's rise to greatness 1660-1763*, ed. by Stephen B. Baxter, (Berkeley, 1983):109-49. See also Morrice:467. The text of the declaration is from *CJ*, 10:28-29.

102. *CJ*, 10:30.

103. *LJ*, 14:127-28; *CJ*, 10:30; Rawl D1079, fol 19b; *London Intelligencer* no. 10(12/ 16 Feb. 1688/9); *CSPD William and Mary, 13 Feb. 1689 – April 1690*:2

104. *LJ*, 14:128-29; *CJ*, 10:31; Grey, 9:84-106; Morrice:470, 475, 477; John Reresby, *Memoirs and travels of Sir John Reresby*, (London, 1904): 340-41; *CSPD William and Mary, 13 Feb. 1689 – April 1690*:1; Lois G. Schwoerer, 'The transformation of the 1689 Convention into a Parliament,' *Parliamentary History* 3(1984):57-76.

105. Lois G. Schwoerer, *The Declaration of Rights, 1689*:267-80 for a detailed study of the passage of the Bill of Rights; Clayton Roberts, 'The constitutional significance of the financial settlement of 1690,' *Historical Journal* 20(1977):57-76; Jennifer Carter, 'The Revolution and the constitution,' In *Britain after the Glorious Revolution*, ed. by Geoffrey Holmes (London, 1969).

106. Balcarres:18-19; P. W. J. Riley, *King William and the Scottish politicans*, (Edinburgh, 1979):11.

107. HLRO Willcocks Papers Sect VI Letter 19, Yester-Tweeddale 8 Jan. 1689; *Procs*, 2:293-7 reprints a contemporary account of the meeting including Arran's speech; Stowe 370, fols 15, 20, 25 for a record of Hamilton's presence at the meeting of the Lords; G. W. Iredell, *The law, custom and practice of the Parliament of Scotland with particular reference to the period 1660-1707* (London Ph.D, 1966):95-103 for conventions.

108. Balcarres: 21; HLRO Willcocks Papers Sect. VI Letter 20, Yester-Tweeddale 7 Feb. 1689.

109. Balcarres:25; *APS*, 9:5; Robert S. Rait, *The Parliament of Scotland*, (Glasgow, 1924):95.

110. *APS*, 9:5-6; Procs, 1:1; P. W. J. Riley, *King William*:12.

111. *APS*, 9:6; Balcarres:23-4; Morrice:509.

112. *APS*, 9:8-10; Procs, 1:5.

113. *Procs*, 1:7; Balcarres: 28-30.

114. *APS*, 9:12-13; *Procs*, 1:15.

115. *Procs*, 1:20.

116. *APS*, 9:22; *Procs*, 1:18-19.

117. *APS*, 9:23.

118. *APS*, 9:33-34; *Procs*, 1:21-25; Balcarres:35-36.

119. *APS*, 9:37-41; *Procs*, 1:30-36; Balcarres:36.

120. *APS*, 9:43-45, 48, 60; *Procs*, 1:37-40, 50.

121. *Procs*, 1:52.

122. *APS*, 9:62-63; *Procs*, 1:52-3, 57; Morrice:548.

123. The description of the ceremony is from *Procs*, 1:85-89; the texts of the documents are from *APS*, 9:38-40 (declaration); 45 (grievances); 48 (coronation oath); 60-61 (letter).

124. Melville's remark is quoted by James Halliday, 'The Club and the Revolution in Scotland 1689-90,' *Scottish Historical Review* 45(1966):144; the voting figures are in P. W. J. Riley, *King William*:9.

125. *APS*, 9:95, 98; it is not clear which sceptre was used because the Honours of Scotland were unavailable until Gordon surrendered Edinburgh Castle on 14 June, G. W. Iredell, *The law... of the Parliament of Scotland*:102-03; William and Scotland are described by James Halliday, 'The Club...' and P. W. J. Riley, *King William*; for the abolition of the Articles, see Iredell:179-82.

126. Morrice:437; *CJ*, 10:12.

127. Clarendon, 2:252-62 for the published version; Alan Simpson, 'Notes of a noble lord, 22 January to 12 February 1688/9,' *English Historical Review* 52(1937):87-98; Laurence Echard, *The history of the Revolution* contains material from this text and also prints tables from Pepys MS 2179. There is a copy of the text in BL Add MS 31956 fols 7-16.

128. Henry Horwitz, 'Parliament and the Glorious Revolution,' *Bulletin of the Institute of Historical Research* 47(1974):50-2 for the text.

129. Lois G. Schwoerer, 'A Jornal of the Convention at Westminster began the 22 of January 1688/9,' *Bulletin of the Institute of Historical Research* 49(1976):244 for the correct order of speakers on 28 January.

130. Schwoerer, 'A Jornall': 242-63; the text is 248-63.

131. Lois G. Schwoerer, 'Press and Parliament in the Revolution of 1689,' *Historical Journal* 20(1977):551 for the quotation relating to Mr. Blaney.

Notes of a Noble Lord

PEPYS LIBRARY MS. 2179, pp. 41–60.

Notes of a Noble Lord accompanying
the foregoing Journals

January 22d 1688/9

No prayers today[1].

After ye Prince of Oranges letter was read, it was moved that assistants might be appointed, by whome their Lordships might be advised in matter of law, as there should be occasion. The Masters of the Chancery were upon the wool-sacks, but no Judges appear'd. The Lords proceeded severally to name whom they thought proper to be assistants. Several of ye Judges were named, but 'twas objected, that most of them had given their opinions for ye dispensing power; that some of them had pleaded against my Lord Russell; that others had a hand in setting ye fine upon ye Earle of Devonshire. Either of which acts was at this time lookt-upon as sufficient cause to render a man uncapable of any employment. At last it was ordred that ye late Lord Ch. Baron Montague, Sir Robt Atkyns, Sir Wm. Dolben, Sir Creswell Levinz, Sir John Holt, Sir Edward Neville, Mr. Wm. Whitlock, Mr. George Bradbury, and Mr. Wm. Petyt do attend this House as assistants till there are Judges. Lord Nottingham very much opposed Mr. Bradbury's being one, saying he was not worthy to carry a bagg after some that were named. The truth is, he has but an ordinary character among those of his profession; but by ye interposition of the Earl of Dorset, who first named him, he was allowed of.

Wednesday January 23th 1688/9

Prayers were said by ye Bishop of Bristoll [*marginal note*: Sir Jonathan Trelawny]; he omitted the prayer for the King.

Thursday January 24th 1688/9

Prayers were said to-day by ye Bishop of Bristoll; he omitted the prayer for the King[2].

Fryday January 25th 1688/9

Prayers were read in the House by ye Bishop of Oxford [*marginal note*: Dr. White]: he read the prayer for ye King. At which my Lord Halifax was very uneasy, and said to some Lords that stood by him, this must not be: but he took no publick notice of it.

After the House was called over, the Earl of Berkley took notice, that there were severall peers there who had never been introduced, and particularly named my Lord Griffin, who stood up in his place, and said, hee was created by ye King a few days before he went away; that he had his writt of summons to Parliament; and his patent was at ye door ready to be produced. Upon this grew a debate; some Lords averring that no Peer could sitt till hee was introduced, others alledging, that the introducing contributed nothing to the right of peerage, instancing that those Peers who had been created by ye late King Charles ye 2d in ye time of his exile, came into ye House of Lords upon His Majesty's Restoration, without being introduced. It was further said; this was no Parliament, and that they could not be introduced but in Parliament. But notwithstanding all that was said, severall Lords still called to Lord Griffin, Withdraw: and none were more violent than Lord Lovelace and Lord Delamere. But at last it was agreed, that those Lords who had not been introduced formerly, should be now introduced, as near the usual form as could be. And then immediately the Lords Lovelace and Delamere notwithstanding ye fury just before, introduced ye Lord Griffin.

Certainly it must seem strange when men will give themselves leave to consider, that a Peer should be introduced in ye House of Peers, when that King's authority who created ye said Peer was pretended to be sett aside; and when the Lords did not pretend to be a Parliament, nor to meet by the King's authority[3].

This being over, it was moved to proceed upon ye consideration of the state of ye nation; and that tomorrow might be appointed for that purpose.

This motion was seconded by my Lord Nottingham and others but it was opposed by many Lords, particularly by ye Earl of Devonshire who said, ye House of Commons had appointed to goe upon that businesse on Monday next; and therefore he moved, the Lords would not enter upon it till Tuesday; by which time we should be able to gather some lights from below, that might be of use to us.

This was seconded by ye Marquess of Winchester and Marquess of Hallifax and others but opposed with great warmth by ye Lords Nottingham, Chesterfield, Clarendon, Rochester, Abingdon and others; with great reflection upon ye Lord Devonshire's motion, as if the Lords were only to take aim from ye gentlemen below. But it was carried, that Tuesday should be appointed to consider of the state of the nation and then ye House adjourned till Monday.

Monday January 28th 1688/9

The Bishop of St. David's [*marginal note*: Dr Watson] was going to read prayers. My Lord Halifax whisper'd him to omitt ye prayer for the King, as improper at this time; but ye Bishop told him plainly, he would not omitt it. Whereupon my Lord Halifax acquainted the House, and moved that prayers might be suspended till further order: which was accordingly ordered[4].

Tuesday January 29th 1688/9

After ye message by Mr. Hampden the House was putt into a committee to consider of the state of the nation, according to ye order of Friday last. The Earl of Danby was in ye chair.

The first matter proposed was, That ye government should be carried on by a regency, and under ye stile of King James ye 2d: which after a long debate was carried in ye negative by 2 votes[5].

The Committee was interrupted in ye aforesaid debate, by another message from ye House of Commons; which ye House agreed to, as appears by the Journal; and then ye House went again into a committee.

After ye debate concerning ye regency was ended, and reported, and agreed to by the House; in regard it was late (for it was eight of ye clock at night) it was moved that ye committee might sitt againe tomorrow in ye afternoon: which was opposed by several Lords, and by many of ye Bishops, upon account of ye day's being appointed to be observed, by act of Parliament. But nothing could prevail; and so ye House was adjourned till tomorrow afternoon.

Wednesday January 30th 1688/9

Afternoon
There was no sermon in ye Abbey-Church for the House of Peers, because ye Lords had appointed none, perhaps through forgetfulness[6].

The House adjourned tomorrow 3 in ye afternoon because it was ye Thanksgiving Day.

Thursday January 31st 1688/9

The Bishop of St Asaph was appointed to preach at ye Abbey before ye Lords, but being indisposed with a cold, Mr. Gee preached for him, who gave no satisfaction[7].

The House was in a committee upon ye last clause in ye vote sent from ye House of Commons, And that ye throne is thereby vacant – vide page[8]

It took up a very long debate, till near 11 at night and then adjourned till 10 tomorrow morning.

In this debate, several peevish and malicious things were spoken of ye King. All of which the collector of these notes will not undertake to remember; but some particulars are not to be forgot.

The Lord Mountague spoke to this effect, I am so perfectly satisfied of the Throne's being vacant, that I have a dispensation within myselfe, without ye help of one from My Ld. Jefferys, or Sir Edward Herbert, and therefore I do declare (said he) That from this day I look upon my selfe to be absolved from all allegiance to King James.

What Lord Delamere said ought likewise to be remembered which was to this effect, I have long thought my selfe absolved from my allegiance to King James; I am satisfied I owe him none, and I resolve never to pay him any; And if King James comes againe, I will fight against him, and will die single with my sword in my hand rather than pay him any obedience.

Fryday February 1st 1688/9

The Lords sent down their amendments to ye vote of ye House of Commons of ye 28th of January last, upon which they sat so late yesterday. But ye Commons were up before ye messengers came; and ye Lords adjourned till tomorrow morning.

Saturday February 2d 1688/9

My Lord Halifax acquainted ye House, that just then a letter was put into his hands by ye Black Rod, directed to him, to be communicated to ye Lords Spirituall and Temporall: That he was told it came from ye Lord Preston, and he knew that ye superscription was of my Lord Preston's hand-writing. He asked ye pleasure of ye House, whither it should be read. Some cried, Read it, Read it; others cried No, No. Then ye Black Rod was asked, who gave him ye letter. He answer'd, Mr. Warr my Lord Preston's secretary, who was at ye door. Mr. Warr was then call'd in and asked, whence that letter came? He answer'd my Lord Preston gave it to him, and bid him take care to deliver it safe to my Lord Marquess of Halifax. That he had been at his Lordship's house, but my Lord was come from home. That he then came down to Westminster, and desired ye Usher of the Black Rod, to deliver it to his Lordship: and this was all he could say.

Mr. Warr was then directed to let my Lord Preston know, that this House required him to attend them presently. Within halfe an hour my Lord Preston came; he was called in, and asked what letter that was which he had sent to ye House? He answered, that yesterday at 3 of ye clock in the morning, a Scotch gentleman, one Mr Hayes, came to him, when he was in bed, and gave him a packet from ye King. When he open'd it, he found 'twas only a cover to himselfe, and 2 letters in it, one to their Lordships, and ye other to ye House of Commons; and this was all he knew. My Lord Preston was then asked where Mr. Hayes was? He said, truly, he could not tell where he was at present, but would undertake, hee should wait upon their Lordships on Monday, if they pleased. And accordingly it was ordered he should then attend: and so my Lord Preston withdrew.

The Lord Viscount Nieuport mov'd, that the House would forbidd ye observing ye 6th of this month, which was ye day King James came to ye Crown; saying it would be very odd to have solemn prayers now at Church for King James's coming to ye Crown. And accordingly it was ordred, that the 6th of Febry ye day of King James's coming to ye Crown, should be no more observed.

Just as ye House was rising, my Lord Lovelace offer'd a petition which ye Clerk took. It was moved by a certain Lord[9] [*marginal note*: Lord Clarendon], That, according to ye Standing Order, he would open it, and acquaint ye House with ye contents of it and by whome it was signed. This was seconded by ye Lord Ferrers. Upon which my Lord Lovelace withdrew ye petition, saying that it was not signed, but there should be hands enough to it.

Some Lords who had lookt upon this petition, found it came from ye rabble, of whom there were great numbers come this morning to Westminster: to which they were encouraged (as some of them said) by Lord Lovelace. William Killegrew was in the Head of them.

Monday February 4th 1688/9

The House was informed, that Mr Hayes was at the door: who being called in was asked where he had the letter he brought to my Lord Preston out of France? He answer'd, when he left Paris (which was on this day was a se'nnight) ye King told him, ye night before, when he went to receive His Majesty's commands, that he had a packet for my Lord Preston, and bidd him call to my Lord Melfort for it. Which he did; and that was all he could say. He was then askt, where my Lord Melfort gave him ye packet for my Lord Preston? He answer'd, at St Germains in France: and then was ordred to withdraw.

Some Lords moved ye letter might be read: but others opposed it, making reflections upon its coming from Lord Melfort; as if coming from his hands, made ye letter unfitt to be read. And in truth, there seem'd a great coldness even in those who had appear'd most zealous in ye King's cause, after my Lord Melfort was named.

Among other angry reflections that were made, ye Lord Viscount

Nieuport (who had been as peevish as any body) said, I hope this House will not read every private man's letter, and I look on this as a letter from a private person; for he from whome it came is no more King here. And so there was no more said of ye letter.

It will seem strange hereafter, that ye House of Peers (where there were so many who had appeared zealous for ye King) should refuse to read a letter from him, because it was given to ye messenger by my Lord Melfort. But such was ye animosity of some, even against ye King himselfe, and ye grief that others had, to find that his Majesty still made use of my Lord Melfort, and the matter fell as is here related.

Tuesday February 5th 1688/9

After ye conference, ye Lords satt till between 3 & 4 in the afternoon, in expectation of hearing from ye Commons: the House was not so much as adjourn'd during pleasure, but the Speaker continued upon ye Woolsack, though there was not ye least intimacion from ye Commons, that they desired ye Lords to sitt.

My Lord Halifax was often called upon, and urged by severall Lords to adjourn. But so unfair he was in ye chair, that he would do nothing but what he pleased. At last, after much importunity & clamour, he was in a manner forced to say, that if wee did not hear from ye House of Commons within half an hour, he thought it would be best to adjourn. So much hast was his Lordship in, and so much zeal did he and others show to unsettle ye old and sett up a new government; that they thought every hour's delay a ruin to ye undertaking which some of them had made. At length not hearing from ye House of Commons, about $\frac{1}{4}$ of an hour before 4, the House adjourned till 9 tomorrow-morning.

Wednesday February 6th 1688/9[10]

After ye free conference, the Lords entred into debate, whether to agree with ye Commons or not. All was said by ye Lords on one side that could bee thought of against agreeing with ye Commons, and to support ye succession, this being an hereditary monarchy. But all that was said was violently opposed by ye other party, most eminently by my Lord Halifax, who thought he answer'd all ye weighty reasons of ye other Lords with the pretence of necessity: saying that ye Crown was only made elective pro hâc vice, and then reverted into its own hereditary channel againe.

This argument of necessity (which will always be esteem'd a weak one by sober men) and all his others were substantially answer'd by ye Earl of Nottingham and severall other Lords. But ye stream was grown so strong since yesterday; and ye confusion, or rather consternation, was so great, that nothing could be heard, and it being late the general cry was, the question, the question.

At length, after a very long debate, the question was putt, whether to agree with ye House of Commons in ye word abdicated, instead of ye word deserted, and to the words that follow, and that the Throne is thereby vacant.

It was resolved in ye affirmative.

The contents for agreeing withe the Commons were 62, the not-contents were 47.

It may seem strange that this question should be thus carried, considering that in ye former debates, the majority had been ye other way, particularly on ye 31st of the last month, and on ye 4th instant. But under one pretence or other, several Lords, who had hitherto voted for ye King, being unwilling to change ye government, were not in ye House at puting ye Question. The Earl of Chesterfield, tho at ye conference, went away before ye question; as likewise did ye Bishop of Bristoll[11], Lord Ferrers, and Lord Godolphin, the latter telling some of his friends, that he was to attend ye Prince of Orange at ye Treasury; an undeniable evidence certainly, that he had rather ingratiate himselfe with a new master, than support his old one, to whome he owed his present station in ye world. The Earl of Burlington was not in the House today, being ill with ye gout; he had always voted for ye King, and had no mind to change. The Lords Weymouth and Hatton did not appear today. The Earl of Yarmouth, ye Lords Coventry and Crew, who had always voted for ye King, went away before the question. All imaginable pains were taken, to bring all ye other Lords who could be found out to ye House. The Earl of Lincoln, who had never appear'd this meeting, came today, and took an occasion to declare that he came to vote as ye Earl of Shrewsbury and ye Lord Mordaunt should direct him[12]. Such a declaration at another time, and from another man, would have been taken notice of; but now all irregularitys were pass'd by unregarded. The Bishop of Durham, who hitherto had been only twice present at these debates, came today to give his vote against ye King, who had raised him.

The Throne being now declared vacant, ye next business was to fill it. It was proposed, that ye Prince and Princesse of Orange might be declared King and Queen. Which was opposed, and strongly contested and took up a great debate, but at length that question was putt, and it was carried in ye affirmative.

Notwithstanding this falling off of some, and ye absence of others, I verily believe there were above 30 negatives. And leave was askt and granted, for all who would, to enter their dissents as appears by the Journal[13]. It being near 7 at night the House adjourned till 10 of ye clock tomorrow morning.

The collector of these notes, happening to sit by a noble earle[14] (a man of great honour and worth) said to him; How comes it to pass, my Lord, that we have differ'd in this last vote since wee have gone together in every point throughout these debates. The Earl replyed, I have not changed my mind, and I look upon this day's work, to be ye ruin of ye Monarchy of England, for we have made ye Crown elective, and I know not where it will end. But there is an absolute necessity of having a government, and I doe not see a prospect of any other than this. We must not leave ourselves to ye rabble. This notion prevailed with several to acquiesce; fearing they should be otherwise ruined; as they pretended[15].

Thursday February 7th 1688/9

In the morning several of the Lords mett before ye sitting of ye House, to enter their dissents; which could not be done yesterday, the Journal-Book not being made up; but must (by ye usage of Parliament) be entred before the rising of ye House ye next sitting, as part of ye proceedings of ye preceding day.

The Earl of Nottingham had prepared reasons to justify our dissenting from ye vote of ye 28th of January past: which some of ye Lords approved very well; others would have some things altered; and some would have no reasons. So it was thought most advisable among ourselves to enter our dissents without giving reason; hoping thereby to gaine ye more of our companions to subscribe with us. But no more would sign than ye 38 mentioned in ye Journal: some Lords making one excuse or other, and some not coming to ye House today; and afterwards they cannot subscribe. These reasons which were prepared by my Lord Nottingham, though not entred in ye Journal, do hereunder follow, which this collector copied, from Lord Nottingham's paper in his own handwriting.

The collector of these notes then moved several Lords to enter their dissents to ye other vote which passed yesterday, for ye declaring ye Prince and Princess of Orange King and Queen. But none would do it as appears by the Journal.

The votes of yesterday being sent to ye Commons ye Lords adjourned till 4 in the afternoon; when they mett, but did nothing, as appears by ye Journal. At 7 at night not hearing from the Commons, ye Lords adjourned till tomorrow morning[16].

Reasons prepared by ye Earl of Nottingham:

1st – Because tho ye King can resign his Crown by consent of Parliament, yet neither ye Parliament nor ye whole people of England have authority to depose him without his own consent; the King being Supream, and therefore there can be no superior to him.

2ndly – Or if ye Parliament could depose him, yet ye Monarchy of England is hereditary by ye fundamental constitution of this government, and has been often declared by Parliament to be so.

3dly – No act of ye King alone can abrogate the right of his heirs without Act of Parliament; and therefore the Throne cannot be now vacant.

4thly – The consequence of the vote is, that ye Monarchy is elective; which is contrary to ye original constitution of ye government, and destructive of it, and ye peace and welfare of the nation[17].

Saturday February 9th 1688/9

When leave was askt for any Lords to enter their dissents to ye alterations made by the Commons to ye vote for declaring ye Prince and Princess of Orange King and Queen: severall Lords seem'd resolved to shew their dislike to every vote that tended to ye disposing of ye Crown. But I did not much believe they would be so resolute, as to enter their dissents against ye alterations: since every one had refused to do it against ye vote itself, when it passed on ye 6th of this month[18].

Monday February 11th 1688/9

Before ye sitting of ye House, ye collector of these notes moved several Lords to enter their dissents to ye vote which passed on Saturday concerning ye alterations to ye vote for declaring the Prince and Princess of Orange King and Queen. But nobody would do it; Every one saying it would signify nothing, and was to no purpose. So soon were men's minds changed, and their zeal cool'd, for reasons best known to themselves.

The collector then proposed to those Lords, who had in all these votes been of the same mind, that they would all agree, by consent to leave ye House.

But ye Earl of Pembroke said, by no means; it would be of ill consequence; the Government must be supported, or else we should be all ruined.

My Lord Nottingham said, we must support ye Government as well as we can, and ye Lords can never answer it, if they leave ye House.

Another noble Lord said, He would not run ye risk of losing his estate, and therefore would continue coming to the House, that he might be in a capacity to serve his country. And it is most certain, that ye apprehension of great severitys from ye new Government, upon those who should quitt ye House, prevail'd upon many to continue going thither, tho they did not approve of any of ye proceedings.

The Earl of Clarendon said, he could not take ye oaths which were now settled; and therefore when they came in force he must leave the House.

Many were of opinion, that if ye 55 Lords, who had voted against ye Throne being vacant on ye 31st of January last; and ye 150 of ye House of Commons who had been of ye same mind in that vote, had immediately left their respective Houses, it would have discomposed our undertakers, and have putt ye Prince of Orange upon new councels. But there was a fate upon us[19].

Tuesday February 12th 1688/9

In ye morning came ye news, that the Princess of Orange was come into ye river. Whereupon ye collector of these notes went immediately out of town, and went no more to ye House of Lords: for when he came back, ye oaths were in force.

Notes

The following footnotes contain the additional material from the published text of Clarendon's diary (see above, p. 68)

1. 'Lord Marquis of Halifax was appointed Speaker *pro tempore*'. (p. 252)

2. 'The standing committees were named, &c. *Vide the Journal*. Lord Halifax desired Mr. Brown to search, and report to-morrow, whether Lord Manchester had a mace when he was speaker *pro tempore*. Lord Nottingham was not in the House to-day, but was gone a-hunting'. (p. 253)

3. 'I cannot imagine, what made the turn about my Lord Griffin, except it was that the violent party had no minde to lose my Lord Carteret; who had never been introduced; and of whom, I believe, they were sure: the Duke of Northumberland likewise had not been introduced before'. (p. 253-4)

4. 'My Lord Newport informed the House, that my Lord Castlemain was in Shropshire; and so setting forth how dangerous a man he was, that he had been ambassador at Rome, &c. he moved he might be brought up in custody; which was ordered'. (p. 255)

5. The diary includes a list of the 49 lords who voted for a regency. (p. 256)

6. 'In the afternoon I went to the House of Lords. The House was in Committee upon the vote from the House of Commons, and agreed to put in the word

'deserted' instead of the word 'abdicated'. (p. 257)

7. 'I was not at church'. (p. 257)

8. 'and after much debate, they came to this question, that instead of 'the throne is thereby vacant' should be inserted 'the Prince and Princess of Orange should be declared King and Queen'. Then the previous question being put, whether this question shall be now put? it was resolved in the negative: contents 47; not contents 52. Then the question was put, whether to agree with the House of Commons in these words of the vote 'that the throne is thereby vacant'. Resolved in the negative; contents 41; not contents 55. Thirty-five of the contents entered their dissents'. (p. 257)

9. Identified in the diary as Lord Clarendon (p. 258)

10. 'The Commons desired a free conference with the Lords upon the subject matter of the last conference: which was presently agreed to. I think, all impartial men who were present, will own, that the Lords had by far the better of the argument, both upon the point of reason, and according as the law now stands'. (p. 260)

11. Bishop of Oxford in the diary (p. 261)

12. 'The Earl of Carlisle was brought upon his crutches: the Lord Lexinton, who came into England but three days ago'. (p. 261)

13. 'Lord Nottingham moved that new oaths might be made instead of the old ones of allegiance and supremacy; which, he believed, few would take to a new King. Upon which a committee was named and ordered to withdraw immediately; who quickly brought in two new oaths; which, with the vote, were ordered to be sent to the House of Commons for their concurrence'. (p. 261)

14. 'Earl of Thanet' (p. 261)

15. 'The Earls of Huntingdon and Mulgrave had all along voted against the King. The Bishop of Ely went to supper with me; we had not eaten all day. I think this was the most dismal day I ever saw in my life. God help us: we are certainly a miserable, undone people'. (p. 262)

16. 'The House of Commons were busy in preparing new articles of Government to be laid before the new King, that he might know upon what terms he was to have the crown'. (p. 262)

17. 'Feb. 8. Friday. I went to the House of Lords: but there was very little to do; and besides I had but little heart to take notice of any thing'. (p. 262)

18. 'I went again to Westminster, but concerned myself in nothing. This day, as well as yesterday, was spent in the two Houses in adjusting the new Instrument of Government: the contents whereof is in the Journal. The Lords sate till near five o'clock'. (p. 262)

19. 'The new frame of Government went on smoothly, and was almost perfected; so that I resolved to go no more to the House of Lords as things now stood'. (p. 262)

Danby's notes of the debates in the Lords on 29 January

50   PARLIAMENT AND THE GLORIOUS REVOLUTION

APPENDIX

British Library (formerly British Museum), Egerton MS. 3345, bundle 3.[1]

Ld Clar:	By what act has ye k: abdicated ?
	If abdicated [is] that was—then [death] ? K never dies, can do no wrong
	World abroad nor maior part[2] will be pleased
	The Oath of Allegiance is to bind being taken
	The statute of 12th C: 2^d
	Statute of 13th C: 2^d
Ld Delamer	K: went because hee dared not to stay ye Justice of ye nation
B^p Ely	The Commons vote is like the Accumulative Treason there being no par
	ticular therein amounting to a forfeiture & therfore not altogether
	If k^g take a monastick vow is a forfeiture
	If k^g have abdicated that is nò vacancy
	K^g is K^g before coronation [instance] Sr Walter Rawleighs case
	Ja 48 the Com^s having voted to proceed ag^t ye k^g sent to y^e
	Lds who threw it out wth indignation & voted[3]
	The Com^s voted
Ld Montagu	to agree wth ye vote because none can be safe but
	those who contributed towards our slavery
Ld Abingdon	to make Ld Montagu name who has spoke ag^t the
	Protestant Religion
Ld Clar:	To defend ye B^{ps} ag^t the calumny of having bin
	the Persecutors of Protestants ag^t Ld Montagu & Ld Oxford
	then he spoke to ye Allegiance & the Recognition of K^g
	James his right
	The same scandall as when ye K^{gs} Judges were arraignd
	Read a p^t of Princes declaration
	one k^g murdered another abdicated in our time
Ld Mordant	To have the dangers considered in wch we were 6 months ago
Ld Nottingham	supposing k^g to have done all that is suggested the
	conclusion not right that the k^g has forfeited
	That k^g cannot forfeit
	nor can we take the forfeiture
	This method tends to absolution of ye Governm^t viz of
	the Constitution of L^{ds} & Comons
	Cannot iudge of the k^g 22. Ed. 3 cannot be adiudged
	That k^g can dissolve Parlm^t & yett Parlm^t may iudge
	him makes Judges how can they iudge him
	The Pretence of ye late times was but ye k^g being coordinate

[1] I am grateful to the Trustees of the British Library Board for permission to print these notes in Danby's hand. They are written on both sides of two folios, and I have rearranged the four sides to make sense of the proceedings. Since the notes are very rough and the writing at times difficult, abbreviations have not been extended. Doubtful readings are enclosed in square brackets.

[2] 'maior part' at home ?

[3] '& voted' struck through.

PARLIAMENT AND THE GLORIOUS REVOLUTION   51

some things a Parlm^t cannot do viz cannot make the
k^g absolute can^1 abrogate themselves or ye house of Comons
so neither can they lay aside ye k^g
To know whither k^g can forfeit 1. H. 6 reason why
they reiected Guardian to P^c of Wales
whatever forfiteable is alienable
K^{gs} Crowne is his inheritance qu^{re} how forfitable
By same power may unmake as well as make & is [Trustee]
to ye L^{ds} will
Take care of not subverting y^r owne Constitution
To whom the forfeiture ?
Force & not volontary withdrawing
not abdicated Scotland & the danger if they dissent and
to how great a degree
If forfeit for his heires the whole Constitution is dissolved &
Every man has Equall right & Equall power

Ld Delamer	K^g a Trustee & may therefore be called to an account
Ld Hallyfax	The impossibility of subsisting if nothing can be done without a king To shew either that there is no danger or to shew a Remedy
Ld Wharton	what have we done all this while by putting the administration &c: to disputte [ ]^2
Ld Rochester	If Throne vacant then the Crowne Elective A meanes to secure the Governm^t without going to this extreamity wch the vote impels That K^g cannot governe moves for a Regent That he cannot sweare to a new k^g
Ld Falconbrige	Impracticability of this k^{gs} Governm^t but not ready for the question of the vote till more debate whither any abdication Dereliction wth ye Seale manifest The vote not well worded to [amend] that
Ld Hallifax	Debate of the Regency the best method King more then a name, the word comprehendes a Government Many Expectations of whi^3 Kings returne to Governm^t whilst under a Regent The Princes figure very great already This of Regent lookes more like change of ye Constit[ution] then the other
Ld Rochester	Regency a great addition to ye Princes figure if dureing the k^{gs} life
Ld Pembrok	Question whither k^g can lay himselfe aside whither he has derelicted or throwne away the Governm^t Comparison to goods throwne overboard Right to plead if appeare in a yeare & a day Cannot comply wth the Oath of right & Lawfull

^{1} 'can' not 'abrogate'? ^{2} Indecipherable word.
^{3} 'whi' struck through.

52   PARLIAMENT AND THE GLORIOUS REVOLUTION

Ld Nottingham   That the best Remedy wch comes nearest to the
formes of our law
Regent is administration of all the legall powers w^ch
the k: [can] legally had
K has forfeited his Power but consider where to place itt
wth safety
Avoides P^c Wales, Oath of Allegiance, will unite us
K^g will loose the revenue
inconveniencies in making a king viz: H: 7: troubled
by denying wifes right
Power of right appears by the attempts to restore R: 2^d &C
moves for a Regency

Ld Hallifax   What figure to ye Prince if but during K^gs life
Regent is a Judgm^t upon a king
did not scruple concealem^t of Treason
If can make a k^g may sweare him right & Lawfull so as not
to be scrupled by such

Ld Nottingham   How safe wth a new king: what would an act of
Parliam^t do an act by K: de facto not Obligatory
Whither not for our Interest that he be but Regent
The States will be more Jealous of a King then a Regent
All Judgm^t the k^gs, but must be given by Officers all processes
the k^gs & yett to be done by others
All Power in the k^g in minority & yett cannot officiate
If captivated by his Enemies may use the k^gs name

Ld Delamer
Ld Lovelace
Ld Clarendon   more danger by a Crowne then a Regent ought to Examine
matter of P^c of Wales before proceed further

Ld Nottingham
Sr R^bt Atkins   Regent ye same as Guardian & Protector & is a Subiect &
liable to triall

Grey's debates

DEBATES

IN THE

Houſe of Commons,

From the Year 1667 *to the Year* 1694.

[THE Prince of *Orange* having publiſhed, at the *Hague*, *October* 24, 1688, a Declaration of the Reaſons inducing him to appear in Arms in the Kingdom of *England*, for preſerving of the Proteſtant Religion, and for reſtoring the Laws and Liberties of *England, Scotland,* and *Ireland*, (*which ſee in the Journal*) his Highneſs landed with his Forces at *Torbay*, on *November* the 5th following; and making from thence directly towards the City of *London*, he arrived there on *Tueſday, December* 17; and, on the 23d of the ſame month, he iſſued forth an Order, deſiring all ſuch perſons as had ſerved in any of the Parliaments of King *Charles* II. to meet him at St *James's* on *Wedneſday, December* 26; and that the Lord Mayor, Aldermen, and fiſty of the Common-Council of the City of *London*, would attend there likewiſe. According to which Order, many of the perſons above-mentioned met at St *James's*, at the time prefixed; when his Highneſs, in a ſhort Speech, told them, " that he deſired them to meet him there, to adviſe the beſt manner how to purſue the ends of his Declaration, in calling a free Parliament, for the preſervation of the Proteſtant Religion, &c." His Highneſs being departed, the Members then preſent adjourned to the Commons Houſe at *Weſtminſter*, where the Right Hon. *Henry Powle*, Eſq; was appointed to take the Chair. The Aſſembly then taking into conſideration what had been propoſed to them by the Prince of *Orange*, after ſome Debate, came to ſeveral Reſolutions; one of which was, " to return Thanks to his Highneſs, for coming into this Kingdom, expoſing his perſon, and adventuring ſo great hazards for the preſervation of our Religion, Laws, and Liberties." Another was " to deſire him to take upon him the Adminiſtration of public Affairs, both Civil and Military, and the diſpoſal of the public Revenue;" and a third was, " to deſire him to cauſe Letters to be written, ſubſcribed by himſelf, to the Lords Spiritual and

VOL. IX.   B   Temporal,

2   *Debates in Parliament in* 1688.

Temporal, and to the several Counties, Boroughs, &c. for calling a Convention to meet on the two and twentieth of *January* next." And an Address was ordered to be drawn up accordingly. The Association entered into by several Lords and Gentlemen at *Exeter, December* 19, was afterwards brought in, and signed by all the Members present.

Wednesday, December 26. *In the Afternoon.*

The Address above-mentioned was brought in by Mr *Hampden*, and agreed to by the Assembly, *(see it in the Journal,)* and on

Thursday, December 27.

It was presented by the Chairman to the Prince of *Orange*; for which his Highness returned them his hearty Thanks, but deferred his Answer till the next day,

Friday, December 28.

When he promised them " to endeavour to secure the Peace of the Nation, till the meeting of the Convention, for the Election whereof he would forthwith issue out Letters, &c." Such Letters were accordingly issued; and on

Tuesday, January 22, 1688-9,

The Convention met at *Westminster* *; when, after Mr *Powle* had been chosen Speaker, the following Letter was presented to the House by Mr *Jephson*, the Prince's Secretary, and read by Mr Speaker :

[" *Gentlemen,*

" I have endeavoured, to the utmost of my power, to perform what was desired from me, in order to the public Peace and Safety ; and I do not know that any thing hath been omitted,

---

* It was upon the appointed time, the longed-for 22d day of *January*, that the Grand Convention met; not only with the expectations of the *British* dominions, but of all the neighbouring Kingdoms and Nations. Being divided into two Houses, as usual in Parliament, (of whose rules they were strictly observant) they immediately proceeded to the choice of their Speakers. In the House of Peers, the Marquess of *Halifax* carried it against the Earl of *Denbigh*; and in the Lower House, Mr *Powle* was unanimously chosen; though it was expected that Sir *Edward Seymour*, who had so early joined the Prince at *Exeter*, would have stood in competition with him. Both Houses had their Clerks, and several Officers, as in a regular Parliament.

Echard.

which

Debates in Parliament in 1688. 3

which might tend to their Preservation, since the Administration of Affairs was put into my hands : It now lieth upon you to lay the foundations of a firm Security for your Religion, your Laws, and your Liberties.

"I do not doubt but that, by such a full and free Representative of the Nation as is now met, the ends of my Declaration will be attained : And since it hath pleased God, hitherto, to bless my good intentions with so great success, I trust in him that he will complete his own work, by sending a Spirit of Peace and Union to influence your Councils, that no interruption may be given to a happy and lasting settlement.

"The dangerous condition of the Protestant Interest in *Ireland* requiring a large and speedy Succour, and the present state of things abroad, oblige me to tell you, that, next to the danger of unseasonable Divisions amongst yourselves, nothing can be so fatal as too great Delay in your Consultations.

"The States, by whom I have been enabled to rescue this Nation, may suddenly feel the ill effects of it, both by being too long deprived of the service of their Troops, which are now here, and of their early assistance against a powerful enemy, who hath declared War against them : And as *England* is, by Treaty, already engaged to help them upon any such exigencies, so I am confident, that their chearful concurrence to preserve this Kingdom, with so much hazard to themselves, will meet with all the returns of friendship and assistance, which may be expected from you as Protestants and *Englishmen*, whenever their condition shall require it."]

[Debate.]

MR *Garroway*.] All *England* is sensible of the great deliverance that we have had from Popery and Slavery by this generous Expedition of the Prince of *Orange*. I need not urge Arguments to give him Thanks; and, in the mean time, till we can proceed to a Settlement of the Nation, and till the Lords and Commons shall make farther application to him, desire " that he will be pleased to take the Administration of the Government upon him."

Mr *Hampden*.] I do concur in the Motion. As the Prince's Letter requires haste, so I would have no time lost in considering it, so as things may not be precipitated which require due deliberation. Be pleased, in the mean time, to thank the Prince, &c. for the great

action

4		*Debates in Parliament in* 1688.

action he has done in delivering the Nation from Popery and Slavery; and, in the fame words, to defire him to continue the Adminiftration of the Government, till the Lords and Commons fhall make farther application to him.

Col. *Birch.*] " That Thanks fhould be returned to the Prince, for his Deliverance of us, *&c.*" I would not have it fo; but, " that God has done it by his means." I could never have believed, fome months fince, what God, by his hand, hath wrought for this Kingdom.

Several other Motions were made for an Addition to the Queftion.

Sir *Thomas Lee.*] Nothing will fave your time more than to let two or three Gentlemen withdraw, and pen you an Addrefs, *&c.* upon the Debate of the Houfe.

Mr *John Howe.*] I think it as proper for us to fay, by whofe means we were brought into Popery and Slavery, as by whom we were delivered out.

The Lords fent a Meffage, with an Addrefs much of the fame nature with that above debated, for the Concurrence of the Houfe; which, with fome little variation, was agreed to by both Houfes.

Sir *Henry Capel.*] This Affembly has been chofen with freedom. There has not been a better Election a great while, without force of the Lord-Lieutenants. You have done a great deal in one day, but this is not enough; fo confider the word " Adminiftration;" 'tis but a fmall Truft you repofe in the Prince; 'twill roll, and be uncertain. The Prince has told you who has helped him to come over hither, the Proteftants. I have feen quick Bills for Money pafs here, to fight againft Proteftants: I hope we fhall now fight with them. His Troops are wanted in *Holland*. I hope you will not neglect a day to confider them: The Proteftants abroad are uneafy till they hear how we proceed. The whole thing of " an actual War with *France*," which I have feen here debated, we could
						never

Debates in Parliament in 1688. 5

never arrive at. I have obferved that we have not had above a hundred and fixty formerly, at giving great Sums; whereas, now we have no King, we are a full Houfe. Therefore pray take the State of the Nation into confideration as foon as you pleafe.

Sir *Thomas Clarges.*] The matter before you is of the greateft weight; therefore I hope you will proceed with prudence and warinefs. Whole Counties, as yet, have no Members : And, that there may be no imputations upon us, and that all exceptions may be taken away, I would have this great affair debated in a full Houfe.

[On filling up the Vacancies of the Houfe.]

Mr *Hampden.*] 'Tis proper to refolve upon filling the Vacancies of the Houfe. I would not preclude the Motions for it; but 'tis the Order of the Houfe, on a Vacancy, to fend your Letter for filling up that Vacancy, *&c.* If you apply to the proper Officer, he muft have a Seal; but now he has none, fo cannot execute your Order. Make a general Rule for filling the Vacancies here, that, upon fuch a Motion, Application may be made to the Prince for his Letter to fill up that Vacancy.

Mr *Seymour.*] We are in fo unfortunate an age, that it has improved Precedents, efpecially on miftaken grounds. There never was a Letter fent to the Chancellor for a Writ to fill up a Vacancy, but by a Warrant from the Speaker of the Commons of *England* affembled. " You are to take care to chufe, *&c.*" It muft be firft made known to you, and it is the eafieft way by Warrant or Order from you, and not to trouble the Prince upon this occafion.

Sir *Thomas Clarges.*] A Warrant from this Houfe is a Warrant for the Lord Keeper or Chancellor, and he has always obeyed it, and thought it fufficient authority to fend out a Writ. Now you are here as a Convention, which is a refemblance of a Parliament. The King, before he calls a Parliament, fends his Writ to chufe Members : After you have fat here, then your Precept;

B 3

6   *Debates in Parliament in* 1688.

cept; and now that we are fat here, you may fend your
Warrant or Letter to the Coroner.

The Speaker.] Anciently, you fent to the Lord
Keeper or Chancellor, to iffue out his Writ, &c. There
was, I remember, a great controverfy [in 1672] about
my Lord Chancellor *Shaftefbury* fending out Writs to fill
Vacancies, on his own Motion, before he had notice from
this Houfe *. There are two ways now propofed; one
for a Letter from the Prince to the Coroner, and the
other for the Speaker to fend his Letter in your name,
&c. I am ready to put the Queftion which way you
pleafe.

Ordered, That the Prince be defired to fend new Circulary
Letters to fome places where the old ones have mifcarried.

[*January* 23, and 26, omitted.]

Monday, *January* 28.
[On the State of the Nation.]

Col. *Birch.*] It has been moved, by one or two,
" that the Speaker leave the Chair." I have known it
moved, in granting Money, and all ordinary bufinefs,
" that the Speaker leave the Chair;" but to leave it now,
in a great bufinefs, you will make it twice as long. I
move you to confider, that, as it will hinder the work,
fo it will lower the greatnefs of it, and make it lefs
than it is.

Serjeant *Maynard.*] 'Tis a great Affair now upon
you. 'Tis never done till debated firft in the Houfe.
How many propofitions will happen at a Grand Committee, without your directions firft! You muft, at a
Committee, know whereupon to go. Firft confider of
the bufinefs, and then refer it as occafion requires.

Sir *Edward Seymour.*] What refolution foever you
take, I would not have you go out of the method of
ufual proceedings. I know how ftrait-laced, in fuch
a great matter, men will be in the Houfe, where they
can fpeak but once. 'Twill look as if you were not wil-

* *See Vol.* II. *p.* 2.

ling

Debates in Parliament in 1688. 7

ling it fhould take effect, as if ill done. But that it may freely be done, pray leave the Chair, to debate freely the Eftablifhment of the Nation.

The Speaker left the Chair.

[In a Grand Committee.]

Mr *Dolben* *.] I take leave to remind you of the Order of the Houfe on *Monday*, " to confider of the State of the Nation ;" but not at the fame time to debate the Remedies for the Misfortunes we are fallen under. Firft, confider the Condition of the Nation, as to that which concerns the Vacancy of the Government, by the abfence of the King. I tell you freely my opinion, that the King is demifed, and that *James* the Second is not King of *England*. For I lay it down as an undoubted propofition, that, when the King does withdraw himfelf from the Adminiftration of the Government, without any provifion to fupport the Commonwealth ; when, on the contrary, he ftops the ufe of the Great Seal, by taking it away with him, this amounts to what the Law calls " Demife," *id eft*, a ceffion ; and " demifed " is " deferted the Government." This is evident in Law, as it is evident in Reafon and Authority. The meaning of the word " Demife" is *demiffio*, laying down ; whether actually relinquifhing the Government, or paffively by death ; in either of which cafes, 'tis "a Demife." In the neceffity of Government, all thefe cafes have the fame confequences. When the interruption is in the Adminiftration, or 'tis demifed ; where there is the fame mifchief, there muft be the fame remedy. 'Tis the fame thing for the King to withdraw his perfon, which makes a Parenthefis in the Government. By withdrawing the Seal, the Chancery ceafes, and no Juftice can be obtained. The Common Pleas cannot be poffeffed of any Caufe, without an original Writ out of Chancery ; and when thefe fail, the Law fails ; and, by confequence, 'tis a Demife, for want of Adminiftrators of the Government ; which

* Son to the late Archbifhop of *York*.

B 4   the

the Law cannot fuffer. *Qui ceffat regnare ceffat judicare.* There is one Authority in the Rolls, *inftar omnium*, in the cafe of *Ed.* IV. There was a rumour that the Earl of *Warwick* advanced towards him ; he fled from *Nottingham* beyond fea ; which was a clear Demife, and all proceedings in *Wefiminfter-Hall* ceafed, and it was judged a Demife. In 14 *Henry* VI. there are many Refolutions of Caufes difcontinued, by that Demife ; *remanfit fine die*, becaufe *le Roi fe demife*, in effect *felo de fe*. Writs of Attachment were difcontinued, becaufe Juftices came not into the country, and the King went beyond fea, without leaving a Lieutenant. The great Oracle of the Law, Judge *Littleton*, pronounced this departure of *Edward* IV. a Demife. Perhaps it may be objected, that *Edward* IV. did return again to the Adminiftration of the Government, and refumed the Government by conqueft, not in a legal way, but by the fword—There are two other Authorities that carry force in them. *Edward* II. refigned the Crown, but by *dureffe*; yet he made the Refignation the 25th of *January*, and immediately it was judged a Demife. *Richard* IId's Refignation was *per minas*, yet that was judged a Demife (as in *Raftall*) *Quod recordatum de regimine regni fui fe demifit R. II. &c.* Thefe Precedents feem ftronger in our cafe, which is a voluntary departure, without *dureffe*. But that our King was frighted or forced away, others can better tell ; but, by what is notorious to the World, there is a fufficient conviction that it was not Force ; but that he did abandon his palace by night, and did go to fea, and was taken and returned again to his own Guards, that Papifts might not raife any difturbance in the apprehenfion of his being detained prifoner. But this weighs moft with me ; that it was not probable that he was driven away by Force, when he ftole away from his Guards, and repeated the attempt to be gone. There is the King's Letter to Lord *Feverfham*, wherein he is obliged to follow the Queen. We have not only our Law in the cafe, but the authority of foreign writers.

Debates in Parliament in 1688. 9

writers. By the Civil Law, when the King does voluntarily abandon the Government, 'tis a Demife, and Ceffation of the Government, according to *Grotius*, and other learned writers, by many Arguments from the Law of God—*Grotius* lays down fome : *Si princeps habet imperium pro direlicto*, &c. he is but a private man then, he certainly ceafes to be a Prince. Not that he was negligent in the Adminiftration of Government, but did direlict ; and we argue well, that a Direliction is a defertion of the Government. *Hoffman*, the Civilian, fays, " If a Prince relinquifhes the Government, he ceafes to be a King." Regularly, I muft end with a Motion; which is, that you will pafs a Vote, that it is the Opinion of the Committee, " That King *James* the Second having voluntarily forfaken the Government, and abandoned and forfaken the Kingdom, it is a voluntary Demife in him."

Sir *Richard Temple.*] This learned Gentleman has faid enough to convince us, that the gravity of this Committee is great, and that we have liberty to deliver the thoughts in every man's breaft. I fhall farther declare, that the King has endeavoured to deftroy the Government of the Nation in Parliaments, by practifing to get Votes before they meet, and to turn all out of the Government, who would not comply with him in Corporations to deliver up their Charters. This has been fo notorious, that I fhall not mention where; though it has been the Rights and Privileges of the People, yet they fhall not be chofen till they declare they will deftroy the Government. How has *Weftminfter-Hall* been tutored, Judges packed for purpofes, and turned out, unlefs they affert power in Kings to difpenfe with the Laws, fo that *Weftminfter-Hall* was become an inftrument of Slavery and Popery, ordinary Juftice deftroyed, and extraordinary ways promoted, in that little and fhort time of the late King *James*'s reign! When a King attempts to deftroy the roots of Government, he differs in nothing from a Tyrant. All he has done may be reduced to that head of the deftruction

10   *Debates in Parliament in* 1688.

ftruction of the Church, by fufpending the Ecclefiaftical Laws, to deftroy all that will not comply with
Popery. The mifchiefs are fo recent and confpicuous,
that, when you come to give Reafons, you will fatisfy the
Nation that King *James* has rendered himfelf inconfiftent with Government. If there be not a Vacancy,
and he has left the Government, what do we do here?
He has quitted the Government, without affurance of
any thing: He has fuppreffed the Parliament Writs:
He has taken away the Great Seal; and here is an apparent end of the Government. The King is fallen
from the Crown, and may think he is under an Obligation of Confcience to break the Laws againft Popery.
He may fay, " I will never live in that torture :" And
if he has faid fo, would any man doubt but that this is
a Renunciation of the Government? All his actions
have tended this way. If he be recalled, he will do the
fame thing again, and tell the World, " This is not from
the Lords, but a company of miferable men of the
Houfe of Commons, and they may go home again;
for the King can do no wrong, nor can forfeit his
Crown by Male Adminiftration."—But fuppofe the cafe
were of an Infant, or Lunatic, the Nation may, in that
cafe, provide for the Government; and, were the King
a perfon that took care of the Government, he would
never have left the Nation thus. He has taken none,
and therefore it is our duty to do it.

Sir *Thomas Lee.*] When you have put the Queftion,
" That there is an Avoidance in the Government," then
your fecond part is, how to provide for it.

Mr *Finch.*] The Queftion now is of Vacancy in the
Government: That of the Right and Title to fill it
up comes too late after the other Queftion. Your
Queftion is, Whether the Right itfelf is gone?

Sir *Chriftopher Mufgrave*.*] As to the matter of depofing Kings, I fhall leave that to the Long Robe, to
exercife

---

* A Gentleman of a noble family in *Cumberland*, whofe life had
been regular, and his deportment
grave. He had loft a Place in King
James's time; for though he was
always a high Tory, yet he would
not

Debates in Parliament in 1688.　　11

exercife their abilities upon. I live near a Kingdom
(*Scotland*) where I know not how ill neighbours they
will be, if they concur not with your fenfe. I would
be clear, whether the intention is to depofe the King;
and, if he has forfeited his Inheritance to the Crown,
I would know from the Long Robe, whether you can
depofe the King, or no.

Mr Comptroller *Wharton**.] I am glad Gentlemen
have explained themfelves. The Gentleman makes a
queftion, whether the King may be depofed; but,
whether he may be depofed, or depofes himfelf, he is
not our King. 'Tis not for mine, nor the intereft of
moft here, that he fhould come again. Abdication and
Direliction are hard words to me, but I would have
no loop-hole to let in the King; for I believe not myfelf nor any Proteftant in *England* fafe, if you admit
him.

Sir *Chriftopher Mufgrave*.] I believe we are in great
danger, fhould the King return again; but I would
willingly know the opinion of the Long Robe; and I
hope they have that candour and tendernefs, that they
will clearly give their thoughts in this great and extraordinary affair.

Serjeant *Maynard*.] I know not the meaning of this,
but I am afraid of a meaning. The Queftion is not,

not comply with his defigns. He
had, indeed, contributed much to
increafe his Revenue, and to offer
him more than he afked; yet he
would not go into the taking off
the Tefts. Upon the Revolution,
the Place out of which he had been
turned was given to a man that
had a good fhare of merit in it.
This alienated him from the King;
and he, being a man of good judgment, came to be confidered as the
Head of the Party; in which he
found his account fo well, that no
offers that were made him could
ever bring him over to the King's
interefts. Upon many critical occafions, he gave up fome important
points, for which the King found

it neceffary to pay him very libe-
rally.　　　　　　　　　*Burnet.*
　* Eldeft fon of Lord *Wharton*,
to which title he fucceeded on his
father's death. He was one of the
firft of rank who joined the Prince
of *Orange* on his landing, and, upon his advancement to the Throne,
had confiderable Places under him,
as he had alfo in the reign of Queen
Anne, being appointed Lord Lieutenant of *Ireland*, and created Earl
of *Wharton*, &c. In 1714, he was
appointed by King *George* I. Lord
Privy Seal, and foon after was created a Marquefs. He died in 1715,
and was father to the late Duke of
Wharton.

whether

12   *Debates in Parliament in* 1688.

whether we can depofe the King; but, whether the King has not depofed himfelf. 'Tis no new project; our Government is mixed, not monarchical and tyrannous, but has had its beginning from the people. There may be fuch a tranfgreffion in the Prince, that the People will be no more governed by him. All Governments, both military and civil, he difpofes of, and becaufe he afked a Million for life, and we afked, the laft Parliament, but that fome Officers, not qualified by Law, might be removed from their Places, the Parliament was diffolved—'Tis a miftake, that *Ireland* was conquered; it was yielded to *Henry* II. by calling him to take poffeffion of it; and for five hundred years it was part of the Monarchy of *England*. The laft Rebellion was by the influence of the Priefts and *Jefuits*, and in 1641 the Proteftants were all maffacred. They flew 200,000 Proteftants; and all that has been done in *Ireland*, would have been done in *England*. All authority, civil and military, was in *Irifh* hands. Was this done like a King of *England?* What fhall we think of this? *Ireland* to be in Popifh hands! Can the King give away that Kingdom? This has been long creeping upon us. There is no Popifh Prince in *Europe* but would deftroy all Proteftants; as in *Spain*, *France*, and *Hungary*; and in *Spain* they deftroyed a gallant young Prince (Don *Carlos*) whom they fufpected to incline to the Proteftants; and now they would make *Magdalen* College a new *St Omers,——The reft the Compiler could not hear.*

Mr *Harbord.*] If the Queftion be, whether you have power to depofe the King, that may tend to calling him back again, and then we are all ruined.

Mr *Howe.*] Some of the Counfel talk as if they were inftructing Juries. I wifh they would come plainly to the point.

Sir *George Treby.*] I am forry for this heat in a matter that requires our utmoft deliberation. 'Tis no lefs a Queftion than, whether we fhall be governed by
Popery

Debates in Parliament in 1688. 13

Popery and Arbitrary Government, or whether we fhall be rid of both. One Gentleman would have the Long Robe declare, whether we have power to depofe the King; though he fpeaks pertinent, yet it is not proper now; for we have found the Crown vacant, and are to fupply that defect. We found it fo, we have not made it fo. Mr *Finch* would have it, the King going out of his Wits, not out of the Government. He knows the cafe; we are fallen out of the King's hands, and the Government muft be provided for, before you go any other way than what was firft propofed—But, to what has been faid of "our not reprefenting the fourth part of the Nation, accounting women and children, and all perfons not Freeholders, of 40 *l. per annum*, who are part of the Nation, and in a Convention ought to be reprefented, when the Government is to be difpofed of," I fay, we reprefent the valuable part, and thofe that deferve a fhare in the Government. You have advifed the Prince of *Orange* to take upon him the fupreme Authority of the Adminiftration of the Government. The condition of the Nation is incumbent on you to provide for; and I am in confcience fatiffied, that the King has loft his legal Government, and is fallen from it. That King that cannot, or will not, adminifter the Government, is no longer King; and this King neither will nor can; which are fufficient reafons to declare the Throne vacant. There are but two parts in Government, to command and obey the Legiflature; but it is by the people's confent we make Laws; and the King, in executing them, affumed a power to difpenfe with the Laws in a lump. He difpenfed with the Statute of Provifors; and the confequence was, the Pope fent a Nuntio hither; and the confequence is, he declares "he can no longer nor farther treat with his people in Parliament." As foon as that is done, he affumes an inherent indifpenfible Authority to vacate all your Laws, difpenfe with the Act of Uniformity, and fet up the Ecclefiaftical Commiffions:

14   *Debates in Parliament in* 1688.

miffions: No authority is above them; they judge
without Appeal; they would have deprived all the
Proteftant Bifhops and Minifters in *England*, and filled up
their Bifhopricks and Livings with Popifh Priefts—The
cement of the Government is for the People to depend
upon the King for the Adminiftration of the Government,
and the People for the execution of Laws, prefervation
of their Grants and Charters. The King, by this difpenfing power, might have packed Members of Parliament, like the Parliament of *Paris*, which is in the
nature of Regifters, only to record the King's Will
and Pleafure by his Dragoons; fo, by this time, we
might have been chofen by Regulators or Dragoons;
and Parliaments would have reprefented none of the
People, except Papifts. When the Conftitution of Parliament is thus invaded, inftead of redrefs of Grievances
we fhould have no Parliament called but of fuch as
made Grievances. If the Prince of *Orange* had not
refcued us from Popery, we fhould have delivered up,
by Law, both Religion and Kingdom. The height of
the Article againft *Richard* II. was, " That he would
have the Laws in his own breaft, and packing of Parliaments." It was the judgment of King *James* I. in
the Parliament of 1607, " That, when a King breaks
in upon his Laws, he ceafes to be a King." It was the
great Argument, in the Exclufion Bill. What hurt can
be done by a Popifh King, is in the Royal Office only;
but it is impoffible in the reft of the Offices of the Government; for no Papift could come into them by
Law, becaufe of the Tefts: And this was the judgment of King *James*'s friends then, and that it was
that preferved the Crown to him. How far this is a
renouncing the Crown, is the Queftion. This was
King *James* I.'s own judgment; he is fallen from
the Crown, and is under an obligation of confcience
to break thefe laws—I think it was an error to let
him into the Throne, and I would not do another in
not keeping him out. Our Deliverer has taken care
                                                    of

Debates in Parliament in 1688.   15

of us; therefore put the Queftion, " Whether King *James* II. has not made an Abdication of the Government, and that the Throne is void."

Sir *Thomas Clarges*.] To fay " that the Crown is void," is a confequence of an extraordinary nature. The confequence muft be, we have power to fill it, and make it from a fucceffive Monarchy an elective; and whether a Commonwealth, or alter the defcent, is yet ambiguous.   How came we hither the 22d of *December*, but to confer with the Members of former Parliaments?   I told them then, " It was to confider how to purfue the ends of the Prince of *Orange*'s Declaration, according to his Letter."   And the advice ended, to call a Convention by the Prince's Letter; that fo a full and free Reprefentation of the people might advife to profecute the ends of the Declaration, which would be tant-amount to a legal Parliament.   I defire the Prince's Declaration may be read.—(*which was done.*)

Sir *William Williams*.] Should you go to the beginning of Government, we fhould be much in the dark : Every man in town and country can agree in fact of the ftate of things.   'Tis plain that King *James* II. is gone out of *England* into *France*; that is a plain fact. 'Tis a wilful, voluntary, or mixed action.   I hear of no direction for Adminiftration of the Government, when the King left the Kingdom; how he has difpofed either of Courts of Juftice, or of the Parliament.   If this fact be true, he is become ufelefs, and has left no remedy to preferve the peace of the Kingdom.   This is partly the State of the Nation; and in that Kingdom where we had always difrelifhed him in feveral Parliaments, he has left feveral Places void in the Government; then what is to be done in this cafe?   I propofe it to be the firft ftep, to declare, " That *James* the Second, by withdrawing himfelf from *England*, has deprived the Kingdom of *England* of the exercife of Kingly Dignity."   Can any man deny all this ?

16   *Debates in Parliament in* 1688.

this ? Then the confequence is, we are deprived of a King.

Mr *Somers* *.] What you do in this cafe will fatisfy the World abroad, if it be like other cafes. *Sigifmund* King of *Sweden*'s cafe is parallel to ours. King *James* the Firft (upon an occafion moft have heard of) protefted, " That if his Pofterity were not Proteftants, he prayed to God to take them from the Throne." *Sigifmund* made the like imprecation. He was fo 'confiderable as to be chofen King of *Poland*. After the Crown of *Sweden* defcended to him, he fent to take the Government upon him : He returned, when he had changed his Religion, and brought *Jefuits* along with him, who were refty, and would difturb the Government, and invade the Laws, as they have ever done. The King prepared to force his way to the Crown ; but before they came to a Battle, they entered into a Treaty, and the King promifed to call a Parliament, and that Religion fhould be fettled ; but before they met, he withdrew to the Kingdom of *Poland* : So they fettled *Charles* VIII. upon that Throne. Firft and laft, the matter was jefuited, to change Religion,

* Member for *Worcefter*, and e-qually celebrated as a Lawyer, a Statefman, and a Patriot. Having diftinguifhed himfelf as Counfel for the feven Bifhops, and been fuc-ceffively Sollicitor and Attorney-General; in 1693 he was appointed Lord Keeper, and in 1698 was created Lord *Somers*. After being twice ineffectually attacked by the Houfe of Commons, he was difmiffed from his Places, on a change of the Miniftry, in 1700 ; and in 1701 was impeached by the Houfe of Commons, but honourably acquitted by the Houfe of Lords. In the reign of Queen *Anne* he had the chief hand in projecting the fcheme of the Union, and in 1708 was made Lord Prefident of the Council, but was again difmiffed, on the change of the Miniftry, in 1710.

" He held the Seals (fays *Burnet*) feven years, with a high reputation for capacity, integrity, and diligence, and was in all refpects the greateft man I had ever known in that poft. He was very learned in his own profeffion, with a great deal more learning in other profeffions, in divinity, philofophy, and hiftory. He had a great capacity for bufinefs,with an extraordinary temper ; for he was fair and gentle, perhaps to a fault, confidering his poft ; fo that he had all the patience and foftnefs, as well as the juftice and equity, becoming a great Magiftrate. He had always agreed in his notions with the Whigs, and had ftudied to bring them to better thoughts of the King (*William*) and to a greater confidence in him." He died (without iffue) in 1716.

                                                              fubvert

Debates in Parliament in 1688. 17

fubvèrt the Government, and to withdraw from the Kingdom. That withdrawing of *Sigifmund* was much lefs than ours. He went to the Kingdom he came from ; ours has withdrawn to another Kingdom, which has always been againft the intereft of *England*, and he cannot come out of the *French* King's power without his confent, and all to his advantage. Some have taken notice of things before, and fome fince, his defertion : But the King's going to a foreign Power, and cafting himfelf into his hands, abfolves the People from their Allegiance. He fent an Ambaffador* to *Rome*, received a Nuntio from thence, received a foreign Jurifdiction, and fet up *Romifh* Bifhops in *England*, that the Popifh Religion might intervene with the Government, thereby to fubject the Nation to the Pope, as much as to a foreign Prince. *Ireland*, which has coft *England* fo much Treafure to reduce, and now to deliver it up to the *Irifh*, to fubject it to a foreign Power ! And to do things by fuch hands, as, by the Conftitution of the Kingdom are incapable ! The hands were as much out of the way as the defign—Juft like *Sigifmund*, after he had left the Kingdom, to fend away the Seal, call a Parliament, and then defert the Nation !—My Motion is, That you will appoint a Committee to draw a Vote upon the Debate.

Serj. *Maynard.*] The difference is in words only : I will fpeak to the laft only. I am not of opinion that the King, being a Papift, has made himfelf incapable of the Crown.

Mr *Finch.*†] You have had variety of Motions, and have well collected them. Give me leave to examine the Motions ; and I afk pardon if I differ in fome things. 'Tis moved, that, by acts done by the King, he has loft his Crown that way ; by going away, he has abdicated the Crown, and made a total refufal of the Government. 'Tis moved to vary the ftate of the Queftion, and only for the prefent to declare the

* Earl of *Caftlemaine.*
† Second fon to the Earl of *Nottingham*, and removed from being Sollicitor General in 1686. In 1702 he was created Ld *Guernfey.* In 1714 Earl of *Aylesford*, and was grandfather to the prefent Earl.

VOL. IX.   C   Throne

18   *Debates in Parliament in* 1688.

Throne vacated. What Queſtion, in point of Law, there is between "*demiſed, abdicated,* and *deſerted,*" the conſequence can be but one and the ſame : If it be meant "Vacancy in the Throne," and you muſt fill it, and that it is devolved upon the People, that is, I believe, farther than Gentlemen would go : I believe no body will urge that ſo far, the Conſtitution of the Kingdom and Government not admitting it—If we were in the ſtate of Nature, we ſhould have little title to any of our eſtates—That the King has loſt his Title to the Crown, and loſt his Inheritance, is farther than any Gentleman, I believe, has, or will explain himſelf. The proviſion you will make will be but little acceptable to ſuch a foundation. The conſequence is but this ; ſince the Monarchy is hereditary, be it vacated, or whatever you will call it, the deſcent is the conſequence of all. No man will ſay the Monarchy is elective, let the Adminiſtration be ever ſo ill, and that the King has no more in the Monarchy than the exerciſe of it. If by neglect, or male-adminiſtration, he can forfeit no more than is in him, then this conſequence is no more, than that his perſonal exerciſe of the Crown is gone ; but ſtill it muſt ſubſiſt ſomewhere. This is of the higheſt conſequence that ever any Debate was here, for Law and Religion to be eſtabliſhed ſure and firm. However we may weather it, Poſterity may curſe our memory in after-ages, if we fail in this weighty matter. What to propoſe is difficult. I will not go about to ſay that what the King has done is any way juſtifiable. Here has been an actual invaſion of our Religion and Properties, when they did get men in to give up the whole Rights of the Kingdom. Theſe are things of a high nature, and call for your timely aſſiſtance. Conſider the difficulty that will ariſe in the conſequence, to ſay, that the King has made a total Renunciation of the Kingdom. That the King may renounce, all agree, that ſuch Renunciation muſt be voluntary and public—And whether ſuch Deſertion be an Abdication ? If he has loſt it,
the

Debates in Parliament in 1688.   19

the Monarchy will either be hereditary or elective, and here will be confequences. I am not of opinion that you fhould fend Propofals to the King; it will not confift with the fecurity of the Nation. Suppofe the Kingdom under a ftate of Infancy, or Frenzy, the fafety of the Government is in the unanimous opinion of the Nation. It is not hard to fay, that the Parliament muft provide for the Adminiftration of the Government, but to call this " a direct forfeiture of the Crown!"—I will not excufe the King, and fay he can do no wrong; but would avoid all doubts, and not fay, in real common parliamentary conftruction, that the King can do no wrong, or that he has forfeited his Crown by male-adminiftration—But fuppofe it the cafe of a Lunatic, or Infant, the Nation may provide for the Government; and were the King a perfon that took care of the Government that he ought to have taken care of——

Sir *Robert Howard*.] I differ in the circumftances of what has been faid, though I agree in the main. There is an inconvenience in refting upon the word " Demife." *Richard* II. would have no Laws but what were in his own breaft; but our King would not be fatisfied with arbitrary Government in the Laws Temporal, but in the Laws of the Church too, thereby to influence our fouls as well as our bodies; and, by an arbitrary Government, to fubvert the Civil and Ecclefiaftical Power; and 'twas no wonder, when a *Jefuit* and Papift fat in Council, that all Corporations were fubverted, and Parliament-men clofeted. This was the defign of *Rich.* II. to try Sheriffs, to pack a Parliament, to make the people own their deftroyers—But if the Demife of the Government fail, where is the foundation we are upon? It muft be fomewhere. By a legal and juft tryal, no man has wrong done him. The King has none done him, in difpofing of the Government, for he acts as a private man, he ought to act from his Laws—When he acts by his Will, and not by the Laws, he is no King; for he acts by Power and Tyranny. I have heard, " that the King has his Crown by

Divine

Divine Right," and we (the People) have Divine Right too; but he can forfeit, if he break that pact and covenant with his People, who have Right, by reason of their Election, as well as in the name of Mr King—This original of power, resistance or non-resistance, is judged by the power resolved by People and King—The Constitution of the Government is actually grounded upon pact and covenant with the People. If this be so, what remains but that the King has made Abdication of the Government, and at one time has lopped off both Church and State? Could he have compassed Liberty of Conscience, he would have cut off Church and State at one stroke, and settled Popery. Here has not been one thing unattempted to destroy us: And if this be so, 'tis my opinion that here is an Abdication of the Government, and it is devolved into the People, who are here in civil society and constitution to save them. And if Divine Right does consecrate all these violations of our Laws, 'tis strange! If the King be of another Religion from his people, and makes a combination with a foreign Power, shall he carry all away with him to destroy us? I am of opinion, " that *James* II. has abdicated the Government*."

Mr *Pollexfen*.†] The Question that has been proposed is, " Whether, by a voluntary departure of the King, the Government is demised?" I would not have Gentlemen surprized by the word " voluntary going away;" there is more meant by that than you suppose. There is a descent of the Crown, if a voluntary departure; and then what do you here, if you admit that? But if it be a " Demise," then the Crown is full by succession; and then too what do you here? If Force has been upon the King, and then he fly, will you call this " a voluntary departure?"—Was it " voluntary "

---

* Sir *Robert Howard* entertained the Committee with a long harangue; and he was the first who ventured to assert the Vacancy of the Throne, and the Breach of the Original Contract, by a continued series of illegal acts (many of which he enumerated and displayed) throughout the whole course of King *James*'s reign. *Echard.*

† An honest and learned, but perplexed Lawyer. *Burnet.* He was soon after made Lord Chief Justice.

his

Debates in Parliament in 1688. 21

his flight from *Salisbury* to *London?* The stronger did chase the weaker. If this is "voluntary," what means the noise of Arms? And is all this "a voluntary driving away?" I would not have you catched with this, to entangle the Debate. 'Tis an unnecessary Question, to carry at first sight; and if the Crown be vacant, trouble yourselves no farther in the matter—If the Crown be demised, you must think of the succession of it.

Mr *Dolben.*] I would not be thought to catch the House, by any Motion from me. I must still call the King's departure, when he needed not, and might have stayed, though there was "noise of Arms," yet if the King would not stick to his Laws, nor redress the grievances of his people, I must call that "a voluntary Demise." 'Tis true, upon a Demise, there must be a Descent; but the Question is, whether the Crown be vacant, now the King is departed, and no body to fill it up.

Sir *James Oxenden.*] 'Tis "a voluntary departure" in the King, to go away, and stir up foreign Princes to bring a foreign Power to destroy us. I cannot call it otherwise.

Sir *Henry Capel.*] 'Tis said, "the King might have stayed, and called a Parliament." But Popery and a Protestant Government are inconsistent. I move, that you will vote, that the Crown is vacant.

Sir *Robert Sawyer.*] The Gentleman that first moved in this Debate, put it upon "a Demise." "Devolution" and "Abdication" seem to be the same thing called by various authors. You have been moved for other words, and in case of "Abdication," it is not difficult. As to the next step, there is a great difference between the Throne being vacant by Abdication, and Dissolution of the Government. The Vacancy of the Throne makes no Dissolution of the Government, neither in our Law, nor any other. If the Government be fallen to the People, which People we are, what do the Lords and we here? If it be devolved upon the People, we have nothing to do here; we are not

C 3   the

22	*Debates in Parliament in* 1688.

the People collectively : We are Representatives of the People in the three Estates of the Nation, and the King. And our Oaths of Allegiance, which we take before we sit, are to the hereditary succession of the Crown ; the third Estate, which is the House of Commons, represents the Freeholders and Burghers, who are not the fourth part of the Kingdom. If the Government be devolved to the People, Copy-holders, Lease-holders, all men under 40 *s.* a year are People—What needs the advice of the Lords to reduce things to a settlement ? Is it not then the right of all the People to send Representatives, and our sitting under this frame of Government is void, as we ought not to be here, so it restores not the rights of the Kingdom—Restore those rights by what free Parliament we can, in such a form, and frame, and constitution as the Government will admit. What do the Lords there ? Are they Representatives of the People ? No ; of their own Estate only. If the Government be devolved upon the People, what do the Lords there ? And we are not the People. Once a Government did dispose of Crowns. And they were not the fourth part of the Kingdom that disposed of the Crown in 1648. This has not only relation to ourselves, but to another Nation, *Scotland*—If we proceed on a sandy foundation, we shall destroy all we do. The People have a judgment of assent or dissent, but not a superiority of determination. If he relinquish the possession of the Throne, but not the Title, whether does that amount to " an Abdication " of the Government ? I take the King's departure out of the Kingdom to be " an Abdication " of the Government. He refuses to govern, that acts otherwise than the Laws direct. And he that will go out of the Kingdom, does make an Abdication and Dereliction of the whole Government. In all I have read, I never met, in so short a reign, the Laws so violated, and the Prerogative so stretched. In his Declaration, he wishes that all his subjects were Catholics, and, if in his power, would certainly have effected it ;
									we

Debates in Parliament in 1688. 23

we muft all have been Catholics, or not fafe. The Church and State were turned topfy-turvy. As to his fuborning a Parliament, this and *Richard* II. are the only inftances I have met with, that fo we might have had neither Liberty nor Property in the Nation—His intention was to govern without Law. The Proteftant Religion here was interwoven with all the Proteftant States of *Europe*; and that principle juftifies the Prince of *Orange's* coming over, and all that joined with him ; which intereft, if it fall, all falls with it. From the time the King has withdrawn, here has been no application made from him ; and therefore I believe he has no intention to govern, according to the Conftitution of the Government : Therefore no obligation remains upon us to him, in cafe this be an Abdication of the Government.

Mr *Bofcawen.*] I have hearkened to *Sawyer* a great while, but I know not how to underftand, " that the fourth part of the people of *England* are not here reprefented," and " that this is not a Parliament." I would know of him, what other way he can propofe of calling a Parliament, than what has been in calling this ? I am of opinion, that, if we fit here till he finds a way to fit better than as you are, you may fit till doomfday. Gentlemen, in former Parliaments, may remember they were told, " that the King could not be true to his Religion, if he did not what he has done :" And I believe none are willing to go into *Egypt* again: To fettle things now, is the way to maintain both your Laws and Religion—If the King's going away be a Demife, then you muft fupply the Throne—And here is not only the King, but a little one beyond fea too, that will pretend. I would fay no more, but " that the Throne is void ;" then take the beft way you can ; and there is but one to defend you from him that is gone, that endeavoured to deftroy your Laws. We muft not fight with a bulrufh : Therefore declare " that the Throne is void," and fill it. And pray put the Queftion, " That the Throne is void."

C 4

Sir

24.   *Debates in Parliament in* 1688.

Sir *William Pulteney*.] I fhall fpeak fhort to the Queftion, whether " Abdication," or " the Throne void,"
I would have both in the Queftion, for what he has
deftroyed was without making any provifion for the Adminiftration of the Government.   We come to fupply
what he has taken from us.   Have not you made another determination of putting the Government into
another's hand for the prefent, which you have already,
in effect, declared " a Demife?"

Mr *Howe*.] People were not free from flavery till
the Tyrant ran away.   I will not fay that any King may
have the fame guilt, but we may have the fame fears
of Popifh Lord-Lieutenants fet over us :   Therefore
put into the Queftion all this.   The laft ufe he made of
the Great Seal was to pardon malefactors, that have
reduced you to this condition.

Mr *Finch*.] I defire to explain myfelf.   'Tis infi-
nuated as if, from what I fhould have faid, a loop-
hole may be left for the King's return.   I am fo far
from that, that I think there can be no fafety in the
King's return, by unanimous confent of the Nation.   I
think the Government not fafe by his Adminiftration;
But all men will agree to be fecured.   I did fay no more.
I did not mean to capitulate, but to eftablifh things
by fuch a Regent during the King's life; if there may
be fuch a fecurity, all men will agree to it, and this
is no loop-hole to let in the King again to the Government; for the King, by going away, *&c.* and his male-
adminiftration, ought not to be trufted; and we may
fear that, in the Regency, power may be exceeded :
Therefore we have a right to demand fecurity, that
we be invaded no more :   Yet the difpofing of the
Crown is another Queftion.   All men can agree, that
there is no fecurity in his return.   But whether his
Adminiftration does fo ceafe as to lofe his Titles, every
man muft fwear to his Vote, that he whom you fhall
place on the Throne is lawful and rightful King.

Sir

Debates *in Parliament in* 1688.   25

Sir *Robert Howard*.] As to the fucceffion of the young Gentleman beyond the feas, if he dies, *France* will find another for you.

Refolved, That King *James* the Second, having endeavoured to fubvert the Conftitution of the Kingdom, by breaking the original Contract between King and People, and, by the advice of *Jefuits*, and other wicked Perfons, having violated the fundamental Laws, and having withdrawn himfelf out of this Kingdom, has abdicated the Government, and that the Throne is thereby become vacant.* [Which was agreed to by the Houfe, and the Lords concurrence was defired.]

Tuefday, *January* 29.

Mr *Garroway*.] Great numbers of fhips have taken in freight for *France*. I would have you addrefs the Prince of *Orange* to ftop them. Our Trade with the *French* King is to our difadvantage ; and now that King *James* is there, our mariners may be ftopped.

Mr *Bofcawen*.] I would not barely addrefs the Prince to ftop thofe fhips, but with it fend our Reafons for it.

Mr *Hampden*.] I would have it part of the Addrefs, " That the Prince would pleafe to ftop thofe fhips, by fome fpeedy courfe, that are going to fetch Wine from *France* ;" left the *French* King ftop your fhips and men too.

Mr *Pilkington*.] When the Wines are bought up, then you will have an embargo upon your fhips in *France* ; and both Wine, Money, and Ships will be gone. And farther I defire, " that the Prince of *O-range* will take care that no fhips go for *Ireland*," whither, I believe, fhips are gone down the river.

Mr *Sacheverell*.] An Embargo at this time to be general would be of ill confequence : To run that trade into one hand at this time, the Merchants will fuffer by it.

Mr *Love*.] I defire the Prince may be moved, " that a few fhips may cruize upon the *Irifh* coaft, to give encouragement to the Proteftants there."

* The above complicated Refolution (when ratified by both Houfes) was perhaps the moft remarkable of all the *Englifh* Records.   *Echard*.

Lord

26   *Debates in Parliament in* 1688.

Lord *Falkland**.] The Prince has ordered ſhips to
cruize upon the *Iriſh* coaſt, and in the *Channel.*

. Col. *Birch.*] I trouble Wine as little as any body;
but I have found by experience that claret will be
drank, and Money ſpent, and not only in brandy but
linnen. Nineteen parts in twenty of the *French* com-
modities we pay ready Money for. If any Gentleman
can, let him find a way to reduce that trade to ba-
lance—And it has been, that nothing from that Kingdom has been but by way of exchange. I would have
the Committee of Trade ſit, to take this into conſideration : I would have no Embargo, but ſave your Money, and that will do your work againſt this hereditary enemy of us and the Empire.

Reſolved, That a Committee be appointed to conſider of the
Trade between this Kingdom and *France,* &c. and that an Addreſs to the Prince of *Orange* be prepared, to deſire him to
lay an Embargo on all ſhips going out of this Kingdom for
France.

In a Grand Committee. On the State of the Nation.

Col. *Birch.*] When I conſider the extraordinary hand
of God that brought us hither, and the freedom we
are here met in, it amazes me ; and I am not able to
comprehend this work of God in ſuch an extraordinary manner ; and, concerning King *James*'s depoſing
himſelf, 'tis the hand of God. Theſe forty years we
have been ſcrambling for our Religion, and have ſaved
but little of it. We have been ſtriving againſt *Anti-
Chriſt,* Popery, and Tyranny. If we go through with
this work, let every one underſtand what he means :
Therefore I ſhall tell you what I mean. King *James* I.
was ſo fond of the *Spaniſh* match (though that proved
a *French* match at laſt) that he loſt the *Palatinate* by
it : Then followed pulling Members out, and committing them to priſon. When once King *Charles* I. mar-

---

* Grandſon to the celebrated Lord *Falkland,* killed in the Civil Wars.
This Lord was afterwards a Privy Counſellor and a Lord of the Admi-
ralty, and died in 1694. He was grandfather to the preſent Viſcount.

ried

Debates in Parliament in 1688.   27

ried a Papift, all things, from that time forward, went
the contrary way; all things tended to Popery and a
Civil War.   At laft I was in it, and, I thought, on the
right fide—(I am fure, I endeavoured to make it fo before I left it.)   When the two Eftates remonftrated, and
begged that the Cuftoms might not be levied without
Law, and Ship-money, there were fmooth tongues in
this Houfe then to carry it on—Then came the breaking
the Laws and Liberties, when things were near a conclufion—It was not the fault of the Minifters of the
Church of *England*; nay, nor the Non-conformifts, but
Popery was in the box, and Idolatry.   I remember
what was faid in this Houfe, when the late King *James*
was married to this Queen: " Men will follow their
intereft; and it was his intereft to deftroy the Proteftant Religion, our Laws and Liberties." Popery will
not profper but in an arbitrary, tyrannical foil.   If
there had never a book been written on this fubject,
yet men may fee, that, if God had not ftopped him, we
had been led like fheep to the flaughter.   If then we
are like to be ruined, if governed by a Popifh Prince,
my Motion is, "That you will vote it inconfiftent with a
Proteftant State to be governed by a Popifh Prince."

Sir *Richard Temple*.] I hope this will have no Debate; for we have found by experience, that a Popifh
King is inconfiftent with the Government of a Proteftant Nation.

Sir *Patience Ward*.] The profpect of a Popifh fucceffor was that which laid all the plots againft the life
of the late King *Charles*, and the Proteftant Religion.

Sir *Robert Sawyer*.] This Debate is preparatory to
what farther you intend to do.   I move, " that you will
vote it inconfiftent with a Proteftant Government to
have a Popifh Prince." There is a poffibility that a Papift may be faved, and a poffibility that a Popifh King
may govern well; but where the Papifts govern the
King, 'tis next to an impoffibility that the Government
fhould be Proteftant.

Mr

28   *Debates in Parliament in* 1688.

Mr *Dolben*.] There is nothing in Statute nor Common Law againſt a Popiſh Prince, but it is againſt the intereſt of the Nation.

Major *Wildman*.] The Lawyers tell you, " there is neither Common nor Statute Law againſt a Popiſh King ;" but the Government of this Kingdom of *England* is an independent Supremacy, that neither foreign Potentate, either eccleſiaſtical or civil, has any thing to do here. There is no Popiſh Prince but does acknowlege the Pope to be ſupreme ; but 'tis Treaſon to acknowlege that Supremacy here : Therefore to ſay, " that there is no Statute Law, &c." is ſtrange to be averred by the Long Robe. I move, therefore, that you will not only declare it to be againſt the intereſt of the Proteſtant Religion to be governed by a Popiſh Prince, but " that it is againſt our Law." Our free independent Government is not conſiſtent with a Nuntio from the Pope. Four hundred years together we have laboured to keep the Church of *Rome* from our Government. 'Tis inconſiſtent with the Law of *England* to be governed by a Popiſh Prince.

Sir *Robert Sawyer*.] Will that Gentleman ſay, " that the Laws four hundred years ſince, and ſome in *Henry* VIII's time, were inconſiſtent with the Popiſh Government ?" I am ſure, without doors, it will be ſtrangely thought of, if *Henry* VIII. ſhould not be ſome time a Popiſh Prince.

Major *Wildman*.] *Henry* VIII. renounced Popery utterly. We ſpeak of Princes holding Communion with the Church of *Rome* ; and you may lay the word " Papiſt " aſide.

Mr *Hampden*.] I have a great deference to the learned perſon ; but the Pope's Supremacy was never heard of before the firſt Nuntio came into *England*, at the inſtance of *William* the Conqueror, who found his Clergy high, and therefore he got a foreign power over them, but complained afterwards, as the greateſt Grievance, of the Pope's power in Appeals, upon which the Statute of Proviſors was made. *Henry* VIII. was
the

Debates in Parliament in 1688.   29

the firft Prince that totally fhook off the Pope's power, and the grounds juftified him, being againft the Conftitution of the Government ; and all agreed to it, and the Laws againft Nuntios from the Pope. Q. *Mary,* not foon, prevailed with Cardinal *Pole* to come over for Nuntio. I defire the Queftion as moved, *&c.*

Lord *Falkland.*] For the honour of your proceedings, let what you do to-day be confiftent with what you did yefterday. If it be inconfiftent with the Law to have a Popifh King, purfue your Vote of yefterday.

Refolved, That it hath been found, by experience, to be inconfiftent with the fafety and welfare of this Proteftant Kingdom, to be governed by a Popifh Prince.

Mr *Wharton.*] You refolved, by Vote, yefterday, "That the Throne was vacant ;" and I fuppofe every Gentleman, and thofe few that were againft the Vote, are now for filling the Throne, and re-fettling the Government ; and I hope it will be done as near the ancient Government as can be. 'Tis a matter of the greateft weight, and deferves the greateft confideration. Confider of it a thoufand years, and you cannot caft your eyes upon a perfon fo well to fill it as the Prince and Princefs of *Orange.* To them we owe all our fafety ; moft of us, by this time, muft either have been flaves to the Papifts, or hanged. I hope, that, for the future, we fhall have fecurity and prefervation from them, and put them in a condition of faving us from our dangers for the future. As you did yefterday, fo I defire you will now call upon the Gentlemen of the Long Robe to put you in fome way practicable. I have read the ftory of *Philip* and *Mary* ; that was not a good reign, and fo not a good Precedent ; but I hope we fhall be all happy under King *William* and Queen *Mary.*

Lord *Falkland.*] It concerns us to take fuch care, that, as the Prince of *Orange* has fecured us from Popery, we may fecure ourfelves from Arbitrary Government. The Prince's Declaration is for a lafting foundation

30   *Debates in Parliament in* 1688.

tion of the Government. I would know what our foundation is. Before the Queftion be put, who fhall be fet upon the Throne, I would confider what powers we ought to give the Crown, to fatisfy them that fent us hither. We have had a Prince that did difpenfe with our Laws; and I hope we fhall never leave that doubtful. The King fet up an Ecclefiaftical Court, as he was Supreme Head of the Church, and acted againft Law, and made himfelf Head of the Charters. Therefore, before you fill the Throne, I would have you refolve, what Power you will give the King, and what not.

Mr *Garroway.*] We have had fuch Violation of our Liberties in the laft reigns, that the Prince of *Orange* cannot take it ill, if we make conditions, to fecure ourfelves for the future; and in it we fhall but do juftice to thofe who fent us hither, and not deliver them up without very good reafon.

Sir *William Williams.*] When we have confidered the prefervation of the Laws of *England* for the future, then it will be time to confider the perfons to fill the Throne. The Prince's Declaration has given us a fair platform. Some of your Laws have been very grievous to the people, though not Grievances; and perhaps thofe occafioned Arbitrary Government. Thofe are to be redreffed. Becaufe King *Charles* II. was called home by the Convention, and nothing fettled, you found the confequence. *Charles* II. was a young man, in the ftrength of his youth, and, you know, much Money was given him, and what became of it? The Act of the Militia is worthy your confideration, and he in whofe hands you will put it fhould be our Head. I take it to be your fecurity to fettle your fafety for the future, and then to confider the perfon. I now fpeak for all *England.* I would confider purging Corporations, and arbitrary Power given the late King by the Judges: Weak Judges will do weak things; their mafter commands them; they read no books, and know nothing to the contrary. I could give many more inftances.

Sir

Debates in Parliament in 1688.   31

Sir *Richard Temple*.] I hope you will not leave till you fee how we got out of our rights. Secure your liberties, and you cannot better recommend the Government to one to fucceed than by fettling thefe things. I will reduce my thoughts to three heads effentially neceffary : 1. Encroachment upon Parliament, (though in the hands where you will place the Government there may be no danger) to fecure pofterity; and you may have time to call perfons to account that break Parliaments, when they will not do what pleafed; to provide for their certainty and frequency, and that perfons obtain not Pardons when they have ruined the Nation ; and to provide for Elections of Parliaments, that Corporations may not be made tools to nominate whom they pleafe ; to provide againft a Standing Army without confent of Parliament, not in Peace, when there is no War nor Rebellion. An Army was no part of the Government till the late King's time. The Militia-Act was made ufe of to difarm all *England*. 2. Your care fhould be, that *Weftminfter-Hall* be better filled with Judges, and not, under pretence of the King's Prerogative, to give away all. That the Judges be " during life," and that they have Salaries inftead of Fees : That Sheriffs make not unjuft Returns of Juries, and that *Weftminfter-Hall* have as little power as you can. Formerly *Weftminfter-Hall* decided not great cafes, but left them to Parliament. The Judges now do not only *Lex dicere* but *facere*. In new and difficult cafes, this will be the way to preferve you from what they are bid to judge. 3. The Coronation-Oath to be taken upon entrance into the Government ; and, as we are fworn to our Kings, fo they to be fworn to protect us. Purfue the ends of the Prince's Declaration, with fome fuch fecurities as I have mentioned, that thefe things may be taken care of; to recommend to pofterity what you have done for them.

Mr *Bofcawen*.] We know, that the Prince's Declaration purfues all thofe ends mentioned. But Arbitrary Govern-

32   *Debates in Parliament in* 1688.

Government was not only by the late King that is gone, but by his Minifters, and farthered by extravagant Acts of the Long Parliament. The Act for regulating Corporations was upon a fpecious pretence to fecure the Crown, but had the end with the Commiffions for regulating Corporations. Though ever fo loyal, yet if they differed from the defigns of the Miniftry, they were put out. The Militia, under pretence of perfons difturbing the Government, difarmed and imprifoned men without any caufe : I myfelf was fo dealt with. There is a Claufe in the Militia-Act, for a week's tax after 70,000 *l.* for trophies, and not to exceed it ; but as it is now practifed, two or three years have been collected together, without regard to the Act. Arbitrary Power is ill in a Prince, but abominable to one another. The Triennial Bill for Parliaments was but a device, when we were going into flavery ; but by fuch an Act, if we have no redrefs of Grievances (as Mr *Vaughan*, of this Houfe, then faid, who was as much for the King as any) " better to have no Law at all." I move, that thefe things may be taken into confideration.

Refolved, That, before the Committee proceed to fill the Throne, now vacant, they will proceed to fecure our Religion, Laws, and Liberties.

Serjeant *Maynard.*] I agree to the Vote ; but I fear, if we look fo much one way on Arbitrary Government, we may fit five years, and never come to an end of what has been moved. One fays, " in the *Saxon* time, the people were much puzzled. One King made one Law, and another King another." Another drives at a new *Magna Charta.* The former Parliaments cared not which way they run, fo Penfions were paid— The management of the Militia was an abominable thing — Many fpeak, in Coffee-Houfes and better places, of fine things for you to do, that you may do nothing but fpend your health, and be in confufion—Take care of over-loading your horfe, not to undertake too many things. I would go only to things
obvious

Debates in Parliament in 1688. 33

obvious and apparent, and not into particulars too much. (*Not well heard.*)

Lord *Falkland.*] We muft not only change hands, but things; not only take care that we have a King and Prince over us, but for the future, that he may not govern ill. Some, perhaps, are diffatisfied with the Power, fome with the Army—'Tis for the people's fake we do all, that pofterity may never be in danger of Popery and Arbitrary Power.

Mr *Sacheverell.*] Since God hath put this opportunity into our hands, all the World will laugh at us, if we make a half fettlement. As the cafe ftands, no man can tell thatwhat he has is his own. Unlefs you look backward how men have been imprifoned, fined, feverely dealt with; the fame may happen to other Gentlemen. We muft look a great way backward. I cannot find three Laws, from twenty years upwards, that deferve to be continued. In the great joy of the King's Return, the Parliament overfhot themfelves fo much, and to redrefs a few Grievances they got fo much Money, that they could live without you; Penfions were agreed for fo much in the hundred for all they gave; Warrants of Commitments, Arms taken from perfons, &c. They were ill-affected to the Government, becaufe they endeavoured to chufe perfons they liked not. You may look back a great way; but fecure this Houfe, that Parliaments be duly chofen, and not kicked out at pleafure; which never could have been done, without fuch an extravagant Revenue that they might never ftand in need of Parliaments. Secure the Right of Elections, and the Legiflative Power.

Mr *Pollexfen.*] Firft make a Settlement of the Laws, that they may be afferted, and thofe muft all be confulted by Lords and Commons, and then fettle the Crown. Every man fees the nature of this propofition; if this be to confound you, 'tis a dreadful propofition: I am as much for Amendment of the Government as any man, and for repreffing the exorbitances of it; but the way you are in will not fettle the Government, but reftore King *James* again. If but a

34   *Debates in Parliament in* 1688.

noife of this goes beyond fea, that you are making
Laws to bind your Prince, it will tend to confufion.
The greateft enemy you have cannot advife better.
One Kingdom is gone already, and this is in confufion.
Some of the Clergy are for one thing, fome for another ; I think they fcarce know what they would have:
And the more we divide, the more it makes way for
the Popifh Intereft. Popery is the fear of the Nation,
and all that have voted againft Popery may fear Popery—But now we begin to forget it. Formerly it was
thought impoffible that Popery fhould come in, and
that the Tefts would keep it out—But how can we
bring to pafs all thefe Propofals, before he is King ?
We cannot ; and when he is King, perhaps he will
not pafs thefe into Laws—To ftand talking, and making Laws, and in the mean time have no Government at all ! They hope better things from our actions abroad, and a better foundation of the Proteftant Intereft. The Prince's Declaration is the caufe
of your coming hither, that the Kingdom may be eftablifhed, and the Laws and Government fecured from being fubverted again. If we ftand talking here, we fhall
do as ftrange things as thofe who prevailed by Arms
in the late times ; and, not coming to a Settlement,
it ended in their own deftruction, and never came into
any fettled Government ; fo the Authority of the King
fwept away all at laft. We lately had a Bill of
Exclufion ; it was talked of fo long, that both parties
fuffered, one formerly, the other fince. A Law you
cannot make till you have a King. The thing you go
upon is not practicable : One Gentleman is of opinion
" to take away all Laws fince this King came to the
Crown;" another *(Chriftie)* " to make a new *Magna Charta*." If you fit till all thefe Motions are confidered, we
may think to make our peace with King *James* as well
as we can, and go home.

Mr *Garroway*.] I would not draw this Debate out
at length ; fomewhat muft be done : A great many
things have been named by feveral perions to be re-
                                        dreffed.

Debates in Parliament in 1688. 35

dreffed. I hope we do not go about to fit here till all be done. All we can do for the prefent is, to reprefent to the Prince that thefe things may be done, and, under fome fhort Heads, to prefent the Prince with what you would have done to give fecurity to the Government ; and let an Oath be adminiftered to him ; and in a few days you may come to your end.

Mr *Seymour.*] We fhall fuffer by our doing more than by reafon of not doing at all. Will you think fit to leave the difpenfing power unqueftioned in *Weftminfter-Hall ?* Though the clock do not ftrike twelve at once, muft it not ftrike at all ? Will you do nothing, becaufe you cannot do all ? Will you let men go on in the fame practices they have formerly ? Will you eftablifh the Crown, and not fecure yourfelves ? What care I for what is done abroad, if we muft be flaves in *England,* in this or that man's power? If people are drunk and rude below, as was complained of, muft that ftop Proceedings in Parliament?

Sir *Thomas Lee.*] I find there is a difference in the Committee, how to word the Queftion. I know not how to propofe words to reach every man's fenfe. If you put it fo general, how our Liberties have been invaded, perhaps a few days will ftate it. There was an opinion, formerly, of the Long Robe that muft be exploded, " That the King may raife what Army he pleafes, if he pay them." That is the fupport of flavery, when there is other fupport to the King than the people's affections to their Prince.

Col. *Birch.*] I am as much afraid of lofing time as any body : Whereas diforders of the Army in *Ireland* are fpoken of, they will be ftill worfe, unlefs provifion be made to keep us from Slavery and Popery. I differ from what Gentlemen fay, as to the time it will take you up. I think it will not take you a day's time, when you have filled the Vacancy of the Throne. Prepare what you would have repealed, and prefent it. As to the Faft moved for, I know not what we fhould faft for—I will not call to-morrow * *Sunday,* for

* *January* 30.

36   *Debates in Parliament in* 1688.

I do not find it called fo in books: I would fit to-
morrow, and I hope to make an end to-morrow. There
is a Tax called Hearth-money ; take that away, and
the Prince will have ten times more fafety than in all
his Army ; and that may be in one line.

Mr *Hampden*, jun.] You are, by Order, to confider
the State of the Nation. Though you have voted,
that King *James* has abdicated the Crown, you have
not done all ; we are ftill free, and not tied by Oaths.
The time preffes hard, on many accounts ; and to rife
without doing more than filling the Throne that is vacant, is not for the fafety of the people. 'Tis neceffary to declare the Conftitution and Rule of the Government. In the late Convention, there was a Vote
paffed, " That the Government was in King, Lords,
and Commons." I move that the Journal may be in-
fpected. You have voted, " That King *James* has
violated the Conftitution of the Nation," call the chief
Governor what you will.

Mr *Harbord*.] You have an infallible fecurity for
the adminiftration of the Government : All the Revenue is in your own hands, which fell with the laft
King, and you may keep that back. Can he whom
you place on the Throne fupport the Government
without the Revenue ? Can he do good or harm without it ? 'Tis reafonable that you fhould be redreffed by
Laws ; but unlefs you preferve your Government, your
Papers cannot protect you. Without your fword, how
will you be fecured from the dangers from *Ireland*,
and the mutiny of the Army ? All may be loft, whilft
you are confidering.

Sir *Richard Temple*.] We here reprefent all the Nation. Place the Government in fome perfon, and then
provide for the reft.

Sir *Chriftopher Mufgrave*.] In juftification of your
Vote yefterday, to declare your Grievances, you are to
declare wherein King *James* the Second has broken the
Laws, and whom you have put by the Government.
You muft have wheels, before you can put the cart
                                                          upon

Debates in Parliament in 1688. 37

upon them. In the firft place, put the Queftion, " That you will proceed in afferting the Rights and Liberties of the Nation ; and that you will appoint a Committee to bring in general Heads of fuch things as are abfo- lutely neceffary for fecuring the Laws and Liberties of the Nation."

[A Committee was appointed accordingly.]

Wednefday, January 30.

[Dr *Sharp* * preached before the Houfe.]

Mr Speaker informed the Houfe, that Dr *Sharp* prayed for the King by the Title of " his moft excellent Majefty, &c."

Lord *Fanfhaw.*] The Clergy are fubject to another jurifdiction, and you cannot cenfure them here for what they do in the Church.

Serjeant *Maynard.*] Dr *Sharp* is one of the firft men that has made a breach upon your Vote. He has not done well: But I will not fpeak of your jurifdiction in this matter ; but let him not have the Thanks of the Houfe for his Sermon.

Sir *John Thompfon* †.] I would not fingle out Dr *Sharp,* when almoft all the Clergy do the fame thing.

The Speaker.] Becaufe he that preached this Ser- mon, contradicts your Vote, which caufed me to take notice of it : I take notice of it, to prevent fu- ture reflections. You vote one day, and 'tis contra- dicted in the Pulpit another. You will have a Sermon preached before you to-morrow by Dr *Burnet*; there is no danger of him ; but I took notice of this, to prevent others.

Mr *Howe.*] This prayer of Dr *Sharp*'s, to put a con- tradiction upon your Vote, will encourage the Priefts to knock our brains out. The Vote we made is con- trary to Paffive Obedience, and this man preaches it up. I move, that the Speaker may have the Thanks of the Houfe for informing us of it.

* Rector of *St Giles's,* and Dean of *Norwich,* one of the moft popular preachers of the age. *Burnet.* He was made Archbifhop of *York* in 1690. † Created Lord *Haverfham* in 1690.

38   *Debates in Parliament in* 1688.

Mr *Pelham.**]- I would not put a reflection upon this Gentleman; he has fuffered for the Proteftant Religion †; and your Vote not being printed nor publifhed, he could have no notice of it. I move, " that he may have the Thanks of the Houfe for his Sermon."

Sir *Chriftopher Mufgrave.*] No body ought to take notice of our Debates; and it has been complained of that your Votes have been made public. I wonder that this fhould be thought a crime in this Doctor. Is not there a Law, whereby they are enjoined to pray according to the Rubric? Shall your Vote difpenfe with an Act of Parliament?

The Speaker.] What I have informed you is not concerning the prayer in the Liturgy, but in his conceived prayer before Sermon.

Sir *Chriftopher Mufgrave.*] The Canon obliges it; and 'tis ftrange if by this you fhould enfnare many people. I think we have great obligation to this Gentleman; and you know that a Prelate was under fufpenfion himfelf for not fufpending him †. All true Proteftants have the greateft obligation in the world to encourage this Gentleman, and I defire that no difcouragement may be put upon him.

Sir *John Knight.*] *Reads the printed prayers for the day (which have reference to the Liturgy)* Shall we lay a charge upon the Doctor, when he is obliged by the printed prayers? I move, " that he may have the Thanks of the Houfe for his Sermon."

Sir *Edward Norris.*] I move, " that the Doctor may have Thanks for his Sermon againft Popery;" and let

---

* Eldeft fon of Sir *John Pelham*, whom he fucceeded in the title of Baronet, in 1702. After having been fucceffively a Commiffioner of Cuftoms, and a Lord of the Treafury, he was created Lord *Pelham*, by Queen *Anne*, in 1706, and died in 1711. He was father of the prefent Duke of *Newcaftle*.

† Dr *Sharp* having preached againft Popery, the Bifhop of *London* was required by the Court to fufpend him for it; which the Bifhop declining, as contrary both to Law and Juftice, he was fummoned himfelf before the Ecclefiaftical Court, and fufpended *ab officio* for his difobedience.

the

Debates in Parliament in 1688. 39

the prayers alone till there be farther directions about them.

Sir *William Williams.*] Now you are putting the previous Question, I shall not interrupt it.

Sir *John Lowther.*] 'Twill look oddly to give the Doctor Thanks, in contradiction of your Vote; and the Lords Concurrence you have not yet to it; and yet it cannot be taken notice of. I would not put the previous Question, because some Gentlemen may not know what it means. [*This gave distaste, and was by some hissed at. It fell.*]

[*January* 31, *Thanksgiving Day.* Dr *Burnet* preached before the House.]

Friday, February 1.

Mr *Hampden*, jun.] I hear Orders are contested. If you, Mr Speaker, mistake Orders, you are not the first in that Chair that has done so, nor will be the last. The Gentleman has began not upon mistake of argument, but is mistaken in fact, and you may rectify him; as in any fact as to Order, a man may be mistaken, and you may rectify him. Pray let us not dispute lesser things, but think of greater matters, and put this off our hands.

Sir *Joseph Tredenham.*] I would not have new Orders put upon us. I appeal, whether the Chair did ever judge matter of fact? If it be so, because we are told so, there's an end of all. A Member may be mistaken, but before you judge him, give him leave to justify himself.

The Speaker.] I think *Tredenham* totally mistaken. If a Gentleman runs into discourse unnecessarily, and not to the purpose, I am to rectify him.

Sir *Richard Temple.*] 'Tis not judging matter of fact; but when a man goes on with a mistake of the fact, you may rectify him. And so why should you spend time to rectify a discourse?

The Speaker.] I cannot judge a mistake, but I may rectify it.

Sir

40   *Debates in Parliament in* 1688.

Sir *Jonathan Jennings.*] I sat near the pulpit : The Reader prayed the whole prayers through, upon which I took particular notice of the pulpit. I hope I am rather miftaken than to fay you are. Under favour, without giving you contradiction, the Doctor prayed " for the King's Majefty, and all the Royal Family."

Thanks were voted to Dr *Sharp*, and Dr *Burnet*, and they were defired to print their Sermons.

Mr *Levefon Gower.*] I move, that you will give the Thanks of this Houfe to the Clergy ; that great body that oppofed Popery by their preaching and writing, and have been inftrumental in bringing us hither. I move, that you will thank them " for what they have done for defence of the Proteftant Religion in King *James* II's reign."

Mr *Finch.*] I move, to thank them for refufing to read the Declaration, in oppofition to the pretended Difpenfing Power.

Mr *Dolben.*] Likewife, I would have them thanked that oppofed the jurifdiction of the Ecclefiaftical Commiffion.

Col. *Birch.*] I would have the addition of one word, to make the thing true ; make it, " Such of the Church of *England* as refufed to read the Declaration."

Refolved, Nem. con. That the Thanks of this Houfe be given to the Clergy of the Church of *England*, who have preached and written againft Popery, and refufed to read, in their Churches, the late King's Declaration for Toleration, in oppofition to the pretended Difpenfing Power, claimed in the reign of the late King *James* the Second*, and have oppofed the late illegal Ecclefiaftical Commiffion.

Mr *Finch.*] If the word "late King" be neceffary in the Vote; I am not againft it ; but, whether is it material to the end of your Vote ? If it be immaterial, there is no reafon why you fhould ufe it.

Sir *John Thompfon.*] You have faid, that the Throne is vacant ; and will not now the thing moved, to

---

* In the Journal it is, " the late reign of King *James* the IId."

leave

Debates in Parliament in 1688. 41

leave out the word "late King," overthrow the consequence of your Vote, being infinitely material?

Sir *Robert Sawyer.*] I move, that your Vote may be
sent to the two Archbishops, to be communicated to
the Clergy.

[Which was ordered.]

Mr *Wharton.*] I am extremely pleased with your
Vote of Thanks to the Clergy, &c. who have behaved
themselves gallantly in opposition to Popery: This
leads me to a Motion for the Thanks of this House
to such of the Army who have behaved themselves so
bravely in opposition to Popery and Slavery. Com-
parifons are odious; but I think it more extraordinary
in men of their education. Churchmen are paid for
it, but the Army was for another purpose. This was
from God's hand; and I desire they may have the
Thanks of the House.

Mr *Palmes.*] I desire likewise, that the Officers of
the Fleet may have the Thanks of the House.

Mr *Wharton.*] I would not have the Thanks of the
House, as is moved, be given to the Army by the
Prince of *Orange.* Is he your servant? Let it be by
the General Officers of the Army.

Resolved, Nem. con. That the Thanks of this House be given
to the Officers, Soldiers, and Mariners, in the Army and
Fleet, for having testified their steady adherence to the Protestant Religion, and being instrumental in delivering this Kingdom from Popery and Slavery; and also to all such who have
appeared in arms for that purpose.

The Speaker.] *(Upon a Motion for gratifying the
Army, &c.)* I think this Motion is unseasonable, and
more proper for another time; it implying Money.

Mr *Garroway.*] I would go no farther in this Motion; for by retaliating upon the Papists here what they
do upon the Protestants in *Ireland,* you will make a
Massacre in *England*; several of the *Romish* Religion
have joined with the Protestants in *Ireland* for sup-
pressing *France,* &c. I would have *Jennings,* who made
the Motion, carry it to the Prince of *Orange* to consider

42   *Debates in Parliament in* 1688.

fider of it; but I would leave nothing upon your books
of it. *(The Gentleman moved only upon hearfay.)*

The Lords fent down the Vote, &c. and agreed to it all, except " the Vacancy of the Throne."

Saturday, February 2.

Sir *George Treby* reports the Heads of the Articles of Government; *(which fee in the Journal.)*

Serjeant *Maynard*.] Informations in the *King's-
Bench* are of feveral forts; I would not have the Queftion upon them general*, but fay what Informations
are a Grievance, and what not; elfe I know not whither they may go. Suggeftions are Informations, for
the benefit of the Court; therefore confider what.

Sir *George Treby*.] I may make a long difcourfe of
Informations in the *King's-Bench*, not long practifed,
nor much to be commended. This is grown to a
mighty vexation (unlefs in popular actions in *Middle-
fex*.) If a man does not appear, he is outlawed. Sometimes, for a foul fact, the Court orders an Information.
But, though fome Informations be thought mifchievous,
yet the Committee rather chofe to leave it to the pen-
ning of a Law to provide an Act, than to make a Report in particular.

Mr *Pollexfen*.] Thefe are but Heads, and no Law.
The taking away Informations in the *King's-Bench*
may be very mifchievous. .If you take them away in general, there may be a thoufand cafes wherein there can
be no remedy. The matter is only for a defence from
oppreffions of Informations in the *King's-Bench*.

Mr *Hampden*.] All Informations in the *King's-Bench*
are taken away for the prefent, for want of a Great
Seal. But taking away the abufes of them is the intent. I hope you intend not to take all away, but intend this memorandum as a claim, and the abufes to
be redreffed.

* *Article* 22. " Informations in the Court of *King's Bench* to be taken
away."

Sir

Debates in Parliament in 1688. 43

Sir *George Treby.*] If Informations be indifferently taken away, though the title be general, you may make reftrictions. This is not confined to the Court of *King's-Bench*, but in the Exchequer there are vexatious Informations that may be taken away.

Mr *Finch.*] I would have it run thus: " Abufes in Law by Informations to be remedied."

Mr *Garroway.*] Several words have been offered, as " Abufes, Vexations, &c." but who fhall judge it? Put it, to have a mark of infamy upon it in general, and then you may qualify it in a Bill.

Col. *Birch.*] If this takes fo much time here, what will it do in the Houfe of Lords? Therefore pen it clearly.

Mr *Sacheverell.*] Informations are not ufeful at all, where the matter may be tried by Indictment, by a Jury, and the party may know the matter he is accufed of. This is in the nature of a declaratory Petition of Right, and muft go to the Lords; but thefe Propofals do not. 'Tis a ftrange tendernefs of fome Gentlemen, when things are laid down as Heads only, and I wonder this fhould have fuch countenance here.

Mr *Hampden.*] Retarding of Juftice, exacting exorbitant Fees upon Informations, &c. and a word called " Difpatch," comes to more than the Fees themfelves.

Serjeant *Biggland.*] I would have notice taken of buying and felling judicial Offices, to keep honeft men out, and put others in; and the Sheriff's Office to be confidered, which influences the whole Government. Bailiffs and Sheriffs muft gain, when they buy their places; and if no care be taken of buying Offices, you will never have good Adminiftration of Juftice.

Mr *Sacheverell.*] I would have the Law againft buying and felling Offices made more effectual, by another Law; and I defire it may be general to all Offices.

Sir *George Treby.*] Some Provifos, in the Statute of *Edward* VI. againft it, are ineffectual. I move, that buying and felling Offices may be effectually provided againft.

Mr

44   *Debates in Parliament in* 1688.

The Speaker.] Some Offices are as lawful to sell as a man's private inheritance. When you come to draw the Bill, you may provide as you please.

Serjeant *Maynard*.] I would have the Act of *Habeas Corpus* considered. If a Jailor be false, the prisoner may lie for ever by commitment of the Council-board.

Sir *William Williams*.] I have known Returns as false as possible. When a man is innocent, there must he lie, be the accusation ever so false. I move, that the person may take issue upon it, that the Return is not true, and that the person may traverse the legality of the Return.

Mr *Paul Foley*.] Not only upon *Habeas Corpuses*, but upon *Mandamuses*, and the same liberty to traverse as upon a *Habeas Corpus*.

Mr *Hampden*.] Nothing has been more practised, nor more have suffered under, than when upon an Indictment the Fine is begged. He that begs it turns Prosecutor presently; this makes way for a great deal of mischief. A great man of the Law would never sign any such Grant, as a most mischievous thing. Ordinarily, on a bare accusation, the Fine would be begged. I would have it declared, that, before conviction, there shall be no begging of the Fines.

Mr *Boscawen*.] This is grown a general practice; when the Fine is begged, it encourages perjury, and instructing of witnesses. I would not only have it declared against Law, but some new penalty, that whoever begs such a Grant be fined.

Sir *William Williams*.] I would go farther; that all Grants of Fines for Misdemeanor shall be void.

The Speaker.] Many of these things are against Law, but in these Heads you only renew your Claim.

Resolved, That begging of Fines, &c. is illegal and void, &c. and such as beg them shall be punished; and that the abuse of collecting the Hearth-Money be redressed.

The Speaker communicated to the House, " That he had received a Letter from Lord *Preston*, and desired to know what he should do with it. It was directed " To the Speaker of the
Honourable

Debates in Parliament in 1688. 45

Honourable Houſe of Commons, aſſembled in Parliament at *Weſtminſter*."

Sir *Henry Capel.*] I would have the Letter laid aſide.

Sir *Thomas Lee.*] This Letter, coming thus to you, gives you a good occaſion to go on with your other proceedings. You know the perſon from whom you received it, and you may lay it aſide.

[The Letter was from King *James*, incloſed in Lord *Preſton*'s Letter.]

Mr *Rowe.*] I have a Petition from great numbers of perſons, for crowning the Prince and Princeſs of *Orange* King and Queen. I deſire that it may be read.

Serjeant *Maynard.*] Here's a Petition proffered you from you know not whom, nor for what; if you read it, the Parliament is without doors, and not here.

Sir *Edward Seymour.**] This Petition is of an extra-ordinary nature: You are now on as great a Debate as ever Parliament was. *(It was upon the word " Abdi-cate, &c. and the Throne thereby become vacant;" which the Lords left out of the Vote from the Commons.)* The Lords were threatened yeſterday by the Mob, and they are not yet diſperſed. They are for a King—but make uſe of miſerable people. If your Debates are not free, there is an end of all your proceedings. You are to ſit ſure here, elſe there is no other way than to go home into the country. What comes from you is the reſult of reaſon, and no other cauſe. As your Debates muſt be free, ſo muſt your Reſolutions upon them; which cannot be, unleſs ſome care be taken to preſerve you from the Mob.

* Formerly Speaker, &c. His father dying in 1688, he ſucceeded to his title. In the preceding reign, though he had zealouſly oppoſed *Monmouth*, and his adherents, yet he was no leſs warm in oppoſing Arbitrary Power, and was one of the firſt Gentlemen in the Weſt of *England* that went over to the Prince of *Orange*. In 1691 he was appointed a Lord of the Treaſury, and was Comptroller of the Houſhold to Queen *Anne*. He died in 1707, and was great grand-father to the preſent Duke of *Somerſet*, and grandfather to the preſent Earl of *Hertford*.

Lord

46　　　　*Debates in Parliament in* 1688.

Lord *Fanſhaw.*] You have had a Letter from Lord *Preſton:* I would ſend to him to know the contents of it.

The thing paſſed off without farther Debate.

On the Lords Amendment to the Commons Vote, *viz.* inſtead of " abdicated," " deſerted ;" and leaving out " the Throne thereby become vacant."

Sir *Richard Temple.*] You have conſidered the word " abdicated " as the only proper word. As for " deſerted," I appeal whether 'tis a proper concluſion to the premiſes. The Lords have left out the whole concluſion in the matter. They have agreed " that King *James* has ſubverted the Conſtitution of the Government, has violated the original contract, and has withdrawn himſelf, *&c.*" Conſider whether this be a proper concluſion. By doing theſe acts, he has moſt plainly " abdicated the Government;" by the premiſes plainly, by ſubverting the Conſtitution, he will govern by an Arbitrary Power, though ſworn to rule according to original contract. The hour he does it, 'tis a renunciation of the Government. *Hottoman*, and all approved authors, call this " Abdicating the Government." *Henry* VI. upon fear of the Earl of *Warwick*, went out of the Kingdom, and left it ; and that, by all the Judges, was judged " a Demiſe." I deſire you will not agree with the Lords.

Mr *Hampden.*] The diſpute with the Lords is about a word changed. 'Tis your word now, the word of the Houſe, and I was ever of opinion the moſt proper word. " Forſaken, forfeited," and other words, were mentioned here ; but, I think, " abdicating " was in requeſt among the *Romans.* When a parent " abdicated " his child, he gave him no maintenance : Though the child never forſook the father, yet if he deſerved it, he was " abdicated." If you ſay ſuch things have been done as violating the original Contract, *&c.* is not " Self-Abdication" more than Deſertion ? If it comes to be diſputed, you will then ſee the value of
the

Debates in Parliament in 1688. 47

the word. Should you fay, King *James* has deferted, is gone from *Rochefter*, and may come again, for doing a thing, juftly to be abdicated, the Queftion is, whether you will retain or change your word; agree or not agree with the Lords.

Sir *Thomas Clarges.*] This is a great bufinefs before you; all tends to the fettlement of the Nation. Union is fo neceffary at this time, that I hope we fhall agree with the Lords in the Amendments. "Defertion" feems more proper than "Abdication," which is not fo needful nor proper. As for precedents, it muft be voluntary. That of *Charles* V. and the Queen of *Sweden*, tant-amount to that of *Alphonfo* King of *Portugal*; his Government was deftructive to his people. *Edward* II. committed all manner of irregularities and oppreffions, by the advice of wicked counfellors, to fubvert all the Laws of the Nation. In *Riley*'s Collections of Records, the Parliament at *Briftol*, upon report that the King had forfaken the Kingdom, (*deceffit regno*, as the words of the Record are, had left the Kingdom,) by unanimous confent, elected the Duke of *Aquitain Cuftos regni*. Therefore I move to agree with the Lords in the word "Defertion."

Mr *Finch.*] I would agree with the Lords, &c. for thofe very reafons offered againft it. The departure of *Edward* IV. out of the Kingdom was judged "a Demife;" (*and fo repeats the Vote.*) If you fay King *James* deferted the Kingdom, the Queftion is ftill entire; whether he did "abdicate" or "defert," is not material. There is good reafon why you fhould agree with the Lords; and I take "defert" to be the more proper word: I am fure 'tis moft proper to agree with the Lords. But whether "deferted" or "abdicated," I would not differ with the Lords; for the confequence is entire to you, and you may agree.

Sir *Richard Temple.*] I am mif-recited, and therefore defire to be rectified. I did not fay "that King *James* deferted the Kingdom," but "the Government." His

renun-

48   *Debates in Parliament in* 1688.

renunciation is by fomething done by fact, not by folemn inftrument.

Lord *Falkland.*] If this Vote be grounded merely
upon the King's leaving the Kingdom, he may come
again, and refume the Government. But " Abdication" relates to breaking your Laws ; and though the
Lords ftand by the Premifes, yet they defert the Conclufion, in leaving out " the Throne vacant." I would
therefore not agree with the Lords.

Mr *Dolben.*] The Precedent I cited the other day,
and inferred my opinion upon was, that *Ed.* IV's w th-
drawing himfelf from the Kingdom and the Government, was a Demife, and it was fo judged by the opinion
of all the Judges ; and from all confiderations together,
you pronounced it an " Abdication" in King *James.*
But barely " a Demife," and "a withdrawing," without the confideration of all the breaches he had made
in the Government, the Houfe did not call it, but the
word " Abdication." I would agree with the Lords
if I could agree with ourfelves, and our own fenfes,
firft. The Lords have fo far concurred with your
Vote, " That King *James* has broken the original Contract betwixt the King and People." The Premifes
muft agree with the Conclufion ; ours is the more proper inference, and we muft ftand by it.

Sir *Robert Sawyer.*] Authors that write of " Abdication" fay, " to defert " is " to abdicate." All that
the Lords mean by " Abdication," you mean by
" Defertion."

Sir *Robert Howard.*] " Defertion" is a *Latin* word,
and " Abdication " is another. If there be no more
intended by the Lords than the word, then the King
has only deferted the Government, and the Throne is
not vacant ; and the King may have the help of a Regency. They are both *Latin* words alike, and both
Englifh : " Abdication" arifes from " vacated." If it
be not fo, the Lords have made room for their laft A-
mendment, " That the Throne is not vacated."

Mr

Debates in Parliament in 1688.   49

Mr *Tipping.*] The Lords are of opinion that the Throne is full, but they tell you not who is in the Throne. I am sorry to hear of a great number that would bring the King back again ; how pernicious that would be to all good Proteſtants, you may eaſily judge. I am ſure 'twill be of ill conſequence to join the Prince of *Orange* with him in the Throne, But I believe the true reaſon of this diſagreeing with your Vote is the delay that the Houſe has made, that they proceeded not to fill the Vacancy of the Throne. If you had proceeded ſpeedily to fill the Throne, poſſibly you would have had another Anſwer. Put the Queſtion of diſagreeing with the Lords, and then declare, " that you will ſupply the Vacancy of the Throne."

Sir *Thomas Littleton.*] The Lords cannot expect that we, who have ſaid the Throne is vacant, ſhould not intend to fill it up : The beſt way is, to go on and fill it up, and put all out of doubt.

The Queſtion being put, That the Houſe do agree with the Lords in theſe two Amendments, it paſſed ſeveraliy in the Negative, *Nem. con.*

Sir *Richard Temple.*] No doubt but you can maintain your Reaſons for your Vote, at a Conference. If the Throne be full, what do we here ? I move you to prepare Reaſons, *&c.* for the Lords at a Conference.

A Committee was appointed accordingly.

Monday, *February* 4.

Mr *Hampden* reported the following Reaſons, from the Committee, why the Commons cannot agree with the Lords Amendments of their Vote of the 28th of *January.*

" 1ſt, Becauſe the word " deſerted" does not expreſs their meaning ſo fully, it importing no more than a " removing," which is expreſſed by the word " withdrawing" in the ſentence before ; therefore they conceive the word " abdicated " a more proper word, importing " a renouncing of the Crown, *&c.*"

" 2dly, They think they need not alter the word " vacant," becauſe their Lordſhips addreſſed the Prince of *Orange* to take upon him the adminiſtration of affairs, and to ſend Circular

50 *Debates in Parliament in* 1688.

Letters for this Convention to meet ; and their Lordships appointing a day of Thanksgiving, and concurring that a Popish Prince
is incapable to govern, &c. justifies the Commons herein."

" 3*dly,* Because there is no person on the Throne, from
whom the subject can have regal protection, therefore they
owe no Allegiance to any ; and consequently the Throne is
vacant *."

[Debate.]

Sir *Joseph Tredenham.*] I agree " that the Throne
is vacant," but I cannot agree it to be " entirely vacant ;" we have no such thing in our Government as
an *interregnum,* and so no entire Vacancy.

Sir *Thomas Lee.*] I appeal to the Chair. Consider
the Orders of the House ; now that the House has resolved that the Throne is vacant, no man can speak
against the foundation of your Vote.

Sir *Joseph Tredenham.*] Since the Speaker says, 'tis
Order, I must acquiesce.

Sir *Robert Howard.*] I hear that the Viceroy of the
Corporations, Mr *Brent,* is bailed ; and, upon his bailing, is fled. Upon this, the Sollicitor General (*Burton*†)
is fled, after he had brought in a bill of 1700 *l.* for
murdering of *Cornish* at his Tryal ‡. I move you to
send for Sir *James Smith,* who bailed *Brent,* to give
you an account of it.

Sir *William Cowper.*] I have heard of 3000 *l.* bail
given in the *King's-Bench* : 'Twas my own case, for
no offence but only for being for the Bill of Exclusion
in this House.

Sir *George Treby.*] Sir *James Smith* is an Alderman
of *London,* and, I believe, will give you some account
of himself. If you please to signify your pleasure, I
shall give him notice.

Ordered, That Sir *James Smith* be sent for.

* These Reasons are differently worded from those printed in the journal.

† *Burton* was a fitter man to have served in a Court of Inquisition, than in a legal Government. *Burnet.*

‡ *Cornish,* who had been Sheriff of *London,* in King *Charles* the IId's reign, was seized on, tried, and executed, in a week, in 1685, on a false accusation of being guilty of that for which Lord *Russel* had suffered. *Burnet.*

Col.

Debates in Parliament in 1688. 51

Col. *Birch.*] If any Gentleman had fpoken my fenfe, I would not have troubled him. On *Saturday* you a- greed on Articles to be fent to the King, &c. things of vaſt confequence; and, if made public, they are like to have another manner of effect. We have been fcrambling a long time. for our Religion and Proper- ties; and fhall thefe things lie there, and no more? Put fome Title to them, and fend them to the Lords im- mediately.

Major *Wildman.*] Confider not to make a feparation of your Votes, before you fend them to the Lords. Diftinguifh thefe as new Laws, and thofe as ancient. Things of Right and of Grace will have no effect, without diftinction. In the Petition of Right, the Commons refufed to have new Laws, but claimed what they demanded *ab origine.* Therefore I move that they may be feparated.

Mr *Hampden.*] The Lords ufed to take Notes at a Conference; of late years they have defired your Pa- per; but our Paper was privately delivered to the Clerk, not to the Lords; and the Houfe approved it. I defire your direction, whether I fhall deliver the Pa- per to the Lords, but not to be entered upon your Book as Order.

Sir *Thomas Lee.*] I move you to put fome Title to the Heads you agreed the other day, to be of fome ufe to you. You are moved to draw them into the form of the Petition of Right. Some of the Heads are not to be remedied, but by new Laws; and you cannot fend them to the Lords till put into a new method; but as for thofe things wherein the ancient Rights are infringed, thofe require no new Laws. New claims of Laws already made, they'll not have the credit till taken up by both Houfes. Things laid afleep, or ill exercifed by the late Government, we lay claim to.

Sir *Henry Capel.*] I defire to revive that Motion. We have been branded often with Alteration of the Government. 'Tis our right to aſſert our Freedom. 'Tis likely, whoever you fhall inthrone will thank you

E 2   for

52   *Debates in Parliament in* 1688.

for giving light into the miscarriages, of the last Government.   And we only assert our Rights and Liberties, pursuant to the Prince's Declaration.

Sir *Richard Temple.*] Those things will go with your
Instrument of Government.   The Throne must be
actually filled before you deliver that Petition ; and you
are well moved to make a separation in the Heads.

It was ordered accordingly.

Tuesday, February 5.
Sir *James Smith* at the Bar.

The Speaker.] The House is informed, that you have
bailed Mr *Brent*, a Papist, and a busy one.   They
would know on what terms you bailed him.

Sir *James Smith.*] I bailed him, because there was not any
Information against him, but that he was a Papist.   He pressed
hard upon me to bail him, which I could not refuse.   He was
taken in a private lodging, near *Old Fish-street*, concealed.   I
committed him as a *Roman Catholic :* I kept him in my house
till Sir *William Waller* had acquainted the Prince of *Orange* that
he was taken.   He brought me word, that the Prince would
not meddle in it : Then I committed him to the *Compter*, till
Sir *William Waller* had brought a Charge against him, which
he brought not ; and then I thought I might bail him.   I consulted the Recorder, and acquainted him with what I had done,
and he advised me to bail him.   There was no body joined
with me in bailing him, having nothing farther against him,
till Sir *William Waller* charged him with endeavouring to alter
the Government.   It was a general Charge, and Sir *William*
undertook Witnesses to prove it.   I bailed him in 1000 *l.* and
500 *l.* the sureties 250 *l.* a-piece, to appear at the next
Sessions of the Peace.   I have sent to his bail for his appear-
ance, and they doubt not but he will appear.

Sir *John Hanmer.*] I am informed that there is such
matter expressed in the Commitment, that he could not
bail him.

Sir *John Guise.*] There is one *Rogers*, who is called
the Post-Boy * of *Magdalen* College, was brought before Sir *George Treby*, and he let him go without bail.

* Rather *Post-master*—A scholar of the house so called.
Ordered,

Debates in Parliament in 1688. 53

Ordered, That Sir *James Smith* do attend this Houfe again to-morrow, with a copy of the Warrant of Commitment of Mr *Brent*, and a copy of the bail, &c. and that the Keeper of the *Compter* do alfo attend with the original Warrant of Commitment.

Mr *Hampden* reports the Conference.

Earl of *Nottingham, who managed.*] The Lords have defired this Conference with the Houfe of Commons, to declare they defire to be united to the Commons in affection, and to be as infeparable in opinion as they are in intereft. The Houfe of Commons are a wife body, &c. and I hope they will agree with the Lords in this great conjuncture of affairs.

Mr *Hampden.*] I hope I fhall be excufed, if I report it not to Lord *Nottingham*'s advantage. " The Lords agree not to the word " abdicated ;" they do not find it to be a word in our known Law of *England*; therefore they would ufe fuch words as are underftood according to the Law, to avoid doubtful interpretation ; the word " abdicate" being a Civil Law word, inftead of " violated," " deferted, " &c. which does exprefs the confequence of withdrawing. To the fecond Amendment, " and that the Throne is thereby vacant ;" though the Lords have declared that the King has deferted the Government, yet with no other inference, than that the exercife of Government ceafed ; and the Lords would fecure the Nation againft King *James*'s return, and no fuch Abdication ; though King *James* II. ceafed to be King, yet there could be no Vacancy in the Throne, the Monarchy being hereditary, and not elective. No act of the King can deftroy the fucceffion of his Heirs, and fuch perfons to whom of right the fucceffion of the Crown belongs*."

* In this Conference, according to the fenfe of the whole Nation, the Commons had clearly the advantage on their fide. The Lords had fome more colour for oppofing the word " abdicate," fince that was often taken in a fenfe that imported the full purpofe and confent of him that abdicated ; which could not be pretended in this cafe. But there were good authorities brought, by which it appeared, that when a perfon did a thing upon which his leaving any office ought to follow, he was faid to " abdicate." But this was a critical difpute ; and it fcarce became the greatnefs of that Affembly, or the importance of the matter. *Burnet.*

E 3   Sir

54   *Debates in Parliament in* 1688.

Sir *Thomas Clarges.*] Thefe Reafons of the Lords feem to me to be fo cogent, that they deferve to be ferioufly weighed. I take the Crown to be heredita-ry, and that King *James* has "abdicated" the Crown, and the pretended Prince of *Wales* being in the power of the *French* King, and the Throne vacant, the Crown ought to proceed to the next Proteftant fucceffor.

Serjeant *Maynard.*] Enter the Paper, and then you may difpute the matter farther. In the mean time, 'tis a fad thing, that the whole welfare of the Nation muft depend upon a word of a grammatical con-ftruction.

Mr *Harbord.*] The *Dutch* have fent their beft troops to our affiftance; and the King of *France* is to rendez-vouz his Army the 10th of *March*, and we are under unfortunate delays here of fettling the Government. I can expect no other, when a fort of men are amongft us, that have been guilty of blood and our misfor-tunes, &c.

Sir *Thomas Clarges.*] I concur with *Harbord*, to give things fair expedition. I hope we are not in fo great danger, the Government being fettled in the Prince of *Orange*, and he being trufted with the Treafure of the Nation. I hope to-day we fhall make fome Settlement, and nothing can be of greater ufe than unity, elfe all will crumble to nothing. The eyes of the whole King-dom are upon us; and fince the Clerk is poffeffed of the Lords Reafons for not concurring in your Vote, I would read them, &c. I hope we fhall come to a happy conclufion.

On the firft Amendment, "deferted" for "abdicated," &c.

Mr *Ettrick.*] Though King *James* has "deferted" the Government, and the Prince of *Orange* has taken the Adminiftration of the Government for the prefent, yet it can have no other inference, than that the exer-cife of the Government is ceafed; and no act of King *James* can deftroy the fucceffion of his Heirs. If
the

Debates in Parliament in 1688.   55

the Throne be vacant, the Allegiance is due of right where the fucceffion belongs.

Sir *Thomas Clarges.*] I agree with the Lords Amendment. I take the Crown to be hereditary, and not electiye, as appears in all our Law-books. By this Vacancy, I underftand only that the King has abdicated from himfelf, and divefted himfelf of the right of Government, and that the Government comes to the next Proteftant Heir in fucceffion; (I explain myfelf) to the Princefs of *Orange*—I will fpeak freely. If the Throne be vacant, ftrictly taken, the Kingdom is elective, and we depart from the fucceffion. The King has not only divefted himfelf of the Government, by breaking the original Contract, and by his exceffes in the Government, but has taken away the child, if it be his, into another Kingdom: And if the Crown be defcended to him, there may be great advantages to the *French* King, who may act for him in *Scotland.* We are not debating for ourfelves, but for all the King's dominions. I am glad the Lords have explained our Vote, and I would proceed with all fpeed to a fettlement of the Kingdom. We are not now making fucceffors, though a Parliament has power to do it; which we have not, being but a Convention.

Sir *Jofeph Tredenham.*] "That the Throne is vacated," is no longer the Queftion, but "whether a fucceffion of the Crown, or that the Crown is elective," was the Queftion offered yefterday; and any body then might have offered objections to your Reafons: But the natural Queftion now is, whether agree, or not agree with the Lords? The Crown was always fucceffive, never elective. There have been feveral Demifes of the Crown, as in *Edw.* II. and *Rich.* II. yet always the next Heir to the Crown has fucceeded. —I will not fay any thing of the mifcarriages of the King, but we have a proper cure for them. I thank God, we have a Proteftant Heir to the Crown. Of the Prince of *Wales* I fhall fay the lefs, becaufe much has been faid by *Clarges*; and 'tis the opinion of the Houfe,

E 4   that

56   *Debates in Parliament in* 1688.

that there is a legal incapacity, as well as a natural. In the Princess of *Orange* there is no incapacity; she is a Protestant; and as for her being a woman, Queen *Elizabeth* was so, and reigned gloriously. I would be grateful to the Prince of *Orange*, for the great things he has done for the Nation; but is this the way, to erect a Throne to the ruin of his Princess? To abdicate his Title, and make a perpetual difference betwixt them, will be no compliment to him. His matrimonial right was the argument that brought him over; and therefore, whilst we compliment him, I would not put a disreputation upon what he has so generously done, to put the Crown singly upon this noble Prince's head! No man can be grateful that is not just. This Prince is too generous not to be just. *Scotland* must have a share of this Election; and as long as we stand firm to the Succession, there is no reason to doubt but *Scotland* will close with us. But we have much reason to doubt their concurrence, when our own Constitutions do not justify what we do. If the head be dead, what is the body? If not dead, a monster. " Making a breach upon the fundamental Laws, by being seduced by the *Jesuits, &c.*" If the Government be subverted, the whole mob may have some more right than we—When there is such a fermentation in the Nation, our proceedings should not countenance such a disorderly proceeding. *Alphonso*, King of *Portugal*, was deposed for Lunacy, *&c.* and his brother succeeded him in the Throne. But when you eradicate the Succession, all the Crowns in *Christendom* will concern themselves. It will make such an earthquake, that all the Protestants in the World will fare the worse for it. The Prince will lose all the glory his generous conduct has obtained. There is no other way to have peace and quiet, but by recognizing the Princess, who has no legal nor natural impediment.

Serjeant *Maynard*.] This Gentleman has spoken very well, but not to the point in question. This may be well prepared, against that comes to be the Question
of

Debates in Parliament in 1688. 57

of filling the Throne, being vacant. Here is a great
miftake on all fides—Who can think the Crown is
elective, when eight or nine hundred years ago, the
Crown was feized to the King, his Heirs, and Suc-
ceffors ?—" That the King has abdicated the Crown "
is paffed, (the Lords have agreed it.) The Queftion
is now, " Whether the Throne be vacant ?" And the
Queftion, Whether vacant to King *James* cannot be,
Whether vacant to perpetuity. " Vacant" is as if he
now was dead, but not perpetually vacant. Will you
have the former King come again ? Then he muft do
as he did—Therefore there was a neceffity to fupply
the Government for the time. When you come to
fpeak to the point, how can the Crown defcend when
the father is living ? The Lords are clearly miftaken
in our Vote : We mean not that the Monarchy is elective—But thus far we muft fill up the Throne, or have
no Government. If the Throne be not fallen vacant,
in the prefent tenfe, utterly now, how will you fill it
up ? But how muft be the next Queftion. 'Tis not
filled, therefore vacant.

Sir *Robert Sawyer.*] Though the Throne be vacant,
yet that the fucceffion is not void, the Lords have
given fuch forcible Reafons, that we muft fight againft
Law and Confcience, if they be laid afide. The Lords
think the word " abdicate" to be otherwife underftood.
Confider the legal effect of the Throne vacant. Upon
the furrender of the Crown by *Richard* II, *Henry* IV
was declared King—*(and reads the words of the Record.)*
The Throne was vacant by his furrender, and *Henry* IV
claimed the Crown as his inheritance, and the Lords
and Commons afferted his Title, and confented that
he fhould reign. Suppofe the King had entered into
a Monaftery, this is a civil death ; when he re-
nounces the civil adminiftration of the Government,
there is a civil death, as well as a natural ; though
living, yet in effect dead : The vacant poffeffion filled
with a fucceffor, who claimed not by conqueft but defcent. You muft explain yourfelves in your Vote,
whether

58   *Debates in Parliament in* 1688.

whether the Throne be vacant as to a perfon, or the whole fucceffion gone ; and that lets you into an Election. This the Lords think. We fight but with words. If we mean no more by " the Throne being vacant," than that the laft King has renounced the Government ; if we mean that the Succeffion is good, the Lords Reafons cannot be oppofed. No man can queftion, that the Kingdom of *England* is fucceffive. Soon after the Conqueft, the Kingdom was unfteady : There was a potent faction in the Church at that time ; but, in all times in Hiftory, you found the Succeffion did prevail. In *Henry* VII's time, and *Henry* VIII's, the Right of the Crown was declared hereditary. Can the King alter that Right ? Can either, or both the Houfes, without the King, alter the fundamental Conftitution of the Kingdom ? It will be a great injury to the fucceffor to give away the Crown from her ; you'll fully all the Prince of *Orange*'s glory. He came not hither to break through all your Conftitutions ; he deferves all you can poffibly do for him, but to give him what we cannot do—! A Title he muft defend as well as he can : And for all he has done to give him nothing ! If by " the Throne being vacant " you mean that the Succeffion is out of doors, I defire you would exprefs your meaning plainly.

Serjeant *Maynard*.] In Queen *Elizabeth*'s time, an Act paffed, " That it was a crime to maintain, that the Parliament could not difpofe of the Crown," in the Queen of *Scots* cafe. In *Edward* II's laft Parliament, (when the *Spencers* governed) the Lords fent to him to know " whether he would renounce the Crown ? If he would not, he fhall take it to whom the lot fhall be." *(The reft the Compiler could not hear.)*

Col. *Birch*.] Some are not of education anfwerable to fpeak amongft thefe learned Gentlemen. I muft confefs I am one of thofe ; yet I fhall fpeak according to the reafon I have. I am glad Gentlemen have fpoken fo plainly of the fucceffion of this noble Lady, and to have it there fettled, though the confequence is endlefs ;

Debates in Parliament in 1688. 59

lefs; it firft puts us by all our hopes, what God has put into our hands will be taken away all at once. Say Gentlemen, " This is a facred Succeffion, and muft not be altered." I heard a Queftion the other day, whether the Government was not *jure divino*, and that was over-ruled; and if you have not more room than you had, nothing can over-rule you. But I hold, that, *jure divino*, the Lords and Commons cannot do an un-juft thing. We have taken from one brother to give to another, and it has not been queftioned to this hour. The Lords have not agreed the Throne to be vacant; and, if fo, where is the Government? Had you fpoken plain *Englifh* t'other day, that the difpofal of the Crown was in the Lords and Commons, there had been no room for this Debate; and you, by that authority, had inftances in all times (and 'tis *Præmunire* to hold the contrary) and then you might have talked of the Suc-ceffion. I will never move you to an unjuft or irra-tional thing : You are bringing upon you that which is fled; and there's a Prince of *Wales* talked of; and if he be not fo, you will never want a Prince of *Wales.* God has brought us from Popery and Tyranny; and, at this rate, nothing will content us but to go into it again. You have Heirs in *Spain*, in *Savoy*, and all up and down, and where more I know not; and poor *England*, for want of fpeaking one plain word, will be ruined, you and your pofterity. Say but where your power is, and the Debate is at an end. There may be claims to the Crown, but their claims will fignify no-thing; for the Lords and Commons have other thoughts. " O! but you take away Heirs and Suc-ceffors!" I never knew that a man yet living had Heirs. I have none, and am living. If this be thus, what can you fay? You ftop all claims to the Crown; for 'tis vacant, and fallen to the Lords and Commons, and no Title can fall to any body. By the Statute of Queen *Elizabeth*, and Acts of Parliament in all times, it lies here. And take it into your hands, where God, in his Providence, has given it you. I will conclude, that

that the power of difpofing of the Crown is in the
Lords and Commons; and by virtue of that power
fill the Vacancy, And I would not agree with the
Lords in leaving out "The Throne is vacant."

Mr *Finch*.] The words of your Vote muft be, "agree
or not agree with the Lords, that the Throne is vacant." The precedent words, "That King *James* has
abdicated, *&c.*" whether you will agree to the Lords
Conclufion, adhere or not. Whatever is faid, whether
the Kingdom be elective or not, if you adhere to this
Conclufion, you conclude that the Government is an
elective Monarchy. One of our Reafons to induce
the Lords to concur to our Vote is, that they have already affirmed as much; and whether the Throne be
"abdicated" or "deferted," in both thefe cafes the
Throne is vacant. By "abdicated," we intend no o-
ther conftruction but that the Throne is vacant. By
breaking the original Contract with the People, he has
made the Throne void as to himfelf. Either you mean
the fame thing, or fomething more; and I would have
it fpoken in plain *Englifh*. And though no one reafon
has been offered againft the Monarchy being hereditary, yet it infers more power devolved on the Lords
and Commons. What is this but to make the Monarchy elective? It has been faid, "who ought to
have this Allegiance paid, will in due time be confidered;" but 'tis moft proper to confider it, when the
confequences do appear. 'Tis a doubt that your Vote
may mean that the Throne is vacant for ever; therefore clear that Queftion, whether the Monarchy be
hereditary or elective: I fear our Reafons have gone
fomewhat that way. Whoever is againft agreeing with
the Lords, concludes that the Throne is vacant, not
only to King *James* the Second, but to every body elfe.
I will not trouble you with arguments, whether the
Crown is elective or hereditary; for 'tis beyond all
queftion, our books are fo full of it, acknowleging
the fucceffion of the right heirs. The Statute of *Ed.* III.
declares, "the King's children ought to inherit the
                                                    Crown,

Debates in Parliament in 1688.   61

Crown, though born *ultra mare*," and so is a Law for ever. I hear it said " *Nemo est hæres viventis.*" There are civil deaths as well as natural. If the Throne be vacant as to King *James* II, then he is civilly dead, or else 'tis in the power of any King of *England*, by his Abdication, to destroy the Succession. For the King, Lords, and Commons to limit the Succession! 'Tis an act of Supreme Power unbounded, and I cannot say what they cannot do. But for us to limit the Succession, is plainly to say we may chuse a King : And is this called that prudence we ought to act with, to destroy that Constitution of the Government, which we came here to maintain ?

Sir *Richard Temple.*] I have great disadvantage to speak after so learned a Gentleman; but I observe he has used more learning to draw you from the Question than to bring you to it. But we are determining the consequences of the Lords Amendments, before we agree that the Throne is vacant. . You are told, " you cannot declare the Throne vacant, without hazard to the Monarchy, which has been transferred from one branch to another." No man goes about to change the Monarchy; but there have not been seven Kings but where the right line has been removed; so that there is no dispute nor ground whether the Monarchy be hereditary. Though the Crown should be vacant to the King and all his heirs, yet 'tis no more than transferring the Crown from one family to another. The Kingdom of *France* had three races, which succeeded in the Monarchy. These Gentlemen would anticipate the day to you of naming a Successor. The learned Gentleman that spoke last would have no farther Vacancy in the Throne but to King *James* II. If by your Reasons to the Lords for retaining the word " vacant" in your Vote, the Throne be full to the immediate Heirs; there is an end of your Debate, and your being here. Is it full? Then the Lords would ha[?] [?]een it, and not put the Government into other

If Gentlemen aim at what they say, for a Protestant

62   *Debates in Parliament in* 1688.

teftant line, how will you come at it? And you have
a pretended Brat beyond fea, whom you cannot fet
afide; and the King may have more children legiti-
mate, and how will you fet them afide? But fome fay,
"Set all but Proteftants afide"—But if the Parliament
have no authority to make it otherwife, you have no
way to prevent falling under a Popifh fucceffor. If
the Throne be full, we have no authority to fit here;
all we have done is to arraign the Lords and ourfelves.
Therefore I would not agree with the Lords, but declare the Vacancy.

Sir *Robert Howard.*] If we negleft this opportunity,
now put into our hands, of fettling the Nation, 'tis
probable we may be no more a people; and 'tis pretty
nigh, whether thefe learned Gentlemen, that fpeak
againft Elections of our Monarchs, have not been the
moft violent Electors of all: They throw upon us a
difficulty how we come by that Conftitution. Is it not
elective, to take one, and leave another? Election limited with fuch narrow notions is a poor fupport. As
for thofe arguments, I hope we fhall preferve the Monarchy by filling the Vacancy, and not fay, who muft
fucceed—Are we not thrown upon this?—Can a child
make Abdication, or a child in the belly of the mother?—They would chufe like the Day of Judgment,
one fhall be taken, and the other left—The Lords are
bold with the fucceffion of a Papift, that none fhall
fncceed to the Crown. Under the nice notion of the
Princefs, if there fhould be occafion for defence of the
Nation, upon a filent fteerage you are drawn upon
rocks—If you ufe the hand that delivered you thus,
you invite him to be gone; and by his compliment to
us, he may lofe all here, and hazard the Proteftant intereft abroad. Thefe arguments are good in quiet
times; but where a divided inheritance is the cafe—Inftance in one thing from Kings defcents—All things
are not fo clear as we could wifh; but let us preferve
ourfelves, which muft be our fupreme Law. If we
part with "the Crown not being vacant," you part
                                                    with

Debates in Parliament in 1688.   63

with all; and then you may hope hereafter, that your Conftitutions will not be violated.

Mr *Bofcawen.*] No man fays, 'tis my right to the Succeffion. The Commons only fay, " the Throne is vacant." We do not impofe any fenfe upon the Lords. We fay not 'tis vacant to the Prince of *Wales*, or o-thers, but vacant. The arguments that are ufed, 'tis faid, are dangerous as to *Scotland*; but this objection was made in the Exclufion-Bill. Upon the whole, you are mafters of your Vote, and no man does fay the Crown is elective; but, in an intricate cafe, the Parliament muft fay, where is the moft Right; and the Parliament that is to nominate the right Heir is *tant-amount* to Election. Confider what is leaft exceptionable; we impofe not upon the Lords; you fay, 'tis vacant, without diftinguifhing, and nothing lefs than to fay the Kingdom is elective. Public fecurity ought to be confidered, and in that we all agree.

Mr *Pollexfen.*] If this difcourfe had been made fooner, perhaps we had been much forwarder. If the Queftion had been, whether you will ftick to your former Vote, the time had been better fpent than in Speeches. When you were then upon the Debate, if any man had faid the Crown was full, you would have had both Law, and Adminiftration of Juftice; but 'tis now referved till the Throne be full. And then we are all fubverted, and return to King *James*, and fo to Popery, if we fill not the Throne. To talk of Regencies, is to fay, then fure there is no Vacancy. Letters, Papers, and the Pulpit, beats a pace confufion of your principal end, which the three Kingdoms, the Proteftant part of the World, are interefted in. But left what has been faid fhould make impreffion, I fhall anfwer, firft, 'tis pretended that this Vote does make ours an elective Kingdom. All men love their Monarchy, and if you make men believe that it is elective, you will catch a great many. No man ever dreamed of this; but if the cafe happen by extraordinary diforder in the Government, that the King is driven out of the
Nation,

64   *Debates in Parliament in* 1688.

Nation, fay what you will that the King is driven out, yet to fuppofe a defcent, by what Law is there any that this does?—This makes Kings faften themfelves, and will foon make way for *James* to come in. If there be any fuch Law, what an unreafonable thing it is! If the King, by mif-government, is driven out of his Kingdom, fome body fhall fucceed; put me fuch a cafe—'Twill be a difcouragement to any to defend his country from Slavery and Tyranny, if this be the confequence. If he takes arms to deliver his country, and he prevail, he is hanged—All our Lives, Fortunes, and Religion, are at the King's pleafure, as his Council have told him; and his fubjects drive him out. I have as much inclination to the Princefs of *Orange* as any body, but you do not really mind the good of your Country, and the Proteftant Religion. If fhe be now proclaimed Queen, can any thing be more defirable than that her hufband be joined with her in the Government?—Now, if you fettle the Crown on her, and we are to fecure a Title we cannot make, if any tranfient iffue fhould arife, fhe is gone, and he will be in War with her Father to defend her Title— And does any think the Prince of *Orange* will come in to be a fubject to his own wife in *England*? This is not poffible, nor ought to be in nature. If you ftay till the Princefs pleafe to give the Government to the Prince, you gratify the Prince, by taking away his wife from him, and giving her the Kingdom. If we are for unity and the Proteftant Intereft, I hope this marriage was made in heaven, and I hope good effects of it. That marriage, thus made, fhall never be feparated by my confent.

Mr *Wharton.*] I fpeak for myfelf; let every one do fo too: I own driving King *James* out, and I would do it again. Let every one make his beft of it.

Mr *Williams.*] I take this Queftion to be for the unity of the Lords and Commons in this great conjuncture. Let the power be where it will, I fpeak for all *England.* All agree, that the late King *James* II.

                                                    has

Debates in Parliament in 1688.   65

h as departed from the Throne, and that his reign over us ceases. If the Lords are of opinion that the reign of King *James* is ceased, we are all agreed. The Lords say, he shall never return again; they are not for his returning again to his Government: I am not for the Monarchy of a Child; I am not for one to subvert the Laws of the Government. If this may be done by the Lords and the Commons, I would agree.

The Question being put, That this House do agree with the Lords in the second Amendment, it passed in the Negative, 282 to 151.

[A free Conference was desired.]

Wednesday, February 6.

Sir *William Waller* attended the House, and gave this account of Mr *Brent*, viz. " That, by common fame, Mr *Brent* was a very obnoxious person. He went to Sir *James Smith*, and informed him, that he was a great criminal, and desired his Warrant to apprehend him. Accordingly he was apprehended, and he desired Monsieur *Bentinck* to acquaint the Prince of *Orange* with it. Mr *Harbord* brought him word, that the Prince would have him proceed against him as the Law would bear. He took Major *Wildman*'s advice: He could not charge him but upon common fame, and, in general, that he was an obnoxious person, and corresponded with Priests and *Jesuits*, and was busy in regulating Corporations; the truth of which was notorious, and doubted not but to produce evidence of it. He said, he could not commit him to *Newgate*, but would to the *Marshalsea*. He told him, Mr *Bradon* might probably make something out against him. He asked *Smith* what was become of the Prisoner? He told him he had great friends of some Lords, who would appear for him, and he could not refuse him Bail. Those Lords he had done some kindness to, and they had sent to him."

Sir *James Smith* brought a copy of the Bail, and the *Mittimus*, viz. " To receive *Brent* into custody for High Treason, in corresponding with Priests and *Jesuits*, and subverting the Government, in advising *Quo Warrantos* against Corporations." There was no proof made of any particular thing against him, more than what was brought in by *Waller*.

The Speaker.] High Treason is particular matter, and you cannot bail a person so charged, by the Statute

66   *Debates in Parliament in* 1688.

of *Weſtminſter*. Treaſon is not bailable but by two Juſtices of the Peace.

Sir *James Smith*.] *Waller* undertook, that perſons ſhould ac-cuſe him ; and I committed him in the mean time.

The Speaker.] You ſay, " Great perſons appeared and wrote for him :" What did they write, and by whom was it written ?

Sir *James Smith*.] Lord *Devonſhire* and Lord *Danby* were friends to *Brent*, and they deſired me to bail him.

The Speaker.] You took ſmall Bail for a perſon ſo accuſed.

Sir *James Smith*.] I took 1500 *l*. Bail in all, which I did by the advice of the Recorder, who ſaid, 1000 *l*. Bail for *Brent*, and 500 *l*. for the Sureties, was ſufficient. At preſent, I do not remember the perſon who came to me from the Lords, but had ſeen him ſeveral times. I did not aſk his name.

Sir *Robert Cotton*.] It concerns me, for the ſatiſ-faction of the Houſe, to remind you of raiſing Bail to an exceſſive height in Lord *Delamere*'s caſe, and aba-ting it in this.

Sir *William Williams*.] I would have an account from *Smith*, or ſome deſcription, of the perſon who came from theſe Lords.

Sir *Robert Cotton*.] Lord *Delamere* was accuſed of Treaſon in the *King's-Bench*. I was one of his Sureties in 10,000 *l*. Bond. He was afterwards committed to the *Tower*, and brought his *Habeas Corpus*, and then was bailed in 20,000 *l*. Bond, with Sureties ; and *Smith* has bailed *Brent* in this ſmall ſum. This riſing and falling of Bail is remarkable.

Sir *William Portman*.] *Brent* is a notorious offender, and I look on him as the author of much of our miſ-chief, and I hope you will make him an example.

Sir *George Treby*.*] I was in hopes you would have called me to riſe, becauſe my name has been uſed by *Smith*. I will give you a true account of this matter. Coming out of the Court of Aldermen, *Smith* aſked

* Recorder of *London*.

me

me " what he fhould do with *Brent*, whether he fhould bail him ? There was a great complaint againft him, but no Evidence: Whether he fhould bail him, or no, and what Bail he fhould take ?" I told him, I wondered there fhould be no Evidence. I advifed him to keep him in prifon for a reafonable time, and give notice to the Profecutor to bring Evidence. " You may apprehend him, and keep him in cuftody till the Profecutor produce his Evidence, and Examination had ; but longer than that you muft not detain him. And this not being purfued, he muft be bailed, and, in ftrictnefs, he ought to be difcharged. In all Bail, the Condition of the perfon is to be proportioned. If there be no Charge upon Oath, the Bail may be the lefs. If he be kept a reafonable time, and no Profecutor appears, it is reafonable to bail him." The cafe appears thus to be : A man charged or chargeable with Treafon, the Profecutor brings no Evidence, nor can have any. If I had faid more, I had not exceeded the Law.

The Speaker.] You find abfolutely, that the Commitment was for Treafon. If a Felony be committed, and common fame be upon a perfon, it is juftifiable to commit him. Whether *Smith* hath done what he fhould do in this matter, I leave it to the Houfe to determine. I queftion whether, if he bail where it is not juftifiable, he is not fineable in the *King's-Bench*.

Mr *Carter*.] The Treafons were committed in *Weftminfter* ; and *Smith* needed no farther Information in general, where there was fuch a notoriety.

* * * * * * *] *Smith* aggravates his crime by his Warrant, which fpecifies Treafon exprefsly. And he did *Brent* wrong, unlefs he had ground fufficient for it, I defire a courfe may be taken with him by this Houfe.

Sir *Thomas Clarges*.] We cannot commit any man, but in cafe of our Privileges. As in the cafe of the Popifh Plot, let fome Juftices of the Peace examine this Gentleman, and commit him.

68   *Debates in Parliament in* 1688.

The Speaker.] I obferve the date of the Recognizance to be the 24th of *January*, two days after your
fitting, &c. 'Tis ftrange he fhould do it at that time.

Sir *George Treby*.] I fee myfelf reflected on. I fhall
anfwer for myfelf: I had no Fee in this cafe; and if
I had, I fhould be fatisfied, when I die, that it was well
taken. It has been my cuftom, if I could not ferve
a Caufe, to return that Fee. I have had the honour
to be a Member in this place thefe twelve years. I
have had offers of preferment to the beft Office of the
Law, coloured over with telling me I was a man of
Parts and Law, and fteered to the Proteftant Religion;
but I would then take no Place, and no Bribe. They
preffed me farther, " Will you truly preferve the King
in his Prerogative ?" I not only loft all advantages
for my non-compliance, but was in danger of my life
too—'Twas the Queftion, " What faid the Recorder
in the Popifh Plot ?"—I defended the Charter of *London*, and the cafe of the Sheriffs of *London*. They told
me, " If you will be eafy, no Place fhall be too good
for you. You fhall be Chief Juftice of *Chefter*, Mafter
of the Rolls, &c." This fhows at what rate they would
have purchafed Betrayers of the Liberties of their Country.
I was not only expofed to the frowns of the Court,
but purchafed their indignation, that I was an enemy
to the King and Government. I was always againft a
Popifh King, to get a Popifh Parliament; and thought
all would be deftroyed, unlefs a Popifh King was deftroyed. This I have done, and thus I have fuffered;
and would not have Perjury in my pocket for the Empire of the World. After all I have done and fuffered,
now to fay, " I have advifed to take Fee-Bail for a
Malefactor," what a little perfidious thing would this
have been? I am concerned not to be reproached nor
expofed for my faithfulnefs to the Government.

Sir *Robert Clayton*.] If there has been any corruption in this matter, it lies in another place. The Recorder is not fo weak as to do it. I would have *Smith*
committed, not by us, but by a Juftice of the Peace.

Lord

Debates in Parliament in 1688. 69

Lord *Falkland*.] It was eafy to have had Evidence againft *Brent*. The Letters fent to Corporations were fufficient. I would apply to the Prince, that *Smith* may be committed to the *Tower*.

Sir *William Williams*.] I hear it faid, " We cannot commit a Delinquent." If we do not lay hands on *Smith*, it may be of pernicious confequence. I would commit him to the *Tower*, and the Commons may juftify it.

Mr *Dolben*.] Though I am unwilling to differ from one of my Profeffion, I cannot agree to Commitment from this Houfe but for Breach of Privilege—I would apply to the Prince, &c.

Sir *John Guife*.] I would not do too much, nor too little, in this cafe. *Smith* was to blame not to commit *Brent* for fo great crimes ; and he might have ealled another Juftice of the Peace to his affiftance. I would have him left in the Serjeant's hands, and I hope you will not let him flip, without putting him into the Serjeant's hands.

Sir *Thomas Lee*.] You are making a queftion, what Power the Houfe has, and what to do with this man— I fhall inform you of the practice in former times— In order to Impeachments, you have committed men, and when they have broken your Privilege, and in order to bring a man to the Houfe of Lords to be tried, &c.

Sir *Thomas Clarges*.] Several perfons were accufed of High Treafon in the Popifh Plot, and you fent to the Chief Juftice to examine and commit them.

Sir *Thomas Lee*.] I would remind *Clarges*, that, at the Tryal of Lord *Stafford*, Members withdrew to take Informations upon Oath. The confequence fell out to be, Sir *William Pulteney* took the Examinations, the Lords pretended Jurifdiction in it, and the Houfe loft a point.

Mr *Wild*.] I was with Lord *Danby* and Lord *Devonfhire*, and they fay, " they never fent fuch a Meffage to *Smith* in their life."

The

70   *Debates in Parliament in* 1688.

The Speaker.] In the 18th of King *James*, there were Impeachments of Monopolies, and the Houfe fent for men in Cuftody, and they were committed till Examination.

Ordered, That Sir *James Smith* be committed to the Cuftody of the Serjeant at Arms.

Thurfday, February 7.

The Lords agreed to the Vote of " Abdication," and " the Throne vacant."

Earl of *Wiltfhire**.] Now that the Lords have agreed "the Throne vacant," I hope you will proceed to fill the Throne. The perfons formerly named are the moft proper that can be. thought of, the Prince and Prin-cefs of *Orange*. I have not parts able to fet out their merits, and what we owe this great Prince for deli-vering us from Popery and Slavery ; and there is no way to fecure us from the return of it, but by placing them on the Throne, and to preferve the ancient Go-vernment. You have been told here of going about to make this an ·elective Government ; but I believe nobody here is of any other opinion, but that the Government is in King, Lords, and Commons.

Major *Wildman*.] To prevent Anarchy, nothing can be better than. to proceed to nominate the Prince and Princefs of *Orange* King and Queen of *England*.

Mr *Palmes*.] I rife not to oppofe the Motion, but to hear what the Committee will report of the Preli-

---

* Eldeft fon to the Marquefs of *Winchefter*, afterwards Duke of *Bol-ton*. Having gone over to *Holland* in the reign of King *James*, he came back with the Prince of O-range, and was very inftrumental in the Revolution. In 1690 he made the campaign with the King in *Flanders*, and was afterwards ap-pointed Lord Chamberlain, Colonel of Foot, and one of the Lords Juf-tices of *Ireland*. In 1699, he fuc-ceeded to the title of Duke of *Bol-*ton ; and in the reign of Queen *Anne* was Warden of the *New Foreft*, Go-vernor of the Ifle of *Wight*, &c. In 1715, he was appointed (by King *George* I.) Lord Chamberlain ; and in 1717 was declared Lord Lieute-nant of *Ireland*. He was alfo twice one of the Lords Juftices, during his Majefty's abfence in his *German* dominions, and died in 1721. He was Grandfather to the prefent Duke.

minary

Debates in Parliament in 1688. 71

minary Heads. I know not whether you will preclude the Committee, by going fo foon to this Vote. They are preparing the Heads, and will be ready with them prefently.

Mr *Wogan*.] Before you proceed to the Article of Invefture, let the prefent nomination of the Prince and Princefs of *Orange* be for life, &c. and the Heirs of her body, not as it was in *Philip* and *Mary*.

Mr *Bofcawen*.] We are upon as great an affair as ever was before a Houfe of Commons; and I hope we fhall be unanimous. It concerns us for the dignity of the Houfe. It is worthy your confideration, whether you will call the Committee down, or ftay till they have done.

Mr *Hampden*.] Do not any thing in hafte. I would let the Committee confider well what muft be for the benefit of all pofterity, when you are dead and gone; and I hope your Refolutions and Rules will be orderly. I believe all the Gentlemen are agreed what to do; but things of this nature cannot be done as with Counfel in a Chamber, and a Clerk only to write. In fo great a bufinefs, pray let us do orderly things. You may call to the Committee, to fee what they have done; or you may order them to go on, if they have not finifhed.

Mr *Wharton*.] I am forry for fo long a Debate of this. I would not go on without calling the Committee down; but would not lofe all thefe Heads the Gentlemen are doing, but act as a wife Affembly.

The Lords fent down the following Vote, and Oaths to be taken, inftead of the Oaths of Allegiance and Supremacy, &c; to which they defired the Concurrence of this Houfe:

[" *Die Mercurii*, 6 *Feb.* 1688.

" *Refolved*, by the Lords Spiritual and Temporal, and affembled at *Weftminfter*, That the Prince and Princefs of *Orange* fhall be declared King and Queen of *England*, and all the dominions thereunto belonging."

F 4   " I *A.B.*

72   *Debates in Parliament in* 1688.

" I *A. B.* do fincerely promife and fwear, that I will be faithful, and bear true Allegiance, to their Majefties King *William* and Queen *Mary.* So help me God.

" I *A. B.* do fwear, that I do from my heart abhor, deteft, and abjure, as impious and heretical, this damnable Doctrine and Pofition, that Princes excommunicated or deprived by the Pope, or any authority of the See of *Rome,* may be depofed or murdered by their fubjects, or any other whatfoever: And I do declare, that no foreign Prince, Prelate, State, or Potentate, hath, or ought to have, any Jurifdiction, Power, Superiority, Preheminence, or Authority, Ecclefiaftical or Spiritual, within this Realm. So help me God.

" That thefe Oaths be taken by all perfons, when tendered to them, of whom the Oaths of Allegiance and Supremacy ――― * be abrogated."]

In the Afternoon.

Sir *George Treby* reports Heads from the Committee †, *&c.* The Committee were divided in opinion, whether you fhould declare " That no Pardons fhould be pleadable to an Impeachment in Parliament," nor would countenance Pardons to perfons who may not have deferved them, nor for recording the Heads in Chancery, till you refolve what ufe to make of them.

Sir *Robert Sawyer.*] Now you are providing new Laws for your future fafety, 'tis proper to mention a new one, *viz.* " That no Popifh Succeffor fhall be capable to inherit the Crown of *England,* and no Papift capable of fucceeding to the Crown."

Col. *Tipping.*] If the Prince and Princefs of *Orange* and Princefs *Anne* die without iffue, the Crown will defcend to the Queen of *Spain,* and the Pope may difpenfe with Religion, and the Dutchefs of *Savoy.* Therefore I move, " That none that have been Papifts fhall be capable to inherit the Crown."

Col. *Mildmay.*] I would have it, " Have been, or fhall be, a Papift,"

Sir *John Guife.*] You have agreed the Throne to be vacant, but have had no confideration when you will fill it; and then will be the moft proper time to confider this.

* So in the Journal.
† See thefe Heads at large in the Journal.

Lord

Debates in Parliament in 1688. 73

Lord *Dumblaine*.] King *James* has had the misfortune to go out of the Throne. I have been always againſt electing a Monarch, and againſt coming into a Commonwealth ; therefore I would firſt fill the Throne. It cannot be filled unleſs vacant. I aſk pardon for my miſtake the other day, in my Vote, " that the Throne was not vacant." I have great obligation to [the Prince] and have ſhowed my duty to him—You cannot do too much for him.

Sir *Robert Howard*.] I would leave out the word " ſhall, *&c.*" There is a great deal of difference between one that turns when the ground is falling under him, and one that longer ſince has given good teſtimony of his Religion. I would not have you ſo penned up as to exclude all poſſibility of converſion.

Sir *John Guiſe*.] There is a great deal of difference between a Peer (in his converſion) that has a ſingle Vote in the Lords Houſe, and the King, that has his Negative Voice in paſſing Laws.

[*Reſolved*, That Proviſion be made for the Settlement of the Crown, that no Papiſt may ſucceed or be admitted thereto ; nor any perſon that hath made or ſhall make profeſſion of being a Papiſt.]

Mr *Sacheverell*.] I would go farther than to declare the Prince and Princeſs of *Orange* King and Queen : I would declare who ſhall have the Adminiſtration of the Government, if they divide ; and then, whither the Government ſhall go after. I would never leave it precarious.

Mr *Paul Foley*.] I ſecond the laſt Motion. If the Prince and Princeſs of *Orange* be declared King and Queen, in the nature of joint tenants and ſurvivorſhip, and not in intention to put by the Lady *Anne*, I agree to it. I would have them declared for their lives, and the longer liver of them ; and declare the Entail afterwards.

Sir *Robert Sawyer*.] I would declare him King in her right,

Sir

74   *Debates in Parliament in* 1688.

Sir *Richard Temple.*] I am ready to agree to fill up the Throne, as the Lords have propofed. If you declare any body King, the queftion is, whether you will not come too late. I thought it your intention, when you filled the Throne to do thefe things, which will be too late afterwards. You are told, when once the King is in the Throne, without Limitation, it is to him and his Heirs. If you declare them King and Queen, either the Prince is in right of the Queen—How will this be underftood? If he be King *de facto*, it is more than you intend. Such Limitation as to preferve the Right to the Princefs and her Heirs—I would ftay there, but let the Committee add, " We know none fo fit as the Prince and Princefs, and therefore we take the Crown to be fitter to be trufted with nobody than him who has delivered us." If they be declared King and Queen jointly, no Difpatch nor Letter can be fent but muft be jointly by the Prince and Princefs.

Col. *Birch.*] I move you to draw up a fhort Inftrument of the Heads of your Intention, to be comprehended within that Inftrument.

Mr *Sacheverell.*] I do not fuppofe this Inftrument of Government to be a new Limitation of the Crown, but what of right is ours by Law. Settle us in fuch a ftate that we may defire the Prince of *Orange.* We fhould make no Conclufion before the Premifes are agreed.

Sir *Thomas Lee.*] The matter fingly before you is, the Report from the Committee. It propofes a method of Declaration of the Rights of the Subject to go along with the Declaration of filling up the Throne, and there it will fall naturally. I would adjourn till to-morrow, and poftpone the Claufe of the Crown. As to what fell from *Sawyer,* if you adjourn the Debate, then the next thing will be to fill the Vacancy; and then how far this nomination of two perfons who fhall have the Adminiftration of the Government, that there be no ftand in the Government, fhall extend, whether

Debates in Parliament in 1688.   75

whether in his own right, or in right of his wife.
'Tis abfolutely neceffary, when you agree with the
Lords, to explain yourfelves in the Limitations.

Mr *Hampden.*] I agree with *Lee* to come to a refolution, before you fend to the Lords, after filling the
Throne, and the Oaths being confidered. 'Tis not
only honourable but fafe, and no dreadful coufidera-
tion in it; it may be foon done : But do not pafs it
firft, and explain it after.

Friday, February 8.

The Houfe took into confideration the Vote of the Lords,
[of the 6th of *February* inftant, fent down to this Houfe for
their Concurrence.] *See p.* 71-2.

Serjeant *Holt.*] As far as I underftand the Queftion, I would concur with the Lords; but the Vote
ftands in need of an Addition, or Explanation, as to
the Adminiftration of the Government. Suppofe only
the Prince of *Orange* as Hufband to the Queen; he
would have the Adminiftration, as the power of the
Hufband over the Queen, as Queen *Mary*, notwithftanding thefe Articles. Then if the cafe be fo of the
King only as Confort, it will be much more when the
King is joint tenant. But to prevent all doubts, I
would have the fole Adminiftration of the Government in the Prince of *Orange*, otherwife there will be
confufion in the Government; one may command one
thing, the other another; and who fhall be obeyed?
And the Government may be loft. I move, therefore, that the Prince of *Orange* may have the fole Adminiftration of the Government during the Coverture.
'Tis neceffary that you come to exprefs the Limitation;
unlefs you do fo, fome may make conftruction that
fhe is Heir to her Anceftor, and the Crown defcends
to her; therefore it is neceffary to declare that the
King and Queen, and the Survivor of them, have the
Adminiftration of the Government. What Eftate then
has the Prince in the Crown? He will have an Eftate
of

76   *Debates in Parliament in* 1688.

of Inheritance without Limitation. If one fits in the Lords Houfe by Writ of Parliament, if it be without Limitation, his Heirs fhall fit after him. I prefume it is not your intention, that the Limitation fhall be to the Prince's Heirs by another wife. 'Tis your defign to fecure the Nation againft Popery, and the ill confequences of it. Therefore I would exprefs the Limitation mentioned, and fo fhall you fhow your regard and kindnefs to the Royal Family, and you will be vindicated from all afperfions abroad of deftroying the Royal Family. The Prince has hazarded all for us; and if you make him Confort only to the Queen, you will reduce him, upon her death, to a private condition. And this will be no gratitude to him that has redeemed us from our misfortunes. Therefore I would limit the Crown to him for life, (as above;) and thereby you will lay a foundation of fecurity to the Nation.

Sir *Thomas Littleton.*] If the Adminiftration of the Government fhould only be in the Prince, the great defign of the Kingdom will be fruftrated. The power of the Parliament of *England* being once afferted, it will eftablifh our foreign affairs. If it be not a time now to ftrengthen our Intereft againft *France*, we fhall never be preferved, but fall into the fame misfortune we were in, in the late King's time: And I would have *Ireland* inferted into the Lords Vote.

Mr *Bofcawen.*] I am not againft inferting *Ireland*; but obferve that the Debate be whole. But why will you leave out *France, Jerfey, Guernfey,* and *Sark?* I would put it into the former ftyle, *France* to precede *Ireland*; let it be drawn into form by the Long Robe, as to Entail of the Crown, and all the reft that follows.

Mr *Hampden.*] If you go on thus from word to word, you will lofe all your time, and change often. I would debate it firft, and then, upon the inclination of the Houfe, draw it up according to your Amendment. I would not leave out *France, valeat quantum valere poteft*; and the Limitation of the Crown, as has been proposed.

Debates *in Parliament in* 1688.   77

propofed. Gentlemen may debate upon it as long as they pleafe, and then you may draw up one entire Vote.

Sir *Richard Temple.*] If after Debate you fhall have fuch Amendments as cannot be made at the Table, then fome Gentlemen may withdraw to form it. None of the Motions are oppofed, to continue the Regal Style and Title ftill to all the Dominions mentioned. If all are agreed in the main, fome Gentlemen may withdraw to put it into form.

Mr *Garroway.*] This muft be commited at laft, but let the Debate go on, to give the Committee a handle to procced upon your direction, and it will go current. The Lords have voted' " That the Prince and Princefs fhall be declared King and Queen of *England.*"

Sir *Thomas Clarges.*] The Queftion is agreed; but I would debate the Qualifications. 'Tis moved, " that the Adminiftration of the Government fhall be for the Prince's life." Suppofe, upon any military occafion, the Prince fhould be out of the Kingdom, fhall not the Adminiftration, &c. then be in the Princefs, during that time ? The Act of Parliament of the 1ft of *Philip* and *Mary* is worth your confideration. I would look over that Statute; and I think what I offer is fit to be received.

Sir *Henry Capel.*] I am glad the Houfe is fo unanimous in this great affair. Says *Clarges,* " In the abfence of the Prince, the Adminiftration of the Government fhould be in the Princefs, &c." We have feen that cafe, and it is no extraordinary thing at all. 'Tis neceffary that the Adminiftration be in one man, and no perfon in *Europe* more fit than the Prince. I offer only, becaufe feveral Entails are mentioned, " that after the Prince and Princefs, to the Heirs of the Princefs; and for default of her Heirs, to Princefs *Anne,* &c; then, after her Heirs, to the Heirs of the Prince of *Orange*; and after them to be left indefinite."

Sir *George Treby.*] As to *Clarges's* Motion of " the Prince going out of the Kingdom," there is no great
need

78   *Debates in Parliament in* 1688.

need to provide for that, for the Law has done it already. The King may conftitute a *Locum tenens,* and 'tis moft probable he will conftitute his Confort. In the Limitation of the Entail of King *Philip* and Queen *Mary,* it was to the Heirs of her body, the Remainder to the Heirs at Law; and now with this fpecial Provifo, excluding all Popifh Succeffors.

Sir *Chriftopher Mufgrave.*] To the Motions, after the Entail mentioned, I do entirely concur, and then to be left indefinite. As for the other Motions, you may pafs them over in filence. I am for the Gentlemen of the Long Robe to withdraw, and pen the thing moft to your fenfe: But it will much expedite the work, if, before they withdraw, you fet down the particular Amendments you make to the Lords Vote in your Paper, that they may concur with the fenfe of the Houfe.

Serjeant *Maynard.*] Sometimes the perfons conftituted to manage the Government in the King's abfence are called "the King's Lieutenants;" fometimes "Guardians of the Kingdom." Though the King go abroad, yet the Government may go on. I have often feen, when there has been an unanimous confent of the Members in a thing, that Gentlemen need not withdraw, but it may be mended at the Table.

Sir *Thomas Clarges.*] I know, by the Law of the Land, the King in his abfence may conftitute a *Cuftos Regni,* and in 1 *Philip* and *Mary* it was limited by that Act. Confider then, whether it may not be enacted, that the Queen be *Cuftos, &c.* in her own right, and not at the pleafure of the King.

Mr *Pollexfen.*] I know that the Law of the Land has fufficiently provided for the Government, in cafe of the King's going beyond fea. Here you go about to make an Alteration of the Law, in appointing a *Cuftos, &c.* Suppofe the King and Queen have a mind to go beyond fea, which may probably happen; or if the Queen cannot, by ficknefs, undertake the Regency; if the King cannot provide againft this, you break
into

Debates in Parliament in 1688. 79

into the Laws; the King being actually King, and the Queen actually Queen: Will you alter your Law already made? We are all of one mind; therefore spend no time, but appoint the Committee to draw up Amendments to the Lords Vote — *(Which was done accordingly)*

Mr *Somers* reports from the said Committee several Amendments to the Lords Vote. *(See the Journal.)*

Sir *Robert Howard.*] I am not for entangling the matter. Though we are in haste to settle the Rights of the people, yet the next best thing is to support them. I would make a declarative part of your known Rights, and cause the Committee to make a Connexion of your Rights.

Serjeant *Maynard.*] 'Tis clear they are your own Rights; you declare, and the Lords must have time to consider of them.

Sir *Richard Temple.*] I am for saving time, and explaining what is designed to do, *viz.* your declaratory Rights you have passed, and those are connected with your Vote; and the Prince has set them out in his Declaration; but where you desire new Laws to be made, it must be done by itself. You will not go up with your Vote to the Lords, to declare the Prince and Princess King and Queen, and nothing with it. If you will give the Committee leave, they will connect it all at once.

Major *Wildman.*] No man is more zealous to assert our Rights than I am; but consider, if there be such a necessity to send them to the Lords, and they must examine them paragraph by paragraph, and perhaps they may say they have Rights of their own Peerage that are not provided for, in what manner can we concur with the Lords in declaring the Succession? Whether is it not expedient, that this House carry to the Prince our fundamental Rights—And the Lords no way consent—and we never part with one *punctum*

of

80   *Debates in Parliament in* 1688.

of them—Whether neceſſary at this time to wave the
Lords, and ſend them to the Prince?

Mr *Hampden*.] I differ in this of aſſerting your
Rights; I would do it in the beſt manner. But to
object " that time will be loſt in ſending them to the
Lords :"—Can a Houſe of Commons do things as a
Warrant from a Juſtice of Peace is done? Conſider
the progreſs of the Prince of *Orange*'s ſecond Declaration—No Remedy but a full Declaration of our Grievances in Parliament : But to go to the Prince alone,
without the Lords! I remember, upon all occaſions, when
your Rights have been aſſerted, that you have gone to
the Lords. King *James* has done this and this, in violation of them ; and you, therefore, preſent the Prince
of *Orange* with the Crown. Is it not natural to preſent the Prince with what you are aggrieved with, and
ſuffer, under all theſe Infringements of your Rights ?
Yet you delay ſending them, becauſe the Commons
fear the Lords will not agree to them. When do you
think the Lords will agree ? Are not the Lords concerned as well as you? And with this prejudice to
the Lords, you will ſend them no Acts of Parliament :
You would do it, and have no time to do it. Can it
be better done, than when you preſent the Crown connected with this, becauſe the Prince has protected
you, and you have an entire confidence in him? It
may be ſaid, you have no great mind to your Rights,
for they can ſtay for them, you ſee : As you deſire
the reputation of a grave and wiſe Council, that repreſent the Kingdom, let the Committee connect the
Heads of the Articles, and repreſent them all together.

Mr *Eyre*.*] I would not prevent going to the Lords
with the Heads of your Articles. If you divide theſe
Papers, the Lords may agree to us in one, and not in
another ; and may you not be told, that theſe things
are ancient Flowers of the Crown, and cannot be
parted with ? I would not have our purchaſe, like the
Indians, to give Gold for Rattles. I would have the
King and Queen rule in the hearts of their ſubjects,

* Soon after made a Judge.

                                                    and

Debates in Parliament in 1688. 81

and the Harmony betwixt the Crown and the People tune together. Had you given the Committee that power to connect both together, all this Debate had been ended.

The Committee reported the Inftrument of Government, with the declaratory Grievances, to which, with fome Amendments, the Lords agreed.

[*February* 9, Omitted.]

Monday, February 11.

Mr *Somers* reports the Lords Amendments of the Articles, at Conferences.

Sir *Thomas Lee.*] This does arife from a miftake. Informations in the *King's-Bench* in our Paper were laid in King *James*'s time, whereas they began in King *Charles*'s.

Mr *Pollexfen.*] The word "Information" fhould have been "Profecution."

Sir *George Treby.*] I would confent to explain it, but not to leave it out. This Article was put in for the fake of one, once in your place, Sir *William Williams,* who was punifhed out of Parliament for what he had done in Parliament; and by divers other arbitrary and illegal Courfes. I hope you will not leave out "clofeting the Members of Parliament."

Serjeant *Holt.*] "Informations" cannot ftand in the plural, profecuted in King *Charles* the IId's time. As for that Profecution of Lord *Peterborough* of the *Scandalum Magnatum quam tam,* &c. 'twas a private Action, and not an Information, whereby the King had no Damage.

Sir *William Williams.*] All that matter did arife in Parliament, and the Profecution in King *James*'s time, and I was fined 10,000 *l.* and damage to the Party. There is the cafe of Lord *Lovelace,* and the cafe of Lord *Devonfhire.* The cafe of Lord *Lovelace* was upon a recognizance, and he pleaded privilege of a Peer, &c.

Mr *Eyre.*] I am for afferting our Liberties, but unneceffary delay will wound the Nation we come

VOL. IX.   G   hither

hither to heal. All we provide for is againſt Informations for what is done in Parliament. I would agree
with the Lords.

Sir *George Treby*.] This will be declaring that *Magna
Charta* is *Magna Charta*, redreſſing what was never
violated.

Mr *Howe*.] The door was opened in King *Charles* II's
time, and the goods were ſtolen in *James* II's time.
As great a door, nay greater, was opened to Popery in
Charles II's time than in *James* II's. And if we may
judge greater things by ſmall, under the Popiſh Kings
there was leſs partiality than thoſe that came in, in
their ſtead. Not to be tedious as well as imperti-
nent, I would leave that clauſe out.

Sir *William Pulteney*.] I believe this doctrine of
queſtioning Parliament-men was begun in *James* I's and
Charles I's time.

Serjeant *Maynard*.] The great Act for ſecurity of
Religion, and of the whole Nation, which makes a
diſability upon any Papiſt to take an Office or Employment, was taken away by the Diſpenſing Power.

Serjeant *Holt*.] I conceive you cannot agree to
omit the word " Diſpenſe," which was the great and
crying Grievance of the Nation. Eſpecially in the
caſe of Sir *Edward Hales*, to let in Papiſts to Employments againſt an Act of Parliament. From a Diſpenſation to a particular Perſon, it would come to a
general Suſpenſion. The Lords take no notice of
Hales's Diſpenſation. Diſpenſation in any caſe has no
ſolid foundation in Law ; it may vacate all Grants. I
agree to have the word qualified, but not totally left out.

Sir *Thomas Lee*.] Prohibition of Importation of Wool
and Logwood were diſpenſed with to one in favour.
All theſe things have begun upon low beginnings. I
give only general Inſtances.

Mr *Finch*.] I cannot agree with the Lords in leaving out " Diſpenſation*." Diſpenſation was to the

* The Lords gave this Reaſon for leaving out " Diſpenſing, *&c.*" " it
might in ſome caſes tend to the prejudice of the Subjects Patents depending upon *Non obſtantes*."

Act

Debates in Parliament in 1688. 8₃

Act of Uniformity before Sufpenfion, which was actually done in the Declaration. Sufpenfion had an ill beginning in Error, and therefore had no foundation. 'Tis dangerous to fay that all power of Difpenfing is illegal; you may undo many perfons. 'Tis not a proper way of remedy to fay that all power of Difpenfing is illegal.

Serjeant *Maynard*.] Confidering the fhortnefs of the time, and the danger we are in, I would agree with the Lords; but I would make a Declaration, that it be confidered in another Parliament.

Major *Wildman*.] Difpenfations are rather *permiffa* then *licita*, and the foundation not good from the beginning.

[*Wednefday, February* 13.

The Lords and Commons agreed " That the Prince and Princefs ♦f *Orange* fhould be proclaimed King and Queen of *England*, *France* and *Ireland*, *&c.* to hold the Crown, *&c.* during their Lives, and the Life of the Survivor; the Regal Power to be exercifed by the Prince; and after their Deceafe, the Crown to devolve to the Heirs of the Body of the Princefs; in Default of fuch Iffue, to the Princefs *Anne*, and the Heirs of her Body; and for Default of fuch Iffue, to the Heirs of the Body of the faid Prince of *Orange*." And they were accordingly proclaimed King and Queen the day after (the 14th) with great folemnity, both Houfes of Parliament attending in the Proceffion.

Friday, February 15.

The Speaker reported, That what his Majefty was pleafed to fpeak on *Wednefday* laft to both Houfes, (when they prefented to the King and Queen their Declaration of Right *) was to the effect and in the words following : " This is certainly the greateft proof of the Truft you have in us that can be given; which is the thing which makes us value it the more; and we thankfully accept what you have offered to us.

---

* Both Houfes of Convention in a full body attending their Highneffes in the Banqueting Houfe, this great Inftrument was read with a loud voice by the Clerk of the Crown; after which the Marquefs of *Halifax*, Speaker of the Houfe of Lords, made a folemn Tender of the Crown to their Highneffes, in the Name of both Houfes, the Reprefentative of the Nation. *Echard.*

G 2 " And

84   *Debates in Parliament in* 1688.

" And as I had no other Intention in coming hither than
to preferve your Religion, Laws, and Liberties, fo you may be
fure that I fhall endeavour to fupport them; and fhall be willing to concur in any thing that fhall be for the good of the
Kingdom, and to do all that is in my Power to advance the
Welfare and Glory of the Nation."

And that thereupon the Lords and Commons went immediately to proclaim the King and Queen.

Refolved, That the humble Thanks of this Houfe be returned
to the King and Queen, *&c.* for their Majefties gracious
Anfwer,

Adjourned to *Monday.*

Monday, February 18.

His Majefty acquainted both Houfes in a Speech, reported
by the Speaker, " That the Condition of his Allies abroad,
and particularly that of *Holland*, was fuch, that without fome
fpeedy Care they would run great Hazard. That the Pofture
of Affairs here required alfo their ferious Confideration; and
that a good fettlement at home was neceffary, not only for
their own Peace, but for the fupport of the Proteftant Intereft
both here and abroad: That, particularly, the ftate of *Ireland*
was fuch, that the Dangers were grown too great to be ob-
viated by any flow Methods. The moft effectual ways to prevent thefe Inconveniences, and the forms to bring thefe things
to pafs, muft be left to them."

Thanks, *&c.* were voted to his Majefty.]

Tuefday, February 19.

In a Grand Committee on the King's Speech.

Mr *Medlycott.*] To prepare ourfelves againft any
foreign Invafion, or inteftine Troubles at home,
there will be a neceffity of raifing Money, which
muft be done in a parliamentary way. And if
we ftay to call a new Parliament, it will be too late;
therefore I move to turn this Convention into a
Parliament. This being not convened in the Royal
Name, I hope formalities will not be infifted upon
to lofe the fubftance. Refolving fuch an Affembly
into a Parliament is not without Reafon nor Precedent,
                                        both

Debates in Parliament in 1688. 85

both formerly and lately. After the Death of *William* the Conqueror, *Robert* being in *Normandy*, *William Rufus*, the second brother, was declared King, by a mutual stipulation betwixt the King and People, in the nature of *Magna Charta*. In the 12th of King *Charles* II, a Convention was called at that King's instance when beyond sea: 'Twas called by desire of the King, when at *Breda*, and after 'twas convened several Acts passed; some were confirmed by the subsequent Parliament, and some not; and those not confirmed were thought valid by the Judges. I infer from thence that the Subjects may upon emergencies meet as well as if called formally by Writ, when forms cannot be had; and move to have an Act to declare this a Parliament to all intents and purposes.

Sir *Robert Sawyer*.] We are to consider the King's Speech, *&c.* for a speedy Settlement of the Nation; and the only way to come at this is a free Parliament; and Money being the great matter to consider of, it cannot be raised without a Parliament. There are some Precedents spoken of, which, if they would at all come up to our case, I should agree to. What is mentioned of *William Rufus* is mistaken as to the case of a Convention. There was no Parliament seven days after he was elected: *Lanfranc*, Archbishop of *Canterbury*, and the rest of the Bishops and Clergy, were especially concerned in it, and by them he was declared King. As for the Precedent spoken of, of the Convention in *Charles* II's time, that Convention was originally a Parliament, and by the seal of that time called to meet in Parliament, and had all the formality of the consent of the People; nay every Act of Confirmation, in the subsequent Parliament, styles them a Parliament at their first meeting; they were called by the Government *in esse* at that time, and were returned as such; and to this Parliament, before they did any thing, the King signified his Approbation of their meeting; and when the King came into *England*, he called them

G 3   a Par-

86   *Debates in Parliament in* 1688.

a Parliament. There was then a King *de Facto*, and
a Government *de Facto*, and by his confent 'tis a Parliament, and that gives it the virtue of a Parliament.
The calling it one way or other alters not the cafe;
but the fingle thing I infift upon is the People's confent. We reprefent the People to this fpecial purpofe;
that now, upon King *James*'s withdrawing, we are called hither to fupply that defect; and we can proceed
no farther, till a free Parliament with the People's confent be called. If this body may continue to act as a
Parliament, without breach of Elections of the People, I fhould be for it. It cannot be done unlefs we
break our Truft. Therefore as that of *Charles* II. was
a Parliament by the King's confent, therefore I
move that the King may be advifed to iffue out new
Writs to call a Parliament.

Mr *Bofcawen*.] I appeal to the Houfe whether *Sawyer* be miftaken, or no, in feveral things he has faid.
I will fay farther, that the People, who fent us hither,
do not only affert the Goverment, but would have us
prevent running back from whence we came; and
now that we are got to the Top of the Hill not to let
all fall! I have not contributed to invade the Liberties of the People, and am as far from it as that
Gentleman. But that Convention which brought in
Charles II. was not fo much a Parliament as this Convention. A Parliament is nothing but *parler le ment*.
That Parliament was called by fome Members included,
and fome excluded, the Long Parliament, by the Seal
from the Keepers of the Liberties of *England*; and
then with fuch Limitations, that fuch and fuch were
only to be returned, as if they were taking Tefts;
none that had been engaged in the King's party during the War, nor the fons of them, unlefs they had
given Teftimony of their Affections to the Government; which renders that Parliament as far from freedom of choice, as white is from black. And in the
Bill for Triennial Parliaments, the Chancellor was of
courfe to iffue out Writs, and for defect of his if-
                                                    fuing

Debates in Parliament in 1688. 87

fuing them out, the Officers of the Country were to do. it by themfelves; from whence I gather that their is no fuch effential thing as a Writ for chufing Members. If you take the Advice of the learned Gentletleman (*Sawyer*) to call another Parliament, and diffolve this, *Ireland* may be loft; and the King of *France* would give 100,000 *l*. to accomplifh it. I am jealous there is a Snake hid in the Grafs, and that there is fomething more in this, than we fee. Confider, if this be no Parliament, then you may fuppofe that the Throne never was vacant, and that 'tis now full; and how will you get a Parliament? And fome look on the other fide the Water. Upon the whole, I would confider the relief of *Ireland*, and to affift *Holland*, which has helped to preferve us, and take up this Debate for the prefent. No other defign can be in this, but to put us all to ftand upon our guard again, and fight out our way, and be upon no bottom: If we retract, and go fo far as is moved, we fhall be all ruined, and go back again to our misfortunes.

Sir *Thomas Clarges*.] I am not of *Bofcawen's* mind. I hope I may fay I never did any thing to infringe the liberties of the People; and though the wind has been in my face, Gentlemen that were never in the Parliament.before know, whither this matter may be carried. In the two laft reigns, there was making diftinctions of Perfons here; we were reproached that we voted againft the King, when we gave our Votes freely according to our Judgments, and that, by thefe Practices, we reprefented but part of the People, and not the whole Nation. I meant no otherwife than that the King fhould govern well. I brought in the *Habeas Corpus* Bill, and what I fay now is with my confcience and mind. As to what is now in Debate, I hope we may have a free-chofen Parliament in twenty five days, the formality of forty days from the Teft of the Writ to the Election not being neceffary. In the Affembly at *London* before this Convention, the propofition was, how the Prince of *Orange* might come to a free Parliament.

G 4 liament.

liament. 'Twas advised, that Letters should be sent from the Prince into the Counties and Boroughs, &c. in order to the Choice of a free Parliament; and I gave my Voice for it preparatory to that: And since it has been voted here, that the Throne was vacant, I am satisfied, though I was then against it. I question whether, upon this change, our Alliances do subsist against that great Monster the *French* King, who invades the *Hollanders*—I hope the Revenue, which is 2,200,000 *l.* may support *Ireland*—When you met the 22d of *January*, and proposed that the Prince should have the Administration of the Government, you omitted one great thing; *viz.* to advise him to possess himself of the Revenue. I propose now that all the Revenue of *James* II. may be used by the King, and there will be no fear of running back from whence we came, as you have been told; but by not calling a Parliament, we put all to hazard, and that the Money we shall raise will not be paid; and will the Judges in *Westminster-Hall* declare this to be a Parliament? I sat in the Parliament of 1660, which had Qualifications from the Members, but they were not observed. 'Twas summoned in *March* to meet the 25th of *April*—Here was then a King *de Jure* kept out by wilful means—The Convention, in 1660, had Letters from the King, who recognized them a Parliament, and it was never called a Convention by the King, nor by any Act of Parliament; and the Acts afterwards ran " Whereas by Act of Parliament, &c." Lord Chief Justice *Hale*, who sat in that Parliament, was of opinion, it was a Parliament, and that they were under the trust of the People, and the Writs that called us, were not called " no Writs;" and if you make this a Parliament, you elude the Prince's Declaration, which says, " No Money to be raised but by Parliament." Can it have any other meaning than that Writs shall be issued out to chuse a Parliament; and shall we give occasion to say that the King enters into the Government by Prerogative, and our parting with our
Privi-

Debates in Parliament in 1688. **89**

Privileges? It has been said, " How can we have a free Parliament chosen in time? The necessity of affairs cannot bear it." I can consent to an Ordinance, or any declaratory Instrument, that the Oaths and Test ought to be taken by Members, before admitted: And when a free Parliament shall meet, I doubt not but they will ratify what we shall do; and now, that there is a Revenue for the present necessity of affairs, and a new Great Seal now made to issue out Writs of Summons, who would put this upon a mere point, whether this be a Parliament, or not?

A Bill was sent from the Lords to prevent all doubts and disputes, which may arise concerning the assembling and sitting of this present Parliament; which was read the first time.

Mr *Hampden.*] I hope this Bill will tend to your Settlement. I observe, the Lords make it more frequent to read Bills twice in a day than here. The House of Commons are always strict to their Order; and I would not be thrust on by the Lords to hasten the reading this Bill. I move, that it may be read again to-morrow morning. [*Which was ordered.*]

Sir *Edward Seymour.*] I see Gentlemen speak here under great disadvantages. If they are not free in this Convention, what shall we do in Parliament? When Gentlemen speak with Reflections, and cry, " Hear him, hear him," they cannot speak with freedom. I speak not this to the Chair (the Speaker) who keeps Order well, but to what passed at the Committee. Shall you put it into the power of the Lords to lay aside any of your Debates, by sending you a Bill down? I would not remove Land-marks to Posterity. If you are satisfied that this is not a pretended necessity, but really; not in name, as the Ship-money was made, of necessity, which disturbed all your Laws, I would have you leave the Chair, and go into a Grand Committee, for freedom of Debate, to establish our security upon a good foundation. 'Tis not four or five hundred Votes can do it; but to arrive at the knowlege of this matter, I desire to go into a Grand Committee.

Sir

90   *Debates in Parliament in* 1688.

Sir *Henry Capel.*] The Chair has taken care of Order; and I have seen no disorder to-day. When *Seymour* was in the Chair, I have heard "Hear him, hear him," often said in the House. *Seymour* says, "He would not have us tied up by the Lords to what they do." I take it, the Lords and Commons are to take care of the Government, and we ought to agree with the Lords as soon as we can. Had the Committee begun upon Heads, we might have gone on; but by degrees we are gone into the matter of the Lords Bill. *Seymour* told you, "That it was necessity that first brought on the Ship-money:" But it was the practice of ill Ministers and Lawyers, who turned old Rolls to ill Interpretation against the Liberties of the People. If ever there was a necessity to warrant making us a Parliament, there is one now. Are we in Peace? Is the state of *Christendom* in so good a case as we can boast of? *Seymour* tells you of "the Great Man of War." If you sit not here as a Parliament, the King of *France* will give Millions to make a Separation in the Nation.

Sir *Thomas Clarges.*] I am called up by what fell from *Capel* about Peace, &c. I hear no War declared yet, but I would put nothing to hazard: You may have a Parliament in three weeks; and we are better justified in that than any other method. The Revenue for the present will supply *Ireland*. We have forces already in pay, besides those the King brought in. I am glad to see so many worthy persons promoted to Dignities; and I believe they will preserve our Privileges—But as to the method lately taken, to make distinctions, and to be pointed at in *Westminster-Hall*, as one of the hundred and fifty against the Throne vacant; to have printed papers of men of one side and the other; yea, the Peers,—I hope the Gentlemen of the Council will prevent these distinctions.

Mr *Hampden.*] We are collaterally launching into what is not resolved on by the House; to talk of the Formality of calling a Parliament in less than forty days—

Debates in Parliament in 1688.   91

days—But pray keep your own Formalities. The Motion to adjourn the Debate muſt properly be put; or put any thing regularly, and I will ſerve you to an *And* and an *I.* If you debate this, you would all day long debate what you reſolve not, *viz.* Whether you will debate it, or not.

Sir *Robert Howard.*] You have already reſolved to read the Lords Bill to-morrow, and then the proper Debate will ariſe that you are upon to-day. I have heard no arguments to-day to diſcourage the Debate. We are obliged to read the Lords Bill a ſecond time. Put the Queſtion for Adjournment.

Sir *Richard Temple.*] I hope we may arrive at all the ends that any Gentleman can deſire. To-morrow, at the Grand Committee, you will have all the freedom of Debate you can deſire ; and I would not anticipate the Debate till it be regularly before you. But it is a ſtrange thing I hear from *Sawyer,* " That we cannot ſpeak for the Bill at the firſt reading," which you may throw out. Is it not a hard thing to ſpeak againſt it, and not for it ?

Sir *Chriſtopher Muſgrave.*] Gentlemen tell you, that the Queſtion is, Whether adjourn, or not : But with great ſubmiſſion, I affirm, Reaſons may be given why you ſhould not adjourn. You are told, " When you read the Bill to-morrow, you have the ſame liberty as now ;" but then your Bill is to be committed by a Queſtion, and that is gaining the point. The point then is only agreeing with the Committee ; but when it comes to the Houſe, you may throw it out, or not. 'Tis a matter of the greateſt conſideration, that there ſhould be freedom in Debate. Some men can declare their thoughts at one time ; others are not ſo happy, but muſt ſpeak oftener. If then it be neceſſary to ſpeak twice, God forbid but a Gentleman ſhould do it! But if not, no man here can believe you are inclined to make this a free Parliament. I would proceed to the conſideration of the King's Speech.

S r

92   *Debates in Parliament in* 1688.

Sir *Edward Seymour.*] I fpeak to Order. 'Tis not the Lords Bill you are upon by Order; 'tis the King's Speech, and you cannot reftrain it.

Wednefday, February 20.

Sir *Henry Capel* delivered a Meffage from the King, to haften the matters before the Houfe recommended in his Speech. After a long filence,

Lord *Falkland.*] The laft part of the King's Speech ought to be confidered firft, as I take it. If we have not the power of a Parliament, we can go upon nothing. There are Precedents to juftify the Lords Bill that they have fent us. We have great works upon our hands; as that of the Relief of *Ireland,* and to affift our Allies, *&c.* and the Nation is in an unfettled condition. The Lords Bill is a foundation for us to build upon; and I move, that we may follow the Lords example.

Mr *Howe.*] We have had learned difcourfes upon this fubject yefterday, and Precedents were brought us. If the matter arife upon what is Law, I fhall not fpeak to that part, nor what has been done formerly, but to what is fit now. I refpect our Anceftors, who always followed the neceffity of affairs. 'Tis unreafonable in a fick man not to take any phyfic but what has been prefcribed him formerly. We are come out of the greateft tide; and, to prevent the danger, let us throw a good defence againft it; but if we cannot make a perfect one, it is our malicious enemies that throw it down. The *French* King was fo formerly, and our own late King, a Papift, now in *France.* There is a certain fort of Loyalty, called " Paffive Obedience," preached by fome of our Clergy, who would pick holes in our bank to keep out the tide. They fay, " Neceffity has no Law;" let us make one for it, and agree to the Lords Bill.

Serjeant *Maynard.*] I do not wonder that men are filent in a matter of fo great confequence. On the confe-

Debates in Parliament in 1688. 93

confequence of this Debate to-day will not only be the fafety of the Nation, but the Proteftant Religion abroad. We make not a ftep, but we are told of errors in the method, ftill to put a ftop to it. Here has been a great ado about words, " the Crown vacant," and " Abdication." And we have been told what the People were, and "that we muft look to our fafety" (by *Sawyer*;) but you are paft all thefe; and now you are moved to make this Convention a Parliament; but I think, we are one already. What is a Parliament, but King, Lords, and Commons ? Pray read the 1 Chap. of 12 *Charles* II. When the King came in, that Convention, (or call it what you will) *Refolved*, " That, without a Writ from the King, they are a Parliament," notwithftanding they had no Writ from the King. 'Tis grounded upon the greateft Law in the World, the Law of the twelve Tables of the *Romans*: *Salus populi fuprema lex efto.* All Laws muft give place to that Law: 'Tis the great Law of all Self-prefervation. Now read that Statute of the 25th of *April.* [*The Statute was read.*] When the King came in, the 20th of *May*, the Parliament had no Writ to call them. We fat here, before this King was declared, and we are fo far like that Parliament. I fhall hearken to the Debate, and give my opinion.

Sir *Thomas Lee.*] I would not trouble you, but that I find you entirely at leifure. Says *Maynard*, " You cannot make this a Parliament, becaufe you are one already from the beginning." If nobody be againft it, pray let the Speaker take the Chair.

Sir *Robert Howard.*] Here feems a general fatisfaction in what has been faid : Therefore report it to the Chair.

Sir *Edward Seymour.*] If I were fatisfied this was a Parliament, I would not go about to offer reafons againft it. If I am put on that ftrefs, to fay my opinion, I will not juftly move to exceptions. If I do not fully come up to their fenfe, I hope they will give me their pardon, as I fhall do to them. If you concluded

cluded " the Vacancy of the Throne," I am concluded
by it. For the prefervation of the Proteftant Religion, thofe ways are moft prudent that are moft legal
and lafting. This Bill from the Lords began there ;
on *Monday* it was twice read, and came down here on
Tuefday : 'Tis a great rarity, and much done in little
time ; and I never faw a Bill of fo different a nature.
It makes every man in as high a nature criminal as the
Law can make it. You declare yourfelves a Parliament, and the Law fays, you are not a Parliament ;
and fo we are all liable to the Statute of the Tefts, and
all incapacitated to fit here : And then thofe who were
for difpenfing with the Penal Laws, and joined in thofe
things, you bring yourfelves under the fame capacity.
I would have the Gentlemen of the Long Robe tell
you, whether, if you declare yourfelves a Parliament,
you are not liable to the Statute. When it is neither
legal nor prudential to do it, whether then is it neceffary ? That Statute, which *Maynard* mentioned, could
not make that a Parliament which was none before.
That Parliament had the confent of the King *de Facto*
and *de Jure* ; there wanted only the King's Writ of
Summons. If they fay, you were no Parliament before, what Record will make you a Parliament now, is
no where to be found. The Law requires, that the
Sheriff return the Jury of *Nifi Prius*, and the Criminal, *&c.* who are not always the beft men of the county. Suppofe the Bench impannel the beft men in it,
there is the Subftance, the Judge, and the Bench, but
there is not the form. Neceffity is a great commander,
but an ill companion, and a worfe counfellor. And
this Houfe muft expect, in other cafes, never to want
that argument. Some Precedents have been fpoken
of, to induce this method ; one of *William Rufus*,
(which is of no authority to govern you) how the
Nobles did affift him againft his brother *Robert*, who
claimed the Crown ; but that was no Parliament, nor
had the power of a Parliament. The only Precedents
mentioned are thofe of *William Rufus*, and the 12th of
                                                Charles

Debates in Parliament in 1688. 95

Charles II. They made not themfelves a Parliament, but in relation to the Long Parliament that diffolved itfelf, and that done with a *ne trahatur in exemplum.* When the people are called together, by fuch Writ as this, I am bold to fay, there are no Precedents—It has been faid, out of doors, this is by the Precedent of *Edward* III. I find that matter totally miftaken: *Edward* II. was driven out of the Kingdom by his fon and his mother: He abfconded, and by a wind was driven into *Wales*, and her fon was *Cuftos Regni.* And the firft Act of *Edward* III. does declare, " That, whereas the late Lord *Edward* II. by the general advice and affent of his Earls and Barons, had voluntarily re-moved himfelf out of the Realm, they declare *Ed.* III. Regent of the Realm." I would not, as other Gentlemen fay, ftick at Precedents, and think that you are as well qualified to make Precedents as to follow others. Yet there is no neceffity to remove ancient Land-marks, and to let our purfes run out at the back-door. Our condition is attended with many difficulties; *Ireland* is in ill condition, and we hear nothing from *Scotland* but uncertainty. The King of *France* has been the Devil and walking Ghoft in every Parliament. What could you expect from *Ireland?* They will own no obedience to the Prince of *Orange*, but when he is crowned. They are fo far from coming to you, that they are driven from you. The perfon *(Hamilton *)* was fo
far

* Lieutenant General *Hamilton* was fent over to *Ireland*. He was a Papift, but was believed to be a man of honour, and had great intereft with the Earl of *Tyrconnel.* So he undertook to go over to *Ireland*, and to prevail with the Earl of *Tyrconnel* to deliver up the Govern-ment; and promifed that he would either bring him to it, or that he would come back, and give an ac-count of his Negotiation. This ftep had a very ill effect; for be-fore *Hamilton* came to *Dublin*, the Earl of *Tyrconnel* was in fuch de-fpair, looking on all as loft, that he seemed to be very near a full refo-lution of entering on a Treaty to get the beft terms he could. But *Hamilton's* coming changed him quite. He reprefented to him, that things were turning faft in *Eng-land* in favour of the King; fo that, if he ftood firm, all would come round again. He faw, that he muft ftudy to manage this fo dexteroufly, as to gain as much time as he could, that fo the Prince might not make too much hafte, before a Fleet and Supplies might come from *France*. So feveral Letters were wrote over by the fame ma-nage-

far from bringing them over to obedience, that he makes it his endeavour to keep them from you. I speak with good intention to the Protestant Religion in *Ireland,* which is in danger to be gone with him. Through all the course of my life, I had rather have unkindness than carry an ill thing about me. A great many Preliminaries ought to be thought of; you will not think fit that *England* should be at all the Charge to reduce *Ireland :* You know formerly there were Adventurers, and you may raise a great deal of money that way. There are two ways to reduce *Ireland ;* present supply of Arms, and Money; but, if not, such as will preserve you, and master them : They will be masters of whatever you send, if you attempt, and fail in the attempt ; and it will be hard to reduce it after. I speak this, not thinking there is a necessity for Money to carry it on. The present Revenue will go a great way towards it, together with the public security ; and no doubt but loyal *London* will supply their Prince upon this exigency, and will supply fully, rather than let the work stand still. We are called as a Council, and may so continue ; for we have no declared enemy, and are in a condition of Peace till War be declared ; and there is none, and we have no League—Can we re-

gagement, giving assurances, that the Earl of *Tyrconnel* was fully resolved to treat and submit. And, to carry this farther, two Commissioners were sent from the Council-board to *France.* Their Instructions were to represent to the King the necessity of *Ireland*'s submitting to *England.* *Tyrconnel* pretended that, in honour, he could do no less than disengage himself to his master before he laid down the Government. Yet he seemed resolved not to stay for an answer or a consent ; but that, as soon as this Message was delivered, he would submit upon good conditions : And for these, he knew, he should have all that he asked. With this management he gained his point, which was much time ; and he now fancied, that the honour of restoring the King would belong chiefly to himself. Thus *Hamilton,* by breaking his own faith, secured the Earl of *Tyrconnel* to the King, and this gave the beginning to the War of *Ireland.* Those who had advised the sending over of *Hamilton,* were much out of countenance ; and it was believed that it had a terrible effect on Sir *William Temple*'s son, who had raised in the Prince a high opinion of *Hamilton*'s honour. Soon after that, he, who had no other visible cause of melancholy besides this, went into a boat on the *Thames,* near the bridge, where the river runs most impetuously, and leaped into the river, and was drowned. *Burnet.*

quire

Debates in Parliament in 1688. 97

quire any thing to be done, before the King be civilly dead, and parties not in being? I speak not this to reflect on him that has done so much for us. I would not only have him paid the charge he has been at, but have *England*'s bounty too to go along with him. *England* has done formerly for *Holland*, as *Holland* has done now for *England*. But I should be glad to see us a legal Parliament, that we may have the People's hearts along with us; and then we shall be sure of their Money. As a Council, we may sit, and represent to the King, that we are not impowered by those that sent us, and desire him to issue out Writs to chuse a Parliament. The Revenue last year was 2,100,000 and odd pounds; the expences 1,800,000*l*; a large proportion of it to the Fleet; many Pensions, and for Secret Service; I hope we shall hear no more of that: Besides the Privy Purse 150,000 *l*. You have sufficient for all your difficulties, and need not turn yourselves into a Parliament for that. In the *Palatinate* War, you had a Committee to manage it—And you may have time to digest all for *Ireland*, and Writs may go out. In the mean time we may sit as a Council. and this will bring us into no difficulties. I have delivered my opinion, and now do what you please.

Serjeant *Maynard*.] If *Seymour* speaks confusedly, I must answer him confusedly. He seems to speak with great reason at first sight; but, looked into, 'tis just nothing. I will answer him to what is material as well as my old memory will run along with him. "When we cannot have a legal Parliament, how shall we possess that which is legal?" He spoke of the Statute, &c. and Tests: The objection is true; no Parliament can sit here, till they have taken the Oaths and Tests: But, under favour, that will not come to our case; that Oath was to the late King, and now, what Oath can we take to a King out of the Throne? You remember what he did, and your Vote upon it. Can we swear still? I hold it impossible to take that Oath, and that Act does cease of itself. I do not say

VOL. IX. H we

98   *Debates in Parliament in* 1688.

we make ourſelves a Parliament. But if this be declared a Parliament by a Parliament of the whole Nation, who dares ſay againſt it ? 'Tis impoſſible to
take the Oath of Allegiance, without being perjured
ipſo faƈto. I would have *Seymour* anſwer me, as I do
him. Shall I ſwear to an impoſſibility ? A man in a
wilderneſs, and out of his way, aſks, Where is the
high-way ? That Gentleman cries, Where is the Law ?
When we cannot find it, we muſt have recourſe to the
Law of Nations. *Salus Populi ſuprema·Lex eſto.* Says
Seymour, "There is no neceſſity to make this a Parliament ; there is no King, nor any declared enemy beyond ſea :" But he that would deſtroy his own People
for Religion, I am ſure, is no friend of ours. Is he not
an enemy that receives all that go from us in diſcon-
tent ? I would not have you entangled with a fine
Speech ; I hope we ſhall not farther diſpute upon words,
as we have done ſome weeks, but neceſſity puts us upon the beſt way we can take. All the event of this
will be to make a difference betwixt the Lords and us.
I will not ſay it is *Seymour*'s intent, but what greater
difference can there be than when the Lords ſay we are
a Parliament, and we ſhall ſay, we are not a Parliament ? There is a great danger in ſending out
Writs at this time, if you conſider what a ferment the
Nation is in ; and I think the Clergy are out of their
wits ; and, I believe, if the Clergy ſhould have their
wills, few or none of us ſhould be here again ; and
never any Popiſh Prince but would not only be
the deſtruƈtion of the Proteſtant Religion, but the
Proteſtants muſt go to pot ; as in *France*, *Bohemia*,
and *Hungary* ; and all by the inſtigation of the Clergy.
What is a Parliament then ? The Convention was not
called by the King's Writs legally, yet were declared
a Parliament ; and you will not declare yourſelves no
Parliament, unleſs you are out of your wits.

Mr *Eyre*.] The matter you are upon is of great conſequence ; therefore I hope you will purſue thoſe coun-
ſels which tend moſt to peace. The way to thoſe ends
is full of difficulties. I ſhall not meddle with politic

Debates in Parliament in 1688.   99

confiderations (with *Seymour*) but the proper matter
now before you. The objections againft the Lords
Bill return upon them that made them. If we are
not conftituted a Parliament under thefe circumftances
now, we may never have one in *England* more——
13 *Charles* II, " No Members are to fit till they have
taken the Oaths by the Statute 5 *Elizabeth*; and the
Oaths not taken voids the Election :" Then all thofe
Elections were void; unlefs thofe Acts are repealed,
how will you ever come by it ? Muft not the next
Parliament make themfelves one by a Law ? But if a
falfe ftep muft be made, why fhould it not be by us,
whilft our wounds yet bleed, and not leave it to another body of men to heal, fix weeks hence, and the
wound paft remedy ? Being to build as of old, with
weapons in our hands, as the *Jews* did, I would not
lay them down till we have built in fecurity. We are
in an infant Government, if I may fo ftyle it; it muft
be preferved by the hand that brought it up. Are we
fure our fucceffors will be of our mind? Nay, the
prefent ferment of the Nation, which time may quiet,
may be fo hot as to give up their own fecurity. The
prefent neceffity is great, as great as the fupport of
our Honour, Religion, and Country—Neceffity abro-
gates all Laws. The Precedents of this, that are demanded, are not to be expected : 'Tis not in every
King's reign that he abdicates the Government. As
to the Precedents of *Edward* II, and *Richard* II, none
of thefe come to our cafe immediately : Neceffity gave
them a fanction ; and where there is the fame Neceffity,
there is the fame reafon. We are as full a Reprefentative as can be had; by the call of the Prince's Letters, we have the beft Reprefentative of the People
that could be had. Is the difference of a Writ and a
Letter put into the fcale with the fafety of the Proteftant Religion ? We may *pay tythe of mint, anife
and cummin, and neglect the greater matters of the Law.*
Tares may be fown whilft we are abfent ; which to
prevent, and bring forth Peace, fo luckily brought

H 2   to

100   *Debates in Parliament in* 1688.

to the Birth, I would have the Lords Bill read a fecond time.

Sir *Robert Sawyer.*] As to what *Maynard* faid with
reflection on the Clergy, I defire to take off that reflection. They have as great a fubmiffion to your
Vote as can be. I fpeak of the Clergy of *Cambridge.*
I had a Letter from *Cambridge* yefterday, (the place I
ferve for), which gives me notice, that they are very
well fatisfied with what you have done; and if they
had time, they would have petitioned for a Parliament
to be chofen; and I have authority from them to let
you know they are to give Money to fupport the Government; and I know how to give my Vote. The
Oaths muft be taken, or elfe all we have done is void;
therefore whether you will do it now like thofe in authority.

Sir *Thomas Clarges.*] I ftand up with great trouble.
As I am now advifed, if this Convention be turned
into a Parliament, 'tis the greateft difservice you can
to the King. I would preferve both his Honour and
Safety. If any thing be wanting in the Revenue, nothing can fupply it but a Parliament. You may have
a Parliament in twenty five days; 1,200,000 *l.* may be
raifed for *Ireland* and *Holland*, all the charge of the
Government, and for Provifion for the Royal Family.
We may fpare a Million, if fuch a Sum be requifite, to
affift us for the prefent, and for other things they may
keep cold for a month. If this be fo, we are not in
fuch Danger as to fly out of the Window. Some things
neceffity has drawn us into; thofe are of the leaft neceffity; but to raife Money is the greateft thing. I
hope 'tis that the King expects from us, and that we
are not trufted to do by thofe that fent us. If the
Revenue for a month be employed, though War
with *France*, an enemy to all Religion and Goodnefs—
In the reign of *Charles* II, the Parliament did fettle a
Revenue on the King's two Brothers; the Officers of
the Revenue told us, that it was not 200,000 *l.* a year.
A great man told a ftory, that a fum of Money was
                                                        pai d.

Debates in Parliament in 1688. 101

paid, and wanted a Crown; the party would have told their Money, but the other would not let him. They would not let the Committee then examine it, for certainly they would have found it more. Where there is a neceffity to give, I will give as plentifully as any body, but let us do it fairly, and by full Authority. As we are, we fhall have no credit upon it; when we come again we may be a lawful Parliament; and I believe the people will fend you again.—A merry man faid once in this Houfe, " Some can ftop and turn managed horfes." As for the Clergy of *London*, they are as learned as any fince the time of the Apoftles. The Church of *England* brought us in *Charles* II, and ftood conftant in thefe laft Tryals—I ever thought thofe laws too hard to prefs mens confciences—They ftood like Apoftles in *Magdalen* College cafe, which is remarkable— I hope the vacant Bifhoprick of *Salifbury* * will be filled with one of that College. *Salus Populi* is *fuprema Lex*, you are told, but if ever you break down the hedges of the Government—And properly we cannot agree with the Lords.

Serjeant *Maynard*.] There is only one Queftion to be infifted on, whether we are a Parliament, and what we fhall do when we are a Parliament. *Clarges* fpeaks honeftly, as I believe he thinks. As for the Clergy, I have much honour for high and low of them, but I muft fay they are in a ferment, there are Pluralifts among them, and when they fhould preach the Gofpel, they preach againft the Parliament, and the Law of *England*—I did not fpeak againft the Clergy in general. I hear no man that feconds *Clarges*'s Motion; therefore put the Queftion for reading the Lords Bill.

Col. *Birch*.] I have heard a Debate of this nature forty years ago, and I ftand amazed at it: I will not bring the Precedents of *Edward* II, and *Henry* IV, to juftify our proceedings, but what I remember of my

---

* Vacant by the Death of Bifhop *Ward*. Dr *Burnet* was advanced to it.

H 3   Know.

102   *Debates in Parliament in* 1688.

Knowledge. I hope we ſhall not fall under this Debate now, and not forty years ago, when we were under much harder circumſtances, when any little words dropt then, about the validity of that Parliament, they were ſmiled at, and not worth an anſwer. When *Oliver* was propoſed to be made a King here, that was laughed at then ; and I believe this Debate will be ſo now. I intreat a little of your Patience ; that of 1660 Parliament was not ſo clearly called as this. Cavaliers were excluded by thoſe that had power to do it, and they did it. 'Twas called by Writ from the Keepers of the Liberties of *England*, that brought us hither. Then all the learned Gentlemen here, Sir *Mathew Hale* and the reſt, were of opinion, 'twas a Parliament to all intents and purpoſes, and nothing of a Convention was ſpoken of ; and to work they went, and very vigorouſly, and not one Queſtion was made of the legality of that Writ, and that Parliament gave two Aſſeſſments of 60,000 *l. per menſem*, before that Act came in to declare it a Parliament ; but there was a great deal more done before the King came in, all the Acts that could be done that were neceſſary, and if one word was ſpoken againſt it, 'twas ſmiled at. That objection about the Oaths has ſome weight ; but in that Parliament of 1660 not an Oath was taken : About ſix weeks after, the Duke of *Ormond* gave the Oaths to the Members, which was far from any Regularity ; and at the opening that Parliament, there were not above eight or nine Lords in the Houſe. There was a Faſt ordered, and a Thankſgiving, and Conferences with the Lords, and not one word of queſtioning the validity of that Parliament ; and now that God has done this for us, to make difficulties when really there is none, I cannot ſee them, from what has been practiſed. Now to ſhow you the Conſequence ; for Money ſhould you ſtay for another Parliament, if you get one in three weeks, a Plot may be upon you, in the interim, and then you will have difficulties ſtill, and perhaps more than are on you now.

                                                                And

Debates in Parliament in 1688.   103

And will you, by throwing away this opportunity, void all the bleffings God has given you? You have, by God's providence, a King that denies you nothing, and now we would be fcrambling again for Religion. I fee a wheel within a wheel in thefe things. I would look on the wheel within my eye. But fuppofe another Parliament go on where we leave off, another Parliament (it feems) muft have the thanks for what has been done, and not you; they muft be the white boys. You have it before you, go on, make your Prince love you; but it feems you fhall not do it, and a fucceeding Parliament muft make a fine hand of this work for you. When once *May* comes, it will not be pleafant fitting here. Many worthy Gentlemen formerly have loft their lives by it. Great Revolutions may be in one year—And you are loft for your Allies, Religion, and all you have. This over-runs all; think on this ferioufly, and go forward with heart and hand: God has done it all; let us not throw it down again. From the beft of Precedents, that of 1660, you are a Parliament; you make not yourfelves a Parliament. Pray go on and read the Lords Bill.

Sir *Thomas Lee.*] I, think we are a much better Parliament than that of 1660. I would know where the Writ was then that called the Lords? Parliaments are not the fame things they were from the beginning; they have had variations. Was not the Prince of *Orange* invefted with legal Authority by you? And the returns of us hither recorded? If you are not a Parliament, how can you reprefent the People in a parliamentary manner, and then what becomes of your Inftrument of Government, and what elfe you have done? The Laws againft Popery, and the Teft, were made when you had no profpect of King *James*'s Abdication; and where were the Oaths of Allegiance, &c. when thefe Gentlemen went in to the Prince? I believe the People like you fo well, they will either fend you again or better. *Clarges* has told you, you cannot raife Money, and, at the fame time,

H 4   tells

104   *Debates in Parliament in* 1688.

tells you, the Revenue may be raifed for prefent ufe.' We are told of relief of *Ireland*; and what next muft be told? You are no Parliament, and you raife the King's Revenue. The King may fearch for his Revenue, and will find it no more legal than now, and no Oaths taken—I fay that you are and were a Parliament, from the beginning.

Sir *Richard Temple.*] I fhall offer fomething not yet touched upon. Has any man faid yet we are not a full and free Reprefentative? Formalities are wanting, you are told, but they are fuch as could not be had; your Elections were as free as ever. No Precedent was ever of a freer. In the Parliament of 1660, there were Qualifications for the Members, and the Lords were not called by Writ, and (a greater thing,) a Commonwealth called it, which was quite another Government. There was a time when Parliaments met without Writs, and King *John*'s was the firft called by Letters, as now, and nobody having fhowed any thing againft the Authority that called you, I will not labour it. In *Henry* IV's time, the fame Parliament was called again, and they raifed Money. When the Affembly of Lords and Commons met, the Prince faid " he would advife with them of the beft manner to call a free Parliament;" and they advifed him to fend his Letters. Have not you done the greateft thing, and now ftumble at the lefs? How you can juftify all you have done, if you are not a Parliament called in as good a manner as could be, admits no Anfwer.

Sir *William Williams.*] 'Tis ftrange we fhould be here a month, and now queftion whether we are a Parliament. If we are called by all the power of *England* a Parliament, then certainly we are fo. Taking it for granted that you could not have fuch a Writ as is ufual, can you be better called? I am forry there fhould now be fuch a Debate. If you fay you are no Parliament, you immediately pafs Judgment againft yourfelves; you make yourfelves the greateft fools, and fomething elfe, and act like children; you have

                                                    acted

Debates in Parliament in 1688. 105

acted without call, and all you have done is void. It will be a ftrange Queftion upon your books.

Sir *Henry Capel.*] I would encourage and affift this King that defires to live with Parliaments. Leave him not alone fix Weeks, but let it not be upon your Books that there is any Queftion upon this matter.

Mr *Pollexfen.*] I can fay no more than what has been mentioned. That nothing may appear on your Books on this occafion, put the Queftion for the Speaker to take the Chair.

Sir *Chriftopher Mufgrave.*] I think you cannot put the Queftion for the Chair. If you confult the Order, 'tis about nothing of the Bill from the Lords, but only " to confider the King's Speech." That is all I have to fay at prefent.

Mr *Bofcawen.*] I agree, we can take no notice of the Lords Bill at the Committee; you are only to confider the King's Speech, and I defire to-morrow you will go upon it. And when the Speaker is in the Chair, you may call for the Lords Bill.

Sir *Thomas Lee.*] Many without doors difcourfe fo much of difference in opinion here in this matter, that I would therefore have the Queftion on the Books.

Sir *George Treby.*] I am fully fatisfied that you are a Parliament. For the honour of the Houfe, declare you are a Parliament; though not for the honour of thofe that oppofed it, yet for yours. If you confider the Prince's Advice, in his Letter, he defcribed a Parliament; whoever denies us to be a Parliament, denies there is either King, or Lords, and Commons. Declare yourfelves one, and you will do yourfelves right, and defeat the defigns of your Enemies.

Mr *Godolphin.*] I am forry to differ from feveral in this great Affembly. I have heard it faid, " If this be not a Parliament originally, we cannot make ourfelves one." I believe thofe who fent me hither, have given me no fuch Authority. I believe we are well chofen, but only for a particular purpofe; which purpofe we have accomplifhed. I am afraid, if Gentlemen look
into

into the Returns by which they fit, they will find they have no fuch form as the old Returns, [*and reads his own Return*] which is thus, " according to the annexed Order and Letter," which is in order to call a free and legal Parliament. If the Gentlemen of the Robe will give it under their hands that this is a Parliament, I will agree; (the Crown, I believe, is worthily placed) but if I am not fatisfied in my Confcience and Judgment that this is a Parliament, I muft be excufed for my Negative. To have every body well fatisfied, your beft way is to faften the King by a legal Parliament. Before you leave the Chair, put a Queftion to eftablifh the Revenue; and that the King may have power to charge it for prefent Emergency, fit and prepare Matters for another Parliament.

Sir *George Treby.*] The main thing that fticks with this Gentleman, *Godolphin*, is the Authority of his Borough, and *Sawyer* had his Authority by laft night's poft *. If *Godolphin* will let me read that part of his Return he has not, if it imports he is a Member of Parliament, he is one, though poffibly, he was not fo fenfible of it before. [*He reads the Words in* Englifh, *tranflated, in the Return*] Here is the plaineft Authority to chufe the Member by the Letter, and all Authority contained in the Return that can be, and I hope this Gentleman will now concur.

Sir *Robert Howard.*] One thing has been omitted; we are all for a Parliament, and yet fpeak againft it. All would have us be doing with Money. And if *Godolphin*'s Borough fent him to treat about Money, and we are not a Parliament, he has the largeft Commiffion I ever heard of.

Refolved, That it is the Opinion of this Committee, That the Lords Spiritual and Temporal, and the Commons, now fitting at *Weftminfter,* are a Parliament.

[Agreed to by the Houfe.]

[*February* 21, Omitted.]

* See p. 100

Friday

Notes of what passed in the Convention ... January 1689

STATE PAPERS.

1688-9.
Tranfcribed
from Lord
Somers's
notes taken
with a pencil.

NOTES of what paſſed in the Convention upon the day the queſtion was moved in the Houſe of Commons concerning the Abdication of King James II. *the 28th of January* 1688-9.

Mr. Dolben.

VACANCY in the government, and the King demiſed.—King withdrawn without proviſion.—Fact clear.—Law plain.—1. The word ſhews it.—2. The ſame reaſon for providing whether his demiſe be merely civil, or whether it be natural, as well as civil.—Chaſm in the adminiſtration.—Total failure of Juſtice.—Authorities.—Edward IV. upon the rumour of the Earl of Warwick's coming, fled: held to be a demiſe, and all proceedings diſcontinued.—Judges learned at that time, Lyttleton one.—*Obj.* Edward IV. returned.—*Anſw.* But that was by conqueſt.—Edward II. reſigned by dureſs, yet adjudged a demiſe in the ſame term.—1 Edward 3. 3.—Richard II. reſigned *per minas.*—Raſt. 528, b.—In this caſe *, departure voluntary.—King acknowledged it.—Did the ſame thing twice.—This conſonant to other laws.—Grotius.—Hottoman.—A Prince ceaſing to adminiſter juſtice, he ceaſes to be King.—Moves, that it is the opinion of the committee, that King James II. is demiſed, by voluntary departure, in conſequence of which the government is without a King.

Mr. Arnold.

Seconded.

Sir R. Temple.

Before he went, deſtroyed all the foundations of the government.—In reſpect to parliament, what arts were uſed!—Turned out all men, who would not comply.—Modelled corporations.—Weſtminſter-hall an inſtrument of ſlavery and popery.—Judges turned out, till the

* *i. e.* James's.

VOL. II.　　　3 F　　　diſpenſing

1688-9. dispensing power owned.——Ordinary justice destroyed, and extra-ordinary relief prevailed.——This is falling from royal powers.——He is a tyrant who acts against his own laws.——Church ruled by ecclesiastical commission law.——Freeholders by martial law.——If no vacancy, how came we here? What steps have been taken towards a compliance?——He suppressed the writs for calling a free Parliament.—Took away the Great Seal.—In breach of his oath endeavoured to subvert the government.——That relinquished, as to the exercise.——Provide for yourselves.——Your resolution already declared, by placing the administration in the Prince of Orange.

Mr. Howe

Thinks it a forfeiture, though he has not the same fears.

Sir R. Howard

Instructed by three worthy persons who have spoken.—Not merely to rest it on *a demise*.——Other English Kings have sucked in the poison of arbitrary power.——That not enough in this instance, our souls must have been enslaved.——Nothing left to subvert.——Usurped all civil and ecclesiastical power.——Violence ever attending his religion,——Corporations.——Closetting.——This Richard the Second's design.——High court of Special Justice, to ruin religious rights, as the dispensing power, the civil.——Ask, if after this a King?——But a King can do no wrong.——This is to quit the part of a King, to act that of a tyrant.——Bracton.——Fortescue.——Every man has a divine right to his life; forfeits it, if he breaks the compact.——So the King.——Compact is the origin of power.——Grotius says so.——People part of the legislative power.——*Abdication* of the government.——Declaration for liberty of conscience would have ruined both Church and State together.——Right devolved on the people, and we must form ourselves.——The King has abandoned us in detestation of his people as poisoned; and meant to carry away from us all means to help ourselves.——Moves some stronger words to be inserted in the question.

STATE PAPERS.

queſtion.——That James II. having endeavoured to ſubvert the conſtitution, by breaking the original contract, &c.

Mr. Pollexfen.

If voluntary going, and nothing more in the caſe, then a deſcent; and if ſo, what do you here ?——If not voluntary, conſider carefully on what to reſt it.——All agree the thrône to be vacant.

Mr. Dolben.

Departure voluntary ſufficient.

Sir James Oxenden.

He went away with deſign to ſtir up all the foreign powers, ſo voluntary.

Sir H. Capel.

Inconſiſtency of our government with a popiſh head.——Queen Elizabeth laid the foundation of a proteſtant government.——Oath of ſupremacy.——Oath of allegiance.——Two principles of popery, 1ſt, No faith to be kept with heretics; 2d, Poſitive obligation to extirpate them.——Papiſts may be fair men, taken one with another; but when church or government concerned, they are in the power of prieſts.

Sir R. Sawyer.

Difference between an abdication and a diſſolution of the government to which the argument of ſome leads.——What then do we here, or the ſecond eſtate in the other houſe ?——We are not the people collectively nor repreſentatively.——We are the third eſtate, in the regular courſe, and the conſtitution monarchial.——Copyholders, leaſeholders, &c. are the people.——Prince's declaration is for a Parliament, which ſuppoſes a conſtitution.——If diſſolution, Lords only repreſent their own vote as individuals, and ought not to meet as an eſtate.—Not in the minds of people to diſpoſe of crowns; but to ſet the government on its true bottom.——Reaſon why we ſhould come here; greater part of the other houſe aſſume it to themſelves to meet, on the ſame principle of *neceſſity*.——So the Prince and

3 F 2   nation

1688-9.   nation judged it..——Writs recalled.——King withdrawn.——No possibility to come at the Parliament.——Formalities used upon a natural demise. We have no power to decide of ourselves, but must give the people's consent.——People must declare what they think of this demise.——*Quest.* Whether this departure so circumstantiated is an abdication?——Thinks so.——Several breaches precedent are certain evidences *quo animo.*——Religion interwoven with the State.——To refuse to govern according to the constitution is absolutely to disclaim the government.——And he who withdraws on such account abdicates.——Never heard of so short a reign so full of violence.——Declaration tells you what was his mind.——Putting all into the popish hands.——Suborning a Parliament.——Richard II. the only instance.——One remedy, as we judged, a Parliament.—— Recalling his writs a continuation of his mind.——At liberty when beyond sea, and yet no application towards administering.

Mr. Boscawen.

We are supposed to be a representative, and can be nothing else. ——In former proclamations it was made out, that he being a King of such a religion as he is, would do as he has done.——King gone away with his seal and child.——Throne vacant.——Should set up him who is most able to govern.——The author of all your mischiefs.——Not to fight with a bulrush.

Sir William Pulteney.

Crown descends not from heaven; then must come from the people.——If error to let him go, to recal him double.——Should attempt it with halters about our necks.——Crown often disposed of by Parliaments.——Dispensing power.——Bringing in foreign jurisdiction.——No wrong done if not by him.——Said to be traiterous to distinguish between power and person, but all governments depend upon it.——To take it into our consideration not to run back.——As little wrong as may be.——Consider your deliverer.

——Do

STATE PAPERS.   4c5

——Do what your pofterity may blefs you for.——Never expect the like game again.   1ʳ88-9.

Sir Thomas Clarges.

Crown void has a confequence of an extraordinary nature.——To make an election, will turn conftitution into a commonwealth.—— The Prince took this to be a full and free reprefentative.

Sir William Williams.

Every man knows King James is out of the kingdom, and in France.——How left it, voluntarily or by compulfion, will not pretend to determine.——No adminiftration left behind him.—— That fails.——The conftitution is broken.—— French intereft repugnant to ours.——Is for declaring, that King James, in having become a Papift, and by withdrawing, has deprived the kingdom of the exercife of kingly government.

Serjeant Maynard.

Some Papifts rule well, fo leave it out.

Mr. Finch.

It is faid that he has loft his crown by acts; and by going away has abdicated.——One confequence can refult from this queftion, What it is?——If that confequence be, that the conftitution is devolved upon the people, few will come up to it.——If that the conftitution is diffolved, believes no wife man will come up to it.——If to declare the throne vacant, is to fay, that he has loft the inheritance, thinks even that further than any one will go.——The fingle confequence is, that James II. is not King.——Then is the throne filled with the next fucceffor.——The monarchy is not elective.—— The monarch can only forfeit for himfelf.——The exercife in him for life; cannot difpofe of or refign the inheritance.——Has difficulties.——Not excufeable, what the King has done.——His going away does not feem a total renunciation.——We are not to fend propofals.——That will not confift with our fecurity.——Suppofe the kingdom under an infant.——Security muft confift in the una-

‡   nimous

1688-9.
nimous concurrence of the kingdom.———Suppose the King misinformed of the constitution, will that be a forfeiture?———King
may endeavour to subvert the constitution, and so render it unsafe
to live under him, because he is so easily abused.———Nation may
provide for the administration in case of lunacy :———So in this
case.

Sir Thomas Lee.

The gentleman is debating the conclusion before he has settled
the premises.———The King may advise his Ministers, instead of being advised by them.

Mr. Finch.

Too late to debate the point I went upon, after this resolution
agreed to.———If the case be, as the gentleman stated it, there is
only a cessation of the exercise.

Sir Chr. Musgrave.

Part of the question is, That the King has subverted the constitution.———But it is clear that remains still.———No answer given to
what has been said.———Demise, abdication, &c. the same things.
———There is an end of that question.———The *right* and the *exercise* must be distinguished.———Have a care of deposing.———A
kingdom near us *, which, if our reasons do not satisfy, they may
prove ill neighbours.———Would be clear, whether it be the intention to depose him.———If he has forfeited the inheritance, how
would we supply?———If not, is under great difficulty as to declaring the throne vacant.

Mr. Wharton.

He is no more our King, whether he deposes himself or not.———
Not for the safety of most here, that he should come back.

Sir Chr. Musgrave.

All are equally in danger; desire to know if the thing may be
done, the King deposed?

* Scotland.

Sergeant

STATE PAPERS.   407

Sergeant Maynard.   1638-9.

Whoever put that queſtion, I know not his meaning; but am afraid of it.——The true queſtion is, Whether the King has not depoſed himſelf?——Put the caſe, and it will appear no new one. ——All mixed government has its foundation in conſent——It is clear, that there may be tranſgreſſions, as will not amount to a forfeiture, but will prove to all that he ought to govern no onger.——The Papiſts pervaded all parts of government.—— The whole revenue was granted to the King by Parliament for life.——What was aſked in return?——Only that Popiſh officers might be diſmiſſed; and we were diſmiſſed inſtead of them.—— If what we are doing is wrong, every man is alike guilty. We have been alike involved in the ſame danger.——It was come to the ſame paſs, as Matthew Paris talks of in King John's time.—— Ireland yielded up: had infatuation enough to have induced him (like that King) to make a 500 years grant of the monarchy of England.——Remembers former times of confuſion; hopes theſe in the end will be as memorable for peace and order.——In the year 1641, Ireland filled with maſſacre and rebellion. —— 200,000 Proteſtants ſlain in a ſhort time; 500,000 left; what muſt have become of theſe under King James?——The native Iriſh, becauſe Papiſts, were let into all employments.——The King would have given away the ſoil; given up 500,000 of his ſubjects.— Was this like an Engliſh King? Can he ſell or give away his ſub- jects?——An Act of Parliament was made to diſarm all Engliſh- men, whom the Lieutenant ſhould ſuſpect, by day or by night, by force or otherwiſe ——This done in Ireland for the ſake of putting arms into Iriſh hands.——The engineer was called the King's Attorney, and bombs his *Quo warantos*.——Every Popiſh King, if he had power, would deſtroy all Proteſtants.——See their condition in —— France, —— Spain, —— Hungary. —— We do not depoſe him.——It is his own act.——If ſeven Biſhops preſent

an

408   STATE PAPERS.

1688-9. an humble petition, it is profecuted as a libel *.——We have feen
all St. Omer's in his Majefty's councils.——This defign was dark,
continued; uniform, to deftroy the Proteftant religion.——This neceffarily complicated with defign to deftroy Proteftants; to deftroy Parliaments.——His religion juftifies and commands this extended ruin.——The *mirror of juftice* fets down the beginning of
this monarchy.——A King chofen and fworn to laws, the conftitution not fubverted in refpect to this right.——To fay *abdicated*
and *void*, the fame thing.——If the government be abdicated, the
throne is vacant.

Sir H. Capel.

Surprifed to go on fo flowly.——We could not prevent this
Prince, before his time, from fucceeding; now we cannot exclude
him, having left us.——No conftitution, which, in cafe of ex-
tremity, may not relieve itfelf.——Will you fet him upon the
throne?——If you limit him, and impofe a regent, you alter the
government.——It is faid, all this was owing to ill advifers.——
If thofe be ill that advife, thofe are faulty who plead for him.——
You have collected the fenfe of the Houfe, and are ripe for a refolution.

Mr. Howe.
Mr. Harbord.
Sir J. Treby.

This is a matter which requires patience and calm thought.——
Queftion is, Whether we fhall be overturned by popery and arbitrary power?——To determine whether we can depofe, is to
enter into a queftion in vain as well as dangerous.——We find the
throne vacant, and do not make it fo.——A worthy perfon inti-
mated that the crown was on the head of fomebody; and that the
King went out of his wits, as with lunacy, not abdicated the government.——If fo, he could have told you who wears it; what
can fupply the government?——Take care whilft we debate of fub-

* Father Petre.

tilties,

STATE PAPERS.

tilties, and ftart at fhadows, left there be not a fpot of ground in this country, on which a Proteftant may fet his foot.——It is faid by another Member, that we do not reprefent a fourth part of the nation, becaufe (forfooth) we are not elected by thofe, who have no fhare in the government by the conftitution of it.——But is it now a queftion, Whether we have authority?——We have exercifed the higheft: difpofed of the adminiftration: appointed a thankfgiving.——The King has renounced his legal government, and fallen from it.——He that will not, or cannot exercife it according to law, is no longer King.——Two parts in government. ——Commanding and obeying.——Legiflative power and executive. ——The difpenfing power introduced into the latter, has overfet the rule eftablifhed by the former.——He cannot now treat with his people in parliament; has infifted on the inherent infeparable authority in the crown to difpenfe.——The High Commiffion Court would have found pretences to deprive Proteftants.—The difpenfing power would have filled the church with Papifts in their ftead. ——As to the legiflature,——when corporations were all diffolved, he might have named his Parliament.——Between the regulators and dragoons, a Parliament would only have reprefented the King or the Papifts.——Where the King infringes the liberty or property of a private man, we may footh, and pacify, and fubmit.——But when the fundamental laws themfelves are invaded; when the malefactors who broke them are, by fraud or force, made the Parliament who frame laws: thefe are violations which fhake off the King.—— Have we then occafion to touch the queftion of depofing?——The higheft article againft Richard the Second was, that he pack'd a Parliament.——In 1607 King James the Firft expreffed his fenfe clearly to the Parliament, when he faid, that the King leaving off to govern according to law, ceafes to be King.——It was a great argument againft the exclufion bill, that no other Papifts befides

VOL. II.   3 G   the

410

1688-9. the King could be in office.——His friends anfwered for him, that the teft law would be inviolable;—yet he pretended only to leave it in force as to the Houfe of Commons.——When petitioned by the Peers concerning it, how loth to yield to them?——See the confequence of the credit which you gave him.——As to the motion, exprefs it as you pleafe.——We are without a King.——I think, in his own judgment, he is fallen from the throne.——He fwore to adminifter the laws, which are free and Proteftant.——But it feems he is under an higher obligation to break them.——Is not this to fay, " My adminiftration muft be a contradiction to my office."—— Is it not a renouncing?——His actions have all fpoken it.——Recall him? his obligations are the fame.——His laft ufe of the great feal was to pardon the malefactors, his advifers.——Moves to infert the words " by advice of Jefuites and other wicked perfons, having violated the fundamental laws, &c."

Mr. Finch.

Queftion, If the King has loft his title to the crown?——I think no man fafe under his adminiftration.——No fafety but in the confent of the nation.——The conftitution being limited, there is a good foundation for defenfive arms.——It has given us right to demand full and ample fecurity.——If there be an expedient wherein all may be fecure, and all agree, that is the beft.——1. We are to examine and inquire of the fucceffion.——2. Every man muft fwear to it as lawful and rightful.——In the prudential part, let what muft occur to you on the fecond head, guide you as to the firft. ——All would be fecure; yet all cannot come up to what fome of us feem inclined to determine in point of right.——Did not mean to capitulate with the King, but eftablifh the government.—— Meant a regent in which all may agree.——That which comprehends moft, will be moft fecure.——Would declare that the King

ought

STATE PAPERS.   411

ought not to be intrufted with the adminiftration; fo fhould be the   1688-9.
queftion.

Sir R. Howard.

A regency and the King are all one.——The queftion, as moved
and amended, takes in the fenfe of the Houfe.——Much is faid of
the fucceffion.——-But we are the people.——And threaten ourfelves
by ourfelves when the queftion is afked, fhall we dare to chufe?
——To talk of preferving the fucceffion as facred, is to fuppofe the
title of the prince.——A thing well cozened.——If he fhould die,
the King of France will find another.

Lord Fanfhawe.

It is faid the King has withdrawn himfelf.——Gone away by
compulfion, in my judgment.——Heard him fay, That he was
afraid of being feized by his own fubjects.——When he was at liberty at Feverfham, he came back.——Afks, if we have power to
depofe?——In law, King can do no wrong; for that reafon minifters are called to account. No occafion for hafte.

Lord Cornbury

Defires the queftion may be explained.

Mr. Roberts.

If the queftion is to have no other confequence than would follow on the King's natural demife, will go *nemine contradicente.*——
Queftion put in the Committee.——*Three negatives.*

Lord Colchefter

Moves to report it prefently.

Sir William Williams

Moves the Houfe to fit to-morrow, and receive the report.

Sir J. Knight.

Arms of France invading all the rights of this kingdom.——Foreign plantations.——Ireland invaded.——Would immediately have
a head.

3 G 2   Mr.

STATE PAPERS.

                                        Mr. Wharton.
To report immediately.
                                        Mr. Wogan.
To-morrow.
                                    Sir Rowland Gwyn.
Time precious, would report now.
                                      Sir R. Sawyer.
To-morrow.
                                     Sir Walter Young.
Immediately.   May do more, now unanimous.
                                      Sir J. Lowther.
Report what done to the Houfe, and confider of it again to-
morrow.   For our honour to proceed deliberately.
                                        Mr. Medlicot.
Security depends on difpatch.
                                      ' *Sir J. Knight.*
Confider the bleeding condition of trade.
Agreed with the Committee by all but one in the Houfe.
                                      Sir R. Howard
Moves to fend up the refolution to the Lords for their concurrence.
                                      Mr. Bofcawen
Seconds.——Mr. Hampden to carry it up.

Refolved, That King James the Second, having endeavoured to
fubvert the conftitution by breaking the original contract between
king and people; and, by the advice of Jefuits and other wicked
perfons, having violated the fundamental laws, and withdrawn
himfelf out of the kingdom, has abdicated the government, and that
the throne is vacant.

                                                    Mr.

STATE PAPERS.

413

1688-9.

Mr. Hampden in the Chair, 29th January.

Colonel Birch.

King depofed himfelf.——Fear upon him from his own guilt.——
Continued attempts upon our liberties.——Nothing left but the difpofing of the people's money, and that challenged as a right laft
Parliament.——From the Spanifh match downwards, Popery has
been coming.——The war followed.——King Charles delivered
himfelf from two of the eftates, by never calling them together for
many years.——Ship-money.——Monopolies.——I will not determine, but he brought the character of his government near to
what was folemnly declared yefterday.——Popery and idolatry
were at the bottom.——When the late King James would marry
this Lady, I afked a great man at that time, Whether he meant to
perpetuate to his family a war with the Houfe of Commons ?——
Popery will not profper but in an arbitrary and tyrannical foil.——
Inconfiftent, ruinous for a Proteftant ftate to be governed by a Popifh
Prince.——Moves to refolve, that it is inconfiftent with the fafety
of this Proteftant kingdom to be governed by a Popifh Prince.

Pilkington.

Seconded.

Sir R. Temple.

Found by experience that the government of a Popifh Prince is
inconfiftent with the ends of government in a Proteftant kingdom.

Sir R. Napper.

Woeful experience.

Sir R. Sawyer.

Inconfiftent with the intereft of a Proteftant kingdom to be governed by a Popifh King.——Law ought to be made; civil and religious
rights interwoven.

Lord

414   S T A T E   P A P E R S.

1588-9.
                                   Lord Faulkland.

Yefterday allowed he was King.——Nothing inconfiftent with our laws.——It is no offence to refufe the teft.

                                      Tipping.

It has been found by experience inconfiftent with the fafety and welfare of a Proteftant kingdom to be governed by a Popifh Prince.

                                Sir William Williams.

A negative on this queftion would be inconfiftent with your vote yefterday.——Paffed *nem. con.*

                                   Mr. Wharton.

Yefterday the throne vacant.——All are for filling it again.—— Adhere to the conftitution as near as poffible.——Bufinefs of the greateft weight.——Pitch on none fo well as the Prince and Prin- cefs of Orange.——Making them as capable of protecting us, as may be.   Philip and Mary, King and Queen; William and Mary, King and Queen of England.   Moves to *fupply the vacancy of the throne.*

                                Sir Duncombe Colchefter.

Our being here owing to the Prince.——Gratitude to pitch upon him.——Seconds.

                                   Lord Faulkland.

I hope we fhall fecure ourfelves from arbitrary government as well as Popery.——Lay the foundation before we raife the build- ing.——Two Kings the conftitution will not bear in a joint fove- reignty. —— We are likewife to fee what regal power is. —— Never leave the difpenfing power doubtful, or the high commiffion fubfifting.——Fundamentals too may be deftroyed, by corrupting Parliaments.

                                   Mr. Garway.

Confider what terms muft be made to provide really and effectu- ally

.S T A T E. P A P E R S.   **415**

ally for our own fafety.——Not deliver up thofe who fent us.—— 1638-9.
But make fuch provifions as may prevent future invaders.

Sir William Williams.

Settle the terms.——Would enact no new conftitution, but
make declaration only, and purfue the old.——If any thing amifs,
find out the caufes.——Then the remedies.——Then the perfons
fitteft to adminifter.——The Prince's declaration ftates much of your
grievances.——The perfon is the laft thing to be thought of.——
In the year 1660, there were many hard laws made grievous to
the people.——Much enhanced the prerogative.——Corrupt judges
and counfellors took courage from them.——That convention often
cried out upon, for taking no better care.——King Charles II. a young
man when called to the crown.——Vaft fums granted.——Militia
act; an antecedent queftion, Whether the power over it in the
crown or people ?——Said to be indecent, that he did not come into
the crown with all its luftre at that time. But now we fpeak for
England.——This is the time to be free, now the throne is vacant.——Corporation Act was arbitrary.——Weak and knavifh
judges will do knavifh things.——They read none of the law books,
and fo read nothing to the contrary.——You have fet an example of
arbitrary proceeding.——Given power to levy a fum of money without Parliament.——Adhere to the ancient conftitution.——We are
to look beyond the conqueft.——Original contract in your votes.

Mr. Chrifty.

A *Magna Charta.*——Coronation oath to preferve the proteftant
religion.

Sir Richard Temple.

Not launch into fuch a fea.——Three heads; 1ft, Provide againft
encroaching on Parliaments for pofterity.—Certainty of them.——
Triennial bill taken away in a thin houfe.——Not only called to
ferve the ends of the crown.——That no pardons may be trumped
upon us.——Election of Parliament fecured, by making corporations

STATE PAPERS.

1688-9.   tions tools.——2d, Standing army settled without consent of Parliament, though no part of constitution.——May be allowed in case of war, invasion, or rebellion.——Militia bill.——Power to disarm all England.——Now done in Ireland.——3d, Westminster-hall must be better filled, with persons who are honest, and are judges for life with fixed salaries.——Take care as to juries; sheriffs; strange fines.——As little as may be of power to be directed by the discretion of the judges, who did not decide great questions formerly, but sent them into Parliament.——That was the occasion of calling Parliaments frequently.——Let the oath of King be taken by them (the Prince and Princess of Orange) before they enter into government.——Prince has called upon you to pursue the ends of his declaration.

Lord Ranelagh.

Prince's declaration, a good foundation to build a settlement upon.——His letter confirms it.

Mr Boscawen.

Arbitrary power exercised by the Ministry.——Acts of long Parliament.——Corporation Act.——That the same with the resolution.——The most loyal or deserving, turned out.——Militia.——Imprisoning without reason; disarming.——Himself disarmed.——Trophy-money, &c.——Triennial bill.——Necessity begot it.——Nothing hindered us from going into slavery but that bill, said by Lord Chief Justice Hales.——Moves, that before the committee proceed to the nomination of any person to fill the vacancy of the throne, they will provide such things as are absolutely necessary for securing our religion, laws, and liberties.

Sir J. Knight.

We shall find the Papists immediately upon us.

Serjeant Maynard.

Two things moved.——One to fill the vacancy of the throne, the other before we fill the vacancy, to make provision for our security.
——Agree

3

STATE PAPERS.

——Agree with the laſt part of the ſecond queſtion, but would not delay to ſupply the throne, left, inſtead of an arbitrary government, we ſhould have none.——It has been ſaid, we muſt go beyond the conqueſt.——Puzzled to find what was law in the Saxon times; tedious and fruitleſs ſearch.——Some particulars well propounded.——Some groſs grievances for which we are beholden to a Parliament, who cared not what was done, ſo their penſions were paid.——Militia Act.——An abominable thing to diſarm the nation, to ſet up a ſtanding army.——Corporation Act carried into execution with a high hand.——If any man offered to ſtir, to remonſtrate, to complain, it was cried out by ſome, the act of oblivion too large.—— Could name them.——Acts of violence.——Corruption of judges, inſtead of *durante bene placito*, ſhould be *quam diu ſe bene geſſerint.* ——But we muſt ſo take care for the future, as not to be loſt at preſent.——The army has been corrupted formerly, may be again. —Let us not delay to ſet the government in motion, under whatever fair pretence, left we give occaſion to moles, who work under ground, to deſtroy the foundations you laid yeſterday.——This is my fear, dictated by the knowledge and experience of paſt times; and this, as a true Engliſhman, who love my country better than my life.—— The things mentioned are obvious in your preſent ſituation, eaſy to be attained.——But it is eſſential, and of immediate neceſſity there ſhould be a King.——The law has ſo bound the King (whether you declare it anew or not) that he can do no wrong, unleſs wicked counſellors adviſe to break it; but in this there can be no miſtake for ignorance.——You are without power, without juſtice, without mercy; other things require time, and admit of it.

Lord Faulkland.

Would juſtify myſelf to thoſe who ſent me hither, as not merely wanting to change hands.——Satisfaction of the people as well as army.——If we act with love of the people we ſhall purſue their intereſt.

Vol. II.   3 H   *Mr.*

STATE PAPERS.

418

1688-9.

Mr. Sacheverel.

Shall be laughed at, if not look after ourfelves now.—When the Prince declares your fecurity fhall be lafting.—No man knows what he can call his own, unlefs you look very far back.——Difarmed and imprifoned without caufe.——Scarce three laws of twenty years deferve to be continued.——Money.——Overfhot themfelves at that time (1660) not to do fo now.——Way to have a good law abolifhed, if you did but name it.——Proved that many penfioners agreed for fo much in the hundred for all they gave.——An old law ftill in force, the Parliaments fhall not be prorogued, till all the grievances be redreffed: when fuch grievances brought in here, we were fent away the next day.——Warrants to take up all Nonconformift minifters, or fuch as were thought to be difaffected to the government, becaufe they endeavoured to chufe members whom they (the court) did not like.——Secure Parliaments rightly and duly chofen.—— Their fitting fo as not to be broken up at pleafure.——No extravagant revenue to be granted as may enable the crown to carry whom it pleafes into elections.——Make falfe returns more penal.——Am for proceeding to thefe things before you fill the vacancy.

Mr. Pollexfen.

Whatfoever things you would declare, will not only require confideration here, but muft be agreed by Lords as well as Commons. ——The propofition excellent in itfelf, but if it have the effect to confound us, a dreadful propofition.——Am as willing as any to apply redrefs to grievances.——But to delay fupplying the government, will reftore the King.——View the prefent condition of the kingdom. If this fhould go beyond fea, that we are bounding the kingly power, before there is one to affume the exercife, what confequence will it have?——Unlefs jealous of friends, your worft enemies cannot hinder you from coming to a fettlement.——See what delay is doing.——This month has loft one King.——The army ready to mutiny.—Every factious intereft will run in there.——Fear
of

STATE PAPERS.   419

of Popery has united; when that is over, we shall divide again.—— It was thought impossible formerly that Popery should come here.—— King James long since seemed to declare, " That cannot be done till I am King."——As to the Prince and Princess of Orange ; you have no reason to mistrust good words, unless it be accompanied with ill actions.——But their actions abroad give me reason to believe them really Protestants.——His declaration speaks the same thing.—— His actions confirm it.——He might have taken the crown, instead of leaving us in debate.——You have no laws till there is a King. ——Those who prevailed by arms, in the late times, in coming to a constitutional government, ruined themselves.——If Oliver had settled into a government, he might have saved his party.——We busied ourselves about a bill of exclusion some time since.——Some for that bill; others for limitations.——We talked so long about it, that we were sent away without doing any thing.——Will there be less talk now on these points of right ?——Besides, your terms may be such at last, that when you come to offer the crown with new limitations, not known before, it may be rejected.——Common destruction will overtake us, whilst we debate these things, without the protection of a legal government.

Lord Faulkland.

No doubt of the Prince and Princess of Orange.——What is done by us before the offer of the crown will be no argument of distrust.——What has been felt in the two last reigns is a sufficient ground for us to proceed.

Mr. Garway.

Somewhat must be done.——Many things named.——Represent our sense to him.——That it may be passed hereafter into laws.

Sir Edward Seymour.

Good things often suffer by overdoing.——Not for making new laws, but declaring old.——Declare against dispensing power; power

420   **S T A T E   P A P E R S.**

of Weſtminſter Hall.——Great part of the revenue depends on the demiſe of the King.——Can we diſpoſe of a crown, and not have power to ſecure ourſelves ?——Not live like a ſlave in England.—— Adminiſtration is in the Prince's hands.——Conſider the end of your meeting.

Sir T. Lee.

The objection is ſpending long time.——Amongſt others, this opinion ſhould be exploded, That the King can raiſe what forces he thinks fit in England, provided he can pay them.——He who firſt broached this doctrine, obtained a great place in judicature.

Sir T. Clarges.

Neceſſary ſomething ſhould be done for common ſafety, and to purſue the Prince's deſires.——Moves, that a committee may be appointed to draw up ſome heads to be preſented to our chief governor, when declared.

Colonel Birch.

If the Prince of Orange would live till we are all dead, we might hope for ſafety under him.——Our ſecurity muſt be in ſettling the government whilſt we have him.——Yet the diſcontents will riſe much higher, if you do not do ſomewhat beſide filling the throne. ——As to the time, it cannot take a day, only to mention them as heads.——We have reſolved to faſt to-morrow (30th of January) we know what we faſt for.——We have often ſat on the Lord's day.——May take up our thoughts to-morrow.——Some ſuch declaration will give you more ſtrength and credit.——By way of addition to what has been obſerved on that head, think hearth-money a badge of ſlavery.——The taking away of that law will bring him more ſtrength than twenty armies.——The queſtion, as juſt moved, is not too general ; may truſt ourſelves.

Mr. J. Hampden.

We make free thus to act for a nation not tied by oaths.—— Know, time preſſes.——They will aſk why the King has abdicated

                                                        9   the

STATE PAPERS.   421

the government.——If you declare the conſtitution, it will be no   1688-9.
law that can bind.——Have looked into the journals, and find the
convention in 1660, was of King, Lords, and Commons.

Sir William Pulteney.

Difficulties on each hand.——Would have a committee appointed
to draw up heads.

Mr. Dolben

Has a reaſon for diſpatch in his hand.——Letter from a noble
Lord in Ireland, that juſt ready to execute.

Mr. Harbord.

Nobody will go farther for maintaining the conſtitution.——A
principal thing is to make examples of thoſe who broke it.——Security infallible.——The revenue is gone by the vacancy.——Cannot
theſe things be doing in the mean time that you ſettle the government?——The Dutch are calling home their troops with impati-
ence.——Factions in the army.——If theſe break out, where are all
your laws and declarations?——Preſerve your government.——It
is the ſword of a King muſt protect you.

Sir R. Sawyer.

Some complain of laws; ſome of the tranſgreſſion of the laws.——
Offences puniſhable in Parliaments, and in ordinary courts.——
Great offences are to be puniſhed in Parliament.——No proviſion:
——Would you make another contract with your Prince than your
anceſtors have done? ——Nothing can be done till it is debated.——
Are you ſatisfied the laws are good?——Declare no power of ſuf-
pending; and that Parliament ſhall ſit ſome ſtated time.——Work
cut out, will employ ſeveral weeks.

Sir R. Temple.

Go on preſently to declare the neceſſary heads.——Convention
of 1660, which brought in the King made ſeveral acts.

Sir

STATE PAPERS.

Sir T. Littleton.

Soon agreed in two things.——1ft, To fill the government.——
2d, To fecure our liberties.——This may be done in a little time
by naming the heads.——Refer it to a committee.

Sir J. Guife.

When fill up *vacancy*, the fame time prefent a declaration.
——Appoint a committee, and at the fame time proceed to nominate.

Sir Charles Mufgrave.

No power to appoint a committee.——Reftrain your queftion.—
Cannot anfwer it to the nation or Prince of Orange, till we declare
what are the rights invaded.——When you declare your grievances,
every man will take them to be the reafon of your vote yefterday.—
Make your wheels before you put the cart on.——Declare your antient government, then fet it up.——Motion, that before the committee proceed to nominate a perfon to fill the throne, That the
Houfe be moved to appoint a committee to bring in general heads.

Mr. Garroway.

An effay has been collected by a worthy gentleman.

Mr. Pollexfen

Reads a paper.——Unlefs Parliaments regulated, no fecurity.—
Claufe about pardons to be added.

Sir H. Capel.

Parliament fo truly Englifh.——No prejudice to the crown in
taking care of our properties.——Security to it.——The crown in-
debted to the proceedings of this day.——Two witneffes to one
fact in treafon.

Sir William Williams.

Collect a queftion.

Sir R. Hobart.

Extravagant bail.——Lord Lieutenants.

Lord

STATE PAPERS.   423

Lord Faulkland.   1688-9.

Exorbitant fines.

Colonel Birch.

The paper only an essay.

Sir H. Temple.

King's Bench.

Tipping.

Council in cases of treason and felony.

Ettrick.

To proceed to nominate, looks like election.

Mr. Poley

Seconds it, not to use the word nominate, as it comes so near electing, in the question about supplying the vacancy.

Mr. Sacheverel.

Declare is too much; the Lords may quarrel.

Sir J. Lowther.

If you make such declaration before vacancy supplied, may admit of another construction abroad, and in France, than intended here. ——Of equal use to you to make such declaration without notice taken, of intention to supply afterwards. So leave out the first part of the question.

Jephson.

Give no occasion to enemies abroad.

Medlicot.

Declare instead of nominate.——Passed *nem. con.*

Lord Faulkland.

Now ready to nominate your committee.——Move the House that the gentlemen of the long robe may proceed.

Sir Thomas Clarges.

Intention that no such thing should be done.——Ordered to report the vote to the House, That it is the opinion of the committee that it is inconsistent with the safety, &c.

8   Mr.

424   STATE PAPERS.

1688 9.

Mr. Hampden

Reports, Firſt reſolution, *nem. con.* To appoint a committee to bring in general heads of ſuch things as are abſolutely neceſſary to be conſidered for the better ſecuring of our religion, and laws, and liberties.

Sir H. Capel

Moved to add theſe words, To the end that we may more ſpeedily proceed to fill up the vacancy of the throne.

Mr. Sacheverel.

No reaſon for it.——Moves to deſire the concurrence of the Lords to the firſt vote.

Mr. Hampden

To carry it up.——Naming the committee, every one to ſtand up.

Sir Joſeph Tredenham.

Exorbitances of *Weſtminſter Hall* moſt complained of.——Not to go upon general words of the long robe.

Mr. Howe.

May be, ſome of the gentlemen of the long robe guilty.

Lord Dunblain.

Long robe as great a grievance as any.

Mr. Harbord.

Committee to meet to-morrow about eight o'clock in the ſpeaker's chambers.

Mr. Jephſon.

Great buſineſs on our hands.   To ſit to-morrow.

Lord Wiltſhire.

Defer filling up the vacancy no longer than the Houſe needs muſt. Sit to-morrow.

Lord Ranelagh.

Not to ſit to-morrow; keep acts of Parliament, not break them. ——Committee appointed to meet to-morrow.

Mr.

STATE PAPERS.   425

Mr. Levifon Gower.

Reflection to fit to-morrow, fo it would be not to fit at all.——
Hope they will difpatch by that time, and we to fit to-morrow at
two o'clock.

Lord Faulkland.
Sir J. Guife.

Seconded.

Sir R. Napper.
Mr. Bofcawen.
Sir R. Howard.

Nothing difingenuous.——Agreed to fit to-morrow at two
o'clock.

A Jornall of the Convention

248   'A JORNALL OF THE CONVENTION

House of Lords Record Office, Hist. Coll. 155, H.C., 1973[2]

[*fo. 1*] A Jornall of the Convention at Westminster begun the 22 of January 1688/9
[*fo. 2*] 1688/9 Munday 28 Jan:
        The Speaker[3] proposes the Vote[4] to be read viz: That on Monday the House
would consider the state of the Nation.

[2] The left-hand margin of the original is headed *Persons that speak*, and contains
the names which are here given in italics. Other marginalia, together with correc-
tions and insertions in the text, are given in the footnotes to this edition. Contrac-
tions in the original have been extended where their meaning is obvious. The last
word of each folio is repeated on the reverse, but omitted here. So also is *28 Jan:*
which appears in the top left-hand corner of each page from fo. 2v. A minimum of
punctuation and capitalization has been added to make the sense clear.

[3] Henry Powle (1630–92), M.P. for New Windsor, Berks., W. (T = Tory. W =
Whig. Following generally-accepted practice, the identification is based upon two
lists that are reprinted in A. Browning, *Thomas Osborne, earl of Danby and duke of
Leeds, 1632–1712* (3 vols., Glasgow, 1944–51), iii. 164–72. NL–T or NL–W indi-
cates that the name is *not in the lists* (NL) and that the partisan designation is,
therefore, provisional, although in many instances it is unquestionably accurate.)

[4] Passed unanimously 22 Jan. 1689: *C.J.*, x. 11. Debate was postponed to 28 Jan.

AT WESTMINSTER'   249

Sir H. Seymor[1] Leave the Chair. Leave the chair.

No No some[2] cryed but carryed in the Affirmative.

House in Generall Mr Hambden[3] to the Chair.

But he did not stir therefore some cald upon Sir William Poltny[4] but most still upon Mr Hambden who excusd himself.

Mr Levison Gowr[5] [who had cald upon Mr Hambden][6] Mr Speaker, to save expence of time I move that Sir W.P. may take the Chair.

Sir William Poltny If that other Gentlemans excuse may be allowd, I humbly move for the same favor, being I'm sure more infirm then[7] he.

The Speaker leaves the Chair. Mr Hamden sits in the Clarks chair. After a great pause *Mr Dolben*[8] speaks to this purpose. That the Kings going away being voluntary amounts to a Demise, Demissio, Derelictio,[9] & moves that A Vote may be passd That the Throne is Void. The Speech was very long & very learned & well deliverd.

Another long pause.

Mr Arnold[10] Mr Hambden I stand up to second that motion that is [*fo. 2v*] made to you to put the question for a Vote.

Sir Richard Temple[11] Recounts the many invasions that have been made upon our Religion, Libertys & Propertys.

upon a motion by Sir Thomas Clarges, a tactical move to give the tories the advantage of discussing the matter first in the house of lords. This manoeuvre was thwarted in the house of lords by the Speaker George Savile, marquess of Halifax (1633–95) and others: Grey, ix. 5; Morrice MS. Q, p. 437; *Correspondence of Henry Hyde, earl of Clarendon, and of his brother Laurence Hyde, earl of Rochester ...* (hereafter *Clar. Corresp.*), ed. S. W. Singer (2 vols., 1828), ii. 252–4.

[1] Almost certainly Sir Edward Seymour (1633–1708), M.P. for Exeter, Devon, T, and not his obscure younger brother, Henry (*c.* 1637–1728), M.P. for St. Mawes, Cornw., T. Grey, ix. 6–7 reports that Sir Edward supported the motion.

[2] Among them were Col. John Birch and Sir John Maynard: *ibid.*, p. 6.

[3] Richard Hampden (1631–95), M.P. for Wendover, Bucks., W.

[4] Sir William Pulteney (*c.* 1626–1691), M.P. for Westminster, Mdx., NL–W. Morrice MS. Q, p. 444 explains that the motion for Pulteney reflected no disaffection for Hampden.

[5] William Leveson Gower (*c.* 1640–1691), M.P. for Newcastle-under-Lyme, Staffs., NL–W.

[6] Square brackets in MS.

[7] *Sic* in MS.

[8] Gilbert Dolben (*c.* 1658–1722), M.P. for Peterborough, Northants., T. Since December Dolben had struggled to reconcile the removal of James II with the obligations imposed by the Oath of Allegiance: Morrice MS. Q, p. 370.

[9] The terms are developed in the lengthy printed accounts of the speech in Grey and Somers and even more fully in the manuscript draft of the speech, in Dolben's hand, found in Brit. Libr., Stowe MS. 840 fos. 1–9. Dolben used 'demise' in its legal sense, meaning the abandonment of the government by the prince by death or overt action. The term implied the devolution of sovereignty, without an interregnum, and was essential to arguments for a regency or for Princess Mary. 'Dereliction' also means desertion of the government by the prince. Quoting Hugo Grotius's 'admirable and perfect book', *De jure belli et pacis*, Dolben argued that a dereliction transformed the prince into a private person: *ibid.* fo. 8.

[10] John Arnold (*c.* 1635–1703), M.P. for Monmouth, NL–W.

[11] Sir Richard Temple (1634–97), M.P. for Buckingham, NL–T. Zealous for William. Fuller accounts of the speech are in Grey and Somers.

250   'A JORNALL OF THE CONVENTION

Mr John How[1] Urges That the Kings Tyranny had before his departure put an end to his Government.

Sir Robert Howard[2] Mr Hamden I desire wee may not rest upon a Demise when wee have sufferd so much in our Religion, Libertys & Propertys, as was well observd to you from above (note Sir Richard T. sate on the uppermost seat). Wee have had Arbitrary Power exercizd upon our Souls as well as Bodys, at least attemted to 'be exercizd. Wee have had Preists in the Caball, A Jesuit in the Councell & whatever has been speciously pretended, still Popery at the Bottom. Wee have had no stop of Violence. A Massacre executed upon our Laws. Corporations subverted. Closetting Members of Parliament & Officers both Civill & Military, & all turnd out who would not promise to give up the only security that we had for our Religion. I can compare the practises of our late unhappy King very fitly to the Action of Richard the 2nd at Nottingham.[3] Wee have had put upon us a spirituall Court of Justice, which renderd our Religion as precarious as our Liberty, & both were given up to the Will of one Man. No Man could plead a Right to any thing that he had. And Whereas there is a Maxim in the Law that the King can do no Wrong,[4] I think tis very true provided you will take it in that sense which many able Lawyers of old[5] have done. That when a King ex mero motu[6] Dos Wrong he thereby ceases to be King. However our Court Sycophants have of late instilld wrong notions of things into the minds of weak Princes, it was the [*fo. 3*] old Maxim[7] of our wise Legislators That God[8] & the Law are above the King. I have heard of a Jus Divinum, & that it has been applied to Monarchy, but I am sure wee have a Divine Right to our Lives, Estates, & Liberty. The Originall of Power was by Pact by Agreement from the People, & sure none ever intended

[1] John Howe (1657–1722), M.P. for Cirencester, Glos., W.

[2] Sir Robert Howard (1626–98), M.P. for Castle Rising, Norf., W.

[3] At Nottingham in Aug. 1387 Richard II launched a policy of revenge against his enemies, summoning the sheriffs of the English counties and Londoners to get a commitment of military and political support in part to pack parliament and putting questions to judges to show that the king was above the law. A recent study is A. Tuck, *Richard II and the English Nobility* (1973). Richard II was mentioned 4 other times on 28 Jan.: Grey, ix. 8, 23; 'A Jornall' fos. 6, 9. The reference would have been readily understood. William Shakespeare's *Richard II* appeared 10 times before 1689, once in 1681 under the title *The Sicilian Usurper*. Tracts concerning Richard's deposition appeared in 1641, 1642 and 1689. Howard himself wrote *The Life and Reign of King Richard the Second* (1681); see H. J. Oliver, *Sir Robert Howard (1626–98): a Critical Biography* (Durham, N.C., 1963), pp. 242–6 for dating and authorship. An expanded version entitled *Historical Observations upon the reigns of Edward I, II, III and Richard II* was licensed without his knowledge, Howard claimed, on 17 Jan. 1689. His *History of the Reigns of Edward and Richard II* appeared in 1690.

[4] The maxim appeared in 15th-century common law and was exploited by 17th-century parliamentarians in their attempts to limit the king by holding his ministers to account. In 1689, as in the earlier Civil War, the maxim was abandoned by critics of the king and embraced by his friends. The concept was referred to 4 times in the 28 Jan. debate (fos. 2v, 6, 8; *Hardwicke Papers*, ii. 411), thereby testifying to its strength. For a discussion of the evolution and political uses of the idea, see C. Roberts, *The Growth of Responsible Government in Stuart England* (Cambridge, 1966).

[5] Among the 'lawyers of old' Howard had in mind was surely Henry de Bracton (d. 1268).

[6] *ex mero motu*: of his own volition.

[7] *Maxim* erased, *Maxim* interlined more clearly.   [8] *When ever a King* erased.

AT WESTMINSTER' 251

perfectly to enslave themselves & their Posterity: but wee have seen Violences offerd to our very Constitution. I look upon it therefore to be above a Demise, A very Abdication of the King; who before he went Hee lopt both Church & State. By liberty of Conscience he let in the Romish Religion. He left nothing un-attemted that might entirely ruin us. In my Opinion the Right is therefore wholly [1] in the people, who are Now to new form themselves again, under a Governor Yet to be Chosen. What should we Do when a King so much Detests his People as to carry away as much as in him lyes [2] all Justice from us by withdrawing the Seals & making no Provision for the Government in his Absence? Is not this an Abdication of it? I do therefore humbly make this Motion: That we passe a Vote That King James [3] the 2nd by Advice of Jesuits or [how you please] [4] some ill Advisers has violated all Laws in Church & State, has subverted & thereby & by withdrawing himself has Abdicated the Government & is no longer our King.

Sir John Morton [5] Mr Chairman [6] I second that Honourable person that spoke last & stand up to move for the Question. [angrily] [7] Pray put the Question Mr Hamden.

Mr Polixfen [8] Professes he could not hear very well & desires to be informd what has been offerd.

Accordingly The Chairman informs him.

Mr Polixfen stood up again but was interrupted by *Mr How* who saith, That the King in his Opinion forfeited his Right to the Crown of England before he went away.

Mr Polexfen I am of Opinion that if the King went away voluntarily there is [*fo. 3v*] a Descent & then wee have nothing to Do Here. But this was no Voluntary Departure which was occasiond by his Fear. If 2 or 3 men that are too strong for me meet me upon the Highway & I give them my mony, Do I voluntarily give it? Can You call the Kings Flight from Salisbury a Voluntary Departure? Hee went away because the Terror of his own Conscience frighted him & he durst stay no longer & then I hope he did not go voluntarily. Mr Hambden I conceive the Crown is Vacant & that wee need not trouble our Heades about a Demise or differ about Words, but wee must all agree in this, That to avoid Confusion to make [9] a Settlement is absolutely necessary.

Mr Dolben Mr Chairman, Altho I have all imaginable Respect & Honor for the Worthy & Learned Gentleman that spoke last, yet I beg pardon if I herein Differ in Opinion from him for I conceive the Kings Departure was Voluntary, for no one can Deny That Hee might have staid if he would, for Terms were Offerd him & if he would but have made good to us what Hee himself Promisd, Hee might have staid if he had pleasd. And I hope I may ask the Question Whether wee may not say the Throne is now Emty?

Sir James Oxenden [10] The King went away to raise France against us, & to raise [11] Ireland against us, & indeed all Europe against us.

---

[1] *entirely* erased, *wholly* interlined. [2] The last 6 words interlined.
[3] *James* interlined. [4] Square brackets in MS.
[5] Sir John Morton (*c.* 1628–1699), M.P. for Weymouth and Melcombe Regis, Dors., W.
[6] *Mr Chairman* interlined. [7] Square brackets in MS.
[8] Henry Pollexfen (*c.* 1632–1691), M.P. for Exeter, Devon, NL–W.
[9] *mabe* erased, *make* interlined.
[10] Sir James Oxenden (*c.* 1643–1708), M.P. for Sandwich, Cinque Ports, W.
[11] *raise* interlined.

252   'A JORNALL OF THE CONVENTION

Sir H. Capell[1] Although I do beleeve That the King might without molestation have staid if he had pleasd, & in that respect his Departure was voluntary for[2] so long as he had sufferd us to enjoy our civill right without Violation & causd Justice to be duly administred, nobody would have molested him,[3] yet I do conceive that a Popish Head is utterly inconsistent with a Protestant Body. A Popish Ruler cannot manage a Protestant Government. If wee reveiw[4] & seriously consider all our Laws since the Reformation, wee shall find cause to beleeve That no Relapse into Popery, No Popish King was ever expected by our Legislators. Wee may say that Queen Elizabeth laid the foundation of our protestant Government, for of the short reign of Edward the 3rd (the 6 I mean) I do not make much account because England fell back into Popery in the day of Queen Mary. The Oath of Allegiance was revivd by Queen Elizabeth [*fo. 4*] and never intended to have the Edge of it turned against Protestants. Wee may safely say That Arbitrary Power was never[5] designd to be brought in by her. Government is a mutuall Contract between the intended[6] Governor & those that are to be Governed, but the 2 Doctrines of the Church of Rome[7] are absolutely destructive to that Contract: for one of them is That no Faith needs to be kept with Hereticks, & the Other That every (Catholick as they call themselves) Popish Prince shall to the utmost of his Power extirpate Heresy by endeavouring to destroy Hereticks. Mr. H. I may say that Clay & Brasse[8] are as consistent together as a Protestant Body with a Popish Head. I know that Papists in communication one with another or even with Protestants are good Neighbors enough, but they become inveterate & intollerable where their Church is concernd: Upon the Whole I must conclude that the Crown is become Vacant.

Sir Robert Sawyer[9] I think the Question is well put, and whether wee call it Demise or Dereliction or Abdication, I think tis all one, Wee mean one & the same thing: but whether tis an Abdication or Dissolution of the Government That I think may be a Question. Here this day wee have confounded them but I beleeve they are not confounded by our Law, or by any Law that I ere yet heard of: & therefore I think the Disposall of the Crown is not in the people, for if it be, What do the 2 Estates do in the other House? Or what Do wee Do here? Wee are not the People collectively or representatively. The Government of England has always been by 3 Estates, Lords Spirituall, Lords Temporall & Commons, & a King, & our Monarchy [*fo. 4v*] is Hereditary, how then shall wee alter it? Or how can wee take upon us to dispose of the Crown? When wee Represent not the 4th part of the People, yet wee shall take upon us absolutely to dispose of the Government & to bestow the Crown where we think fit.[10] I desire it may be considerd how the Government should be made. I say again that wee do not represent

[1] Sir Henry Capel (1638–96), M.P. for Cockermouth, Cumb., W.
[2] *for* interlined.
[3] *so long . . . molested him*, written in the margin, with *x* marking the place in the text where it should be inserted.
[4] *Sic* in MS.   [5] A second *never* erased.
[6] *intended* interlined.   [7] *of the Church of Rome* interlined.
[8] Neither a proverb current in England at the time nor a passage in the Bible, Milton or Shakespeare refers to the incompatibility of clay and brass. For proverbs see M. P. Tilley, *A Dictionary of the Proverbs in England in the 16th and 17th centuries* (Ann Arbor, Michigan, 1950).
[9] Sir Robert Sawyer (1633–92), M.P. for Cambridge University, T.
[10] *Mr* erased.

so many as the 4th part of the Nation, for there are freeholders under 40 shillings a year & all Copyholders, & Women & Children & Servants. All these have no votes in chusing Knights oth Shire or Citisens or Burgesses unlesse they are freemen, & I suppose nobody can deny that they are 3 times as many as those that do chuse us. Therefore they must be consulted before wee can take upon us to dispose of the Crown, if the Right of Disposing it be in the People. But if you will restore the Rights of the People & the Liberty & Property of the Subject, Go to the Prince of Orange's declaration which I desire may be read.[1] There you will find that the Prince of Orange directs wee should maintain the Rights & Priviledges of[2] every body. Pray Mr Seymor[3] consider of it. Will you conclude the Lords? Will you Tye them up & the rest of the Nation to what you do here? This strikes at the root, at the very fundamentall part of our[4] Government. Wee have no such instructions from those that sent us hither, I'm sure I have not for my part. If the People have the Power of disposing of the Crown, which I beleeve they have not, but suppose they had, Wee are not the People. Indeed a 3rd part or lesse of this House did once take upon them to dispose of the Crown. A 3rd part of this House which are not a 4th part of the People, they did alter the Government by strong hand, but you saw what it came to. Twas of no long continuance. Wee ought to consider the Relation which wee have to Scotland & to Ireland, & to all the Protestants abroad, & wee ought to have a Care of wrong Steps. Let us not build upon a Sandy Foundation: for at this rate instead of uniting us wee shall leave our selves in a more miserable condition than wee were in before. Mr Seymor[5] I confesse there seemes to be a Necessity of our being here: wee come here in order to the obtaining a free Parliament, for there was no other way to come at a free Parliament. And tho *[fo. 5]* we are no Parliament our selves yet we are the same Commons as[6] were Parliament Commons. If the Crown be faln, tis just as if[7] the King were dead and then the Crown descends. The next Heir is to be proclaimd,[8] in order to which the privy Councell meet & sit. The Lord Mayor

[1] Prince William's Declaration of Reasons, widely circulated in England and on the Continent in the autumn of 1688, to which Clarges also appealed (fo. 6v), was read according to Grey, ix. 15.

[2] *of* repeated.

[3] Marginal note: *at his calling upon Mr Seymor (who seemed to be very uneasy while Mr D., Sir R. H. and Sir H. C. spoke, & with whom twas thought he had agreed to throw in a bone) the House laughd.* It is almost certain that Sir Edward Seymour and not Henry, in whose views the House could have had little interest, is intended here and on fo. 4v, below. The absence of a title is puzzling; perhaps a deliberate slur or provocation, or a slip of the compiler's pen. Sawyer was out of order to call a fellow member by name. See G. Petyt, *Lex Parliamentaria: or A Treatise of the Law and Custom of the Parliaments of England* (licensed 6 Dec. 1689), p. 169, and H. Scobell, *Rules and Customs, Which by long and constant practice have obtained the Name of Orders of the House* (Dublin, 1692), p. 18. To 'throw in a bone' means to create discord. An allusion to the difficulty which a bone causes when it is placed between dogs. In use since 1562. *O.E.D.*

[4] *the* erased, *our* interlined.   [5] Marginal note: *laughd at again.*

[6] *are* erased, *as* interlined.   [7] *if* interlined.

[8] With the exception, of course, of Charles II, these were the steps followed in the 17th century in proclaiming a king. In previous centuries no such exact formula existed. See E. R. Turner, *The Privy Council of England in the 17th and 18th Centuries, 1603–1784* (Baltimore, 1927–8), ii. 86, 441, and W. Stubbs, *Constitutional History of England in its Origin and Development* (3 vols., Oxford, 1874–8), *passim.*

254   'A JORNALL OF THE CONVENTION

comes to them, what to Do? Not to elect a Successor, but to see if the Councell
will name the Right Person, which if they know to be right then the City joines
with them in it. The People cannot decide, they may indeed Declare who is King.
This Act of the Kings I confesse makes the case very Doubtfull. Tis Hazardous
for us to make a Successor till the People have declard. There may arise a Dispute
who is the next Heir. Wee have indeed a kind of Interregnum at the present.
Tis with us just as it is upon the Decease of a Lord of a Mannor, the Tenants cannot
chuse whom they will to be Lord over them, but if there are severall Competitors
they may chuse to whom to Attorn.[1] I confesse I have had great Doubts within
myself concerning the reason of our meeting at first, till I considerd it seriously
that the Kings going away is an Abdication & dos amount to a Determination of
his Title. Therefore to speak my Conscience, my Opinion is That the Kings
Departure is an Abdication. Those things which were precedent to his going
away Do shew [quo animo][2] Hee did it. His acting so directly contrary to the
Interest of England (which is the true Protestant Interest) & his refusing[3] to
govern according to Law, I look upon to be a totall refusing[3] to Govern: & so was
his withdrawing himself from us, for Hee that withdraws himself from the
Government Dos abdicate the Government. Wee have had very violent Invasions made upon our Rights, No History can parallell so short a Reign so
Violent. How has the Prerogative been stretchd & straind to do the People mis-
cheif, whereas the Prerogative was originally for the sake of the People. The King
told us his mind in his Declaration,[4] where in he wisht that all were Catholicks, &
we know that a King acts usually according to his Wishes: therefore by his good
will [*fo. 5v*][5] if his wishes might have prevaild, wee should all have been Catholicks.
[The House cald out Papists.][6] Our Church & State has been turnd Topsy Turvy.
Hee would have subornd a Parliament which was[7] & is[8] the only Remedy for all
our Greivances. Therefore I Conclude that his first going away was voluntary, &
in effect a Declaration that he would not Govern according to Law & consequently
an Abdication: and That all our Obligations to him are Void if it be an Abdication.
    Mr Boscowen[9] Mr H. I do not understand the Distinction that the Gentleman
made who spoke last, for I desire to know how the People can be better represented.
I think wee represent the people fully, who indeed did originally represent

For the form used in proclaiming Charles II, see G. Davies, *The Restoration of
Charles II, 1658–60* (San Marino, Calif., 1955), pp. 345–6.
    [1] An act whereby a tenant acknowledged the transference of an estate to a new
landlord and agreed to become the tenant of the new lord. The analogy does not
appear again in the written record and it may be presumed that it was considered
inappropriate. According to Sir Matthew Hale, writing in 1668, the law of attornment was 'much out of use': H. Rolle, *Un Abridgment des plusieurs cases et resolutions
del common ley* (1668), preface. For centuries attornment could, in certain circumstances, be compelled. The law was clarified by the statute of 4 & 5 Anne, c. 3, para.
9: *Statutes of the Realm*, viii. 459. See also W. Holdsworth and others, *History of
English Law* (18 vols., 1922–72), iii. 82, 97, 100, 234; vi. 624–5.
    [2] Square brackets in MS.   [3] *-all* of *refusall* erased, *-ing* interlined.
    [4] The Declaration of Indulgence issued by James II in Apr. 1687 and reissued in
Apr. 1688 with order that the Anglican clergy read it from their pulpits.
    [5] A right-hand margin is left on this folio, in which is written, *this margin is left
for no other reason but inadvertency.*
    [6] Square brackets in MS.
    [7] A second *was* erased.   [8] *&* *is* interlined.
    [9] Hugh Boscawen (1625–1701), M.P. for Cornwall, W.

AT WESTMINSTER'   255

themselves & made Laws as now they chuse Knights oth Shire by the Majority of Voices, but that cannot be now they are grown so numerous & therefore they chuse Representatives for them, who represent them all: I do not speak of copyholders whose Lord represents them, nor of the meanest freeholders, much lesse of servants or women or children, but I speak of all that have a share in the Government or are fit to have a share in it, as to the Legislative part by chusing Representatives. [Then he hinted at the bill of Exclusion][1] to this purpose: Now I hope that those that were for that will be thought to have had some reason on their side. Wee were told that there was no possibility of bringing in Popery because the next heires were Protestants, but now wee have got a little One. I think wee have a great deal of reason to declare the Throne is void. I'm sure France has long entangled us, & is now like to make open war against us, & wee have reason to make use of our best weapon, to chuse a King to go before us & to fight our battells, (which was the first occasion of Kingly Government) & that a Woman cannot so well do. But I wish that wee may be unanimous in declaring that the Throne is now Void.

Sir William Poltny [Began to speak & was not heard, upon which the House cryed Speak out.][2] It is a time indeed to speak out & I shall speak my Opinion, which [*fo. 6*] is That there is an Abdication & that the Crown is void. For I doe take it That the Office of a King is an Office originally from the People & not from Heaven, an Office which was intended for their preservation not their Destruction: therefore an endeavour of a King to destroy those People whom hee was entrusted with to preserve them, makes a Cessure of the Trust. It is just as if a Governor of a Citty or Fort should turn the Cannon against the Garrison, in that Case they may lay him aside.[3] I was for the Bill of Exclusion & I thought it an Error to bring him in, Let us not Double our Error by bringing him in a 2nd time. If wee Do wee must een all go to him with Halters about our necks. I conceive there are many Presidents to shew that the Crown has been disposd of by a Parliament. Particularly 1 Henry 4 when an other unfortunate King not fit to govern, I mean Richard the 2nd, had appeald to a forreign Jurisdiction, which in that Parliament was an Article against him & he was deposd. Here wee have had an appeal to forreign Jurisdiction with a witnesse. Wee have sent, I mean the K. did, an Embassador of obedience to the Pope.[4] Wee have had the Popes Nuntio[5] sent to us, Our Government has been under Father Peters.[6] I know there is a Maxim That the King can do no Wrong but I would fain know Whom to blame else for all the Wrong that has been Done us: it has been originally & primarily by no other but the King. By whom else have our Judges been turnd out because they would not serve the Turn till such were found as would? If a King commits Murder with his own hand, who then Dos the Wrong? Tis not indeed a Kingly Act. Tis not a Trayterous Distinction, whatever it has been thought, to Distinguish between a Kings Power & his Person. Tis almost the same thing as in a Constable, if he gets Drunk & abuses or goes about to beat or wound me, I may defend myself: but if he comes in the Kings name armd with the Kings authority I am bound to obey him. The King has evident- [*fo. 6v*]ly abusd his Politicall Capacity, by

[1] Square brackets in MS.   [2] Square brackets in MS.
[3] An analogy repeatedly used in tracts connected with the Militia Bill/Ordinance controversy of 1641–2. For one example, H. Parker, *Observations upon some of his Majesties late Answers and Expresses* (2 July 1642), p. 3.
[4] Roger Palmer, earl of Castlemaine (1634–1705).
[5] Ferdinand d'Adda (1649–1719).   [6] Father Edward Petre (1631–99).

256   'A JORNALL OF THE CONVENTION

invading our Rights, & therefore wee have reason to provide for our own Security: and in doing so wee ought to consider who has been under God our Deliverer, & how great a Deliverance has been wrought for us, & Do that which may be most effectually conducive to our Preservation. If wee be lost now, the Game is in our own hands. When can wee expect to have such a Deliverance again?

Sir Thomas Clargis[1] If by the Crown being void is meant that the Regall Authority is at an end, for my part Mr H I think the Crown is not void. For wee have been left as I may say in the condition of an Elective Commonwealth: & I pray consider what we did upon the 22 of Dec:[2] last, I think twas about that time if I mistake not. Consider into whose hands you did then put the Powr & upon that foot, upon that ground wee are met here now, that is upon the Prince of Orange his letter: And if wee are not a Parliament as some say wee are not; wee are tantamount to a Parliament. I think wee sit here to pursue the ends of the Prince of Orange's Declaration, & therefore I move that the Declaration may be read.

Sir William Williams[3] Wee have appointed this day tis true to consider the state of the Nation, but to consider all parts of the State of the Nation will hold us 7 year, instead of that I conceive the Finall End of our meeting here is to consider which is the best way to secure the peace of the Nation, & in order thereunto wee are to declare That it is a plain Fact That King James 2 is out of England & is in France. How he left this Kingdom, whether voluntarily or urgd by his own feares I do not meddle, but tis a plain Fact that he is gone: & it is another plain Fact That no care was taken by the Prince [House crys out King you mean][4] Ay I mean King James the 2nd to secure the peace of the Nation by maintaining the Judicature of it or otherwise[5] before he went. And if that be True that he is Gone & That he hath deprivd us as far as in him lyes of the Protection & Benefit of the Law, That wee are defective through his Fault in our Judicature, and have no other Remedy, & that he is gone to the French, a nation that has ever been averse to England & wee to them (for we never liked any thing of France but their Wine that indeed wee like very well), What is fit to be Done in this Case? To attain to the [*fo. 7*] knowledge of which the 1st Step will be to remember That he had deprivd this Nation of the exercise of[6] Kingly Government.

Chairman reads the Vote.

Mr Summers[7] There is a Case which I think is in all respects parallell to this, & that is the History of Sigismond King of Sweden,[8] quod vide.[9] [*fo. 7v*] The

---

[1] Sir Thomas Clarges (*c.* 1618–1695), M.P. for Oxford University, T.

[2] Clarges surely meant 26 Dec. 1688 when members of Charles II's parliaments met with representatives of the city of London and, as the house of lords had done on 24 Dec., asked Prince William to take on the administration of the government and call a Convention (*C.J.*, x. 6). The house of lords met on 22 Dec., but reached no conclusions (*Clar. Corresp.*, ii. 233, 235, 236; Morrice MS. Q, p. 385).

[3] Sir William Williams (1634–1700), M.P. for Beaumaris, Anglesey, Wales, W.

[4] Square brackets in MS.   [5] *or otherwise* interlined.

[6] *the exercise of* interlined.   [7] John Somers (1651–1716), M.P. for Worcester, W.

[8] Sigismond (1566–1632) was king of Poland from 1587 to 1632 and of Sweden from 1592 to 1599. Aiming, it was believed, to strengthen the monarchy and reinstate Catholicism in Sweden, Sigismond clashed with his uncle Charles. Defeated in battle, Sigismond fled and was deposed by the Swedish parliament which, in 1604, proclaimed Charles king of Sweden. These events were recounted by A. Nixon, *The Warres of Swethland. With the Ground and Originall of the said Warres . . . betwixt Sigismund, King of Poland, and Duke Charles his Unkle, lately Crowned King of Swethland* (1609), and J. Fowler, *History of the troubles of Suethland and Poland,*

AT WESTMINSTER' 257

imprecation[1] of King James, the Granfather to our late unhappy King, comes
into my mind,[2] and King John the Father of the before mentiond Sigismond
made such a Kind of Imprecation. The People of Sweden did as I said at first
admit him, but after he had violated the solemn promises which he made to them,
that violation was followd by a war under the conduct of Charles, the Uncle of
King Sigismond. But I must crave leave to observe to you That this Desertion of
Sigismonds was much lesse then that of our late King, For he went but into
another his Kingdoms, that of Poland, whereas King James is not gone into
Scotland nor into Ireland, but when he was at his liberty to go whether he pleasd,
Hee chose to go to that place (which of any in the World is most averse to the
interest of England) into France, which makes good the suspition of the secret
Leagues that were between the 2 Kings. But before he went away, Hee did
utterly incapacitate himself to be our King, for how could he be supream Head of
our Church who submitting himself & us to another, a forreign, Head, by sending
an Embassador of Obedience to Rome & by receiving the Popes Nuntio here,
Both which acts are directly against our Laws? Besides which he sent out Popish
Bishop to visit all the Kingdom, & has deliverd Ireland again into the hands of the
Irish hands: and has indeed usd all imaginable meanes to bring us into Popery &
Slavery. I do therefore humbly motion That a Committee be appointed of some
Members to collect the Sence of the House and ...

[House call out][3] No, No, To the orders of the House.[4]

Sir John Mainard[5] Mr Hambden I am against wording the Vote That King
James 2nd being a Papist is inconsistent &c. I desire That word Papist may be
left out in our Vote.

Mr Finch[6] Makes a Question Where the Opinions of the worthy Members that

*which occasioned the Expulsion of Sigismundus the Third, King of those Kingdomes,
with his Heires for ever from the Suethish Crown* (2 edns., 1656), as well as by S. von
Pufendorf, whose history of Sweden was printed in Stockholm in 1688 (translated
into English in 1702), and in *The Causes and Manner of Deposing a Popish King in
Swedeland, Truely Described* (1688). A modern account is C. Hallendorff and A.
Schück, *History of Sweden* (New York, 1970), pp. 188–208.

[9] The journal breaks off and is resumed on the next page.

[1] James I's 'imprecation' or curse is explained by Grey, ix. 16: 'King James I
(upon an occasion most have heard of) protested "That if his Posterity were not
Protestants, he prayed God to take them from the Throne."' The occasion was
almost certainly a meeting of the Council in February 1605 when James, referring
to the Catholics, was reported to have said that 'if he thought his sone and heire
after him would give any toleration thereunto, he would wish him fairly buried
before his eyes'. *Original Letters, Illustrative of English History*, ed. H. Ellis (11
vols., 1824–46), 2nd ser., iii. 216, and D. H. Willson, *King James VI and I* (1956),
p. 223.

[2] After *mind* a space of 2 lines is left.   [3] Square brackets in text.

[4] Somers was out of order to move the appointment of a committee to collect the
sense of members while the House was in Grand Committee, the essential purpose
of which was to explore the wishes of members and whose rules required that before
dissolving a vote be taken on the report to the full House. See Petyt, *Lex Parliamentaria*, p. 218, and Scobell, *Rules and Customs*, p. 23.

[5] Sir John Maynard (1602–90), M.P. for Plymouth, Devon, NL–W. He was appointed serjeant-at-law in Nov. 1660 (cf. compiler's note about the 'Sergeant's
voice', fo. 8v).

[6] The Hon. Heneage Finch (*c.* 1649–1719), M.P. for Oxford University, NL–T.

258   'A JORNALL OF THE CONVENTION

have spoke to this Debate Differ? Gives his Judgmt. Recounts what has been movd [*fo. 8*] and shews what Difference there is between the Throne being demisd &c and that it tends to a Dissolution of the Government. For if you take it as a Dissolution, then wee that sit here Have no right to our Estates, there is a Dissolution of that Right too. But can wee say That King James by this Act of his Departure has lost to himself & his Posterity the absolute inheritance of the Crown? Will any one go about to maintain That Opinion? Wee have ever heard & read That the Monarchy of England was Hereditary, which no act of Violence how great soever committed by the King can forfeit. It must Descend unlesse wee, while wee complain of the Kings violation of our Rights, will our selves violate our very Constitution. It ought to be considerd That This Debate is of the highest consequence. I would not be mistaken, I am far from going about to excuse the King. I own that the violations were very great and that the taking up arms was necessary: but I desire it may be examind whether his going away be an Abdication. Urges the Difficulty.[1] Is not of Opinion to send proposalls. I think tis the same Case as if the King were a Minor or in a Phrensy & thereby altogether unfit to govern. The King was certainly misinformed & abusd by those whom he intrusted under him & by those that were about him, but will that make an absolute forfeiture of his Right? Hee Repeats & explains the Maxim That the King can do no Wrong but saith Hee urges it not. The Kings zeal to Popery makes him indeed unsafe to be trusted, but desires it may be very well considerd what is fit to be done. Concludes it fit the Supream Power should be deposited[2] somewhere, but for his own part dares not undertake to determine[3] this great point.

Sir Thomas Lee[4] Mr H, The Gentleman that spoke last brings you to a 2nd question before you have determind or gone thorow with the 1st.

Mr Finch again Defends his Motion & saith The Question would come too late when the Vote is passd.

Chairman reminds the House what has been said & reads the Question.

Sir Christopher Musgrave[5] Denies the King's subverting the Government, Doubts our Power of depo-[*fo. 8v*]sing the King. Thinks it not for the Honor of this House to attemt what they cannot perform. Would have the Nation near him—Scotland satisfied.

Mr Wharton[6] Denies him to be King. Saith it may be for the safety of some but of few to call him back.

Sir Christopher Musgrave Defends himself. Saith he would only have the House proceed upon good grounds. Desires to know of the Lawyers Whether wee can depose the King. Would have nothing done but what may be safe.

Sir J. Mainard I am of Opinion That the King has deposd himself. And for the Gentleman that spoke last, his Motion That wee should do nothing but what is Safe, I think if the King should come back every one that sits here now would be equally Criminall with any one that should attemt the King's life with a Dagger. All Government had at first its Foundation from a Pact with the People: & here No one can say but That Pact has apparently been broken by the Kings invading & violating Our Laws, Property, Liberty, & Religion, by his putting Papists into all places of trust in the Government as fast as hee could find Papists for them.

[1] Margin: *here I was hindred by a members going by.*
[2] *dep* erased before this word.   [3] *r* interlined.
[4] Sir Thomas Lee (1635–91), M.P. for Buckinghamshire, W.
[5] Sir Christopher Musgrave (*c.* 1631–1704), M.P. for Carlisle, Cumb., T.
[6] The Hon. Thomas Wharton (1648–1715), M.P. for Buckinghamshire, W.

I remember very well the occation of dissolving the last Parliament. Wee desird only that some Popish Officers might be removd & wee were removd our selves.[1] It is 500 year now or thereabouts since Ireland was conquerd, or rather not conquerd but yeelded: and it has been now 500 year in english hands: indeed there was a bloudy Massacre in the year 1641 or thereabout, but after a war it was entirely recoverd again: but now this King has given it away to the Irish papists, & has put the lives of 500000 protestants into their hands. Urges the endeavors usd to new mould all corporations, mentions the Quo Warranto's. Rehearses the Male administration of the Government. The illegall violence usd at Maudlin Colledge.

[Here the Sergeant's voice faild him so as the House called upon him to speak out, but he said Hee could speak no louder & I could hear no more.][2]

Sir H. Capell Mr H. I confesse I am surprizd to heare some Gentlemen who yeeld that wee have been in a miserable Condition, make a Doubt whether our Case admits of any Remedy. It is a great Misery indeed if we can be no way releivd. Im sure it was the Sence of 2 Parliaments before the Crown fell to this unhappy King that it was fit to exclude[*fo. 9*] him: but then wee were amusd with specious pretences of limitations. How will you limit him now? He reflects on him that said the King was ill advisd. Movd for the Question.

Mr How Reflects very much.

Chairman takes him down.

Mr Harbord[3] *angrily* Mr Chairman, By your favor you ought not to take down any gentleman that is speaking before you hear what he has to say. If he saith any thing amisse, he is liable to the censure of the House for it, but ought not to be taken down.[4]

Mr Hamden the Chairman excuses himself. Saith our Debates ought to be managd with Moderation not with Heat & Reflections.

Sir G. Treby[5] Sorry for Heates. States the Question modestly. Reflects (tho not by name) upon what was said by Mr Finch & Sir Christopher Musgrave, going out of his Wits not out of[6] the Government. All protestants at this rate may be destroyd without a Remedy. Excuses our Authority. Reflects on Sir Robert Sawyer.[7] Saith The King has renouncd us. Recites the 2 parts in Government, Commanding & Obeying. The Legislative & Executive power both violated. Is of Opinion that the King cannot be treated with. Recites how The King by the High Commission intended to have deprived all the Protestant Clergy & by assuming a Power to Dispence intended to filled[8] the Church with Popish Preists.

[1] The reference is to the prorogation of James II's only parliament on 20 Nov. 1685.

[2] Square brackets at the left-hand end of 2 lines in the MS.

[3] William Harbord (1635–92), M.P. for Launceston, Cornw., W.

[4] According to contemporary parliamentary procedure, remarks made in debate were subject to the censure of the House, but the Speaker (the chairman of a Grand Committee is not specifically mentioned) did have the authority to rebuke an M.P. for impertinence or 'nipping'. See W. Hakewell, *Orders, Proceedings, Punishments, and Priviledges of the Commons House of Parliament in England* (1641), p. 7; Petyt, *Lex Parliamentaria*, pp. 153, 156, 157, 170; Scobell, *Rules and Customs*, pp. 19, 24–30.

[5] Sir George Treby (1643–1700), M.P. for Plympton Erle, Devon, W.

[6] *out of* interlined.

[7] *Chr. Musgrave* erased.   [8] *Sic* in MS.

260   'A JORNALL OF THE CONVENTION

Touches the regulation of Corporations & quartering Dragoones upon such as were most tenacious of their liberty. That in a little while had those practises gone on the House of Commons would have represented the King only. The greatest malefactors as it was orderd would have been the only Representatives. A Private person may be remedied, but these nationall greivances could not any otherwise then by the Prince of Orange who under God is our only remedy. Recites Richard 2nd only fault, King James 1st Judgement That when a King governs contrary to Law he ceases to be a King.[1] Hints at the Bill of Exclusion. Mentions the pretences of the Duke of York's freinds at the Oxford Parliament that the Test securd our Religion. Makes a Prosopopeia[2] in the name of King James 2nd. [*fo. 9v*] Saith That the last Act the King did with the Seales was to pardon notorious malefactors.

Lord Wiltshire[3] Moves for the Question.

Sir Robert Sawyer Saith some Gentlemen did mistake him, he only desird the Question might not be ambiguous. Thinks the King cannot surrender. Saith the Crown cannot be Void but the Throne may.

Mr Finch Desires to explain himself. Makes a Question Whether 'tis the maleadministration or the going away of the King that is thought to amount to an Abdication ? [Many of the House " Both ".][4] Saith Hee is not for the Kings return but desires Unanimity. Makes a question whether we are ripe for declaring That the King's title to the Crown is voided ? Urges the Oath of Allegiance that the King is acknowledgd rightfull King & many other Difficultys. Saith tho all desire to be secure yet they differ in Opinion as to the way. Reflects on Sir G. Treby & declares he means a Regency & that way will be most safe wherein all shall agree.

Sir Robert Howard Saith tis a fault to speak twice[5] but cannot forbear declaring his Opinion That a Regency is as bad as calling the King back. Reflects on the Gentleman [Sir Robert Sawyer that sat by him][6] that said Wee are not the People. Desires to know Who are then the People ? Saith Wee are afraid of our selves & while wee are thus carefull of preserving the Succession wee shall thro it upon the young Gentleman that is gone over with his Nurse, or wee shall leave it in the power & at the choice[7] of the French King to give us one.

Chairman reads the 1st question, recites the exceptions [have not subverted][8] reads another question leaving out [Papist].[9]

Another speak.

Chair again The 2nd Question.

[1] Both Grey (ix. 14) and Somers (*Hardwicke Papers*, ii. 409) note that Treby said that James expressed this point to the parliament of 1607. Surely Treby was referring to James I's speech delivered to parliament, 31 March 1609: *Political Works of James I*, ed. C. H. McIlwain (Cambridge, Mass., 1918), p. 309. H. M. Chew, 'King James I', in *Social and Political Ideas of Some Great Thinkers of the 16th and 17th Centuries*, ed. F. J. C. Hearnshaw (New York, 1949), p. 120 believes the comment was made to placate parliamentary opinion.

[2] Prosopopeia—'a rhetorical figure by which an...absent person is represented as speaking or acting': *O.E.D.*

[3] Charles Powlett (1661–1722), styled 'Lord Wiltshire' in 1689, succeeded as 2nd duke of Bolton, 1699, M.P. for Hampshire, NL–W.

[4] Square brackets in MS.

[5] It was no fault when the House was in Grand Committee, as Howard surely knew.

[6] Square brackets in MS.   [7] *& at the choice* interlined.

[8] Square brackets in MS.   [9] Square brackets in MS.

Lord Fanshaw[1] Saith never in the House before. Thinks the King went by compulsion, was afraid of his own subjects. King declard so the night before he went. Pleads very much for him. Knows no reason for hast.

Lord Cornbury[2] Pray let the Question be explaind.

Mr Roberts[3] I desire to know which way the Question is put.

Mr Chairman reads The Question: [*fo. 10*] That King James the 2nd by endeavouring to subvert the constitution of the Kingdom by breaking the Originall compact between King & people, and by the Advice of Jesuits & other wicked persons having violated the fundamentall Laws both of Church & State & by withdrawing himself,[4] has thereby abdicated the Government & left the Throne Vacant.

Mr Cook[5] I humbly conceive It is 2 Questions.

House No No.

Chairman Shall I put the Question to this Committee?

House Ay Ay.

Chairman As many as are of Opinion that King James [repeats the Question][6] say Ay.

Most of the House very loudly Ay Ay. One went out just[7] before.[8]

Chairman As many as are of another opinion say No.

Lord Cornbury, Lord Fanshaw, Sir Edward Seymor, No.

Chairman The Ay's have it.

Sir R. Temple Mr Hamden I desire you would report it to the House.

Chairman Shall wee adjorn?

Lord Colchester[9] Pray let us proceed immediately.

Sir William Williams I think wee have done enough for this day.

Sir Richard Temple Pray leave the Chair.

Chairman Shall I make a Report to the House? House Ay Ay.

Sir J. Knight[10] ⎫
Mr Wharton   ⎬ Immediately.
                         ⎭

Mr Wogan[11] Pray let us adjorn till to morrow.

Sir Rowland Gwyn[12] I think we had need lose no time.

Sir Robert Sawyer I think wee had better adjorn till to morrow.

[1] Charles Fanshawe, 4th Viscount Fanshawe (1643–1701), M.P. for Mitchell, Cornw., NL–T.

[2] Edward Hyde, Viscount Cornbury (1661–1723), son of the 2nd earl of Clarendon, M.P. for Wiltshire, T.

[3] The Hon. Francis Robartes (1650–1718), son of the 1st earl of Radnor, M.P. for Lostwithiel, Cornw., T.

[4] *& by withdrawing himself* interlined.

[5] Either John Coke (*c.* 1653–1692), M.P. for Derby, T., or William Cooke (*c.* 1621–1703), M.P. for Gloucester, T.

[6] Square brackets in MS.   [7] *just* interlined.

[8] It was against the rules of the House for a member to slip out. See Petyt, *Lex Parliamentaria*, p. 152, and Scobell, *Rules and Customs*, p. 6. On 28 Jan. the back door to the chamber had been locked (to prevent entering and leaving?) and the key laid on the table: *C.J.*, x. 14.

[9] Richard Savage (*c.* 1654–1712), styled 'Lord Colchester', succeeded as 4th Earl Rivers in 1694, M.P. for Liverpool, Lancs., W.

[10] Sir John Knight (d. 1718), M.P. for Bristol, Glos., T.

[11] William Wogan (1635–1708), M.P. for Haverfordwest, Pembs., Wales, T.

[12] Sir Rowland Gwynne (*c.* 1658–1726), M.P. for Radnorshire, Wales, W.

262   'A JORNALL OF THE CONVENTION

Sir Walter Young[1] I desire wee may go on immediately.

Sir J. Lowther[2] I conceive there is no such great hast. I desire we may adjorn till to morrow that wee may have the concurrence of the Lords.

Mr Medlicot[3] Immediately.

Chair Shall I put you the Question for to morrow?

Sir Thomas Lee Pray Mr Hambden leave the Chair & submit it to the house.

[*fo. 10v*] The Chairman Mr Hambden leaves his Chair. The Speaker reassumes his. Mr Hamden reports.

Sir J. Knight interrupts. [House Agree Agree][4]

The House agrees with the Committee. The Question passes.

Sir Robert Howard I desire wee may send to have the concurrence of the Lords.

Mr Boscowen I second that Motion for the Concurrence of the Lords.

Mr Levison Gowr I humbly propose that a Committee may be appointed to draw up this[5] our Vote to carry up with it to the Lords.

House No No.

Orderd That Mr Hambden carry up this Vote to the Lords & desire their concurrence.

Mr Speaker Pray Gentlemen Attend your Chairman, for the Lords take great notice how Votes are attended.

Mr Hamden carrys up the Vote to the Lords & leaves it & returns.

Sir William Cooper[6] Pray Mr Speaker let us go into a Committee of the whole house to go on with our busnesse.

Sir William Williams I think wee have done enough for this day & may now adjorn.

Sir J. Guise[7] Pray send to know whether the Lords sit.

Word was brought That the Lords were up.

Sir Robert Napper[8] Pray Mr Speaker put the question Whether we shall adjorn.

Speaker Is it your pleasure Gentlemen that I should adjorn? [House][9] Ay Ay. The House is adjornd till 9 to morrow.

[*fo. 11*][10] *Sir Robert Howard* For my part I see no Difference therefore I desire

Mr Garway[11] I desire the Debates may go on to give us a handle in Lord's Votes to amend. Shall be declared that they be immediately King & Queen.

[1] Sir Walter Young (or Yonge) (1653–1731), M.P. for Ashburton, Devon, NL–W.
[2] Either Sir John Lowther (1642–1706), M.P. for Cumberland, W, or Sir John Lowther (1655–1700), 1st Viscount Lonsdale in 1696, M.P. for Westmorland, NL–T. Although damned as whig in Nov. 1688, Lowther is identified as tory by K. Feiling, *History of the Tory Party, 1640–1714* (Oxford, 1924), pp. 227, 235, 257.
[3] Thomas Medlicott (1628–1716), M.P. for Abingdon, Berks., NL–W.
[4] Square brackets in MS.   [5] *for* erased.
[6] Sir William Cowper (1639–1706), M.P. for Hertford, W.
[7] Sir John Guise (Guyse) (c. 1654–1695), M.P. for Gloucestershire, W.
[8] Sir Robert Napier (c. 1642–1700), M.P. for Weymouth and Melcombe Regis, Dors., T.
[9] Square brackets in MS.   [10] This folio contains fragments of remarks.
[11] William Garroway (1616–1701), M.P. for Arundel, Suss., W.

AT WESTMINSTER'   263

Sir Thomas Clargis Is for Qualifications. Against administration of Government during Princes life. Asks if the Prince go to War, may not the Princesse have the Administration?

Sir H. Capell

The debate at large
... at the Free Conference
6 February

THE
DEBATE
At Large,
BETWEEN THE
LORDS and COMMONS,
AT THE
FREE CONFERENCE,

Held in the

Painted Chamber,

IN THE

SESSION of the CONVENTION,

Anno 1688.

Relating to the Word,

ABDICATED,

AND THE

Vacancy of the THRONE,

In the COMMONS Vote.

The Second Edition Corrected.

LONDON
Printed: And Sold by JOHN MORPHEW,
near *Stationers-hall*, MDCCX.
(Price 1 *s.*)

(3)

The DEBATE at Large, &c.

Martis 22 die Januarii, 1688.

IN the Convention met, upon his Highnefs the Prince of *Orange*'s Letters, this Day in the Houfe of Commons. A Motion being made that the Houfe would appoint a Day, to take into Confideration the Condition and State of the Nation.

Refolved, *Nemine Contradicente*, That the Houfe on *Monday* next, at Ten of the Clock in the Morning, take into Confideration the State and Condition of the Nation.

Lunæ 28 die Januarii, 1688.

The Houfe then (according to the Order of *Tuefday* laft) proceeded to take into Confideration the State and Condition of the Nation.

Refolved, That the Houfe do now Refolve it felf into a Committee of the whole Houfe, to take into Confideration the State and Condition of the Nation.

Mr. *Speaker* left the Chair.

Mr. *Hamden* took the Chair of the Committee.

Mr. *Speaker* Reaffumed the Chair.

Mr. *Hamden* Reported from the Committee of the whole Houfe that, having taken into Confideration the Condition and State of the Nation, they had agreed upon a Refolve ; which he Read in his Place, and then deliver'd the fame in at the Clerk's Table, where the fame being Read, was as followeth.

Refolved, *That King* James *the Second, having Endeavoured to Subvert the Conftitution of the Kingdom, by Breaking the Original Contract between King and People ; and, by the Advice of* Jefuits, *and other Wicked Perfons, having Violated the Fundamental Laws, and With-drawn himfelf out of the Kingdom, hath* Abdicated *the Government, and* that the Throne is thereby Vacant.

Refolved, That this Houfe do agree with the Committee, *That King* James *the Second, having Endeavoured to Subvert the Conftitution of the Kingdom, by Breaking the Original Contract between King and People ; and by the Advice of* Jefuits, *and other Wicked Perfons, having Violated the Fundamental Laws, and having Withdrawn himfelf out of the Kingdom, hath* Abdicated *the Government ; and* that the Throne is thereby Vacant.

A 2   Ordered,

(4)

Ordered, That Mr. *Hamden* do carry up the said Resolution to the Lords for their Concurrence. And it was carried up to the Lords, by Mr. *Hamden*, accordingly.

Sabbat. 2 *die Feb.* 1688.

A Message from the Lords to the Commons, by Sir *Miles Cook* and Mr. *Methwin*, Two Masters in *Chancery* attending the House of Lords.

Mr. S P E A K E R,

The Lords have confidered of the Vote of this Houfe of the 28th of January *laft, to which they Concur with Amendments ; unto which Amendments they defire the Concurrence of this Houfe.*

The Amendments made by the Lords to the Votes fent up to them from this House, the 28th of *January*, were Read and are as followeth,

L. 8. Inftead of the Word *Abdicated* Read *Deferted*.

L. 9. Leave out thefe Words, *And that the Throne is thereby Vacant.*

Lunæ 4 *die Feb.* 1688.

To the Firft Amendment, Propofed by the Lords to be made to the Vote of the Commons, of the 28th of *January*, Inftead of the Word *Abdicated*, to infert the Word *Deferted*, the Commons do not agree; becaufe the Word *Deferted* doth not fully exprefs the Conclufion neceffarily infer'd from the Premifes, to which your Lordfhips have agreed; for your Lordfhips have agreed, *That King* James *the Second hath Endeavoured to Subvert the Conftitution of the Kingdom, by Breaking the Original Contract between King and People, and hath violated the Fundamental Laws, and Withdrawn himfelf out of the Kingdom.* Now the Word *Deferted* refpects only the Withdrawing, but the Word *A dicated* refpects the Whole ; for which Purpofe the Commons made Choice of it. The Commons do not agree to the Second Amendment, to leave out the Words, *And that the Throne is thereby Vacant.*

1ft. Becaufe they conceive, that, as they may well inferr from fo much of their own Vote as your Lordfhips have a-greed unto, *That King* James *the Second has* Abdicated *the Government and that the Throne is thereby Vacant* ; fo that if they fhould admit your Lordfhips Amendment, *That he hath only Deferted the Government* ; yet, even thence, it would follow that the *Throne is Vacant* as to King *James* the Second, *Deferting* the Government, being, in true Conftruction, De-ferting *the Throne.*

2dly, The Commons conceive they need not Prove unto your Lordfhips, That, as to any other Perfon, *the Throne is alfo Vacant* ; your Lordfhips (as they conceive) having al-ready admitted it, by your Addreffing to the Prince of *Orange* the

(5)

the 25th of *December* laft, *To take upon him the Adminiftration of Publick Affairs, both Civil and Military ; and to take into his Care the Kingdom of* Ireland, *till the meeting of this Convention.* In Purfuance of fuch Letters, and by your Lordfhips renewing the fame Addrefs to his Highnefs, (as to Publick Affairs : And the Kingdom of *Ireland*,) fince you met, and by Appointing Days of *Publick Thankfgivings* to be Obferved throughout the whole Kingdom, all which the Ccmmons conceive do impply that it was your Lordfhips Opinion, *That the Throne was Vacant,* and to fignify fo much to the People of this Kingdom.

3*dly*, It is from thofe who are upon the Throne of *England* (when there are any fuch) from whom the People of *England* ought to receive Protection; and to whom, for that Caufe, they owe the Allegiance of Subjects ; but there being none now from whom they expect *Regal* Protection, and to whom, for that Caufe, they owe the Allegiance of Subjects, the Commons conceive, *The Throne is Vacant.*

Refolved, That the Earl of *Wiltfhire* do go up to the Lords to defire a Conference upon the Subject matter of the Amendments.

The Earl of Wiltfhire *Reports,* That, he having attended the Lords, to defire a Conference, they had given Anfwer, *That they did confent to a Conference immediately in the* Painted Chamber.

Refolved, That the Committee to whom it was referred to prepare Heads of Reafons at a Conference with the Lords, be the Managers of the faid Conference.

Mr. *Hamden,* Reports, from the Committee appointed to Manage the Conference with the Lords, That they had Attended the Lords at the Conference and Communicated unto their Lordfhips the Reafons why this Houfe doth not Concur with their Lordfhips in the faid Amendments.

Martis 5 die Feb. 1688.

Mr. *Hamden* Reports from the Conference with the Lords, that the Earl of *Nottingham* fpoke to this Effect,

" That the Lords had defired this Conference with the
" Commons, that they might be as happily United to the
" Commons in Opinion, as they are infeparable in their In-
" tereft ; and that they are, at this time, uneafy that they
" cannot Concur with the Commons in every thing ; becaufe
" it is of fo great a Concern to the Nation, and from fo great
" and Wife a Body. That he then delivered what the Lords
had done in Reference to the Subject Matter of the laft Conference, and faid, " That the Lords did infift upon the Firft
" Amendment of the Vote of the Houfe of Commons of the
" 25th of *Jaҥuary* laft, inftead of the Word *Abdicated,* to
" have the Word *Deferted.*   1*ft.* " Be-

(6)

1*st*. " Becaufe the Lords do not find, that the Word *Abdi-*
" *cated* is a Word known to the Common Law of *England*,
" and the Lords hope the Commons will agree to make ufe of
" ſuch Words only, whereof the Meaning may be underſtood
" according to Law, and not of ſuch as will be liable to
" doubtful Interpretations.

2*dly*, " Becaufe in the moſt common Acceptation of the
" Civil Law, *Abdication* is a Voluntary Expreſs Act of *Re-*
" *nuntiation*, which is not in this Cafe, and doth not follow
" from the Premiſes, *That King* James *the Second, by having*
" *With-drawn himſelf, after having endeavoured to Subvert the*
" *Conſtitution of the Government, by Breaking the Original Con-*
" *tract between King and People, and having violated the Funda-*
" *mental Laws*, may be more properly faid to have *Abdicated*,
" than *Deſerted.*

He faid the Lords did Infiſt on the Second Amendment, to
leave out the Words, *And that the Throne is Vacant*, for this
Reafon:

" For that although the Lords have agreed, that the King
" has *Deſerted* the Government, and therefore have made
" Application to the Prince of *Orange, To take upon him the*
" *Adminiſtration of the Government, and thereby to Provide for*
" *the Peace and Safety of the Kingdom*, yet there can be no
" other Inference drawn from thence, but only that the Exer-
" cife of the Government by King *James* the Second is Ceafed ;
" fo as the Lords were, and are willing, to fecure the Nation
" againſt the return of the faid King into this Kingdom ; but
" not that there was either ſuch an *Abdication* by him, or
" ſuch a *vacancy in the Throne*, as that the Crown was there-
" by become *Elective*, which they cannot agree.

I. " *Becauſe, by the Conſtitution of the Government, the*
" *Monarchy is Hereditary, and not Elective.*

II. " *Becauſe no Act of the King alone can Barr, or Deſtroy*
" *the Right of his Heirs to the Crown ; and therefore in Anſwer*
" *to the third Reaſon alledg'd by the Houſe of Commons, If*
" *the Throne be vacant of King* James *the Second, Allegiance*
" *is due to ſuch Perſon as the Right of Succeſſion doth*
" *belong to.*

The Queſtion being put that this Houfe do agree with the
Lords in the faid Firſt Amendment.

It paffed in the Negative.

The Queſtion being put that this Houfe do agree with the
Lords in the faid Second Amendment.

The Houfe Divided.

The Yea's go forth.

The Tellers for the Yea's, Sir *Joſeph Tredenham*, and Mr.
Gwyn. 151.

The Tellers for the No's, Mr. *Colt*, and Mr *Herbert*. 282.

And

(7)

And fo it was Refolved in the Negative.

Refolved, That a free Conference be defired with the Lords upon the Subject matter of the laft Conference.

Ordered, That it be Referred unto,

Sir *Robert Howard*, Mr. *Polexfyn*, Mr. *Paul Foley*, Mr. Serj. *Maynard*, Mr. Serj. *Holt*, Lord *Faukland*, Sir *George Treby*, Mr. *Somners*, Mr. *Garraway*, Mr. *Bufcowen*, Sir *Thomas Littleton*, Mr. *Palmer*, Mr. *Hamden*, Sir *Henry Capel*, Sir *Thomas Lee*, Mr. *Sacheverell*, Major *Wildeman*, Colonel *Birch*, Mr. *Ayres* Sir *Rich. Temple*, Sir *Henry Goodrick*, Mr. *Waller*, Sir *John Guyes*. To Manage the Conference.

Ordered, That Mr. *Dolben* do go up to the Lords, and defire a free Conference with the Lords upon the Subject Matter of the laft Conference.

Mr. *Dolben* Reported, That he having (according to the Order of this Houfe) attended the Lords to defire a Free Conference with their Lordfhips, upon the Subject Matter of the laft Conference, they had agreed to a Free Conference prefently in the *Painted Chamber*. And the Managers went to a Free Conference, at the Free Conference in the *Painted Chamber*.

Mr. H A M D E N's *Speech*.

MY Lords, the Commons have defired this Free Confe- rence from your Lordfhips upon the Subject Matter of the laft Conference, that they may make appear unto your Lordfhips, that it is not without fufficient Reafon, that they are Induced to Maintain their own Vote, to which your Lordfhips have made fome Amendments; and that they can- not agree to thofe Amendments made by you Lordfhips for the fame Reafons.

My Lords, the Commons do very readily agree with your Lordfhips, That it is a Matter of the greateft Concernment to the Kingdom in general, its future Peace, and happy Go- vernment, and the *Proteftant* Intereft, both at Home and Abroad, that there be a good Iffue and Determination of the Bufinefs now in Debate between Both Houfes, and a fpeedy one as can confift with the Doing of it in the beft manner. This way of Intercourfe between Both Houfes by Free Confe- rence, where there is full Liberty of Objecting, Anfwering, and Replying, the Commons think the beft Means to attain this End, and to Maintain a good Correfpondence between Both Houfes, which is fo neceffary at all Times, but more efpecially in the prefent Conjuncture; this my Lords will bring Honour and Strength to the Foundation that fhall be laid

after

(8)

after our late Convulsions, and Discourage our Enemies from Attempting to Undermine it.

It is true, my Lords, the present Difference between your Lordships and the Commons is only about a few Words; but he Commons think their Words so Significant to the Purpose for which they are used, and so proper to the Case unto which they are applied, that in so Weighty a matter as that now in Debate, they are by no means to be parted with.

The Word *Abdicated* the Commons conceive is of larger Signification than the Word your Lordships are pleased to use *Desert* ; but not too large to be applied to all the Recitals in the Beginning of the Commons Vote, to which they meant it should be applied. Nor ought it to be Restrained to a Voluntary Express Resignation, only in Word or Writing, Overt-Acts there are that will be Significant enough to amount to it.

My Lords, that the Common Law of *England* is not acquainted with the Word, it is from the Modesty of our Law, that it is not willing to suppose there should be any Unfortunate Occasion of making use of it : And we would have been willing that we should never have had such an Occasion as we have to have Recourse to it. Your Lordships next Amendment is, that your Lordships have left out the last Words in the Commons Vote, *And that the Throne is thereby Vacant.*

My Lords, the Commons conceive it is a true Proposition, and *That the Throne is Vacant* ; and, they think, they make it appear that this is no new Phrase ; neither is it a Phrase that perhaps some of the old Records may be Strangers to ; or not well acquainted with: But they think it not chargeable with Consequences that your Lordships have been pleased to draw from it, *That it will make the Crown of* England *become Elective.* If the Throne had been full, we know your Lordships would have assigned that, as a Reason of your Disagreement, by telling us who filled it ; and it would be known by some Publick Royal Act, which might notify to the People in whom the Kingly Government resided ; neither of which hath been done ; and yet your Lordships will not allow the *Throne to be Vacant.*

My Lords, I am unwilling to detain your Lordships longer, from what may be better said for your Lordships Satisfaction in these Matters, by those whose Province it is : I am to acquaint your Lordships, That the Commons do agree, it is an Affair of very great Importance. Here are other Gentlemen that are appointed to manage this Conference, and will give their Assistance to bring it, we hope, to a happy Conclusion, in the Agreement of Both Houses, in this so very a Considerable Point.

Mr

(9)

Mr. S O M M E R S.

My Lords, what is appointed me to speak to, is your Lord-ships First Amendment, by which the Word *Abdicated*, in the Commons Vote, is changed into the Word *Deserted*; and I am to acquaint your Lordships what some of the Grounds are, that induced the Commons to insist upon the Word *Abdicated*, and not to agree to your Lordships. Amendment.

1st. The First Reason your Lordships are pleased to deliver, as for your Changing the Word is, *That the Word Abdicated your Lordships do not find, is a Word known to the Common Law of* England *; and therefore ought not to be Used:* And the next is, *That the common Application of the Word amounts to a voluntary Express Act of Renuntiation, which* (your Lord-ships say *) is not in this Case, nor what will follow from the Premises.*

My Lords, as to the First of these Reasons, if it be an Objection, that the Word *Abdicated* hath not a known Sence in the Common Law of *England*, there is the same Objection against the Word *Deserted*; for there can be no Authority, or Book of Law produced, wherein any determined Sence is given to the Word *Deserted*: So that your Lordships first Rea-son hath the same Force against your own Amendment, as it hath against the Term used by the Commons.

The Words are both *Latin* Words, and used in the best Au-thors, and both of a known Signification; their Meaning is very well Understood; tho' it be true, their Meaning be not the same: The Word *Abdicate* doth naturally and properly signify *Entirely to Renounce, Throw off, Disown, Relinquish any Thing or Person, so as to have no further to do with it ;* and *that whether it be done by Express Words, or in Writing,* (which is the Sence your Lordships put upon it, and which is properly called *Resignation* or *Cession*) or, *by Doing such Acts as are In-consistent with the Holding, or Retaining of the Thing ;* which the Commons take to be the present Case, and therefore made Choice of the Word *Abdicate*, as that which they thought did, above all others, most properly express that Meaning : And in this latter Sence it is taken by Others, and that it is the true Signification of the Word, I shall shew your Lord-ships out of the best Authors:

The First I shall mention is *Grotius* de Jure Belli & Pacis, L. 2. C. 4. §. 4. *Venit enim hoc non ex jure civili, ex jure na-turali, quo quisq; suum potest* Abdicare, *& ex naturali Præ-sumptione qua voluisse, quis creditur, quod sufficienter significavit.* And then he goes on, *Recusari Hæreditas non tantum verbis, sed etiam re potest, & quovis indicio voluntatis.*

B   A nother

(10)

Another Inſtance, which I ſhall mention, to ſhew that for the *Abdicating* a thing, it is ſufficient to do an Act which is Inconſiſtent with the Retaining it, tho' there be nothing of an *Expreſs Renuntiation*, is out of *Calvin's Lexicon Juridicum*, where he ſays, (*Generum* abdicat, *qui ſponſam repudiat :*) *He that Divorceth his Wife*, Abdicates *his Son in Law*. Here is an *Abdication* without *Expreſs Words*; but is by doing ſuch an Act as doth ſufficiently ſignify his Purpoſe.

The next Author, that I ſhall Quote, is *Briſonius, de Verborum ſignificatione*, who hath this Paſſage, *Homo liber qui ſe-ipſum ven it*, abdicat *ſe ſtatu ſuo*, that is, *He who ſells himſelf, hath thereby done ſuch an Act as cannot conſiſt with his former Eſtate of Freedom*; and is therefore properly ſaid, *ſe abdicaſſe ſtatu ſuo*.

Budæus, in his Commentaries *ad Legem ſecundam, de Origine Juris*, Expounds the Words in the ſame Sence, Abdicare *ſe Magiſtratu eſt idem quod abire pænitus Magiſtratu :*) *He that goes out of his Office of Magiſtracy, let it be in what manner he will, has* Abdicated *the Magiſtracy.*

And *Grotius*, in his Book *de Jure Belli & Pacis*, L. 1. c. 4. §. 9. ſeems to expound the Word *Abdicare*, by *manifeſte habere pro derelicto :* That is, *That he who hath* Abdicated *any thing, hath ſo far Relinquiſhed it, that he hath no Right of Return to it.* And that is the Sence the Commons put upon the Word : It is an *Entire Alienation of the Thing* ; and ſo ſtands in Oppoſition to *Dicate : Dicat qui proprium aliquod facit* ; abdicat *qui alienat*, ſo ſays *Pralejus* in his *Lexicon Juris*. It is therefore inſiſted upon as the proper Word by the Commons.

But the Word *Deſerted* (which is the Word uſed in the Amendment made by your Lordſhips) hath not only a very doubtful ſignification ; but in the common Acceptance both of the Civil and Canon Law, doth ſignify only a *bare Withdrawing*, a *Temporary Quitting of a Thing*, and *Neglect* only, *which leaveth the Party at Liberty of Returning to it again. Deſertum pro Neglecto*, ſays *Spigelius* in his *Lexicon*: But, the Difference between *Diſſerere* and *Derelinquire*, is expreſly laid down by *Bartolus*, upon the 8th Law of the 58th Title of the 11th Book of the *Code*, and his Words are theſe, *Nota diligenter, ex hac Lege, quod aliud eſt Agrum* diſſerere, *aliud* derelinquire *; qui enim* derelinquit, *ipſum ex Pænitentia non revocat : ſed qui* deſeret, *intra biennium poteſt.*

Whereby it appears, my Lords, that that is called *Deſertion*, which is *Temporary* and *Relievable :* That is called *Dereliction*, where there is *no Power of Right to Return.*

So in the beſt *Latin* Authors, and in the *Civil* Law, *Deſerere Exercitum* is uſed to ſignify *Soldiers leaving their Colours*, Cod. Lib. 12. §. 1.

And

(11)

And in the *Canon* Law to *Defert a Benefice*, fignifies no more than to be *Non-Refident* ; fo is *Calvin's Lexicon, Verb.* Defert. *fecund. Canones.*

In both Cafes, the Party hath not only a *Right of Return-ing* ; but is *Bound to Return again :* Which, my Lords, as the Commons do not take to be the prefent Cafe, fo they cannot think that your Lordfhips do ; becaufe it is exprefly faid, in One of your Reafons given in Defence of the laft Amendment, *That your Lordfhips have been, and are willing, to fecure the Nation againft the Return of King* James ; which your Lord-fhips would not, in Juftice, do, if you did look upon it no more than a *Negligent With-drawing*, which leaveth *a Liberty to the Party to Return.*

For which Reafons, my Lords, the Commons cannot agree to the Firft Amendment, to infert the Word *Deferted* inftead of *Abdicated* ; becaufe it doth not, in any fort, come up to their Senfe of the thing : So, they do apprehend, it doth not reach your Lordfhips Meaning, as it is expreffed in your Rea-fons ; whereas they look upon the Word *Abdicated* to exprefs properly what is to be Inferred from that Part of the Vote to which your Lordfhips have agreed, *That King* James *the Se-cond, by going about to Subvert the Conftitution, and by Breaking the Original Contract between King and People, and by Violating the Fundamental Laws, and With-drawing himfelf out of the Kingdom*, hath thereby Renounced to be a King according to the Conftitution, by Avowing to Govern by a Defpotick Power, unknown to the Conftitution, and Inconfiftent with it ; he hath Renounced to be a King according to the Law, fuch a King as he Swore to be at the Coronation, fuch a King to whom the Allegiance of an *Englifh* Subject is due ; and hath fet up another kind of Dominion, which is to all Intents an *Abdication*, or *Abandoning of his Legal Title*, as fully as if it had been done by exprefs Words.

And, my Lords, for thefe Reafons the Commons do infift upon the Word *Abdicated*, and cannot agree to the Word *De-ferted.*

Mr. Serjeant HOLT.

My Lords, I am commanded by the Commons, to affift in the Management of this Conference, and am to fpeak to the fame Point that the Gentleman did, who fpoke laft to your Lordfhips Firft Amendment.

As to the Firft of your Lordfhips Reafons, for that Amend-ment, (with Submiffion to your Lordfhips) I do conceive it not Sufficient to alter the Minds of the Commons ; or to in-duce them to change the Word *Abdicated*, for your Lordfhips Word *Deferted.*

(12)

Your Lordſhips Reaſon is, *That it is not a Word that is known to the Common Law of* England. But, my Lords, the Queſtion is not ſo much, Whether it be a Word as Antient as the Common Law, (though it may be too) for that will be no Objection againſt the Uſing it, if it be a Word of a known and certain Signification ; becauſe that, we think, will Juſtify the Commons making uſe of it, according to your Lordſhips own Expreſſion.

That it is an Antient Word, appears by the Authors that have been Quoted, and its frequently met with in the beſt of *Roman* Writers, as *Cicero*, &c. And by the Derivation from *Dico*, an Antient *Latin Word*.

That now it is a known *Engliſh* Word, and of a known and certain Signification with us, I will Quote to your Lordſhips an *Engliſh* Authority, and that is the Dictionary ſet forth by our Country-man *Minſhaw*, who hath the Word *Abdicate* as an *Engliſh* Word, and ſays that it ſignifies to *Renounce*, which is the Signification the Commons would have of it : So that I hope your Lordſhips will not find Fault with their uſing a Word that is ſo Antient in it ſelf, and that hath ſuch certain Signification in our own Language.

Then, my Lords, for that Part of your Lordſhips Objection, *That it is not a Word known to the Common Law of* England, that cannot prevail ; for, your Lordſhips very well know, we have very few Words in our *Tongue* that are of equal Antiquity with the Common Law ; your Lordſhips know the Language of *England* is altered greatly in the ſeveral Succeſſions of Time and the Intermixture of other Nations ; and if we ſhould be obliged to make uſe only of Words then known and in uſe, what we ſhould deliver in ſuch a Dialect would be very Difficult to be Underſtood.

Your Lordſhips Second Reaſon, for your Firſt Amendment in changing the Word *Abdicated* for the Word *Deſerted* is, *Becauſe in the moſt common Acceptation of the Civil Law*, Abdication *is a Voluntary Expreſs Act of* Renuntiation. That is the general Acceptation of the Word, and, I think, the Commons do ſo uſe the Word in this Caſe, becauſe it hath that Signification : But I do not know, whether your Lordſhips mean a Voluntary expreſs Act or Formal Deed of *Renuntiation :* If you do ſo, I confeſs I know of none in this Caſe : But my Lords, both in the Common Law of *England*, and the Civil Law, and in common Underſtanding, there are Expreſs Acts of *Renuntiation* that are not by Deed ; for if your Lordſhips pleaſe to obſerve, the Government and Magiſtracy is under a Truſt, and any Acting contrary to that Truſt is a *Renouncing* of the Truſt, though it be not a *Renouncing* by Formal Deed : For it is a plain Declaration, by Act and Deed, though not in Writing, that he who hath the Truſt,

Acting

(13)

Acting contrary, is a Difclaimer of the Truft ; efpecially my Lords, if the Actings be fuch as are Inconfiflent with, and Subverfive of this Truft : For, how can a Man, in Reafon, or Senfe, exprefs a greater *Renuntiation* of a Truft, than by the conftant Declarations of his Actions to be quite contrary to that Truft ?

This, my Lords, is fo plain, both in Underftanding and Practice, that I need do no more but Repeat it again, and leave it with your Lordfhips, *That the Doing an Act Inconfiflent with the Being and End of a Thing, or that fhall not Anfwer the End of that Thing, but quite the contrary, that fhall be Conftrued an* Abdication, *and Formal* Renuntiation *of that Thing.*

Earl of NOTTINGHAM.

Gentlemen, you of the Committee of the Commons, we differ from you indeed about the Words *Abdicated* and *Deferted* ; but the main Reafon of the Change of the Word and Difference, is upon the Account of the Confequence drawn in the Conclufion of your Vote, *That the Throne is thereby Vacant :* that is, What the Commons mean by that Expreffion ? Whether you mean it is fo Vacant as to null the Succeffion in the Hereditary Line, and fo all the Heirs to be cut off, which we fay will make the Crown *Elective ?* And it may be fit for us to fettle that Matter firft, and when we know what the Confequence of *The Throne being Vacant* means in the Vote as you Underftand it, I believe we fhall much better be able to fettle the Difference about the Two Words.

Mr. Serjeant MAYNARD.

My Lords, when there is a prefent Defect of One to Exercife the Adminiftration of the Government, I conceive, the Declaring a Vacancy, and Provifion of a Supply for it, can never make the Crown *Elective.*

The Commons apprehended there is fuch a Defect now ; and, by confequence, a prefent Neceffity for the Supply of the Government, and that will be next for your Lordfhips Confideration, and theirs afterwards.

If the attempting the utter Deftruction of the Subject, and Subvertion of the Conftitution, be not as much an *Abdication* as the attempting of a Father to Cut his Son's Throat, I know not what is.

My Lords, the Conftitution, notwithftanding the Vacancy is the fame ; the Laws that are the Foundations and Rules of that Conftitution are the fame : But if there be, in any par-

(14)

particular Inſtance, a Breach of that Conſtitution, that will be an *Abdication* ; and that *Abdication* will infer a Vacancy.

It is not that, the Commons do ſay, *the Crown of* England *is always and perpetually Elective* ; but it is more neceſſary that there be a Supply when there is a Defect, and the Doing of that will be no Alteration of the *Monarchy* from a *Succeſſive One* to an *Elective.*

Lord Biſhop of ELY.

Gentlemen, the Two Amendments made by the Lords to the Vote of the Commons, are as to the Word *Abdicated*, and as to the *Vacancy of the Throne :* That *Abdicated* may be Tacitely by ſome *Overt-Acts*, that Gentleman, (I think I may name him without Offence) Mr. *Sommers*, very truly did alledge out of *Grotius :* But, I deſire to know, Whether *Grotius*, that great Author, in treating on this Subject, doth not interpoſe this Caution, *If there be a yielding to the Times : If there be a going away, with a Purpoſe of ſeeking to Recover what is, for the preſent Left or Forſaken :* In plain *Engliſh, If there . were any thing of Force or juſt Fear in the Caſe, that doth void the Notion of* Abdication : I ſpeak not of *Male-Adminiſtration* now, of that hereafter.

Mr. Serjeant MAYNADR.

But, my Lords, that is not any Part of the Caſe declared by the Commons in this Vote, when the whole Kingdom, and the *Proteſtant* Religion, our Laws and Liberties, have been in Danger of being Subverted, an Enquiry muſt be made into the Authors and Inſtruments of this Attempt ; and if he, who had the *Adminiſtration* intruſted to him, be found the Author and Actor in it, What can that be, but a *Renuntiation of his Truſt*, and conſequently his Place thereby *Vacant ?*

My Lords, *Abdication* (under Favour) is an *Engliſh Word* ; and, your Lordſhips have told us, the true Signification of it is a *Renuntiation.* We have indeed, for your Lordſhips Satisfaction, ſhewn its Meaning in Foreign Authors ; it is more than a *Deſerting* the Government, or Leaving it with a Purpoſe of Returning. But, we are not, I hope, to go to learn *Engliſh* from Foreign Authors, we can, without their Aid, tell the Meaning of our own Tongue.

If Two of us make a mutual Agreement, to Help and Defend each other from any one that ſhould Aſſault us in a Journey, and that he that is with me turns upon me and Breaks my Head, he hath, undoubtedly, *Abdicated* my Aſſiſtance and Revoked.

Lord

(15)

Lord *Bishop* of EL Y.

The Objection of the Lords against the Word *Abdicated* is, *That it is of too large a Signification for the Case in Hand*. It seems to be acknowledged, that it reacheth a great Way ; and therefore the Lords would have a Word made use of, which (by the Acknowledgment of that Learned Gentleman) signifieth only, *The Ceasure of the Exercise of a Right*.

If there be such a Defect as hath been Spoken of, it must be Supplied ; there is no Question of that.

And I think we have, by another Vote, declared, *That it is inconsistent with our Laws, Liberties, and Religion, to have a Papist to Rule over this Kingdom*. Which I take to be only as to the Actual Exercise and Administration of the Government.

It is *Grotius* his Distinction between a *Right*, and the *Exercise of that Right* ; and, as there is a Natural Incapacity for the Exercise, as Sickness, Lunacy, Infancy, doating Old Age, or an incurable Disease, rendring the Party unfit for Human Society, as *Leprosy*, or the like ; so I take it, there is a Moral Incapacity ; and that I conceive to be a full irremoveable Perswasion in a false Religion, contrary to the Doctrine of *Christianity*.

Then there must be a Provision, undoubtedly, made for supplying this Defect in the Exercise, and an intermediate Government taken care for ; because become necessary for the Support of the Government, if He to whom the Right of Succession doth belong makes the Exercise of his Government unpracticable, and our Obedience to him, consistently with the Constitution of our Religion, impossible ; but that, I take it, doth not alter that Right, nor is an *Abdication* of the Right.

Abdication, no doubt, is by Adaption an *English* Word ; and well known to *English* Men conversant in Books : Nor is it objected, that it is not a Word as antient, and it may be more antient than the Common Law of *England* ; we find it in *Cicero*, and other old *Roman* Writers.

But, as to *Cicero*, I would observe that there is a double Use of the Word ; sometimes it is mentioned with a Preposition, and then it signifies the *Renouncing an Actual Exercise of a Right*, as *Abdicare a Triumpho* : And sometimes it hath the Accusative Case following it, and then it signifies the *Renouncing of the very Right*, as that which was mentioned, *Abdicare Magistratum* ; so that the Signification (as the Lords in their Reason) is doubtful : And such Words, we hope, the Commons will not think fit to use in a Case of this Nature and Consequence, as ours now in Debate,

And

(16)

And befides, the Lords apprehend, that great Inconveniencies will follow upon the Ufe of this Word, if it mean a *Renouncing abfolutely of the Right*.

It feems the Commons do not draw the Word *Abdicated* from his withdrawing himfelf out of the Kingdom ; for then *Deferted* would (no doubt) have anfwered. That *Abdication* is the fame, whether a Man go out of the Kingdom or ftay in it ; for it is not to be efteemed according to the Place, but the Power.

If a Man ftays in the Kingdom, this is *Abdicare* with a Prepofition, *to Abdicate the Exercife of the Government*, but not *the Right of Governing*, according to the Conftitution ; and to fuch an *Abdication* (if it be fo declared) my Lords, I believe, may foon agree.

Then, Gentlemen, there is another Diftinction in thofe Authors that writ concerning this Point, which are chiefly the *Civilians* ; there may be an *Abdication* that may *Forfeit the Power of a King only* ; and there may be *One* that may *Forfeit both That and the Crown too.* It is a Diftinction indeed in other Words, but to the fame Senfe : I will tell you prefently why I ufe it.

Thofe *Abdications* that are of *Power* only, are *Incapacities* ; whether thofe I call Natural and Involuntary, as Defects of Senfe, Age, or Body, or the like ; or Moral and Voluntary, as Contrariety in Religion ; an Inftance whereof there was lately in *Portugal*, which was a *Forfeiture only of the Power*, and not of the *Name* and *Honour of a King* ; for though the *Adminiftration* was put into the Younger Brother's Hand, the Patents and other Publick Inftruments ran in the Elder Brother's Name.

This is, without all doubt, naturally an *Abdication* in the full extent of the Word ; nor do I here (as I faid) confider, whether that the King be gone out of the Kingdom, or ftay in it ; but only, whether he be fit for the *Adminiftration*, which muft be provided for, be He here, or gone away.

But the higheft Inftance of an *Abdication* is, when a Prince is not only unable to execute his Power, but Acts quite contrary to it ; which will not be anfwered by fo bare a Word as *Endeavour*.

I take thefe to be all the Diftinctions of Abdications.

Now if this laft Inftance of an *Abdication of both Power and Right*, take Place in a *fucceeding Monarchy*, the Confequence will be, *That there is a Forfeiture of the whole Right* ; and then that *Hereditary Succeffion* is cut off ; which, I believe, is not intended by the Commons : There is indeed one Inftance of the Ufe of fuch an *Abdication* in *Monarchy*, and that is, that of *Poland* ; and fuch an *Abdication* there makes the *Throne Vacant* ; and thofe with, and in whom the Power is invefted of
making

(17)

making Laws, (to wit the Senate) appoint One to fill it : But that, and whatever other Instances of the like Kind, these may be all of *Elective Kingdoms* ; for though some of them are, or may be in *Kingdoms* now *Hereditary*, yet they were, in those Times, *Elective*, and since altered into *Hereditary Successions.*

But here is One thing that is mentioned in this Vote, which I would have well considered, for the Preservation of the *Succession*, and that is the *Original Compact* : We must think sure that meant of the *Compact*, that was made at the first Time, when the Government was first instituted, and the Conditions that each Part of the Government should observe on their Part, of which this was the most Fundamental, *That King, Lords, and Commons, in Parliament assembled, should have the Power of making New Laws, and altering of Old Ones* : And that being one Law which settles the *Succession*, it is as much a Part of the *Original Compact* as any : Then if such a Case happens, as an *Abdication* in a *Successive Kingdom*, without doubt, the *Compact* being made to the *King*, his *Heirs*, and *Successors*, the *Disposition of the Crown* cannot fall to us, till all the *Heirs* do *Abdicate* too. There are indeed many Examples, and too many Interruptions in the *Lineal Succession* of the Crown of *England* : I think, I can instance in Seven since the Conquest, wherein the *Right Heir* hath been put by : But that doth not follow, that every Breach of the First *Original Contract*, gives us Power to *Dispose* of the *Lineal Succession*; especially, I think, since the Statutes of Queen *Elizabeth*, and King *James* the First, that have Established the Oath of *Allegiance* to the *King*, his *Heirs*, and *Successors*, the Law is stronger against such a *Disposition* : I grant that from King *William* the First, to King *Henry* the Eighth, there has been Seven Interruptions of the *Legal Line of Hereditary Succession* ; but, I say. those Statutes are made since that Time, and the making of New Laws being as much a Part of the *Original Compact*, as the observing Old Ones, or any thing else, we are obliged to pursue those Laws, till altered by the *Legislative Power*, which singly, or joyntly, without the Royal Assent, I suppose, we do not pretend to ; and these Laws being made since the last Interruption, we are not to go by any Precedent that was made before the making those Laws.

So that all that I conceive ought to be meant by our Vote is, *But a setting aside the Person that Broke the Contract : And, in a Successive Kingdom, an* Abdication *can only be a Forfeiture, as to the Person himself.*

I hope, and am perswaded, that both Lords and Commons do agree in this, *Not to break the Line of Succession, so as to make the Crown Elective* : And, if that be declared, that this *Abdication* of King *James* the Second reacheth no farther than himself, and that it is to continue in the *Right Line of*

C   *Suc-*

(18)

Succeſſion, that, I hope, will make all of one Mind in this important Affair.

Earl of C L A R E N D O N.

As I remember, Mr. *Sommers,* who ſpoke to the Signification of the Word *Abdicated,* did Quote *Grotius, Calvin's Lexicon,* and other Civil Lawyers, where the expreſs Words make
it to be a *Voluntary Act* ; and ſo are all the Inſtances that ever
I read or heard of ; that is, there either was ſome *Formal
Deed of Renuntiation,* or *Reſignation* ; or ſome *Voluntary Act
done of the Party's own* ; and ſuch whereby they have ſhewn
they did Diveſt themſelves of the Royalties.

I think truly, Gentlemen, it is very apparent that the King,
in this Caſe, hath done nothing of this Nature: It is indeed
ſaid by that learned and ingenious Gentleman, Mr. *Sommers,*
That it may ariſe from the Facts, that in the Vote it has been
declared he hath done, *Breaking the Fundamental Laws, and
the Original Contract: and endeavouring to Subvert the Conſtitution of the Kingdom.* I will not diſcourſe the Particulars that
have been alledged to make out this Charge ; but I may ſay
this much in General, That this *Breaking the Original Contract,*
is a Language that hath not been long uſed in this Place ; nor
known in any of our Law Books, or Publick Records. It is
ſprung up, but as taken from ſome late Authors, and thoſe
none of the beſt received ; and the very Phraſe might bear a
great Debate, if that were now to be ſpoken to. Mr. *Sommers*
did likewiſe ſpeak ſomething to the particular Caſe, and the
Grounds of the Vote ; he ſaid, *The King is bounded by Law,
and bound to perform the Laws made, and to be made.* That is
not denyed ; I would take Notice, that his Obligation thereunto doth not proceed from his Coronation Oath ; for our
Law ſaith, *He is as much King before he is Crowned, as he is
afterwards: And there is a Natural Allegiance due to him from
the Subjects immediately upon the Deſcent of the Crown upon
him.* And though it is a very requiſite Ceremony, to put him
under a farther Obligation by the Conſcience of his Oath; yet
I think it will not, nor can be denyed but that, as King, he
was bound to obſerve the Laws before ; and no Body will
make that Oath to be the *Original Contract,* as I ſuppoſe.

But, my Lords and Gentlemen, if you do admit that it was
never intended by the Houſe of Commons, to relate any farther
than to this King himſelf, I believe my own Opinion would
concur to ſecure us againſt his Return to Govern us : But then,
Why is there ſuch a Contention about a Word ? Doth all this
imply more than *Deſertion* ?

But it is ſaid, that *Abdication* doth imply a *perfect Renuntiation,* which I cannot ſee how it is in this Caſe, *ſo as to leave*
us

(19)

us at Liberty to supply as we please, and Break the Line of Suc-cession.

Mr. Serjeant *Maynard* says, *That it is not indeed to make the Government perpetually Elective.* I would know what he means by *Perpetually:* Our breaking through the Line now, by a Choice out of the Lineal Course, is an Alteration and a Precedent : And why may not others take the same Liberty we do ? And will not that make it *Perpetually Elective?*

But truly, I think, no Act of ours can alter the *Lineal Succession* ; for, by all the Laws we have now in Being, our Government appears to be *Hereditary* in a Right Line of *Descent:* And upon any Descent, when any one ceaseth to be *King*, *Allegiance* is by Law due to his *Legal Heir*, as *Successor*, as well before Coronation, as after.

I was in great Hopes that you would have offer'd something in Answer to one of my Lord's Reasons against that part of the Vote which declares, *The Throne to be Vacant.*

That no Act of the King's alone can Bar or Destroy the Right of his Heir to the Crown, which is Hereditary, and not Elective. And then, if this Matter goes no farther than King *James* the Second, in his own Person, How comes the *Vacancy* and the *Supply* to be Devolved upon the People ? For if he only be set aside, then it is apparent, whether the Crown is to go, to the Person that hath the next *Right of Succession* ; and consequently there is no *Vacancy.*

Earl of NOTTINGHAM.

Gentlemen, I would not protract Time, which is now so necessary to be husbanded ; nor perplex Debates about any Affair like that which lies now before us : It is not a Question barely about Words, but Things, which are now disputing.

The Word *Abdicated*, it is agreed by Mr. *Sommers*, is a Word of Art ; and he hath told us what its Signification is, from those that are skilled in the Art to which it belongs : He doth acknowledge that it is no Law-word among *English* Lawyers ; nor known to the Common Law : But then, he saith, neither is the Word, used by the Lords, *Deserted.*

I agree to him, that neither the one or the other are Words used in our Law ; but the Inference I would draw thence is this, That we have no Words applicable to this Case ; because we never before had such a Case ; and we must not draw Inferences of Law in such a Case, that are not deducible from Rules well known in our Laws.

I will not Dispute what the Sense of the Word *Abdication* is in the *Civil Law* ; but that it is a *Civil Law* Word is agreed to by me ; and if it be, for that Reason I am against using

C 2						of

(20)

of it ; becaufe I am fo much in Love with our own Laws, that I would ufe no Words in a Cafe that fo much concerns our Legal Conftitution, but what are fetched from thence.

I hope I fhall never fee our cld Laws altered ; or if they be, God forbid we fhould be the voluntary Agents in fuch an Alteration.

But then we are told the Word *Deferted* doth not reach our Cafe; becaufe the Signification of the Word is but a *Temporary Leaving* or *Forfaking of his Power, which he may Reaffume* ; nay, *which in fome Cafes there is a Duty upon him to Return unto.* If that were all, Mr. *Sommers* hath given himfelf an Anfwer to that Objection, out of what he alledges of the Lords Reafons, who have declared, that they are willing *To fecure the Nation againft the Return of King* James *into this Kingdom ; and will therefore concur with the Commons in any Act that fhall be thought neceffary to prevent fuch his Return :* fo that it fhould feem we were agreed in that Matter ; and if that were the Point, we fhould find Words proper foon enough to exprefs our Meaning by. But I find neither of thefe Words will, on the one fide or on the other, be allowed to fignify this Meaning ; therefore we fhould (as I take it) come prefently to think of fome other that would. But the Reafons why my Lords did chiefly infift upon the Alteration of the Word *Abdicated,* was, *Becaufe they did apprehend, that it being a Word not known to our Laws, there might be other Inferences drawn from it than they do apprehend our Laws will Warrant, from the Cafe, as it is ftated in the Fact of this Vote* ; and, *as they conceive, is done in the concluding of the Throne's being Vacant.*

Therefore, I think, it would fhorten the prefent Debate, if we did fettle that Point firft ; and, as we frequently in Parliamentary Proceedings, Poftpone this, and that Paragraph in a Bill, till fome others that may be thought fit to be determined firft be agreed to ; fo we fhould Poftpone the Debate about the Word *Abdicate,* till the *Vacancy of the Throne* be fettled ; for if we were fure that the Throne were, or were not Vacant, we fhould eafily light upon what Word were proper to be ufed in this Cafe.

I fhould therefore propofe, that we might Debate that firft ; becaufe if there be an *Englifh* Word of known Signification in our Law, which fhould fignify no more than *Renouncing for a Man's felf* ; and which would not amount to fo much as *Setting afide the Right of Others,* that Word may be ufed ; and, if no other, the Word *Renouncing* it felf may be taken, which would be beft agreed to.

Acting againft a Man's Truft (fays Mr. Serjeant *Holt*) *is a Renunciation of that Truft.* I agree it is a *Violation of his Truft to Act contrary to it* ; and he is accountable for that *Violation,*

to

(21)

to Anſwer what the Truſt ſuffers out of his own Eſtate : But I deny it to be preſently a *Renuntiation* of the Truſt, and that ſuch a one is no longer a Truſtee.

I beg his Pardon if I differ from him in Opinion, whom I acknowledge to have much more Learning in his Profeſſion than I can pretend unto : But if the Law be, as he ſays, in a *private Caſe*, then I muſt beg leave to forbear giving my Opinion in a Caſe of this *publick Nature* that is now before us, till I know what ſuch a *Truſt* is, and what the Law ſays in ſuch a Caſe.

If indeed you do pretend *That the Throne is Vacant*, and both Houſes agree to that Concluſion, I think it will be no matter what Word is uſed about it : But, if we do not agree to that Concluſion, I think it will be afterwards eaſie to ſhew which is the fitteſt Word to be ſtood upon ; or to agree upon ſome other.

I pray therefore (to ſhorten the Debate) that you Gentlemen would Speak to this Point firſt ; and when that is reſolved, I hope we ſhall eaſily come to an Agreement about the other.

Sir GEORGE TREBY.

I think, my Lords, that we may not conſent to begin at the End, and firſt to enquire of the Concluſion, before the Premiſes are ſettled : For the *Vacancy of the Throne* follows, as an Inference drawn from the Acts of the King's, which are expreſs'd moſt fully by the Word *Abdication*; and to enquire what the Conſequence is, when the Fact is doubtful, from which the Conſequence is to enſue, is beginning at the wrong End ; till we ſtate the Fact, we can aſſign no Conſequence at all to it : Therefore, my Lords, I think the preſent Debate is to begin, where the Difference between the Two Houſes doth begin, and that is at the Word *Abdicated* ; and when that is over, we ſhall regularly come to the other Point in Difference.

We are gone back too far, when we offer to enquire into the *Original Contract*, Whether any ſuch thing is known or underſtood in our Law or Conſtitution ? or, Whether it be new Language amongſt us ? And I offer this to your Lordſhips Conſideration for Two Reaſons,

Firſt, It is a Phraſe and thing uſed by the Learned Mr. *Hooker*, in his Book of *Ecclefiaſtical Polity*, whom I mention as a valuable Authority, being one of the beſt Men, the beſt Church Men, and the moſt Learned of our Nation in his time, and his Works are very worthily recommended by the Teſtimony of King *Charles* the Firſt ; He alloweth, *That Government did Originally begin by Compact and Agreements.*

But

(22)

But I have yet a greater Authority than this to influence this Matter, and that is your Lordships own, who have agreed to all the Vote but this Word *Abdicated*, and *the Vacancy of the Throne*. And therefore so much is enough to be said to that; and go back to Debate what is not in Difference, is to confound our selves, instead of endeavouring to compose Differences.

And truly, my Lords, by what is now Proposed, I think, we are desired to go as much too far Forwards, when the *Vacancy of the Throne* is proposed to be the Question to be first Disputed before the *Abdication*, from which it is Inferred.

But sure I am, it is very much beyond what the Vote before us doth lead us unto, *To talk of the Right of those in the Succession :* For that goes farther than the very last part of the Vote ; and it is still to lead us yet farther, to say any thing about making the *Crown Elective :* For, I hope, when we come to answer your Lordships Reasons, we shall easily make it out, that it is not in this Case ; neither was there any Occasion given by this Vote to infer any such thing : We shall therefore keep to the Points as they are both in order of Place in the Vote, and of Reason in the Thing ; and, as we have done hither, to speak to the Words *Abdicated* and *Deserted,* the Words to be Disputed about in the First Place. Another Lord did give One Reason against the using the Word *Abdicated, Because it is a Word belongs to the Civil Law ;* and said, *He would by no means exchange our own* English *Common Law for that.* I entirely concur with that Noble Lord in that Point ; but he did agree to us also, *That there is no such Word in our Common Law as* Deserted ; that is which should signify, by the Stamp the Law puts upon it, any Sense applicable to the Matter in Hand.

Then if we must not use our Word, because unknown to our Common Law ; neither must we use your Lordships for the same Reason, and so shall be at an intire Loss what Word to use ; and so, indeed, they may well come to consider the Conclusion First, who leave us at Uncertainties on what Terms we are to Discourse ; and there cannot be a greater Confusion in any Debate, than to state a Conclusion without the Premises ; which we must do, if we cannot agree how to Word the Fact we infer from.

My Lords, I shall not much differ from what, in general, has been said concerning the Sense of the Word *Abdicated* ; for it seems to be agreed on all Hands that it is a *Renuntiation :* Neither will I contend for an *Involuntary Abdication* ; because I think it means a *Voluntary Act :* But truly what your Lordships mean, in your Reason against it, by the Word *Express,* I cannot so well understand.

That

(23)

That a King may *Renounce* his Kingſhip, I think, may be made out both in Law and Fact, as well as any other *Renunciation* ; and that, as far as I can diſcern, by your Lordſhips Reaſons, and this Days Debate hitherto, is not intended to be denyed by any : Indeed, ſome of my Lords have told us, *That there 'tis meant of the Exerciſe of a Right which may be Renounced, without Renouncing that Right.* Whether that be a true Diſtinction or no, is not very Material ; but if it be, that the very Kingſhip it ſelf (as including a Right to Govern) may be *Renounced*, and hath been, it will be no Difficulty to make out, by Inſtances in all Countries, not only where the Crown is, or was *Elective* ; but alſo where it was *Hereditary* and *Succeſſive*.

If a King will *Reſign* or *Renounce*, he may do ſo, as particularly *Char.* 5*th*.

Earl *of* PEMBROKE.

That was an expreſs Solemn *Renuntiation.*

Sir GEORGE TREBY.

My Lords, the particular manner of doing it, is (I take it) not Matter in Debate juſt now before us, till it be ſettled whether a King can *Abdicate* at all, or *Renounce* his *Kingſhip* at all ; this then being granted, *That a King may Renounce, may Reſign, may Part with his Office, as well as the Exerciſe of it*, then the Queſtion indeed is, *Whether this King hath done ſo or no ?*

That he may do it, I take it for granted, it being an Act of the Will : Then let us now enquire into the Facts, as ſet out in the Vote, Whether this Will of his be manifeſt ? For that you have heard it may be diſcovered ſeveral Ways ; the Diſcovery may be by Writing, it may be by Words, it may be by Facts : *Grotius* himſelf, and all the Authors that treat of this Matter, and the Nature of it, do agree, *That if there be any Word, or Action that doth ſufficiently manifeſt the Intention of the Mind and Will, to part with his Office, that will amount to an* Abdication, *or* Renouncing.

Now, my Lords, I beg leave to put this Caſe, That had King *James* the II. come here into the Aſſembly of Lords and Commons, and expreſſed himſelf in Writing, or Words, to this Purpoſe, I was Born an Heir to the Crown of *England*, which is a Government limitted by Laws made in full Parliament, by King Nobles and Commonalty ; and, upon the Death of my laſt Predeceſſor, I am in Poſſeſſion of the Throne ; and, now I find, I cannot make Laws without the Conſent of the Lords and Repreſentatives of the Commons in Parliament ; I cannot ſuſpend

Laws

(24)

Laws that have been fo made, without the Confent of my People ; this indeed is the Title of Kingfhip I hold by *Original Contract*, and the Fundamental Conftitutions of the Government and my Succeffion to, and Poffeffion of, the Crown ; on thefe Terms is part of that *Contract* ; this part of the *Contract* I am Weary of, I do Renounce it, I will not be oblig'd to Obferve it ; nay, I am under an Invincible Obligation not to comply with it ; I will not Execute the Laws that have been made ; nor fuffer others to be made, as my People fhall defire, for their Security in Religion, Liberty, and Property, which are the Two main Parts of the Kingly Office in this Nation. I fay, fuppofe he had fo expreft himfelf, doubtlefs this had been a plain *Renouncing* of that *Legal Regular Title* which came to him by Defcent : If then He by Particular Acts, fuch as are enumerated in the Vote, has declared as much, or more than thefe Words can amount to, then he thereby declared his Will to *Renounce the Government* : He hath, by thefe Acts mention'd, manifeftly declar'd, That he will not Govern according to the Laws made ; Nay, he cannot fo do ; for he is under a ftrict Obligation, (yea the ftricteft) and Superior to that of the *Original Compact* between King and People, to Act contrary to the Laws, or to Sufpend them.

By the Law, he is to Adminifter Juftice ; and to Execute his Office according to the Tenour of thofe Laws ; and, the Coronation Oath obligeth him likewife to confent to fuch Laws as the People fhall choofe : But, on the contrary, by that Unfortunate Perfwafion (in Point of Religion) that he hath Embraced, he is oblig'd to Sufpend the Laws that Defend the Eftablifhed Religion, and to treat it, as it has been (as we well know) called, as the *Northern Herefie* ; and, under pain of Damnation to Extirpate it : And, in order to it, did fet and Repeal all the Legal Fences of it, without Confent of Parliament. What the Endeavours and Practices of that kind have been in the laft Reign, I fuppofe, we are not now to be told of, or inftructed in ; and if (as is very Plain) this doth amount to a manifeft Declaration of his Will, no longer to retain the exercife of his Kingly Office, thus Limited, thus Reftrained, then in Common Senfe, as well as Legal Acceptation, he has fufficiently declared his *Renouncing of the very Office* : As for his Departure out of the Kingdom, 'tis not material, whether it was Voluntary or Involuntary ; but it is fufficient, that his acting declares, *quo Animo*, he went away ; he no longer would purfue what he defign'd ; and was fo ftrongly oblig'd unto the contrary, by the Duty of his Office and Relation, and the Obligation of the *Original Contract* ; as likewife his own Coronation Oath, and then he defires no longer to be here.

So

(25)

So that taking both thefe things together, that he will not ;
nay, he cannot (as thus perfwaded in Point of Religion) Govern according to Law ; and thereupon hath withdrawn himfelf out of the Kingdom: It is a manifeft Declaration of his exprefs *Renouncing* and *Parting with his Kingly Office:* And therefore I cannot depart from infifting upon this word *Abdicated,*
which doth fo well correfpond to the Fact of the Cafe, and fo
well exprefs the true Meaning of the Commons in their Vote :
Nor can we Confent to the *Poftponing* this Point, till the other,
about *The Vacancy of the Throne,* be determined ; for this is
the very Foundation upon which we are to proceed, for Efta-
blifhing the Superftructure of the other Conclufion.

Earl of NOTTINGHAM.

This Learned Gentleman that fpoke laft, fays, *It is neceffary to prefer the Premifes before the Conclufion, as being the Foundation to the Superftructure.* Truly, I apprehend, that this
Word *Abdicated* was part of the *Conclufion,* and not of the
Premifes ; the Vote runs thus, *That by Breaking the Original
Contract, having endeavoured to fubvert the Conftitution of the
Kingdom, and having withdrawn himfelf out of the Kingdom,
he has Abdicated the Government, and the Throne is thereby Vacant.*

I take it to be (as I fay) part of the *Conclufion,* the other
part being joyn'd by a Copulative ; therefore that which is but
the other part of the *Conclufion,* is not to be inferred from the
other part of the *Premifes.* But take it to be (as you fay)
that *The Vacancy of the Throne is another Diftinct Conclufion
from all that preceded, as the* Premifes, *and therefore it is to be
confidered laft* ; I would then beg the Favour of You, Gentlemen of the *Houfe of Commons,* to anfwer me one Queftion a-
bout this Point of *Abdication,* Whether you mean by *Abdication,* a Renouncing for Himfelf, or for Himfelf and his Heirs?

If you mean only *Abdication* for Himfelf, it will have a
different Influence upon the Debate and Refolution of the
Cafe, as to the meaning of that You call the *Conclufion* ; for
then, *How can the Throne be Vacant ?*

But if it be meant for Himfelf and his Heirs, then I apprehend it is no more than what you fay at the End, *That the
Throne is indeed Vacant* ; and then this *Abdication* cannot be
part of the *Premifes,* but muft be the fame Thing with, or part
of, the *Conclufion.* I will not undertake to difpute, Whether
a King of *England* may, or may not, Renounce his Kingdom?
For my own Part, I think he can, and I may go fo far in A-
greement with thofe that have fpoken to this Point, *To yield
that he may do it by implicit Acts, contrary to the Kingly Office.*

D   For

(26)

For a *King* to fay, He will not Govern according to Law; and for a *King* to Act wholly contrary to Law, and do that which would Subvert the Conftitution, is (I think) the fame thing.

But then I muft fay alfo, That I think there is a Difference between *Saying fo*, and *Doing fomething* inconfiftent with what the Laws require ; for every Deviation from the Law, is a kind of Breach of the Fundamental Laws; for I know no Law, as Laws, but what are Fundamental Conftitutions ; as the Laws are neceffary, fo far as to fupport the Foundation.

But if every Tranfgreffion, or Violation of the Law, by the Prince's Connivance or Command, were fuch a Breach of the Fundamental Laws, as would infer an *Abdication*, then were it in vain to call any of his *Minifters* or *Officers* to account for any fuch Action.

Then the Action is the *King's*, and not *Their's* ; and then adieu to the Maxim of, *A King's not doing Wrong* : And we may have Recourfe to that other *Refpondent Superior*, as more effectual Satisfaction.

I take this Matter to be fo plain, as to the Diftinction that I have mentioned, that nothing can be more ; and it has been thought fo effentially neceffary to have it clear and manifeft, That thofe Two great Inftances of *Edward* the Second, and *Richard* the Second, were exprefs folemn Renuntiations, and thofe confirm'd in *Parliament* by the *Lords* and *Commons*, by the Act of Depofing them.

Therefore I cannot infer from the Facts enumerated in the *Vote* , That this fhould be an *Abdication* for Himfelf and his Heirs.

But therefore, becaufe in this firft Point it is difputable, what is meant by a Word not of known Signification in the Law ; it might, I think, do well to confider, what is to be inferred from it : And therefore all I have now faid, is only to this purpofe, That either Both make one *Conclufion*, or elfe the latter cannot be inferred from the former.

Sir GEORGE TREBY.

I beg leave to fay fomething to what this Noble Lord has laft fpoke unto : When I call this Point of the *Vacancy of the Throne* a *Conclufion*, I did not mean altogether to exclude *Abdication* from being a *Conclufion* from the Particulars enumerated before ; for, indeed, it is in the nature of a double *Conclufion* : One, from the particular Facts mentioned, That thereby King *James* has *Abdicated* the *Government*.

The other, from the *Abdication*, That thereby the *Throne is Vacant* : By the inftanced Acts, he hath Abdicated the *Go-*

vern-

(27)

verument ; and by his Abdicating the *Government*, the *Throne is vacant*. As to the reſt of that which his Lordſhip is pleaſed to ſay, I perceive he does (as he muſt) agree to me, That a *King* may Renounce by Acts, as well as Words, or Writings.

But then, I would add, and agree with his Lordſhip alſo, *That God forbid, every Violation of the Law, or Deviation from it, ſhould be reckon'd an* Abdication *of the* Government. I deſire to deliver my ſelf from the Imputation of any ſuch abſurd Conceit.

When a King breaks the Law in ſome few particular Inſtances, it may be ſufficient to take an Account of it from thoſe Evil Miniſters that were inſtrumental in it, why ſuch a thing was done, which was againſt Laws ? Why ſuch a Law was not Executed by them, whoſe Duty it was to ſee it put in Execution ? You may, in ordinary Caſes of breaking the Law, have Remedy in the ordinary Courts and courſe of Juſtice.

But ſure ! He does not take this to be ſuch a Caſe, or theſe to be ordinary Violations of the Law : And therefore in extraordinary Caſes, the extraordinary Remedy is to be recurred unto ; for the *King* having a limited Authority, by which he was obliged to keep the Laws made, as to the executive part of the Government, and to obſerve the Conſtitution for making ſuch new Laws as the People ſhould find neceſſary, and preſent him for his conſent ; when he doth *Violate*, not a particular Law, but all the Fundamentals; nor Injure a particular Perſon in Religion, Liberty, or Property, but falls upon the whole Conſtitution it ſelf, What doth all this ſpeak?

He therein ſaith, *I will no more keep within my limited Authority, nor hold my Kingly Office upon ſuch Terms.*

This Title I had by the Original Contract between King *and* People ; *I Renounce that, and will Aſſume another Title to my ſelf: That is, ſuch a Title, as by which I may Act as if there was no ſuch* Law *to Circumſcribe my Authority.*

Where ſhall any Man come to have Redreſs in ſuch a Caſe as this, when the Malefactor comes to be Party, unto whom all Applications for Relief and Redreſs from Injuries ſhould be made, and ſo he himſelf ſhall be a Judge of his own Breaches of Law. This moſt apparently was the Caſe as to the *Quo Warranto's*, which was a plain Deſign to ſubvert the Conſtitution in the very Foundation of the *Legiſlature*.

It is becauſe the King hath thus violated the Conſtitution, by which the Law ſtands, as the Rule both of the King's Government, and the Peoples Obedience, that we ſay, He hath Abdicated and Renounced the Government ; for all other particular Breaches of the Law, the Subject may have Remedy in the ordinary Courts of Juſtice, or the extraordi-

nary

(28)

nary Court of Parliamentary Proceedings : But where such an Attempt as this is made on the Essence of the Constitution, it is not We that have brought our selves into this state of Nature, but Those who have reduced our Legal well-establish'd Frame of Government into such a state of Confusion, as we are now seeking a Redress unto.

Earl of ROCHESTER.

The *Lords* have given their Reasons why they altered the Word *Abdicated* ; because it is a Word not known to the Common Law, and of doubtful Signification : Therefore it would be well if the *Commons* would please to express their own Meaning by it. I believe my Lords would be induced to Agree, that the King hath *Abdicated,* That is, *Renounced the Government* for Himself. If you mean no farther than that ; and if you do so, Why should You not be pleased to explain your selves, that every one may know how the Matter stands, and to preserve a good Correspondence between Both Houses, in such a Juncture and Conjunction as this ?

But if you do mean any thing more by it than *Abdication* for himself only, tho' their Lordships should agree to the using of the Word *Abdicated* ; yet this would prove a greater Argument against their Agreeing in the other Point, about the *Vacancy of the Throne ;* Therefore we would be glad to have you explain your selves what you mean by it.

Then there was a little Pause.

Mr. HAMDEN.

If the Lords have nothing further to offer upon this Point, it will be fit for us to go on to the other Amendment made by the Lords to our Vote.

No Lord offering to speak, the Commons *proceeded to the Second Amendment.*

Mr. SACHEVERELL.

My Lords, Your *Lordships* Second Amendment to the *Commons* Vote, (to wit, To leave out the Words, *And that the Throne is thereby Vacant*) the *House of Commons* cannot agree with Your Lordships to that Amendment ; and they do conceive they have many and great Reasons why they should not do it.

But, my Lords, They very much Wonder how it comes here to be laid upon them (as it seems to be, by one of your Lordships Reasons) That they, by using those Words of *Abdi-*
cation

(29)

cation and *Vacancy*, fignify an Intention of making an Alteration of the Conftitution of the Government.

I would not mifreprefent Your Lordfhips Words, or mifreprefent Your Meaning : But You are pleafed to fay, *That you
cannot agree to fuch an Abdication or Vacancy, as that the
Crown fhould thereby become Elective :* As if the *Commons* had
Thoughts of making the Kingdom Elective, when no fuch
Thing was either meant by Them, or can be deducted from
their Words.

But, my Lords, One Reafon why they differ from You is,
They think (upon the Nature of your Proceedings) they are
in the Right, to infift upon their *Vote*, as they fent it up to
your Lordfhips : And they conceive, as to all the Reafons
your Lordfhips have been pleafed to give them for your Alterations, not One of them hath fo much Argument in them,
as they might well expect.

The *Commons* Reafon for their Difagreeing to this Amendment, was, Becaufe they Conceive (that, as they may well
infer) from fo much of their own Vote, as your Lordfhips
have agreed unto, *That King* James *the Second hath Abdicated
the Government ; and that the Throne is thereby Vacant :* So,
if they fhould admit your Lordfhips Amendments, *That he hath
only Deferted the Government ;* yet, even thence would follow,
It's Vacant, as to King James *the Second :* Deferting the Government being, in true Conftruction, *Deferting the Throne.*

Now, to this they do defire, That your Lordfhips will confider and fee, Whether you give any Anfwer to this Reafon ?
or rather, Whether you do not leave the Matter ftill in the
Dark ; and (in Truth) leave the Nation in a perpetual ftate
of War ?

Your Lordfhips Anfwer to that, altho' you have agreed,
that the King has *Deferted* the Government ; and therefore
you have made Application to the Prince of *Orange, To take
upon him the Adminiftration of the Government, and thereby provide for the Safety and Peace of the Kingdom :* Yet there can be
no Inference drawn from thence, but only that the Exercife
of the Government by King *James* the Second, was ceafed ;
fo, as the Lords were, and are willing, *To fecure the Nation
againft the Return of the faid King into this Kingdom ;* but not
that there was either fuch an *Abdication* by him, or *Vacancy*
in the Throne, as that the Crown thereby became Elective ;
to which they cannot agree. I defire now to know of your
Lordfhips, What part of this Reafon hath given an Anfwer
to what the *Commons* faid in their Firft Reafon ; That they
may very well conclude from their own Vote, as to what
your Lordfhips have therein agreed to, *That the Throne is Vacant, as to King* James *the Second ; Deferting the Government,*
and *Deferting the Throne,* being, in true Conftruction, the
fame.

(30)

same. Inftead of anfwering this Reafon, your Lordfhips come and apply it here, only to a bare *Giving over the Exercife of the Government by King* James : And, pray, my Lords, let us confider where we are.

If the Cafe be fo, then King *James* the Second, who has only left the *Exercife*, continues in the *Office*, and is King ftill; and then all the Acts that we have done in this *Convention*, are wholly (as we conceive) not Juftifiable ; You are in no Place or Station to relieve your felves, or Nation, in this Exigence ; unlefs you will think of fetting up another Regency by your own Authority, without his Confent ; which, I conceive, by the Laws of *England*, you cannot do.

What then follows upon all we have done ? We have drawn the Nation into a Snare, by the Steps we have taken ; and leave all in fuch an Intricacy, as we have no Power, by Law, to deliver them out of ; nor can we anfwer for what we have done, unlefs the King fhould Die, and that would leave the Succeffion uncertain

My Lords, I only apply my felf, to confider the Reafons of your Lordfhips, for infifting upon this Second Amendment ; becaufe, I conceive, your Lordfhips have therein given no Anfwer to the Reafon firft given by the *Commons*, why they cannot agree to your *Lordfhips* Amendment.

Mr. POLEXFEN.

My Lords, your own Reafons (under Favour) do fhew, That your Lordfhips do intend, that the King is ftill in the Government : This, I think, is moft apparent out of your own Reafons.

For, when you have declared, *That the King hath Deferted the Government*, and then fay, No Inference can be drawn thence, but only, *That the Exercife of the Government by King* James *the Second was Ceafed* ; then you do thereby ftill fay, That King *James* the Second is in the Government ; for if only *the Exercife be Ceafed*, the *Right* doth ftill remain : Then am fure we have no Reafon to agree with their Lordfhips in that Point.

Next, my Lords, truly we cannot fee how this thing that you would have can be inferred from your own Vote, That *only the Exercife of the Government by King* James *is ceafed* ; fince you do not fay that he deferted the Exercife of the Government ?

And if your Lordfhips had any purpofe to exprefs your Meaning by a publick Vote, That *only the Exercife ceafed*, furely your Lordfhips would have put in the word *Exercife* there : But when in your Vote you fay, *The Government was deferted*, you cannot mean only the Exercife of it.

And

(31)

And that it is the firft Reafon that the Commons give your Lordfhips, why we cannot by any means admit of your Lord-fhips Amendment, becaufe *Throne* and *Government* are in the true conftruction the fame ; but the Exercife of the Govern-ment only (as you exprefs it) and the Government it felf (if your Reafon conclude right) are not the fame. And we are to reafon from the words expreffed in rhe *Vote*.

Next, my Lords, we fay, It cannot be inferred from the words, as they reft in your Lordfhips Vote, That *only the Exercife of the Government, as to King* James *the Second, did ceafe.*

For if we read that part about Deferting the Government, with the reft of the Particulars that go before, his endea-vouring to fubvert the Conftitution of the Kingdom, breaking the original Contract, violating the Fundamental Laws, and withdrawing himfelf out of the Kingdom ; then can any Man of Underftanding think that this deferting of the Go-vernment can be any thing elfe, but fomewhat that is agree-able to all thofe precedent Acts, which are not a ceafing of the Exercife of the Government only, but a deftruction of the Government it felf.

But befides, my Lords, under Favour, the Adminiftration or Exercife of the Kingly Government is in conftruction and confideration of Law all one and the fame : And I think no body that would reafon aright from thence can fay there is any diftinction between Government and the Exercife of the Government ; for whofoever takes from the King the Exer-cife of the Government, takes from the King his Kingfhip ; for the Power and the Exercife of the Power are fo joyned that they cannot be fevered.

And the Terms themfelves (taking them as the Law of *England*, which we are to argue from this Cafe, teacheth them) are fo co-incident, that they cannot either fubfift without confifting together : If a Man grant to another the Government of fuch a Place, this imports the Exercife of the Government there to be granted thereby.

As if the Iflands belonging to this Crown and Dominion of *England* (as the Plantations abroad) if the King grants to any one the Government of *Jamaica*, or the like, fure no one will fay, that That is not a Grant of the Exercife of the Government there.

So that where-ever a Government is granted, the Exercife of that Government is meant and included, and therefore the fuppofed Diftinction may be fomething indeed, if they be only notionally confidered ; but it is a Notion altogether dif-agreeing to the Laws of *England*.

When your Lordfhips fay in your Reafons, That *the Exer-cife of the Government as to King* James *the Second is ceafed ;*
which

(32)

which as far as you can go in this Point, the Commons can by no means agree to this Reason ; for by the words fo ufed (*the Exercife ceafed*) we apprehend, that you mean the Kingfhip continueth ftill in him, and that only the Exercife is gone.

And if it be fo, and it be utterly unlawful, and as great a Crime (as what Law faith it is not ?) to make away from the King the Exercife of the Government, as to take from him the Government, then it may do well for your Lord-fhips to confider, whether you are not Guilty of the fame Crime and Thing which you would decline by your amend-ment.

The Commons therefore cannot admit, that there fhould be a taking away of the Exercife of the Government from the King, any more than the taking away the Government which (we fay) he hath himfelf given away by *Abdication.* And if King *James* be our King ftill, we cannot by any means agree to the keeping of him out of the Kingdom ; for if it be his Right to be King ftill, God forbid but that he fhould enjoy it, and be admitted to the Exercife of it again.

Then, my Lords, for the Conclufion that your Lordfhips have added to your Reafon (as making it from the very words of your Vote) that it is, *That it would infer fuch a Vacancy in the Throne, as that the Crown fhould thereby become Elective* ; this, we conceive, is a Conclufion, that hath no Premifes either from our Actions, or our Sayings, or our Votes, or any thing elfe in this Cafe ; nay, it is quite vary-ing from all the Premifes : But when fuch a Conclufion can be fhewn to follow from them, then it will be time enough for us to give our Anfwer to it.

But, my Lords, this is that we do infift upon; That if the Right of Kingfhip be ftill (after all that is agreed on both hands) due to him, we cannot in Juftice agree to keep him from it. And if it be not his due Right, but by thefe Acts, his fubverfion of the Conftitution, his breaking the original Contract, and violation of the Fundamental Laws, he hath Abdicated it (as we fay) and this Abdication hath put him by his Right, and fo his Right is gone from him (as we con-ceive it is) ; then, I think, we may lawfully go on to fettle the Peace and Welfare of the Nation.

But the Right to be ftill in him to have a Regency upon him without his own Confent, or till his Return, we take it to be a ftrange and impracticab'e thing, and would be intro-ductive of a new Principle of Government amongft us. It would be fetting up a Common-wealth inftead of our ancient regulated Government, by a limited Monarchy ; then, I am fure, we fhould be juftly blamed : And therefore we can by no means fubmit to your Lordfhips Alterations of our Vote,
upon

(33)

upon any of the Grounds and Reasons that have as yet been offer'd.

Earl of CLARENDON.

As to what Mr. *Polexfen* hath offered, I desire to observe a Word or two, and that is from the Commons Second Reason, for their Disagreeing to their Lordships Amendments.

You say there, That *the Commons do conceive they need not prove to your Lordships, that as to any other Person besides King James the Throne is also Vacant :* Doth not this shew, that the meaning of the Vacancy is a Vacancy throughout, as well as with respect to King *James.* I ask your Pardon if I do not declare my own Opinion about the Vacancy as to him ; but all that I mention this for, is to know your Meaning in this Point, how far the Vacancy is to extend.

You said before, That *He had Abdicated the Government, and thereby the Throne was Vacant.* How is it Vacant ? Is it only as to King *James,* or is it as to him and all or any of his Posterity, or any of those that are in the remainder in the Royal Line in Succession ? If it be as to them too, then it must necessarily follow, that the Kingdom must thereby become Elective still, or the Government changed into a Commonwealth ; neither of which, we hope, the Commons intend by it. And therefore that made me ask before what a grave and learned Gentleman meant when he said it should not be perpetually Elective.

Mr. *Serjeant* MAYNARD.

I am sure, if we be left without a Government, as we find we are (why else have we desir'd the Prince to take upon him the Administration ?) sure we must not be perpetually under Anarchy, the Word *Elective* is none of the Commons Word ; neither is the making the Kingdom Elective the thing they had in their Thoughts or Intentions ; all they mean by this Matter, is to provide a Supply for this Defect in the Government, brought upon it by the late King's Male Administration. And I do say again, this Provision must be made ; and if it be, that would not make the Kingdom perpetually Elective ? I stand not upon any Word, but am for the Thing, that a Provision be made to supply the Defect.

Mr. POLEXFEN.

Do your Lordships agree, that the Throne is Vacant as to King *James* the Second ? If so, or if you will say it is full of any body else, and will name whom it is full of, it will then

E   be

(34)

be time for the Commons to tell what to fay to it. If your Lordfhips will pleafe to fhew that, we'll go on to give it an Anfwer.

Earl of CLARENDON.

Your own Words in your Second Reafon are, That *you need not prove to us, that it is to any other Perfon the Throne is alfo Vacant* : Then how fhould we name who it is full of ? Admit for Difcourfe fake, but we do not grant it, for my part I do not. I fay, taking it to be Vacant as to King *James* the Second, then you ask us, who it fhould be fupplied by : Muft it not be fupplied by thofe that fhould have come if He were dead ?

For, I pray confider, I take this Government by all our Laws to be Hereditary Monarchy, and is to go in Succeffion by Inheritance, in the Royal Line ; if then you fay this Government is Vacant, that would be to put all thofe by that fhould take the Succeffion, and that will make the Kingdom Elective for that time.

You fay, *the Throne is Vacant* ; then I may very well afk who hath the Right of filling up that Vacancy ? We fay, there is no Vacancy ; if there is, pray is there any Body that hath the Right of filling it up ?

Mr. Serjeant MAYNARD.

That is not the Queftion before us, yet that will come properly in debate when we are agreed upon the Vacancy.

The Noble Lord fays, *It is by our Law an Hereditary Monarchy.* I grant it ; but though it fhould in an ordinary way defcend to the Heir, yet as our Cafe is, we have a Maxim in Law, as certain as any other, which ftops the Courfe ; for no Man can pretend to be King *James's* Heir while he is living : *Nemo eft hares viventis.*

Earl of PEMBROKE.

To that Point I think my Lord of *Clarendon* gave an Anfwer, " That it fhould go to the next in the Line that were " to take it, if the King were dead : for as we fhould be underftood, we fhould make it a Cafe of Demife of our Kings, as our Law calls it ; that is, the King is dead in Law by this *Abdication* or *Defertion* of the Government, and that the next Heir is to take by defcent.

You, Gentlemen, afk us who the Throne is full of ; I think it is fufficient to know that there are Heirs who are to take the Lineal Succeffion, though we do not, or cannot pofitively
name

(35)

name the particular Perfon ; and therefore we may well conclude there is no Vacancy.

Suppofe I fhould be told fuch a Gentleman is in fuch a Room, and there I find him, and another Man with him, and I come out and tell you fo, and afk which is he, you may be doubtful which of the two is the Man, but fure the one of them is he ; but becaufe you cannot tell which it is, fhall I conclude no fuch one is there ? If there be a doubtful Title (that is, dubious in whom the Title refides, but a certain Title as to fome one) and I cannot directly name him that hath the immediate Right, yet it is fufficient to prevent the Vacancy, that there is an Heir or Succeffor, let him be who he will.

Mr. *Serjeant* MAYNARD.

But your Lordfhips will neither agree it is Vacant, nor tell us how it is Full. King *James* is gone, we hear or know of no other, What fhall the Nation do in this Uncertainty ? When will you tell us who is King, if King *James* be not ? Shall we everlaftingly be in this doubtful Condition ?

Earl *of* PEMBROKE.

Sure, Mr. Serjeant *Maynard*, you will agree there is one, and no more than one, to whom a Right does belong of Succeeding, upon failure of King *James.* Has he no Heir known ?

Mr. *Serjeant* MAYNARD.

I fay, no Man can be his Heir while he lives. If he has any it is in *Nubibus,* our Law knows none ; and, What fhall we do till he be dead ? It cannot defcend till then.

Earl *of* PEMBROKE.

You agree, That notwithftanding King *Charles* the Second was abroad at his Father's Death, and did not actually Exercife the Government, yet in Law, immediately upon his Father's Deceafe, he was not the lefs Heir for that ; nor was the Throne Vacant.

Mr. *Serjeant* MAYNARD.

That is not like this Cafe, neither becaufe the Defcent was Legally immediate ; but here can be no fuch thing during King *James*'s Life, as an Hereditary Defcent : So that either here muft be an everlafting War entail'd upon us, his Title

E 2   con-

(36)

continuing, and we oppofing his return to the Exercife of the Government ; or we have no Government for want of a Legal Defcent and Succeffion.

Pray, my Lords, confider the Condition of the Nation till there be a Government ; no Law can be executed, no Debts can be compelled to be paid, no Offences can be punifhed, no one can tell what to do to obtain his Right, or defend himfelf from Wrong.

You ftill fay, *the Throne is not Void*, and yet you will not tell us who Fills it. If once you will agree, *that the Throne is Vacant*, it will then come orderly in Debate, how it fhould, according to our Law, be filled.

Earl of NOTTINGHAM.

The Objection (as I take it) that is made to thefe Reafons, the Lords have given for their infifting upon the Amendments is, *That we have not fully anfwered in them the Reafons given by the Commons for their not agreeing to thofe Amendments.*

Mr. SACHEVERELL.

My Lords, we fay you have not fully anfwered the firft of our Reafons.

Earl of NOTTINGHAM.

Gentlemen, I intend to ftate the Objection fo :

That firft Reafon of yours I take to be this in effect, That our word (*Deferted*) being applied to the Government, implies our Agreeing that the King hath deferted the Throne, thofe two being in true Conftruction the fame ; and then by our own Confeffion, the Throne is Vacant as to him.

To this you fay, my Lords have given no Anfwer : Truly, I think it is a clear Anfwer, that the Word (*Deferted*) may have another Senfe, and doth not neceffarily imply *Renouncing* entirely of a Right, but a ceafing of the Exercife. But then, if that does not Vacant the Throne as to him, the other Reafon comes to be confidered, How came you to defire the Prince of *Orange* to take the Adminiftration upon him, and to take care of *Ireland* till the Convention, and to write his Letters circularly for this Meeting ? And to renew your Addrefs to the Prince, and to appoint a Day of Publick Thanksgiving ?

In anfwer to that, my Lords fay, That tho' the King's *Deferting* the Government (as they agree he has done) did imply the Throne to be vacant, yet they might juftly do all thofe Acts mention'd in the Common Reafons ; becaufe if barely
the

(37)

the Exercife of the Government were *deferted*, there muſt be a ſupply of that Exerciſe in ſome Perſon's taking the Admi-niſtration ; and as none ſo fit, becauſe of the Prince's relation to the Crown (and his preſence here) to Addreſs unto about it, ſo none ſo proper to make that Addreſs as the Lords; for in the abſence of the King they are the King and Kingdoms great Council, and might have done it by themſelves without the Commons; but being met in a full repreſentative Body, they joyned with them.

Mr. *Polexfen* indeed has ſaid, *There is no diſtinction in Law between the Kingſhip and the Exerciſe of it.* And, That *it is the ſame Crime, in conſideration of Law, to take away the Exerciſe, as to take-away the Kingſhip.*

I ſhall not diſpute with that Learned Gentleman (whom I very much Honour for his Knowledge in the Profeſſion of the Law) what Offence either of them would be now, for we are not diſcourſing concerning a Regency, how the Government ſhould be Adminiſtred, but we are barely upon the Queſtion, Whether the Throne be vacant, ſo that we may have ano-ther King? But if we ſhould grant a Vacancy, as to the King himſelf, we are then told, the next in Succeſſion cannot take, becauſe no one can be Heir to one that is alive. Yet, I think, the Anſwer given by my Lords before is a very good one, That *tho' the King be not dead Naturally, yet if* (as they infer) *he is ſo Civily, the next of Courſe ought to come in as by Hereditary Succeſſion* ; for I know not any diſtinction between Succeſſors in the caſe of a Natural-Death, and thoſe in the caſe of a Civil one.

For I would know if the next Heir ſhould be ſet aſide in this Caſe, and you put in another, whether that King ſhall be King of *England* to him and his Heirs, and ſo being once upon the Throne, the ancient Lineal Succeſſion be altered? If that be ſo, then indeed it is ſufficiently an Elective King-dom, by taking from it the Right Heir.

If it be not ſo, then I would ask, Whether ſuch King as ſhall be put in, ſhall be King only during King *James's* Life? That, I ſuppoſe for many Reaſons, is not your meaning ; but, at leaſt he muſt be made King during his own Life ; and then if there be a Diſtinction made as to the Succeſſion between a Natural and a Civil Death, if King *James* ſhould die during the Life of the new King, what would become of the Here-ditary Monarchy? Where muſt the Succeſſion come in, when the next Heir to King *James* may not be next Heir to the preſent Succeſſor?

Therefore we muſt reduce all to this point, which my Lords have hinted at in their Reaſons, Whether this will not make the Kingdom Elective? For if you do once make it Elective, I do not ſay that you are always bound to go to Election, but

it

(38)

it is enough to make it fo, if by that Prefident there be a Breach in the Hereditary Succeffion; for I will be bold to fay, you cannot make a ftronger Tye to obferve that kind of Succeffion, than what lyeth upon you to preferve it in this Cafe.

If you are under an Obligation to it, it is part of the Conftitution. I defire any one to tell me what ftronger Obligation there can be ; and that, I fay, is Reafon enough for my Lords to difagree to it, it bringing in the Danger of a Breach upon the Conftitution.

Next, Gentlemen, I would know of you, if the Throne be vacant, whether we be oblig'd to fill it ? if we be, we muft fill it either by our old Laws, or by the Humour of thofe that are to chufe; if we fill it by our own old Laws, they declare, That it is an Hereditary Kingdom, and we are to take the next to whom the Succeffion would belong, and then there would be no need of ftanding upon a Vacancy.

If we are to fill it according to the Humour of the Times, and of thofe that are to make the Choice, that diverts the courfe of Inheritance, and puts it into another Line : And I cannot fee by what Authority we can do that, or change our Ancient Conftitution, without committing the fame Fault we have laid upon the King.

Thefe are the Objections againft the Vacancy of the Throne, which occur to me ; and We, Gentlemen, defire a fatisfaction to them before we agree to the Vacancy.

And, I think, the Anfwering them, will lead us unto that which I take to be the main Point in Queftion, Whether the vacancy of the Throne, and filling it again, will not, as my Lords fay, endanger the turning this Hereditary Monarchy of ours into an Elective one?

Mr. SACHEVERELL.

My Lords, it feems very ftrange to us, that this Queftion fhould be asked us, when we come to fhew, That your Lordfhips Reafons for leaving out this part of our Vote are not fatisfactory, neither do anfwer the Reafons we gave for our not agreeing to your Lordfhips Amendments : And it is much ftranger that we fhould be asked, Whether this Vacancy extends to the Heirs, when you will not tell us, whether it be vacant as to King *James* himfelf.

You put it upon us to fay, the Execution or Exercife of the Government is ceafed ; but you will not fay the Throne is vacant, fo much as to him: And if it be not, what have we to do, to confider, or debate, of any confequence, whether it will infer an Election or not ?

We defire of your Lordfhips that which we think is very proper ; firft, to know whether the Throne be vacant at all ?
If

(39)

If it be, then our Propofition in the conclufion of our Vote is true, *That the Throne is thereby vacant.*

My Lords, I think we come here very much in vain, till this Point be fettled ; What fatisfaction can it be to your Lord-fhips, or Us, or the Nation, to know that fuch things as are mention'd in the Votes have been done by King *James*, and that he has deferted (as you fay) the Government, if he ftill retain a Right to it, and your Lordfhips will not declare he hath no Right, but amufe the Kingdom with the doubtful words of the *Exercife* (as to him) *Ceafing.* If that be all you mean, what need the Queftion be asked, how far it is vacant, for it fhould feem it is not vacant at all.

Earl of NOTTINGHAM.

Will you pleafe to fuppofe it vacant as to King *James*, that is, that he hath no Right ? Then let us go on to the next ftep.

Mr. SACHEVERELL.

That, my Lords, we cannot do, for all our bufinefs is to maintain our own, *That the Throne is vacant.*

Mr. SOMMERS.

My Lords, your Lordfhips, as a Reafon againft the Word *Abdicate,* fay, *It is not a word known in our Common Law.* But the word *Vacant* about which we are now difputing, can-not have that Objection made to it ; for we find it in our Re-cords, and even apply'd in a parallel Cafe to this of ours, in 1 *Hen.* IV, where it is exprefly made ufe of more than once, and there it doth import what I think it doth import in this Vote of the Houfe of Commons, now in Debate, and to re-quire any further or other Explication of it than the Record gives, will be very hard and unreafonable ; for we are here to give the Commons Reafons for maintaining their own Vote, and nothing elfe.

If your Lordfhips pleafe to look into the Record in that cafe, there was firft a Refignation of the Crown and Government made and fubfcribed by King *Richard* the Second, and this is brought into the Parliament, and there they take notice, that the *Sedes Regalis* (thofe are the words) *fuit vacua* ; and the Refignation being read both in *Latin* and *English*, in the Great Hall at *Westminster*, where the Parliament was then affembled, it was accepted by the Lords and Commons.

After that, it proceeds farther ; and there are Articles ex-hibited againft *Richard* the Second, and upon thefe Articles
they

(40)

they went on to Sentence of Depofition and Deprivation, and then followeth the Words in the Record ; *Et confeffim ut con-ftabat ex præmiffis & eorum occafione Regnum Angliæ cum per-tinentiis fuis vacare.* Then *Henry* the Fourth rifeth up out of his Place as Duke of *Lancafter*, where he fat before, and ftand-ing fo high that he might be well enough feen, makes this Claim to the Crown : The Words in the Record are, *Dictum regnum Angliæ fic ut præmitur Vacans una cum Corona ven-dicat.*

After that, the Record goeth on, That upon this Claim the Lords and Commons being afked, What they thought of it ? they unanimoufly confented, and the Ach-bifhop took him by the Hand, and led him *ad Sedem Regalem prædictum, &c.*

Nay, and after all this, it is there taken Notice of, and particularly obferved, that *prius Vacante fede Regali*, by the Leafion and Depofition aforefaid, all the publick Officers cea-fed ; There is Care taken for *Henry* IV's taking the Royal Oath, and granting of new Commiffions.

My Lords, the Commons do therefore apprehend, that with very good Reafon and Authority they did in their Vote de-clare *the Throne to be Vacant.* But as to the going farther to enquire into the Confequences of that, or what is to be done afterwards, is not our Commiffion, who came here only to maintain their Expreffions in their Vote againft your Lordfhips Amendments.

Earl of ROCHESTER.

In a free Conference the Points in queftion are freely and fully to be debated ; and, my Lords, in order to their Agree-ment with the Commons, are to be fatisfied what is meant, and how far it may extend.

You, Gentlemen, that are the Managers for the Houfe of Commons, it feems, come with a limitted Commiffion, and will not enter into that Confideration which (as our Reafons exprefs) hath a great Weight with my Lords, Whether this Vote of the Commons will not make the Monarchy of *En-gland*, which has always heretofore been Hereditary, to become Elective?

That the Vacancy of the Throne will infer fuch a Confe-quence, to me appears very plain : And I take it from the Argument that laft Gentleman ufed for the Word *Vacant*, out of the Record of *Richard* the Second's time, that is cited for a Prefident for that Word. But as that is the only Predfient, yet it is attended with this very Confequence ; for it being there declared, That the Royal Seat was Vacant, immediately did follow an Election of *Henry* the Fourth, who was not next in the Right Line; Did not then this Hereditary Monarchy

(41)

Monarchy in this Inſtance become Elective ? When King *Charles* the Second dy'd, I would fain know whether in our Law the Throne was vacant. No ſure ; the next Heir was immediately in the Throne.   And ſo it is in all Hereditary Succeſſive Governments.

Indeed in *Poland* when the King dies there is a Vacancy, becauſe there the Laws knows no certain Succeſſor : So that the difference is plain, that where-ever the Monarchy is Hereditary, upon the Ceaſing of him in Poſſeſſion, the Throne is not Vacant ; where it is Elective, 'tis Vacant.

Earl of CLARENDON.

I would ſpeak one word to that Record which Mr. *Sommers* mentioned, and which the Lord that ſpeak laſt hath given a plain Anſwer unto, by making that difference (which is the great Hinge of the matter in Debate) between Hereditary and Elective Kingdoms. But I have ſomething elſe to ſay to that Record.

Firſt, It is plain in that Caſe King *Richard* the Second had abſoluʒely reſigned, renounced, or (call it what you pleaſe) *Abdicated* in Writing under his own Hand.   What is done then ? After that, the Parliament being then ſitting, they did not think it ſufficient to go upon, becauſe that Writing might be the Effect of Fear : And ſo, not voluntary ; thereupon they proceed to a formal Depoſition upon Articles, and then comes in the Claim of *Hen.* IV.

After all this, Was not this an Election? He indeed ſaith, That he was the next Heir, and claimed it by Deſcent from *Henry* the Third ; yet he that was really the next Heir did not appear, which was the Earl of *March* ; ſo that *Henry* the Fourth claimed it as his indubitable Right, being the next Heir that then appeared.

But, Gentlemen, I pray conſider what follow'd upon it ; All the Kings that were thus taken in (we ſay Elected, but the Election was not of God's Approbation) ſcarce paſſed any one Year in any of their Reigns, without being diſturbed in the Poſſeſſion.

Yet, I ſay, he himſelf did not care to owe the Crown to the Election, but Claimed it as his Right. And it was a plauſible Pretence, and kept him and his Son (though not without interruption) upon the Throne. But in the time of his Grandſon *Henry* the Sixth, there was an utter Overthrow of all his Title and Poſſeſſion too : For if you look into the Parliament Roll, 1 *Edward* IV, the Proceedings againſt King *Richard* the Second, as well as the reſt of the Acts during the Uſurpation (as that Record rightly calls it) are annul'd,

F   repeal'd,

(42)

repeal'd, revok'd, revers'd, and all the words imaginable u-
fed and put in, to fet thofe Proceedings afide as illegal, unjuft,
and unrighteous, And, pray what was the Reafon ? That
Act deduceth down the Pedigree of the Royal Line, from
Henry the Third to *Richard* the Second, who dy'd without
Iffue, and then *Henry* the Fourth, (faith the Act) Ufurped ;
but, That the Earl of *March*, upon the Death of *Richard* the
Second, and confequently *Edward* the Fourth from him, was
undoubted King, by Confcience, by Nature, by Cuftom, and
by Law.

The Record is to be feen at length, as well as that ı *Henry* IV, and being a latter Act is of more Authority.

And after all this, (I pray confider it well) the Right
Line is reftored, and the Ufurpation condemn'd and repealed.

Befides, Gentlemen, I hope you will take into your confideration, what will become of the Kingdom of *Scotland* if
they fhould differ from us in this Point, and go another way
to work, then will that be a divided Kingdom from ours again.
You cannot but remember how much Trouble it always gave
our Anceftors, while it continued a divided Kingdom ; and if
we fhould go out of the Line, and invert the Succeffion in a-
ny point at all, I fear you will find a Difagreement there, and
then very dangerous Confequences may enfue.

Sir ROBERT HOWARD.

My Lords, the Proceeding and Expreffions of the Houfe of
Commons in this Vote are fully warranted by the Prefident
that hath been cited, and are fuch as wherein there has been
no interruption of the Government according to the Conftitution.

The late King hath, by your Lordfhips conceffion, done all
thofe things, which amount to an *Abdication* of the Government, and the Throne's being thereby Vacant: And had your
Lordfhips concurred with us, the Kingdom had long e'er this
been fettled, and every body had peaceably followed their own
bufinefs. Nay, had your Lordfhips been pleafed to exprefs
your felves clearly, and not had a mind to fpeak ambiguoufly‧
of it, we had faved all this Trouble, and been at an end of
Difputing.

Truly, my Lords, this Record that hath been mention'd of
Henry the Fourth, I will not fay is not a Prefident of Election, for the Archbifhop ftood up, and looked round on all fides,
and asked the Lords and Commons, *Whether they would have
him to be King* ; and they afferted,(as the words of the Roll are)
That *He fhould Reign over them*. And fo it is done at every
Coronation.

As

(43)

As to his Claim, they did not fo much mind that, for they knew that he Claimed by Defcent and Inheritance, when there was a known Perfon that had a Title before him.

For, that which a Noble Lord fpoke of touching the Publick Acts that have been done fince the King left us, I may very well fay, we think them Legally done ; and we do not doubt but that Power which brought in another Line then, upon the vacancy of the Throne by the Leafion of *Richard* the Second, is ftill, according to the Conftitution, refiding in the Lords and Commons, and is legally fufficient to fupply the Vacancy that now is.

That the Noble Lord indeed faid, That your Lordfhips might not only with the Commons advife the Prince of *Orange* to take upon him the Adminiftration, and joyn with us in the other things ; but that you might have done it of your felves, as being in the abfence of the King, the Great Council of the Nation,

My Lords, I fhall not fay much to that Point, your Lordfhips Honours and Privileges are great, and your Councils very worthy of all Reverence and Refpect.

But I would ask this Queftion of any Noble Lord that is here, Whether, had there been an Heir, to whom the Crown had quietly defcended in the Line of Succeffion, and this Heir certainly known, your Lordfhips would have affembled without his calling, or would have either Adminifter'd the Government your felves, or advifed the Prince of *Orange* to have taken it upon him ? I doubt you had been (pardon me to fay it) all guilty of High-Treafon, by the Laws of *England*, if a known Succeffor were in poffeffion of the Throne, as he muft be if the Throne were not Vacant.

From thence, my Lords, your Lordfhips fee where the Difficulty lyes in this matter, and whence it arifeth, becaufe you would not agree the Throne to be Vacant, when we know of none that poffefs it.

We know fome fuch thing hath been pretended to as an Heir Male, of which there are different Opinions, and in the mean time we are without a Government; and, Muft we ftay till the Truth of the matter be found out ? What fhall we do to preferve our Conftitution, while we are without a fafe or legal Authority to act under the fame according to that Conftitution, and in a little time it will, perhaps, through the diftraction of our Conftitution, be utterly irremediable ?

I do not deny, but that your Lordfhips have very great Hardfhips to conflict with in fuch a Cafe, but who is the occafion of them ?

F 2   We

(44)

We all do know the Monarchy is Hereditary ; but how, or what fhall we do to find out the Succeffor in the Right Line ?

You think it will be a difficult thing to go upon the Examination who is Heir ; perhaps it will be more difficult to Refolve in this Cafe, than it might be in another : For though heretofore there have been *Abdications* and *Vacancies*, it has been where the King has been of the fame Religion of the Eftablifh'd Worfhip of the Nation ; and amongft thofe that pretended to the Succeffion, the feveral Claimers have been Perfons born and bred up in that Religion that was Eftablifh'd by Law ; or it may be there have been a Child in the Womb at the time of the Vacancy.

But then, my Lords, there would not be much difficulty to examine, Who fhould Inherit, or what were fit to be done. I confefs, I fay, there are Difficulties of all fides, or elfe your Lordfhips fure would have fpoke out before now : And if you had been clear in it your felves, you would have let the Commons and the World have known it. But it not being clear, muft we always remain thus ? Ufe what words you will, *Fill up*, or *Nominate*, or *Elect*, it is the thing we are to take care of, and it is high time it were done.

My Lords, There is no fuch Confequence to be drawn from this Vote, as an Intention or a Likelihood of altering the Courfe of the Government, fo as to make it Elective, the Throne hath all-along defcended, in an Hereditary Succeffion, the main Conftitution hath been preferved.

The Prefident of *Henry* the Fourth is not like that of Elections in other Countries ; and I am forry there fhould be any occafion for what is neceffary to be done now.

But when fuch Difficulties are upon the Nation, that we cannot extricate our felves out of the Lineal Succeffor, your Lordfhips, I hope, will give us leave to remember *Salus populi eft fuprema Lex*.

And if neither you nor We can do any thing in this Cafe, We, who are met under the Notion of an Affembly or Convention of the States, then have met to no Purpofe ; for after we have Voted our felves to be without a Government, (which looks as if fomething were really intended as to a Settlement) all prefently finks, and we are as much in the Dark as we were before.

And, my Lords, I pray give me leave to fay one thing more : Your Lordfhips fay, You will never make a Prefident of Election, or take upon you to alter the Succeffion.

With

(45)

With your Lordſhips Favour, the Settlement of the Conſtitution is the main thing we are to look after. If you provide for the ſupply of the Defeƈt there, that Point of the Succeſſion will, without all queſtion, in the ſame Method, and at the ſame time, be ſurely provided for.

But, my Lords, you will do well to conſider: Have not you your ſelves already limitted the very Succeſſion, and cut off ſome that might have a Line at Right? Have you not concurred with us in our Vote, *That it is inconſiſtent with our Religion and our Laws to have a Papiſt to Reign over us?* Muſt we not come then to an Eleƈtion, if the next Heir be a Papiſt? Nay, ſuppoſe there were no Proteſtant Heir at all to be found, would not your Lordſhips then break the Line?

But your Lordſhips Vote that is ſo inconſiſtent, you do ſuppoſe a Caſe of the greateſt Conſequence that can be, may happen; and if that ſhould happen to be our Caſe, that the whole Proteſtant Line ſhould fail, would not that neceſſitate an Eleƈtion, or elſe we muſt ſubmit to that which were inconſiſtent with our Religion and our Laws?

If your Lordſhips then, in ſuch a Caſe, muſt break through the Succeſſion, I think the Nation has Reaſon to expeƈt you ſhould take care to ſupply the preſent Defeƈt, where the Succeſſion is uncertain.

My Lords, If this ſhould not be agreed unto, what will be the Conſequence? We that uſed, and juſtly, to boaſt of living under the Beſt of Governments, muſt be left without any one; for, your Lordſhips, it ſeems, cannot agree with us to Supply and Fill up this Gap in it, or tell us who is the Succeſſor: And we muſt not do it our ſelves by Eleƈtion; which is the only way left us to provide for our Settlement.

Truly my Lords, upon the whole, I cannot tell what Condition we ſhall be in, or what we can do farther; but we muſt even part, and break up in Confuſion, and ſo leave the Nation to extricate it ſelf, as well as it can, out of this Diſtraƈtion. But then, at whoſe Door that will lye, I muſt leave to your Lordſhips own Thoughts.

Earl of PEMBROKE.

We have indeed paſſed ſuch a Vote, as that Gentleman ſays, againſt a Popiſh Prince's Reigning over us; but I ſhould think that amounts to no more than a Reſolution, that by a Law to be made we will take care of it in Parliament: Therefore I think that which we aim at, and that which the Conſtitution of our Government does require, is, to put things in a legal Method: And, in order to do it, I would have the legal Succeſſor Declared and Proclaimed, and then a Parliament

(46)

ment fummoned in that Prince's Name, and the whole Matter fettled there.

An Act made by a King *de facto*, is Void as to a King *de jure*; therefore I would have the Conftitution preferved, and would defire, that all that is done in this Matter may be again done in Parliament.

Earl of CLARENDON.

Sir *Robert Howard* was pleas'd to fay, That *by the fame Method that the Throne now fhould be Filled, by the fame the Succeffor fhould be Declared, and the Right Line Settled.* Is not that declaring the Crown to be Elective ?

Suppofe you fay nothing but Fill the Throne, Is it not to take away the Right Line of Inheritance ? And, Will not fuch a Succeffor claim it for his Pofterity ?

Truly, I think, if the Right Line be declared in the fame way that the Succeffor is, then we take upon us to difpofe of the Inheritance of the Crown abfolutely ; which, I think, by all the Law I ever read or could hear of among us, is out of our Power ; and, that neither Houfe, or both Houfes together, have Power to do any thing relating to the Succeffion, but by Act of Parliament ; which the two Houfes by themfelves cannot make.

Sir RICHARD TEMPLE.

I think we are now going too far in this Matter ; the Queftion before us is only, *Whether there be a Vacancy in the Throne*. After we have done with that, I do not fee how this will preclude the Confideration of any Claim to the Succeffion.

Your Lordfhips fay, *You are under great Difficulties upon this Subject*. But, my Lords, till you have declared the Throne Vacant, I muft prefume to fay, I do not fee how it is poffible for any of us to make one Step towards a Settlement.

If there be any Claims to the Crown, that Confideration will be next ; and how to come at them, I conceive we are in the fame Capacity as our Predeceffors were to provide for all Exigencies as fhall emerge, and for the fupplying all Defects in the Government.

It is true by the Acts of Queen *Elizabeth* and King *James*, I. we have the Oaths of Supremacy and Allegiance that are to be, and have been taken by all Perfons.

But, my Lords, there is an old Oath of Fidelity, that ufeth to be required in Leets, and that by the antient Law of *England* every Man ought to take that is Sixteen Years of Age ;
and

(47)

and this was as much obliging to the King, his Heirs and Succeſſors, as any of thoſe later Oaths are ; for they ſeem only to be made to exclude foreign Authorities, and not to infer any new Obedience or Subjection : Therefore I am only ſaying, we are in as natural a Capacity as any of our Prede-ceſſors were to provide for a Remedy in ſuch Exigencies as this.

I do not intend to trouble your Lordſhips any farther than the Words of the Vote lead me.

If the Throne were Full, what do we do here ; nay, how came we hither? I would fain know, whether all that is mention'd in one of our Reaſons of the Adminiſtration being committed to the Prince, and thoſe other Acts, do not all imply, at leaſt, that we are in ſuch a Caſe as *wherein the Throne is Vacant*, otherwiſe, if it had been Full, I appeal to any one, whether we could have aſſembled or acted in any other Name, or by any other Authority, than his that filled it ? Then do not all theſe things declare, that there is a Vacancy ?

My Lords, I have done, having ſaid this, That it is a ſub-ſequent Conſideration, how the Throne ſhall be Filled, and all the Particulars that relate to it remain entire, after this Re-ſolution taken.

But, I think, we are at preſent to go no farther. No Man, I hope, thinks there is a juſt Ground for any Appre-henſion of an Intention to change the Government; I am ſure there is no Ground for any ſuch Apprehenſion : So that we have all the Reaſon in the World to inſiſt, That your Lordſhips ſhould agree with us, that the Throne is Vacant, or we ſhall not be able to move one Step farther towards a Settlement.

Sir THOMAS LEE.

My Lords, So much has been ſaid in this Matter already, that very little is to be added.

But give me leave to ſay unto your Lordſhips, That thoſe Amendments your Lordſhips have made to the Commons Vote are not agreeing with your other Votes, nor any of the Acts done ſince the *Abdication*. Had it been in the common ordinary Caſe of a Vacancy by the King's Death, your Lord-ſhips in *December* laſt would ſure have let us known as much : But is plain you were ſenſible we were without a Government, by your deſiring the Prince to take the Adminiſtration, and to iſſue out his Letters for this Convention.

But, my Lords, I would aſk this Queſtion, Whether upon the *Original Contract* there were not a Power preſerved in the Nation to provide for its ſelf in ſuch Exigencies ?

That

(48)

That Contract was to fettle the Conftitution as to the Le-giflature, which a noble Lord in the beginning fpoke of ; fo we take it to be : And it is true, that it is a part of the Contract, the making of Laws, and that thofe Laws fhould oblige all fides when made ; but yet fo, as not to exclude this original Conftitution in all Governments that commence by Compact, That there fhould be a Power in the States to make Provifion in all Times, and upon all Occafions, for extraordinary Cafes and Neceffities, fuch as ours now is.

I fay nothing now as to the Hereditary Succeffion ; our Go-vernment has been always taken to be Hereditary, and fo declared when there has been occafion to make Provifion otherwife than in the direct Line.

But our Matter is fingly upon a Point of Fact, Whether the Throne be Vacant (as the Commons fay it is) by the *Abdi-cation* of King *James* the Second.

The prefent Vacancy is nearest that of *Richard* the Se-cond, of any that we meet with in our Records; and the Phrafe being there ufed, we infift upon it as very proper. And when that is agreed unto, the Houfe will, no doubt, declare their Minds in another Confequential Queftion that fhall arife in a proper way. But this is all we can fpeak to now.

Sir GEORGE TREBY.

To difcourfe, Whether the Crown of *England* would by this Means become Elective, is altogether unneceffary ; and, I think, your Lordfhips have given no Reafons that are fuffi-cient to make the Objection out, neither any Anfwers to the Commons Reafons for their Vote.

It feems to me an odd way of Reafoning, firft to miftake the Meaning, and then give Reafons againft that miftaken Meaning.

The Queftion is only here, Whether we can make good this Propofition, *That the Throne is Vacant by the Abdication of the late King.*

I confefs, 'tis a melancholy thing to difcourfe of the Mif-carriages of Governments, but 'tis much more afflictive to talk of unhinging all the Monarchy by a breach upon the di-rect Line of the Succeffion, as, if the Crown of *England* did actually defcend to *Lewis* the Fourteenth, it would not be in the Power of the States of this Kingdom to divolve it upon another Head.

A Noble Lord put an Inftance of Two Men in one Room, one of whom was really fuch a one : But though a ftander by could not directly tell which was he, yet it could not be faid

by

(49)

by him, that such a one was not there. But, if you please, I will put this Case :

Suppose there were two Men in one Room, that no one alive could tell which was which ; as suppose this to be the Case of the Two Children of *Edward* the Fourth, that they had been kept close Prisoners by their Uncle *Richard* the Third so long, that there were no living Witnesses able to tell which was the eldest of the Two, that would occasion a Difficulty much as intricate as ours here. One of them must be Eldest, but by Reason of the Uncertainty, must not an Election be made of them ? And could any thing else do but an Election ?

But, I say, the proper single Question here is, Whether we have well affirmed upon the Premises that are mentioned in the former part of the Vote, That he has *Abdicated*, and that *the Throne is thereby Vacant.*

Your Lordships in part agree ; for you say, *He has Deserted the Government* ; then you say, *He is not in it.* And it is as much as to say, He has left the Kingdom destitute of a Government.

Now if there be any Sense in which our Proposition is true, will you deny the whole Proposition, because it may be taken in a Sense that is dubious and uncertain, as to the Consequences.

You cannot say the Throne is Full : If then there be a Doubt with you, to be sure it is not like to be evident to us, especially in this Case, considering who your Lordships are.

You are the Persons that usually are, or ought to be, present at the Delivery of our Queens, and the proper Witnesses to the Birth of our Princes. If then your Lordships had known who was on the Throne, we should certainly have heard his Name from you, and that had been the best Reason against the Vacancy as could have been given.

My Lords, We say no more than our Ancestors have said before us, as you see by the Parliament-Roll, 1 *Henry* IV ; and I must maintain the Record to this Purpose, that the Government is Vacant, and it is there declared, as it is expressed in our Vote: So that we have not invented or coined a Word for our Turn, neither is the Notion new, it is a Word that has been used before in a Case as near this as any can be.

But it is objected, That that should be no President, because of what follow'd upon that Vacancy of the Throne. I desire that your Lordships would read the Record.

The next thing there, is, *Henry* the Fourth cometh himself, and says, *He claimed the Crown as descended from* Henry
G *the*

(50)

the Third, and the Lords and Commons assented. It is true, the Arch-Bishop did propose him (as was usual at Coronations) and he did there actually ask them, *Whether they did chuse him for their King?* They agreed to it, and the Arch-Bishop makes a Discourse upon the Virtues of a Man to Govern the Nation better than a Child; and then he is placed on the Throne. And this I take to be a proper, plain, applicable President in our Case.

But that noble Lord's Objection strikes at the very Heart of it, if the Objection be rightly made, That all these Proceedings, and so consequently the Words and Phrases there used, are all repealed, 1 *Edw.* 4.

My Lords, It is very well known, and readily agreed by us, that *Edward* the Fourth came in in disaffirmance of the Title of the House of *Lancaster.*

As those Times went, whenever there was any Turn in Government (as there were several) there were new and contrary Declarations about the Title to the Crown, made constantly in Parliament; and what one Parliament had settled, another undid.

But then this Advantage we have on our side, that as we have this first President for us, so we have the last; for I need go no farther than the Parliament Roll of 1 *Henry* VII. 12. 16. where the Record is set right again.

The Act for Deposing *Richard* the Second is indeed by 1 *Edw.* IV. Repealed, and saith, That *Henry* the Fourth usurped the Crown, and murther'd *Richard* the Second; and thereupon it proceeds to attaint *Henry* the Sixth. But then comes in *Henry* the Seventh, and 1 *Henry* VII. there is an Act made, that sets aside all the Acts and Attainders made against his Line, and consequently repealed 1 *Edw.* IV, which repealed 1 *Henry* IV.

And I would observe one thing by the way concerning *Henry* the Seventh: He was of the Line of *Lancaster,* and when he came to the Crown, would not endure to have his Crown reckoned only Matrimonial, or suffer the Stile to go in the Names of *Henry* and *Elizabeth,* as he must have done if he had stuck to the Title of the Right Line of Succession; no, he always stood up for his own Title, though he had the Heiress of the House of *York* in his Bosom.

Therefore, my Lords, his Act for restoring the Record of 1 *Henry* IV. again, is as good an Authority as it was before, and somewhat better; for it hath the last Act on its side, which is unrepealed to this Day.

Earl

(51)

Earl of PEMBROKE.

Henry the Seventh had a good Right and Title by Marriage to the Crown, *in re Uxoris.* No one can queſtion but his own Title, as deſcended from *Henry* the Fourth, was an Uſurpation ; and he would not ſuffer any one to preſcribe which Title was beſt, as long as it was acknowledg'd he had one good one.

That this Kingdom is Hereditary we are not to prove by Preſident in the Liſt of our Kings and Queens ; for we ſhall ſcarce find above Three in any direct Line, without ſome Interruption ; and therefore we are not to fetch our Preſidents, or Proofs, ſo far as thoſe Days. And this I ſpeak for the Reaſon which was hinted before.

The Laws made are certainly part of the *Original Contract* ; and by the Laws made, which eſtabliſh the Oath of Allegiance and Supremacy, we are ty'd up to keep in the Hereditary Line, being Sworn to be true and faithful to the King, his Heirs and Succeſſors ; whereas the old Oath was, only to bear true Allegiance to the King. There (I take it) lies the Reaſon why we cannot (of our ſelves) without breaking that Contract, break the Succeſſion, which is ſettled by Law, and cannot be altered but by another, which we our ſelves cannot make.

Sir GEORGE TREBY.

Your Lordſhip is pleaſed to ſay, *Henry* the Seventh's Title by Deſcent was an Uſurpation. I think it is pretty hard to determine what Title he did govern by, ſince though his Wife was the Lineal Heir, yet ſhe had no Part, or ſo much as a Name in the Adminiſtration. And if it were too great an Iſſue to be try'd then, it will be harder to do it now. And it has been ſaid, It was his Mother's Counſel to him, not to declare particularly upon what Foot his Title ſtood.

But, my Lords, if we ſhould allow none for Acts of Parliament but thoſe that were made in the Reigns of Hereditary Kings, and in the Right Line, I doubt we ſhould want the greateſt part of thoſe Laws that compoſe the Volume of Statute-Books, and the Records by which we enjoy a great part of our Inheritances and Poſſeſſions.

G 2   *Mr. Serjeant*

(52)

Mr. Serjeant MAYNARD.

If we look but into the Law of Nature (that is above all Humane Laws) we have enough to juſtify us in what we are now a doing, to provide for our ſelves and the Publick Weal in ſuch an Exigency as this.

Sir RICHARD TEMPLE.

If Laws made about the Succeſſion be ſo obliging, what then ſhall we ſay to the Succeſſion of Queen *Elizabeth*, who had an Act of Parliament (to the keeping of which an Oath was required) againſt both her and her Siſter.

Earl of PEMBROKE.

But to ſhew what Opinion ſhe her ſelf and the wiſe Men of her Times had, and were of, in this Point, there is an Act made in her Reign, and yet in being, which declares it to be a *Præmunire* to affirm, the Parliament cannot ſettle the Succeſſion of the Crown, or alter it. Entails in Parliament have been of the Crown, both Antient and Modern, yet the Authority of another ſubſequent Act has prevail'd againſt ſuch an Entail : So that it ſhould be done, I ſay, in Parliament.

Sir RICHARD TEMPLE.

I think we are in as full a Capacity to take Care of the Government as any of our Predeceſſors, in ſuch an Exigence ; and if we do as they have done before us, that is, not to be called a changing of the Monarchy from an Hereditary to an Elective.

Earl of NOTTINGHAM.

After this long Debate, pray let us endeavour to come as near as we can to an Agreement : We have propoſed ſome Queſtions, about which my Lords deſired to be ſatisfied ; You, Gentlemen, have not been pleaſed to give an Anſwer to them, and We have no great Hopes of getting one from you, as this Debate ſeems to be managed.

On your part you have declared, That you do acknowledge the Monarchy is Hereditary and Succeſſive in the Right Line ; then I cannot ſee how ſuch an Acknowledgement conſiſts with the Reaſons you give for your Vacancy ; for I cannot imagine how a Kingdom can be an Hereditary Kingdom,

and

(53)

and that King who hath Children now in being (at the time of his forsaking the Government) can have the Throne Vacant both of him and his Children.

The Course of Inheritance, as to the Crown of *England*, is, by our Law, a great deal better provided for, and runs stronger in the right Line of Birth than of any other Inheritance. No Attainder of the Heir of the Crown will bar the Succession to the Throne, as it doth the Descent to any common Person. The very Descent, by Order of Birth, will take away any such Defect.

And so was the Opinion of the Great Lawyers of *England*, in the Case of *Henry* the Seventh. Then cannot I apprehend how any Act of the Father's can bar the Right of the Child (I do not mean that an Act of Parliament cannot do it); I never said so, nor thought so; but, I say, no Act of the Father's alone can do it, since even the Act of the Son, which may endanger an Attainder in him, cannot do it, so careful is the Law of the Royal Line of Succession. This is declar'd by many Acts of Parliament, and very fully and particularly by that Statute 25 *Henry* the Eighth, *Cap.* 22, entituled, *An Act concerning the King's Succession* ; where the Succession of the Crown is limited to the King's Issue-Male first, then Female, and the Heirs of their Bodies one after another, by course of Inheritance, according to their Ages, as the Crown of *England* hath been accustomed and ought to go in such Cases.

If then the King hath done any thing to divest himself of his own Right, it doth not follow thence, that That shall exclude the Right of his Issue ; and then the Throne is not Vacant, as long as there are any such Issue; for no Act of the Father can Vacant for himself and Children.

Therefore if you mean no more than but the divesting his own Right, I desired you would declare so : And then suppose the Right gone as to him, yet if it descend to his Lineal Successor, it is not Vacant.

And I told you, One Reason my Lords did stand upon against agreeing to the Vacancy, was, Because they thought your Vote might extend a great deal further than the King's own Person.

But your all owning it to be a Lineal Inheritance, and this Vacancy, methinks, do not by any means consist.

You declare, you never meant to alter the Constitution ; then you must preserve the Succession in its ancient Course : So I did hear a worthy Gentleman conclude it to be

your

(54)

your Intention to do. But by what methods it can be done in this Case by us ? I desire to be satisfied in a few things about this very matter.

I desire first to know, Whether the Lords and Commons have Power by themselves to make a binding Act or Law ? And then I desire to know, whether according to our Ancient Legal Constitution every King of *England*, by being seated on the Throne, and possessed of the Crown, is not thereby King, to him and his Heirs ? And without an Act of Parliament, (which we alone cannot make) I know not what Determination we can make of his Estate.

It has been urg'd indeed, That we have in effect already agreed to what is contain'd in this Vote, by Voting, That it is inconsistent with our Religion and Laws to have a *Popish Prince* to Rule over us.

But I would fain know , Whether they that urge this, think that the Crown of *Spain* is Legally and Actually excluded from the Succession by this Vote ?

No Man sure will undertake to tell me, That Vote of either House, or both Houses together; can alter the Law in this or any other Point.

But because I am very desirous that this Vote should have its Effect, I desire that every thing of this Nature should be done in the ancient usual Method, by Act of Parliament.

GOD forbid that since we are happily deliver'd from the Fears of *Popery* and *Arbitrary Power*, we should assume any such Power to our selves ; What Advantage should we then give to those who would quarrel with our Settlement for the Illegality of it ? Would not this, which we thus endeavour to crush, break forth into a Viper ?

For the Record of 1 *Henry* the Fourth, I acknowledge the Words of the Royal Seat being Vacant are us'd. But since you your selves tells us of it, That *Henry* the Fourth did Claim by Inheritance from his Grandfather, that methinks may come up to what I would have the declared Sense of Both Houses upon this Question ; (to wit) The Throne might be Vacant of *Richard* the Second, but not so Vacant but the Claim of the immediate Successor was to take place, and not be excluded, but entirely preserved.

And *Richard* the Second seems to have had the same Opinion, by delivering over his Signet to them.

Our Laws know no *Inter regnum* ; but upon the Death of the Predecessor the next Heir is King *in uno & eodem instanti.*

It

(55)

It was fo Refolv'd even in *Richard* the Second's own Cafe ; for at his Grandfather's Death it was a Quefti-on, Whether King *Richard* the Second, or the Eldeft Son of his Grandfather then living , fhould fucceed ; and it was Refolved, That he ought to have it, becaufe of his Right of Inheritance: Which is the more remarkable, becaufe of the Conteft.

And when *Richard* the Third ufurped his Crown, to make his Claim good to the Right of Inheritance, he Barftar-dized his own Nephews.

And fo it was in all the Inftances of the Breaches that were made upon the Line of Succeffion, which were fome Seven (but all Illegal) ; for fuch was the Force of the Laws, that the Ufurpers would not take the Crown upon them, unlefs they had fome fpecious pretence of an Hereditary Title to it.

That which I would have Avoided by all means, is, the Mifchievous Confequences that I fear will enfue upon this Vacancy of the Throne, (to wit) the utter Overthrow of the whole Conftitution of our Government. For if it be fo, and the Lords and Commons only remain as part of it, will not this make the King one of the Three Eftates ? Then is he the Head of the Commonwealth, all united in one Body under him. And if the Head be taken away, and the Throne Vacant, by what Laws or Conftitution is it that we retain Lords and Commons ? For they are knit together in their Common Head ; and if one part of the Government be diffolved, I fee not any Reafon but that all muft be diffolved.

Therefore 'tis of very great importance that we come to an Explanation, how far you mean the Throne to be Vacant ; and that if it reach to the King and his Heirs, (notwithftanding all the Acts of Parliament about the Succeffion) we may confider how the Confequences of that will effect the Conftitution ; for I prefume to fay, it may then be in your power as well as to fay, we fhall have no King at all.

I was miftaken by the Gentlemen who took notice of what I faid the Lords might do of themfelves, in the abfence of the King : I would not be underftood to fay, the Government devolved upon the Lords ; but I may fay they are the Government's great Council in the Interval of Parliaments, and may have greater fway by the Privilege of their *Birth*, in the Exigencies of the State : As ap-pears in feveral Inftances, and particularly the firft of *Henry* the Sixth, and during his Infancy.

There

(56)

There was a Cafe put by one Gentleman, about the two Sons of *Edward* the Fourth being kept Prifoners fo long, till it could not be known by any Living Witneffes which was the Eldeft : I would only ask that Gentleman, Whether in that Cafe he would fay the Throne were Vacant ; certainly there would have been One in the Throne.

But then it followeth, that though their fhould be an Uncertainty of the particular Perfon, yet that would not infer a Neceffity that the Throne fhould be vacant.

Upon the whole Matter, you feem to underftand your own words to fignifie lefs than they do really import.

I do not find that you purpofe to make the Kingdom Elective ; and yet you talk of fupplying the Vacancy by the Lords and Commons.

You do not fay, That the King has left the Crown for himfelf and his Heirs ; and yet your words fpeak of a Vacancy, and nothing of the Succeffion ; but you do not tell us what you mean.

Therefore if this matter were explained, that my Lords may know how far the Intention of the Vote reacheth, that it may not abroad, or hereafter, be conftrued to go beyond fuch Meaning, (that is) as to the King himfelf, and not to his Heirs, perhaps there might quickly be a happier Accommodation than can be expected while things remains thus, ftill in doubt, and in the dark.

Gentlemen, If any of you can fettle this Matter in its true Light, it would do very well ; and it is You muft do it ; for the Words are Yours, and fo we muft be told your Signification and Intention by your felves.

If you mean by *Abdication* and *Vacancy* only that the King has *left the Government*, and it is Devolved upon the next Succeffor, that may perhaps fatisfie my Lords, and we may agreee upon fome Settlement.

I muft confefs any Government is better than none ; but I earneftly defire we may enjoy our Ancient Conftitution.

Therefore I again renew my Requeft, That you would come to fuch an Explanation, as may breed an Union between the two Houfes, for the ftrength of your Confultation and Refolutions in this great Emergency.

If the Kingdom were indeed Elective, we were in a Capacity of Electing, but *pro hac Vice*, according to the Conftitution, this Queftion would be greater than what it was before ; but then the great Debate in it would only be, Who fhould firft have the Honour of laying the very Foundation of the New Government.

But

(57)

But as this Cafe ftands upon the Foot of our Ancient Laws, and Fundamental Conftitution, I humbly befeech you to confider, Whether at the fame time that in this way you get an Eftablifh'd Government, you do not overturn all our Legal Foundations.

Mr. PAUL FOLEY.

I hope, my Lords, there is no danger of fhaking our Fundamentals in this Cafe ; but we are purfuing thofe Methods that agree with our Laws and Conftitution : For though the Monarchy of this Nation be Hereditay in the ordinary courfe of Succeffion, yet there may fall out a Cafe wherein that cannot be comply'd with, and a plain Vacancy may enfue. For, put the Cafe the whole Royal Line fhould fail, (as they are all Mortal as well as we our felves are) fhould we in that Cafe have no Government at all ? And who then fhould we have but the Lords and Commons ? and I think that cafe comes neareft to the Cafe in Queftion, where the Succeffor is not known ; for if he had been, we fhould have heard of him before now. And, what is the reafon that it fhou'd then in the former Cafe devolve to Lords and Commons, but that there is no King ? And they being the Reprefentive Body of the Kingdom, are the the only remaining apparent parts of the Government, and are only to fupply the Defect by providing a Succeffor. And, is here not the fame Reafon here ? We are without a King, I am fure I do not know of any that we have : If that fall out to be the Cafe now, that will infer a Vacancy with a Witnefs , and it will be of neceffity that the Lords and Commons take care to fupply it.

Mr. G—— E——e.

My Lords, We are led, and, I think, out of the Way, into a very large Field, hunting after the Confequences of a Vote not yet fettl'd or agreed unto : We have, as I conceive, nothing but the Vote it felf to confider of, or debate upon : We do not intend to prejudice any Legal Right : But what the confequences of this Vote may be, before the Vote it felf be paffed, I believe no Man can reafonably pretend to afcertain, unlefs we have the Spirit of Prophecy.

The Throne may be vacant as to the Poffeffion, without the Exclufion of one that has a Right to the Succeffion, or a diffolution of the Government in the Con-

H   ftitu-

(58)

ftitution; neither will there be room for the Objection of a King *de facto*, and not *de jure*, which fome of the Lords were pleafe to exprefs their Fears of.

This Gentleman that ftands by me inftanced in a Record, and that was miftaken as a Prefident for the proceeding in this Cafe; it was only mention'd by him to fhew, That by ufing the word *Vacant*, the Commons did no more than our Anceftors did before us; and therefore it was not an unknown word or thing to have the Throne Vacant.

We do apprehend we have made a right and apt Conclufion from the Premifes, for otherwife all the Vote is but Hiftorical.

We declare the late King hath broke the Original Contract, hath violated the Fundamental Laws, and hath withdrawn himfelf out of the Kingdom, that he hath *Abdicated*, actually Renounced the Government.

What occafion was there for fuch a Declaration as this, if nothing were concluded from it ? That were only to give the Kingdom a Compendious Hiftory of thofe Miferies they have too well learnt by feeling them.

Therefore there was a neceffity to make fome Conclufion; and none fo natural as this; That we are left without a King in the words of the Vote; That the Throne is thereby *Vacant*, which it may be as to the Poffeffion, and yet the Right of Succeffion no way prejudiced.

But, my Lords, we come here, by the Commands of the Houfe of Commons, to debate the Reafons of their Vote and your Lordfhips Amendments, not to difpute what will be the Confequences, which is not at prefent our Province.

And fo the Conference ended, and the Members of each Houfe returned to their refpective Houfes.

Die

(59)

Die Jovis Septimo Feb. 1688.

A Meſſage from the Lords, by Sir *Robert Atkins* and Sir *Edward Nevill.*

Mr. *Speaker,*
The Lords have Commanded us to tell you, That they have agreed to the Vote ſent them up of the 28th of *January* laſt, (touching which there was a free Conference yeſterday) without any Alterations.

E I N I S.